Offstage Observations

Also by Steven Suskin

Show Tunes: The Songs, Shows, and Careers of Broadway's Major Composers
Berlin, Kern, Rodgers, Hart, and Hammerstein: A Complete Song Catalogue
*Opening Night on Broadway: A Critical Quotebook of the Golden Era of the
    Musical Theatre, Oklahoma! (1943) to Fiddler on the Roof (1964)*
*More Opening Nights on Broadway: A Critical Quotebook of the Musical
    Theatre, 1965–1981*
Broadway Yearbook 1999–2000
Broadway Yearbook 2000–2001
Broadway Yearbook 2001–2002
A Must See! Brilliant Broadway Artwork
Second Act Trouble: Behind the Scenes at Broadway's Big Musical Bombs
The Sound of Broadway Music: A Book of Orchestrators and Orchestrations
The Book of Mormon: The Testament of a Broadway Musical (with Trey
    Parker, Robert Lopez, and Matt Stone)
*Natasha, Pierre & The Great Comet of 1812: The Journey of a New Musical
    to Broadway* (with Dave Malloy)

OFFSTAGE OBSERVATIONS
Inside Tales of the Not-So-Legitimate Theatre

STEVEN SUSKIN

APPLAUSE
THEATRE & CINEMA BOOKS
Guilford, Connecticut

Applause Theatre & Cinema Books
An imprint of Globe Pequot, the trade division of
The Rowman & Littlefield Publishing Group, Inc.
4501 Forbes Blvd., Ste. 200
Lanham, MD 20706
www.rowman.com

Distributed by NATIONAL BOOK NETWORK

British Library Cataloguing in Publication Information available

Library of Congress Cataloging-in-Publication Data

Names: Suskin, Steven, author. | Chapin, Theodore S., writer of foreword.
Title: Offstage observations : inside tales of the not-so-legitimate theatre / Steven Suskin ;
    foreword by Ted Chapin.
Description: Guilford, Connecticut : Applause Theatre & Cinema Books, 2022.
    | Includes index. | Summary: "Offstage Observations: Inside Tales of the Not-So-Legitimate
    Theatre follows a stage-struck teenager as he crashes the gates of Broadway and forges a career,
    keenly observing hits and flops while rubbing shoulders with celebrities famous (and infamous),
    as well as the people who fueled the industry"—Provided by publisher.
Identifiers: LCCN 2021052785 (print) | LCCN 2021052786 (ebook) | ISBN 9781493064632
    (cloth) | ISBN 9781493064649 (epub)
Subjects: LCSH: Suskin, Steven. | Theater critics—New York (State)—New York—Biography.
    | Musicals—New York (State)—New York—History and criticism. | Theater—New York
    (State)—New York—History and criticism.
    | LCGFT: Autobiographies.
Classification: LCC ML423.S955 A3 2022 (print) | LCC ML423.S955 (ebook) |
    DDC 782.1/4097471—dc23
LC record available at https://lccn.loc.gov/2021052785
LC ebook record available at https://lccn.loc.gov/2021052786

for anyone
who has stood on an empty stage
in the dark
and dreamed

or will tomorrow

Contents

CONTENTS

Foreword
by Ted Chapin

STEVEN SUSKIN IS A TRUE THEATRE ANIMAL. I CAN SAY THAT SINCE I consider myself one too. In fact, we grew up at around the same time, so the Broadway he talks about in *Offstage Observations* is the same Broadway that attracted me. Things are different now in many ways, but I still believe, as Steven chronicles in these pages, that careers can be made in the theatre through research, gumption, persistence, risk, politesse, and pursuing anything that looks at the very least interesting and possible.

Nothing was going to be handed to Steven, and he knew that. His stories of coming in from the suburbs as a teenager to catch shows he knew were in previews (when the tickets were less expensive—a tradition that has evaporated), talking his way from the nosebleed seats down to empty seats in the orchestra section, and then sweet-talking his way backstage to meet the performers show gumption. He learns early on that the theatre community can be welcoming. It is not all sweetness and light, or of the highest quality, as he discovers early on with his opinions, which he shares here with candor, explaining in detail what he loved and respected about some shows. Others are brushed aside with a casual phrase of dismissal.

But it is his stories of finding his own way into the Broadway arena that are the most fascinating. He knew nothing would be handed to him. From the start he knew he needed to introduce himself to people he had identified as helpful to his cause. That is how he talked his way into many a job, foremost among them a long-term stint at the office of the great David Merrick. Who does what there is illuminating, and his description of being told to toss out files of clear historic interest in order to make way for a new tenant is almost heartbreaking, until he hints that some of the papers destined for the dustbin ended up in his own briefcase. He is observant and careful, telling some of the unsavory things he learned without commenting too much. And many of his descriptions of how problems were solved—like the solution to Merrick demanding the orchestra in *I Do, I Do* be moved to the pit so they could be seen, or later in his career trying desperately to hold a production of *Hair* together—are amusing and somewhat terrifying. The theatre isn't a place for the timid.

Today Suskin is a respected theatre journalist and scholar who has written many a book examining different aspects of Broadway with great skill. We are all grateful to him for it all. Now he puts himself center stage, and any of us who lived through the Broadway of the 1960s and 1970s will grin with recognition and wince a bit at his version of what we all went through in some form or other.

Prologue

Onstage

ENTER STAGE LEFT

AT WHAT MOMENT IS CHILDHOOD PASSION CEMENTED INTO THE WORK of a lifetime?

My epiphany—if you can call it that—occurred on a Monday in late January 1969. I can't tell you what I did the day before, my sixteenth birthday; but I very well remember what happened the next night.

There was no school that day or Tuesday, for reasons forgotten, so I took the train into the city with my friend Michael to see a show. Our first choice, I determined, was Howard Sackler's new play, *The Great White Hope*. It had been ecstatically received by the critics and would ultimately win that season's Triple Crown: the Tony Award for Best Play, the New York Drama Critics Circle Award, and the Pulitzer Prize.

In those days, there were no such things as phone orders or internet ticketing; unless you knew enough to plan ahead and order by mail (with a self-addressed, stamped envelope), the only way to get tickets was to walk up to the box office window. Yes, you could deal with a ticket broker, but few teenagers had contact with brokers. Besides, I already instinctively viewed ticket brokers as grubby parasites.

We made our way to the Alvin Theatre, which since 1985 has been called the Neil Simon but to me will always remain the Alvin. Tickets were readily available; as I would later learn, serious plays—as opposed to musicals or popular comedies—were unlikely to sell out on weeknights. We took our place up near the back row; moved down to the front mezz

Outside the Alvin Theatre (1968).
PHOTO BY BILL YOSCARY

as soon as the show started; scoped out a pair of empty seats in the first row of the reasonably packed orchestra while watching the first act; and transplanted ourselves for acts two and three.

Now, just because a play goes on to win the Tony, Critics Circle, and Pulitzer, that doesn't necessarily mean that it's *good*; as a longtime awards voter—and having served as a member of the Tony Award Nominating Committee—I can assure you that the certified "best" sometimes means only that it is not quite so weak as the others. But *The Great White Hope* was bruisingly good, provocative, dangerous theatre.

James Earl Jones played Jack Jefferson, a fictionalized version of heavyweight boxing champion Jack Johnson. Johnson was the first Black man to win the title, which he took in 1908 and held through 1915. Race relations in the United States being what they were, a search was launched for a "great white hope" capable of obliterating him.

Johnson—who married a white woman, further whipping up controversy—was larger than life. As was the character of Jefferson, in the play. Jones, in his breakthrough role, proved that he too was very much larger than life—and remained so for decades. He made his Broadway debut in 1958 in *Sunrise at Campobello*, playing a manservant to prepresidential Franklin D. Roosevelt. Jones worked frequently in the intervening decade, with small roles in three subsequent Broadway plays and a fair amount of off-Broadway experience. His most noticeable performance over those years, perhaps, was as Lieutenant Lothar Zogg, the bombardier, in Stanley Kubrick's 1964 movie *Dr. Strangelove*.

Jones was phenomenal as Jack Jefferson. (That April, he would become the first Black performer—male or female—to win a Tony Award for acting in a play.) Old-timers talk of seeing Laurette Taylor in *The Glass Menagerie*, or Marlon Brando in *A Streetcar Named Desire*; for me, Jones in *The Great White Hope* served as the first of not-all-that-many jaw-droppingly unforgettable performances I've witnessed. As Jefferson's world collapsed around him, we watched this strong and thunderous force of nature disintegrate in front of our eyes. My eyes were, by this time, rivetted on Jones from the first row. The image of the actor in the harshly bright lights—the sweat rolling off his brow (onto the people in the first row, mind you), the spit cascading out of his mouth—remains with me.

After the show, I headed to the stage door and presented myself to the doorman, authoritatively asking for Mr. Jones's dressing room. I had learned, in previous escapades, that if you put up a good front you could sometimes talk your way in.

"Just wait in there," he said. "It's dark, watch your step." And he pointed us through the brick archway onto the stage.

The stage! Well, not actually the stage. Rather the offstage area to the left of the proscenium. Dark with shadows, cluttered by scenic pieces on the floor and others tied to the grid high above. Electric cables everywhere. Along the side wall—the Fifty-Second Street wall—was a mass of equipment. Most intriguing was what I could barely make out, through the portals that served as wings: the stage, lit by a big, bare bulb on a standing post. The ghost light.

I had by this point been backstage at a handful of Broadway shows. In each case, though, the dressing room had been on the stage door side of the building. At the Alvin, the star dressing room—the only one on the ground floor—was on the far side, meaning we'd have to actually cross the stage.

We waited. Actors and stagehands in overcoats streamed past us, leaving for the night. (You could easily tell which was which; if they weren't white, they surely weren't union stagehands.) In the meantime, a party of four entered from the street holding *Playbills*; Mr. Jones was expecting them, they told the doorman. They joined us in the wing, middle class, middle-aged white out-of-towners from Cleveland or somewhere.

After a few minutes, a slight man approached. "I'm Mr. Jones's dresser, I'll take you over. Careful of the tracks," he said, pointing to the cuts in the stage upon which pieces of scenery slid on and off during the show.

Off we went, from the dark wing onto the stage of the Alvin with the bright ghost light. As my eyes adjusted, I noticed the auditorium before me, with red exit signs over the fire doors. "This way, please," he said, rushing us along. I continued across the stage, not wanting to miss my chance to meet James Earl Jones but wondering whether I could get back to that spot on the way out.

Past the stage right wall lined with a system of ropes and counterweights, through another archway to a staircase leading up and down. Up a few steps to a landing, through a door with a cardboard gold star and a sign saying "Mr. Jones."

"He's just out of the shower. Take a seat."

James Earl Jones, triumphant, in *The Great White Hope* (1968).
PHOTO BY BILL YOSCARY

The star dressing room at the Alvin looked much like the other dressing rooms I'd thus far visited. Old, tired, coated with too many layers of white paint that couldn't hide the fact that the place was built in 1927. A coiled, knee-high floor radiator, painted white, hissed out steam. A small, crusted window with an air conditioner likely as old as I was, patched in. Some recently purchased wicker furniture in white, a small bar, a half-refrigerator, all of which gave the place a temporary, homey look. A folding screen, a folded-up army cot for napping on two-show days. No makeup counter with mirrors and lights; there was a pair of narrow, louvred doors—painted black—leading to a second room, which was where the dressing table, costumes, and shower were. Through these doors, after a couple of minutes, came James Earl Jones.

And he was in jovial form. You might think that after a grueling three hours—and Jack Jefferson in *The Great White Hope* is as grueling a role as you will find—that the fellow might be tired. On the contrary. He was keyed up, invigorated, and—after a quick shower—ready to enjoy himself. The stockbroker or lawyer or policeman off the beat doesn't go home at five o'clock and slip into bed. It was eleven o'clock at night, but Jones was clearly energized. He must have been hungry, too; you wouldn't want to eat a full dinner before performing this role.

"Good evening," boomed out the voice. Over the years we've grown to know the sound of James Earl Jones, what with his commercial voice-overs for companies like Verizon and CNN ("This is CNN"), not to mention Darth Vader. The voice was unknown in 1969, unless you happened to have just sat through *The Great White Hope*. But it was commanding. And—standing there in that dressing room, on a cold weeknight in late January—jovial.

The Clevelanders shook his hand. They were cousins of his accountant or dentist or some such. How is so and so? asked Jones. "You were really great," they said, proffering their programs for autographs. Then he turned to us.

What can you possibly say to a star, after a performance of this sort, that doesn't sound trite? Especially if you're only a teenager? But Jones was holding out his hand, and my friend Michael was too nervous to speak.

"We're just in high school," I said. "You know, I read the reviews so I knew this show was going to be good. But I don't even know how to describe your performance. You were astounding."

"Well, thank you," he enthusiastically replied. "It's a wonderfully written play, isn't it? Howard Sackler did a marvelous job."

We chatted briefly. "What school did we attend?" he asked in his perfectly modulated tones. "Did we plan careers in the theatre?" The Clevelanders were standing, watching, but after four minutes there was little more I could possibly say other than goodnight.

"Thanks for coming to see us," James Earl Jones boomed after me through the door with the gold cardboard star.

Ghost Light

"Well, we missed the 11:16," said Michael as we crossed the stage.

I stopped center. They call it a ghost light, and I could see why; the theatre, which half an hour earlier was filled with lights and people and a roaring crowd, looked ghostly. As my eyes adjusted, I could make out reds, whites, and burnished gold, lit by the ghost light behind me and the subdued exit signs above the doors.

"Come on," said Michael, already across the stage near the exit.

"Just a minute," I said, "we've got time till the next train."

The seven hundred seats in the orchestra looked like one mass. Three masses, that is, right, left, and center. At the back of the orchestra were two staircases up to the mezzanine. The mezz was smaller than the orchestra but looked even more substantial, like a sea. There was a crossover row in the middle of the mezz, with entrance stairs. Over on house right two rows up, that's where I sat when I saw my third Broadway show, in 1961.

A view from the stage of what I still call the Alvin Theatre (without apology to Neil Simon).

BILL MORRISON COLLECTION / THE SHUBERT ARCHIVE

The dome of the theatre was off-white. Looking to the back wall, I saw the follow spot booth with three windows. I followed the side wall down past the mezz to the boxes. Two on each side; from the edge of the apron, it felt like you could almost touch them. Everything silent, looking like a toy theatre. The orchestra floor was covered with discarded programs and candy boxes, the seats disordered, some folded up, others not. But I couldn't see much of that from where I stood. Just a seemingly, though not actually, luxurious sea of muddy red.

This was the house that Gershwin built—or, rather, that profits from the early Gershwin musicals built. A house that opened with Fred Astaire and his sister, Adele, singing "'S Wonderful" in *Funny Face*. This was the spot from which Ethel Merman launched "I Got Rhythm" in Gershwin's *Girl Crazy*, and later "Anything Goes" in the Cole Porter musical of that title. This is where Porgy and Bess first sang Gershwin's immortal score, where Gertrude Lawrence sang the "Saga of Jenny" in *Lady in the Dark*, where Zero Mostel pranced on the way to the *Forum*. Here stood the Lunts, Helen Hayes, José Ferrer's Cyrano and—just that evening—James Earl Jones in *The Great White Hope*. And now I stood on the very same stage, looking out on the very same seats. Reupholstered over the years, but still.

The air in the theatre is constantly ventilated, of course. But the air above the stage, rising four stories to the grid, is never cleaned; theatre dust, from great performers and great performances, drifts high above and can never be wiped away. And here was I, center stage at the Alvin.

I felt a fresh chill on my face, as if I were looking out from a secluded mountaintop into a welcoming canyon. I wanted to call out in the silence, but that would disturb the mood—and I couldn't soliloquize while Jones was still there, offstage right in his dressing room.

"Let's go!" called Michael.

While I sat watching *The Great White Hope*, and even as I visited James Earl Jones, I already firmly intended to spend my career in show business. Standing on the empty stage of the Alvin—the ghost light behind me, the vast auditorium of shadows enveloping me—I knew that I would and *must* spend my life in the theatre. This was home, and has remained so well into the new century.

Through the Stage Door

SATURDAY IN MARCH

MY FIRST LEGITIMATE STEP THROUGH THE STAGE DOOR—NOT AS IN intruder talking my way in, but by express invitation—was set in motion a year later.

The morning of March 14, 1970, was bright and blustery. Or maybe not. I can tell you that I took a nine-something Long Island Railroad train from my suburb, forty-five minutes from Broadway. Or from Penn Station, anyway. Then the 1 train to Fiftieth Street, a mile up. I would have walked, but I wanted to get to the box office of the Broadway The-atre as soon as possible to buy a ticket for that afternoon's preview of the new musical, *Purlie*.

I can only tell you the date because I know that *Purlie* opened the next evening; if I seem in these pages to come up with more than a few highly inconsequential dates, it's because my inner calendar has always been tied to opening nights on Broadway. (The third book I wrote, in fact, was called *Opening Night on Broadway*.) I can't for the life of me tell you what I did or where I was on my eleventh birthday; but I can tell you where I was the day before at 2:30 p.m.: at the St. James Theatre watching the matinee of *Hello, Dolly!* My father, on a pre-dawn commuter train nine days earlier, read the *New York Times* review and had the good sense to go *not* to work but to the box office. Early, so he'd be near the front when they opened at 10:00 with a line from the St. James all the way down Forty-Fourth Street to the Paramount Building on Broadway—which in those days, before internet ticketing or even telephone orders, meant that he was able to nab a good pair on the aisle for the following weekend.

Why would a seventeen-year-old select a musical like *Purlie*, with no stars, no well-known authors or directors, and no preliminary buzz or word-of-mouth? Preview business, I could tell from my subscription to *Variety*, was poor. Even so, I had a hunch that *Purlie* would be good. Which is common to many of us in the business. What makes you want to see this one, and not that one? Just a sense of . . . something. From the moment you first hear about a musical, which in those days usually came from the preliminary ad in the Sunday *Times*, you think, it sounds good. Or something about it, specifically, just *doesn't* sound good. Or sometimes, you're simply not interested.

Sometimes you can immediately tell from the ad just how good a musical will be. Or not. *Purlie* (1970).

Purlie I wanted to see. I had, several years earlier, stumbled across an obscure 1963 film called *Gone Are the Days!* These things would show up on TV, often late at night; without videotapes or video recorders, you had to watch 'em when they were broadcast. *Gone Are the Days!* was a wickedly funny, if uneven, satire on race relations. I relished the humor as Ossie Davis battled the bigoted Ol' Cap'n for his inheritance, the traditions of the Ol' South crumbling around them. I learned from the opening titles that this was derived from a play, which turned out to be Davis's own *Purlie Victorious*.

Back in junior high school days, I whiled away boring classroom hours reading playscripts that I got out of the nearby well-stocked public library. After seeing the film, I quickly devoured *Purlie Victorious*. I could understand why the play had been a quick failure; Broadway audiences of 1961 and film audiences of 1963 weren't much interested in social satire, at least when the good and wise and clever characters were Black and the villain was a bumblingly doddering white patriarch—who, in retrospect, was likely patterned on some still-sitting US senator or other.

Broadway audiences of 1970 weren't likely to be interested, either; but here was a musical version of *Purlie Victorious*, coauthored by Davis with songwriters from the pop world and a cast of unknowns. Davis collaborated on the book but didn't star in the musical; they had a young actor named Cleavon Little, who turned out to be exceptionally good. By virtue of which he became the first Black actor to win the Tony Award for Best Actor in a Musical—just a year after James Earl Jones won the nonmusical equivalent—and the first virtually unknown actor to win the award.

The box office at the Broadway Theatre had two or three people waiting, which is to say no line whatsoever. I considered the choices. Preview prices, at the time, were lower than the post-opening scale. I had already learned that if you asked for a balcony seat and the house wasn't full, a sympathetic treasurer sometimes had the latitude and inclination to move you down. (This was before the arrival of the half-price TKTS booth in 1973, which is built upon just this sort of discounting.)

I asked if I bought a $2.50 ticket way upstairs, might it be possible to get a slightly better seat?

The matinee was filled with groups, was the reply. But that night at 8:30, the final preview, he could move me down. To the third row of the orchestra; the major critics were coming, and the producer wanted to fill in the front. "It'll be much better from the orchestra," added the treasurer, who clearly loved what he'd seen of the show. "They just put in a new song last night. It's great."

Going to the evening show meant I'd have to take a late train home, arriving past midnight; but a front orchestra seat for the final preview of *Purlie* for $2.50? Of course!

A STAR EMERGES

And yes, that ticket for *Purlie* was well worth it. Not a perfect musical, due to some built-in flaws; but a highly entertaining one, with numerous heights making up for the several weaknesses. The show started deceptively, with a somber funeral. But the gospel hymn was interrupted by brass, with the dancers exploding into a true knockout of an opening number called "Walk Him up the Stairs." They were carrying a coffin, but it soon became clear that they weren't gonna walk him up, they were going to *catapult* him.

Then came a scene in which Purlie—the role Ossie Davis originally wrote for himself—entered and set the tone of the evening. Cleavon Little did not, on his entrance, have the commanding stage presence of Davis, who was an actor to be reckoned with. As soon as he talked and smiled and offered a sidelong glance or two, though, it was apparent that this fellow was wickedly good, and his razor-sharp opening number ("New Fangled Preacher Man") sealed the deal. You can get a good sense of the silkily sly Little by watching the railroad work gang scene—where he sings "I Get a Kick out of You"—in the 1974 Mel Brooks movie, *Blazing Saddles*.

Standing alongside Purlie was Lutiebelle, a fresh-as-the-morning, dew-on-the-melon-patch country girl not too many generations removed from Uncle Tom's Topsy. Which is precisely how Ossie wrote the role in *Purlie Victorious*, as a satirical vehicle for his wife, Ruby Dee. The Lutiebelle of the occasion sang her first song, revealing a big voice and a delectable personality. Glancing at the program, I saw that this was Melba Moore.

I was one of the handful of people in the place who actually knew who Melba Moore was, at least on that Saturday night prior to the rave reviews she was to receive in Monday's papers. When I'd gone to see a matinee of *Hair* a year and a half earlier, I determined to go backstage afterward to meet the cast. Given the crowd at the Biltmore stage door, I realized I'd have to improvise to get in; so I told the doorman that I needed to interview some of the actors for my high school newspaper. "You're supposed to set that up in advance," he said wearily, but he'd see what he could do. And he did; after a few minutes, he came out and said I could go up to see the "White Boys" girls, dressing room #7.

Now, the "White Boys" girls weren't white girls; there were twin songs in the second act called "White Boys" (sung by three Black girls) and "Black Boys" (sung by three white girls). The songs weren't much to speak of, but the "White Boys" girls had one of the most memorable costumes in Broadway lore. Tom O'Horgan, the director, put them up on a high platform, singing and slinking and bunched up like the Supremes. In the middle section of the song, he had them fan out—revealing that the three girls were wearing one, tent-like, red sequined dress. (Tom didn't design the costumes; Nancy Potts did; but this was the sort of wildly outsized idea he regularly came up with.) Enormously explosive laugh, so memorable that we're still talking about the dress and the negligible song fifty years later.

Up I went to the third-floor dressing room of the trio, who turned out to be Lorrie Davis, Emmaretta Marks, and the twenty-three-year-old Melba Moore. First person I ever met called Melba, and still the only one. It wasn't much of an interview, as I didn't have a high school newspaper to write for; for their part, the girls were friendly and seemed amused by this sheltered fifteen-year-old "white boy" from another world.

So when I filed into my seat for the final preview of *Purlie*, I was one of the few people in the house who knew precisely who this Melba Moore was. Except that the sweetly naive Lutiebelle of the evening was nothing whatsoever like the savvy Melba I had chatted with upstairs at the Biltmore; this Melba was smaller, adorable, and meeker. Until . . .

About an hour into the first act, along came one of those moments. That is, one of those rare lightning-like flashes of theatre magic. A book scene—a not especially good book scene—ended, with Purlie leaving Lutiebelle alone onstage to await his return. Music started, gentle music. The lighting began to change; when they go from a full-stage book scene into a solo, they subtly lower the lights on the set while bringing them up on the singer. Melba went over to an auspiciously placed rocking chair and sat, slowly rocking as she hummed.

And then everything stopped. No, the show didn't stop, timewise; it was just an instant, by the clock. But for the audience (and critics) there that night, at the final preview of *Purlie* in 1970, everything did indeed stop as the musical intro ended. Melba steadied the rocking chair, gripping the arms tight. Everyone, twelve hundred or so in the not-so-full house, seemed to lean forward in their seats; you could tell then—before she even started singing—that something remarkable was about to happen. A star was at that moment born, as the saying goes. The remarkable thing about it was that this magic didn't occur as Moore launched into "I Got Love"; the magic happened *before* the song, as she stopped humming and stopped rocking and gripped the arms of the chair. The brief verse ends with her singing the word "love" higher and higher for an octave and a half, like a rocket firing up prior to lift off—at which point she exploded from her chair, and those twelve hundred all but exploded from their seats as well.

I was to see Melba do *Purlie* again, onstage, at the Tony Awards, and in the videotape of the national tour; I saw her do other musicals; I saw other people play Lutiebelle, and even wrote the script adaptation for the 1998 Kennedy Center concert version of *Purlie*. On none of those occasions, though, did I ever again feel the magic of that night.

While *Purlie*—and Melba Moore rocketing to the rafters with "I Got Love"—were the highlights of that March day in 1970, they were not the event that provided my entrance to the other side of the Broadway footlights. That was set in motion several hours earlier, during the intermission of an infinitely less exhilarating theatrical affair.

MATINEE AT THE BELASCO

As I left the Broadway box office that morning clutching my steeply discounted front-orchestra ticket for that evening's *Purlie*, I had nine hours
till curtain time. Which meant I should get tickets to a matinee! My first
choice was clear: *Coco*, with Katharine Hepburn, around the corner at
the Mark Hellinger. Surely sold out, I thought, despite the lousy reviews
they'd gotten in December. But maybe I could get standing room? The
line was long, and there was a "this performance sold out" sign hanging
in the box office window. I already knew that this didn't necessarily mean
there were no tickets; I asked the porter as he swept through the lobby;
he said they might have a single and it was worth waiting. So I waited.
And waited, plotting out my next choice or choices. I finally got to the
front of the line and asked for a single. Nothing. Not even standing
room? Nope, those immediately went to the first people lined up when
they opened at ten that morning, the treasurer said.

It was already past noon, there were two other previewing musicals to
choose from. *Minnie's Boys*, a musical about the Marx Brothers starring
Shelley Winters, didn't sound like it would be too good. *Look to the Lilies*, a Jule Styne musical about a nun and an ex-convict starring Shirley
Booth, sounded worse. (From the moment you first hear about a show, as
I said before, you sometimes just *know* it'll be a stinker.) *Lilies* was on the
way, at the Lunt-Fontanne on Forty-Sixth Street, but saving that as last
resort I went over to the Imperial. *Minnie's Boys* had a line, and a wait,
and no tickets. It was by now 1:30. If I went to try *Lilies*, I was likely to
miss out on getting anything for the matinee. (I later saw both, during
their brief runs: *Minnie's Boys* was poor, with compensatory high spots;
Lilies was altogether somnolent. *Coco*, too, despite Hepburn, was pretty
much awful.)

So I headed east on Forty-Fourth for a preview of something that
sounded so unpromising that they were sure to have seats. One of my
quests, now that I was months away from moving to Manhattan, was to
see a show in every one of the then-thirty-two Broadway theatres. This
was a chance to knock the Belasco off the list. The house that David
Belasco built was rarely booked at the time. That was then; nowadays,

thanks to a spectacular renovation by the Shubert Organization in 2010, it is one of Broadway's jewels.

I was most fortunate, on a snowy winter's day years later when a friend was rehearsing a play there, to scamper around Belasco's abandoned penthouse apartment on the roof. This included a hidden window with a view of the stage; massive built-in mahogany clothes cabinets; a fireplace with tiles reportedly pilfered from the Alhambra in Spain; and the remains of painted panels in the master's bedroom that—with long-gone atmospheric lighting—had been contrived to replicate sunsets in all their splendor. None of this remains easily accessible anymore; the windows were boarded up and central ventilation ducts run through the rooms during various renovations. There were also abandoned theatrical offices and long-disused stage machinery, including a hydraulic lift in the subbasement that was designed to allow relatively instant scene changes. It was still quite clear to me, observing the grimy remnants, just how this cannily devised equipment had worked.

The Belasco tenant on that day when I was looking for something to see prior to *Purlie* was called *Grin and Bare It!* This consisted of two one-acts, *Grin and Bare It!* and *Postcards*. The former was a play of some notoriety. A long-gone writer named Tom Cushing published it in 1931 under the title *Barely Proper: An Unplayable Play*—unplayable because it was set in a nudist colony, with all the characters naked. Forty years later, nudity was big; the off-Broadway musical *Oh! Calcutta!* was the town's hottest ticket. Within the year, it would move uptown—to that very same nearly-impossible-to-book Belasco, no doubt setting the ghost of the so-called Bishop of Broadway howling albeit with eyes closely glued to the bodies onstage.

Some fly-by-night producer unearthed Cushing's unplayable play and figured: $$$! So he hired a hack director and slapped together a cheap-as-dirt production. Plus he added a relatively literary—but not good—two-character curtain raiser. That was just window dressing, or window undressing if you will; you could tell because the preview price was $6.95 for orchestra seats but the ABCs said: "Please Note: First Two Rows Orch. for All Perfs. Previews $10."

So off I went to the Belasco, figuring that at least I'd get to see one of the dwindling number of Broadway houses in which I'd never been. Bought my $2 ticket, for the second balcony. They had no interest in improving my seat, but I felt sure there'd be plenty of room for me to quickly move downstairs. Once ensconced in the balcony, I realized that was not as easy as it sounded; the Belasco was one of the rare theatres with a separate entrance for the top balcony, with no connecting stairs to the rest of the house. (I later learned that there is a secret inner door, but I didn't know that then.) So rather than moving down to the mezzanine or orchestra in the first minutes, I scoped out the front of the orchestra while the actors were flailing through *Postcards*. The front rows, with those higher-priced seats, had couples on the two aisles but nobody in between.

At intermission I sailed down to the street and crossed to the main lobby, mingling with the crowd of smokers. I quickly slipped into the orchestra level and took the empty seat I'd identified from above, four in from the aisle in the second-row center. Nobody batted an eye, so I was safe. I leaned back and relaxed for the remaining minutes of the intermission.

"I can't believe it; they're really giving us the *Barrymore*?"

"Lou says they're doing no business, they got no money. They'll post notice Monday."

"I've always loved the Barrymore."

This from the people directly behind me. The most interesting dialogue I'd heard so far that afternoon.

"When do we need the check for the scene shop?"

Nonchalantly turning my head, I saw the man behind me who was asking about the check, an empty seat with coats, and then two men to whom he was speaking. The man furthest from me, it was impossible not to notice, had short, curly, platinum blonde hair.

"We can stall him."

After a bit of this, the two on the end—who seemed close confederates—started their own quiet conversation. I didn't know what to say to the guy behind me, but this was real Broadway talk. The best I

9

could think of was, "Excuse me, but I couldn't help overhearing. Are you doing a Broadway show?"

"Yes. *A Place for Polly*; we started rehearsals on Monday. Don't tell anyone, but I think we're getting the Barrymore."

"Oh. That's a play?" I asked, never having heard of it but knowing that musicals rarely played the Barrymore.

"A comedy. Starring Marian Mercer."

"Oh, she's wonderful. I didn't know she'd left *Promises*." Which was to say, I might have been in high school but I knew Mercer and *Promises, Promises*—and, after all, I was at a preview of *Grin and Bare It!* So the man, who said his name was David G. Meyers, proudly told me everything there was to know about the show he was coproducing, *A Place for Polly*. One of those plays that instantly sounded worse than awful.

The lights soon went down, taking us head-on into *Grin and Bare It!*—which was indeed very much awful, filled mostly with character people who were decidedly unattractive. There I was at seventeen, already realizing that poor out-of-work actors will do *anything* to earn a paycheck. As pathetic as they all were, one of them—playing an obese French maid—was absolutely grotesque. She got to wear a gauzy apron, at least.

Ten years later, I was in the star dressing room at the Music Box visiting my friend John Cullum, who had taken over the lead in *Deathtrap*. In came castmate William LeMassena, a veteran actor who had started back in 1940 as part of Alfred Lunt's coterie of young men. "You know Bill LeMassena, don't you?" said John.

All I could think was—uggh, that's the guy with the appendicitis scar from *Grin and Bare It!*

The curtain finally came down, to deafening silence. As I turned to leave, David Meyers said, "You seem to see everything. We start previews next month. Come see *Polly* as my guest, I'd love to hear what you think." And he gave me his card.

No Place for Critics

I noticed in Tuesday's *Times* that Murray Schisgal's *The Chinese and Dr. Fish*, at the Barrymore, was closing that week; and in Sunday's *Arts and Leisure* section there was a quarter-page ad for the new attraction. An especially weak-looking ad, with a supposedly comic drawing of a conflicted-looking young woman. Ken Gaston and Leonard Goldberg, with David G. Meyers, present Marian Mercer in *A Place for Polly* by Lonnie Coleman. Previews at the Barrymore starting April 10, opening on April 18. Not wanting to seem too eager, I waited ten days before calling and setting up a ticket for the second preview.

Gaston and Goldberg had already—despite only one Broadway offering—earned a reputation for shoestring, fly-by-night work. Their first show had been a tacky, "all-star" revival of the old farce *Three Men on a Horse*, which played the Lyceum the prior October. "All-star" meaning the original leading player Sam Levene, thirty-five years older, plus every out-of-work comic actor Gaston and Goldberg could get cheap. Directed by coauthor George Abbott, also thirty-five years older and no longer in demand. More on Mr. A. later.

Meyers, who seemed an eager and nice-enough chap from Brooklyn, was trying to break into the producing game. He presumably brought Gaston and Goldberg enough fresh money to get his name over the title.

I went in for the Saturday matinee. There at the box office was a ticket, waiting in my name. A $6.00 ticket with two holes punched in it, which is to say a comp. A good orchestra seat, although I don't suppose there was a *good* seat for *A Place for Polly*. Ten minutes before curtain, Meyers came down the aisle and found me.

"I'm so glad you made it. Enjoy the show. I'm not staying, call me tomorrow and tell me how you liked it." And he was gone. Leaving me with an overnight assignment: figuring out *something* to say. Because *A Place for Polly* was a dismal sex comedy about a charming but neglected woman with a wonderful sense of humor (Polly, needless to say); her philandering husband, a publisher; her sister, a best-selling novelist (and plagiarist, patterned on Jacqueline Susann of *Valley of the Dolls*); a noble young editor; a crusty Broadway producer; and on and on. All of whom stand around at cocktail parties, one in each act, telling lame jokes.

This was the sort of thing would-be producers used to test on the summer stock circuit, occasionally bringing one into town in hopes of making a million. One or two in a million did just that, like *Any Wednesday* or *Butterflies Are Free*; most would barely get through the second act on opening night before closing. Like *A Place for Polly*.

What I did say was something along the lines of how much I liked Marian Mercer, how funny she was. And that I especially enjoyed Alan Manson (as the stock, wise-cracking Jewish producer) and Evelyn Russell (as the stock, wise-cracking Eve Arden type). What Meyers said was something like, yes, we have rewrites we're going to put in, we know what we need to do. And he said, "I bet you've never been to an opening night. Want to come next Saturday? You can maybe help out."

"Not a place for critics."
A Place for Polly (1971).
MAX A. WOODWARD
COLLECTION, MUSIC DIVISION,
LIBRARY OF CONGRESS

I had been to a couple of Broadway openings thus far, but I didn't need to tell him that. *A Place for Polly* could have been *Moose Murders* or *Prymate*; I was definitely going to be there, especially if I could "help out."

The week flew quickly by, or whatever that cliché is. I called Meyers on Wednesday. He said it was an early opening, at 6:30. He had booked a room at the Edison, directly across from the Barrymore, so that he didn't have to go home afterward. (He lived way the hell out in Brooklyn, somewhere.) He might be taking a nap, so I should stop by at 5:00 and make sure he's up. Oh, and he was renting a tuxedo but I should just wear a nice suit if I have one.

I came in Saturday and walked up to the Hotel Edison in an April shower, arriving early. I entered through the Forty-Sixth Street doors, then walked over to the Forty-Seventh side to look at the Barrymore. *A Place for Polly*, the marquee lit up in the rain. A crowd was streaming out of the *Hair* matinee next door at the Biltmore; the Barrymore lobby was deserted. I went back inside, waited in the lobby till 5:00, then called Meyers's room. No answer. Must be sleeping, maybe. Went up to his room, on the fourteenth floor.

The lobby of the Edison was rundown, but the hallway was positively seedy. The hotel had opened in 1931—a lively time to open a new Times Square hotel, with the Depression about to hit bottom—and it looked like they hadn't cleaned the carpet since. The wooden doors were covered with layers of once-shiny white paint, with transoms above; I guess so that back in pre-air-conditioned summer days you could open the slats for ventilation. The slats were now lacquered shut, the whole place grimy and musty. I knocked at the door; Meyers instantly came out, straightening his clip-on bow tie.

"Opening night, this is exciting," I said, without an exclamation point.

"I think we're ready," he said as we crossed the street. "Wait a second."

We stopped in the box office lobby; he passed some ticket envelopes through the window. "These will be picked up," he said to the treasurer. We went out and down the alley to the right of the theatre, through the stage door.

I had managed to get backstage at several Broadway theatres thus far, but this was the first time I didn't have to talk my way in. This time I *belonged* there, if only for a tenuous half hour.

We stood in the entrance hall, beside the pay phone next to the callboard. "I don't know if we'll need you to do anything, but it's good to have you around in case." People came and went, Meyers saying hello or nodding, and a couple of times introducing me. "That's Lisa, our press agent."

Gaston and Goldberg flounced in. "You remember Steven, we met him at *Grin and Bare It!*" Meyers said, although Gaston and Goldberg didn't seem much to care. One of them—Gaston, the short one, I think—was wearing a mink. Or maybe he wasn't; I saw the pair four or five times over the course of a few months, and one of those times one of them was definitely wearing a mink.

Polly was not the only new show in town for the boys; they had an off-Broadway play starting previews the following Wednesday. *Circle in the Water* it was called, one of those naked-boys-at-the-military-school affairs. Very classy. It played eighty-five previews and closed, without bothering to brave the critics. (I suppose I should point out that this Leonard Goldberg was not the same Leonard Goldberg who produced *Charlie's Angels, Hart to Hart*, and other television hits.)

After a while Meyers said, "I've got to wish the actors luck, wait here." So I just stood by the call board as stagehands and dressers came and went, a seventeen-year-old in a suit trying to look like I belonged there inside the stage door at a real Broadway opening. Nobody minded me or noticed me, one way or other. At six o'clock I heard the "half-hour" call over the intercom. Meyers came running down the dressing room stairs.

"Problem. Skipper has a run in her pantyhose." This meant little to me; turned out that Skipper was the nickname of Cathryn Damon, who played the sexy plagiarist. She wore a black see-through outfit in the second act; I remember the wise-cracking producer character watching her enter and saying, with a leer, "If there's anything you don't see, just ask for it." So torn pantyhose could, indeed, be problematic.

"The wardrobe lady's frantic. Go to Smiler's," he said, handing me a ten-dollar bill. That was the takeout deli on Eighth Avenue above

Forty-Fifth, where the stagehands and musicians and hookers got coffee, sandwiches, and other necessaries. "Buy a pair of L'Eggs—they come in those white plastic egg packages. She needs small, the color is called 'nude.'"

"Okay, pantyhose in the egg, small, nude. You sure they have it at Smiler's?"

"Definitely, they have a rack behind the counter." (I suppose the wardrobe lady must have told him.)

"Get a receipt," he yelled after me.

So off I went to Smiler's, which at six on a busy rainy April Saturday night was packed with all sorts of characters. They did indeed have a rack of L'Eggs at the counter, along with other "emergency" items. If I felt awkward asking the jaded clerk at the register for pantyhose, he didn't bat a tired eye. I returned with the egg in a paper bag, gave it to the wardrobe lady waiting by the call board. "Thanks, dear, David said to find him in the lobby."

I went out front, Meyers gave me a ticket, I gave him the change and the receipt. And then—inevitably—*I had to watch the show again.*

Because the curtain time was early and I wasn't invited to whatever passed for the opening night party—it was small, Meyers said, because the budget was tight—I was able to get back to Long Island in time to see the critic on NBC. In those days, believe it or not, four of the local TV stations had theatre critics. The guy on Channel Four that night, Leonard Probst, said, "*A Place for Polly* is not a place for critics, at least not for this one." But by this point, which was about 11:26 p.m., *A Place for Polly* had already folded.

Even so, there I was: still in high school, but I'd already worked on a Broadway show. Not rubbing elbows with the stars, sure, merely buying pantyhose for Skipper Damon in the worst play of 1971. Or at least the worst play since *Grin and Bare It!*

But it was a beginning.

CHAPTER TWO

Passport to Times Square

CROSSROADS OF THE WORLD

I WAS SO BORED BY THE MIDDLE OF TENTH GRADE THAT I DID THE math: if I packed the next year with electives and skipped lunch, I'd have enough credits to graduate. Not quite enough—New York State had a fourth-year English requirement, but I was told that some colleges would waive that. As far as high school was concerned, once I finished my first year of college English, they'd give me a diploma. I didn't care about a diploma, or college, really; I just wanted to start working in the Broadway theatre, and fast. For familial reasons I needed a college degree, but by cutting my senior year of high school it would end that much quicker.

The trick was to get a college to accept me without a high school diploma, which was complicated by the necessity of taking college entrance SAT exams a year earlier than everybody else (without having taken the eleventh-grade courses included on the tests). But I was determined. I learned that the New York University School of Education sometimes accepted students without that final year of English, so that was good enough for me; if I didn't get in, I'd just go back for twelfth grade. I charmed the ancient elocutionist in the admissions department, who reportedly had an affair with John Barrymore back in the mid-1930s, and I was in. Which means that when *A Place for Polly* opened and closed on that evening in mid-April of 1970, I was already booked to move into a Greenwich Village dorm in September.

I called Meyers after the opening to commiserate on the closing. They were not surprised, he said; he knew this might happen, but thought it was worth a try and got his name above the title (although *Polly* turned out to be his final Broadway credit). Meanwhile, he decided to open an office. He was producing an off-Broadway play for the fall, spending the summer on casting and money-raising.

I had spent the prior summers working for my uncle at his Wall Street firm, not because I was interested in finance but because—even at fifteen—I preferred working in an office with adults to summertime activities for teenagers. I planned to go back for the summer of 1970, but a theatrical office sounded ever so much better. Meyers was happy to get free help, naturally, but he also realized that I was dedicated; how many high school students spent their leisure time and dollars going to plays like that past season's *Brightower*, *The Mundy Scheme*, and *Sheep on the Runway*? So I switched my summer address from Hanover Square to Times Square.

To 1545 Broadway, that is. The southwest corner of Forty-Sixth Street, right in the heart of everything. A prime location, a classic-sounding address, but a highly undesirable office building. For good reason. That block—on the western side of the diagonal where Broadway and Seventh Avenue crisscross—consisted of two movie houses. The Astor was on the Forty-Fifth Street side, just across from the legendary Astor Hotel (which was by then a construction site, having been demolished in 1968). The northern end was the Victoria. Both had been built as legit theatres; both had converted to films in 1926, even before the Depression or the advent of sound films. The stage house of the Victoria, which as a live theatre was called the Gaiety, was actually on Forty-Sixth Street; the Broadway frontage included the box office, the entrance lobby, and six stores—all of it topped by five floors of offices.

After switching between films and Minsky's Burlesque, the Gaiety reopened in 1943 reconfigured as the Victoria cinema. Taking advantage of the location, the owners erected a huge, four-story billboard covering half the Broadway block. The Astor management, not to be outdone, erected their own four-story billboard over their third of the block. By 1956, the Astor and the Victoria joined forces with one enormous billboard covering the two buildings; said to be the largest billboard in the world, it was wrapped around the corners so it went from Forty-Fifth Street, up Broadway, and onto Forty-Sixth; not quite, but almost, from the Morosco to the Helen Hayes.

The wraparound Times Square billboard, smothering the windows of 1545 Broadway (between 45th and 46th Streets).
PHOTOFEST

Impressive, yes; if you advertised your movie on that sign, it was *noticed*. But what of the five floors of offices behind the billboard? Well, the view was gone. Many of the windows had been obliterated by the earlier billboards, but the block-long sign was a solid sheet of metal, or hundreds of sheets; what's more, it was covered at the top so no birds could fly in and get trapped. No snow or rain, either. And no sun. The offices still had their windows, and they were functional so you could open them for ventilation; the back of the billboard frame was a foot or so away. But there was no exterior light. What you did get was ambient noise, and plenty of it: Times Square traffic, bouncing between the wall and the metal sign.

So this was not prime rental space; I don't know that people realized the offices were even there, as nothing was visible other than the ground-floor storefronts. Entry was via a door behind the Victoria box office, where there was an elevator and stairs. I took that elevator my first day and headed down a long, dark, but cool hallway. Echoing throughout was the sound of a phonograph record; ah, I thought, someone is playing *Company*. (The Stephen Sondheim/Hal Prince musical opened eight days after *A Place for Polly*, and the original cast album had just been released.)

When I entered the door of the office, there was David Meyers sitting at a desk—next to which was a portable stereo playing *Company*—the electronic sounds of which were even then reverberating off the back of the largest billboard in the world. *Company* would be the incidental music of that office; the record was on all summer, and I don't know why none of the other tenants complained.

BEHIND THE SIGN

The play that Meyers was producing can be disposed of quickly; I was to learn that a majority of plays and musicals optioned for the commercial theatre, worthy or not, were likely never to reach the stage. The specimen in question was called *Sister Sadie*, by one Clifford Mason. One of those mama-on-the-couch plays, to borrow a canny phrase later devised by playwright George C. Wolfe in his *The Colored Museum*. Sadie has a husband, a lover, and a teenage son; she gets the second to kill the first so she can control the third. Something like that. *Sadie* had a director, a star, and even a set design. What it didn't have, and never found, was the money.

They even had a title song. We went one day to a similarly rundown office in a considerably more substantial building at 1650 Broadway, three blocks north. The composer was a fellow named Lincoln Chase. Unimpressive, but he had a pop hit to his credit, a song with which even I—who went out of my way to *not* listen to anything pop—was familiar. You are, too; the title "The Name Game" might not ring a bell, but it's the one with that illustrious phrase "banana fanna fo-fanna." The *Sister Sadie* title song was not so memorable, although I remember it all these years later: "Sister Sadie is a lady, oo-oo-oo, yeah yeah yeah, yeah yeah yeah." Something like that.

The summer was spent in meetings and money-raising, or I should say attempted money-raising. Meyers was unable to get *Sister Sadie* on; it appeared briefly, in the spring of 1972, under other sponsorship, at LaMama. For me, the proximity was a perfect excuse to go and catch up on shows I hadn't already seen. What I remember most was one night when I went to something—can't remember what—that was overlong, so much so that I determined it would be too late to take the train back to Long Island. So after the show, I went back to 1545 Broadway. Up the elevator, down the dark, empty hallway, and into the office. There was an old, cast-off couch, and there I spent the night. A spooky night but kind of magical, alone atop a deserted theatre building with the midnight sounds of Times Square bouncing off the walls.

I also remember an encounter with Gaston and Goldberg, one summer's day at lunch at Joe Allen on the other side of Eighth Avenue. Meyers was smart enough to know, after *A Place for Polly*, that they were not the sort of partners you wanted to have. They were just then embarking on a big-budget musical, which ranks high in the annals of misguided, god-awful fiascos. *Fiddler on the Roof* was still going strong in its sixth year, with two Jewish-theatre-party-specials—*The Rothschilds* (from the *Fiddler* songwriters) and *Two by Two* (from Richard Rodgers, with Danny Kaye as Noah)—competing to be the big fall musical. Gaston and Goldberg planned to top both with *Ari*, a musicalization of the best-selling novel and successful film, *Exodus*.

With money in the bank and rehearsals scheduled for October, Gaston and Goldberg were—for the first and apparently only time—flush. "Life is great," Gaston told me at the bar at Joe Allen, "when you have all this investor money, you gotta *spend* it." They managed to do so, all right. *Ari*, when it finally arrived in January at the Hellinger, was simply terrible. Complete with a concentration camp ballet. The boys produced one final musical a year later, the equally lousy *Heathen!*—a Hawaiian vanity project musical that closed opening night—and that was the end of their Broadway careers.

Joe Allen regularly hung window cards from Broadway disasters on his restaurant walls, and those two musicals immediately earned their place. Gaston opened an upscale gay bar called Rounds, on East

Fifty-Third Street, in 1979, and was dead by 1983. Goldberg had a quicker and even more ignominious fate, if you will: the morning after his thirty-third birthday in 1979 he was found handcuffed in his bedroom with his brains blown out. Seems he had become a drug dealer, produced a soon-to-be released, underfunded big-budget major motion picture (the JFK-assassination thriller, *Winter Kills*) using mob money, and run afoul of the Mafia. Goldberg's partner and coproducer, one Robert Sterling, wound up with a forty-year sentence for drug smuggling albeit with brains intact. But that's someone else's story to tell, not ours.

I ran into Meyers occasionally over the years—looking increasingly scruffy—outside various theatres at curtain time, cadging patrons with the plea "anyone have an extra ticket?" The last time I saw him was at the final press preview of the Royal Shakespeare Company's import of *All's Well That Ends Well* at the Martin Beck, in 1983. Liz McCann and Nelle Nugent were the lead producers.

"There's a man by the stage door asking for comps," said Liz or Nelle (I can't rightly remember which), pointing toward someone with glazed eyes who looked like the male equivalent of what was then called a bag lady. "He smells. If someone gives him a ticket, don't let him in." And that was the last I saw of David G. Meyers.

ME AND THE ME

I have always found that in this business, one thing inevitably leads to another. And so it was in the summer of 1970, as I was preparing to leave my first theatre job (of sorts) and start classes at NYU. Across the hall from Meyers was the office of Jeff Britton, a minor off-Broadway producer who at the time had his one and only hit, a loose-knit musical called *The Me Nobody Knows*. Britton's assistant would stop in on occasion, I expect to escape from her boss. Also popping in was Malcolm Allen, the company manager of *The Me*. The company manager is more or less the on-site business manager of the show, in the office by day and at the theatre by night. They both told me I must go down and see *The Me*. I went to the Orpheum Theatre one night, and liked it a lot.

I moved into my dorm on a Tuesday, with classes starting Thursday. On Wednesday, I paid a final visit to the office and Malcolm stopped in. "You don't ever need any ushers or anything down there, do you?" I asked.

"Yes, matter of fact. Can you start tomorrow?"

And so it was that on my first day of college I started my first paid job in the theatre, as a lowly usher at *The Me Nobody Knows*.

NYU was in a state of transition just then. They were building a grand new library, but it wasn't finished; what passed for a library, during my years there, was spread out among empty space in several buildings. They were breaking ground for a grand new gymnasium, but it wasn't even started; if you wanted to use the gym—which I didn't, ever—you had to take the subway up to the other NYU campus in the Bronx. Dorm space was so tight that the university took a floor in the hotel at One Fifth Avenue and crammed five of us into a one-bedroom apartment. That's where I spent my first year of college.

One Fifth Avenue—which soon thereafter was converted into a high-luxury co-op—was located at the southeast corner of Fifth Avenue and Eighth Street, right above Washington Square Park. I knew the area well, as my paternal grandparents lived at Two Fifth Ave.; I could actually see into their sixth-floor living room from my dorm room window on the fourth floor. The fabled Greenwich Village of the 1920s–1950s started to disappear in the mid-1960s, as hippies displaced bohemians and beatniks. The main stretch of Eighth Street between Fifth and Sixth Avenue still had some of its long-established book and record stores, but the invasion of T-shirt stores, pizza-by-the-slice, and cheap paraphernalia had begun.

Heading east across Eighth Street led you to University Place and Broadway, a few short blocks over; then Astor Place, where the New York Shakespeare Festival had only recently opened the cavernous Public Theater; and then the East Village. St. Marks Place—the continuation of Eighth Street—was then the center of the counterculture. One block more took you to the Orpheum on Second Avenue, one of off-Broadway's most desirable houses. *The Me* opened there in May and was doing sellout business when I arrived in early September.

Ushers are just about the lowest rung of the ladder, theatre-wise, and not a group that typically fraternizes with the talent. But *The Me* was not typical. The cast ranged in age from eleven to twenty-five; at seventeen, I was just about in the middle. The show consisted of writings by underprivileged, undereducated ghetto children, freely adapted and set to music. While some of the cast came in with theatre credits, half were newly discovered amateurs who felt somewhat out of place as working actors. I already had more professional knowledge, for whatever that's worth, than most of them. So I was accepted into the group, such as it was. Which meant, merely, that we would occasionally go for quick meals or to see a movie. The mother of the littlest kid—eleven-year-old Irene Cara—was an usherette at the Rivoli, one of the big movie houses on Broadway. Sometimes she let a bunch of us sneak in through the exit door, and I don't know how she got away with it.

Irene and a boy from Chicago named Douglas Grant were the youngest, and the cutest, and great audience favorites; they actually had the most prominent Broadway credit, having been featured in the 1968 Shirley Jones/Jack Cassidy vehicle, *Maggie Flynn*. Hattie Winston and Northern J. Calloway, talented performers who were clearly well over high school age, had the most important roles in *The Me*; both quickly moved up to Broadway as star replacements, Hattie as Silvia in *Two Gentlemen of Verona* and Northern replacing Ben Vereen in *Pippin*. It was Irene, though, who became the most famous, acting in—and singing the title song of—the 1980 film *Fame*. She also, somehow, won herself a Best Song Oscar in 1984 as one of the songwriters of "Flashdance, What a Feeling."

The work demands of an usher are minimal, with no actual involvement in the production. The other two ushers at the Orpheum were adults with full-time jobs elsewhere; this was just a way to pick up some extra cash, which came to about $20 per week. For me, though, this was a better education than college. I would watch the show closely, performance after performance, noting differing reactions from different audiences, observing when the material worked and when it didn't—and trying to figure out why.

PIXILATED GNOME

The most memorable event at the Orpheum occurred one October Saturday during the early show. (We played the then-standard off-Broadway schedule, with Saturday performances at 7:00 and 10:00.) Midway through the first act I returned to the small lobby; the house entrance doors run parallel to the street, with the box office window at one end and stairs to the balcony at the other. Sitting on the bottom landing was a gnome-like man in his own cloud, wearing a dazed smile beneath what might be described as a jaunty cap. A patron? A street person who wandered in, stoned, from St. Mark's Place? A pixilated gnome? From the looks of him, he could have been any of the above—or perhaps all.

"Can I help you?" I asked.

"Oh, the music is so beautiful, I can't bear to stay inside." The accent was British, with something of a daffily cockneyish lilt.

"This is a wonderful show, you should go back in," I said.

"Just flew in this morning," he said. "Got meetings, tomorrow, for my new show."

"Oh," I said, having already learned that half the people you were likely to meet around the theatre were in their spare time writing a script—which was, of course, extraordinary. "Are you a writer?"

"Yes, we're doing an extravaganza of *Gulliver's Travels*."

Sure, I thought; *Gulliver's Travels* onstage, *that* sounds easy enough.

Looking at this strange little man, I suddenly thought—wait a minute, I just read about this in *Variety*. *Gulliver's Travels*: Lionel Bart!

I was already worldly enough not to say, gee, I love *Oliver!* or gosh, I played Fagin in junior high school. Or anything of the sort. So I just said, "Kermit Bloomgarden, isn't it?" (Bloomgarden was the producer of a long line of important shows, including *The Music Man*—and a tenant at 1545 Broadway.)

"Yes. Larry Gelbart's writing the book. Brilliant genius."

Gulliver's Travels from Lionel Bart and Larry Gelbart did, indeed, sound like it was tantalizing if impossible. The show never got on, in any event; Bart's brain had apparently sizzled in 1965. His last big musical, a written-for-Broadway version of Fellini's *La Strada*, had closed after only one performance in December 1969; while Bart's name was on the score, he had been pretty much absent—reportedly institutionalized, somewhere—and all but three of his songs were cut. Good songs, mind you. But Bart was never to come up with anything of consequence from 1964 until his death in 1999.

From inside the house I could hear Beverly Bremers and José Fernandez singing the plaintive duet, "How I Feel."

"You really should go back in, now. This song is very touching, and the first act finale—'If I Had a Million'—is wonderful. You really don't want to miss it."

"Yes, I'll just sit here a bit longer," said he.

I went off to do whatever it was I had to do, and when I returned Bart was gone. Must have left altogether; I couldn't spot him at intermission or after the show.

Over the years, I've come to appreciate Bart's work; what's good is exceptional, in a rough-hewn way. I didn't know this, in 1970, at which point little of his work other than *Oliver!* was known stateside; but I expect I appreciate and understand the man a bit more, thanks to our unconventional chat.

My two months at *The Me* abruptly ended on November 15. Actors' Equity called an off-Broadway strike, closing down all seventeen shows then playing. It was an interesting situation for the kids in *The Me*; here they were, mostly under twenty, earning a paycheck that—while not what the folks on the Equity council might consider a living wage—was large for non-middle-class city dwellers, circa 1970. Many of the "kids" were clearly outearning their parents, making a substantial contribution to the family budget. And here were some uptown union people, few of whom had ever worked under off-Broadway contracts or cared to, voting to cut off their suddenly established careers.

The strike lasted thirty-one days, during which the decision was made to move *The Me* to Broadway. The show reopened on December 18 at the Helen Hayes Theatre. The original one on West Forty-Sixth Street, which was demolished in 1982—along with four other theatres and the office building at 1545 Broadway—to make way for the so-called Portman Project, resulting in the Marriott Marquis Hotel.

The show went on to a Broadway run of almost a year, turning a slight profit. But not with me. There was no chance of my continuing as an usher; the Broadway theatres at the time used females only. (The one exception was the Music Box, which had male ushers and an impossibly long waiting list for openings.) Even before the Broadway transfer of *The Me* was announced, I did find a job on Broadway—kind of.

Too Little, Too Soon

Back at 1545 Broadway, there was a fellow in the next office down the hall named Bruce W. Stark. I used to go in to chat, but more specifically to gawk at a framed window card (poster) hanging on the wall. This was from a 1967 play called *The Freaking Out of Stephanie Blake*, at the Eugene O'Neill; a photographer by trade, Stark's photographs were used in the show as projections. Stephanie Blake didn't freak out, but star Jean Arthur did, during the second preview; the show closed then and there. Arthur, who gave incomparable performances in such classic films as *Mr. Smith Goes to Washington* and *Shane*, had a similar experience during the 1946 tryout of Garson Kanin's *Born Yesterday*. The star suffered from stage fright so severe that the producers had no choice but to replace her during the tryout, with an unknown named Judy Holliday.

Stark was producing a musical called *Soon*, opening mid-December; the coproducer—and I expect main backer—was Sagittarius Productions, which was the stage name for Edgar M. Bronfman Sr. of the Seagram's distillery. (He was a major backer of *1776*, and Sagittarius was credited as associate producer of *The Me Nobody Knows*.) This was one of those hopeless rock musicals that had no place on Broadway—or off-Broadway—but turned up due to the whirlwind success of *Hair*. *Soon* was booked into the Ritz Theatre on West Forty-Eighth Street. A never-popular Shubert house from 1921, the Ritz had given up after twenty years and in 1943 converted to radio (and later television). ABC moved out in 1965, leaving the place empty. Some non-enterprising landlord bought it in 1970, and planned to bring the house back to life (?) with *Soon*.

But it wasn't Broadway, exactly. There was studio audience seating, left over from the television years, with a restricted capacity of 499; I seem to recall that the boxes were still set up as sound booths and thus unusable. The undernourished Ritz scrounged through a handful of bookings—five flops over three years, none running more than two weeks—and quickly went back out of business in 1973. The Jujamcyn chain bought the house

If the artwork looks suspiciously familiar, that's because David Edward Byrd immediately thereafter replaced the initial art for *Follies* with a similar image of Lady Liberty, albeit with cracked façade. *Soon* (1971).
MAX A. WOODWARD COLLECTION, MUSIC DIVISION, LIBRARY OF CONGRESS

in 1983, eventually springing for a grand renovation capped by a name change to the Walter Kerr. But in 1970, the Ritz was mostly nonunion—it certainly didn't have union ushers—so Stark said I should go over and talk to the house manager.

Why, here and now, should anyone be writing or reading about *Soon*? Long gone, and understandably forgotten. But there were things to note. *Soon* told the story of a rock musician who came to town, joined a band with some other rock musicians, met up with a manager who wanted them to go commercial, etc. Including plenty of groupies, listed in the program as Groupies. What made things interesting, though, was the cast of unknowns. The singer who came to town was a fellow called Barry Bostwick, a year before he starred in *Grease*. His girl was Marta Heflin. One of the boys in the band he joined was a tall and scraggly twenty-one-year-old named Richard Gere.

What made things even more interesting were the problems unfolding through previews. The show, clearly, didn't work—so much so that after two weeks they shut down, fired director/coauthor Robert Greenwald, and went back into rehearsals. (This is a highly uncommon, and highly expensive, proposition.) Greenwald was replaced by Gerald Freedman, who in 1967 directed the original, pre-Broadway production of *Hair* at the Public Theater. Being less than successful, *Hair* was duly rewritten and reborn—with Tom O'Horgan replacing Freedman.

The new book for *Soon* came from Martin Duberman, whose culturally significant *In White America* had opened off-Broadway in 1963 for a five-hundred-performance run. Barred from the premises, was composer/lyricist Scott Fagan. This was problematic; he had been playing one of the leading roles along with Bostwick and Gere. In came a replacement, an Australian singer best known as the then-husband to Liza Minnelli: Peter Allen.

Previews resumed two weeks later, and the show was still no good. They opened on January twelfth, closed on the thirteenth. I still remember *Soon*, but not for Bostwick, Allen, Gere, or Heflin. What remains with me is a song in the first act called "Music, Music."

One of the five Groupies started singing, you couldn't even see who she was, but the voice—a high, sweet, clarion voice—emerged from the clutter and cut through the house. I still can't forget that voice, which belonged to a twenty-two-year-old from Birmingham called Nell Carter.

Blue Coat

After *Soon*, I was eager to keep spending my nights in a Broadway theatre. If ushering was out of the question, why not sell candy?

Two brothers, Al and Selwyn Golub, had the refreshment and coatroom concession at all the Broadway theatres. Not just the Shubert houses but the rest, too, along with Carnegie Hall. The story was that the Golubs started back in the days when the Shuberts had a big room in the basement of the Booth Theatre, where the boys helped mix huge vats of not especially sanitary orange drink. In 1970, theatre concessions was such a marginal operation that nobody else bothered to compete. Nowadays, it has become a real business.

I went for an interview not with the Golubs but with their general manager—a son-in-law, I think—in a dingy office on the second floor of the Consulate Hotel, just next to the Eugene O'Neill Theatre. Yes, they always had openings for new people. Could I work Wednesday matinees? A not inconsiderable request, as many of their employees had full-time day jobs—needed them, because this was a part-time job with minimal pay. Sure, I could. When could I start?

I had determined, being a seventeen-year-old with definite ideas, that I should wangle an assignment to the Majestic. A big, important new musical was scheduled for March, loaded with top Broadway names; I was sure it would be a disaster, so I figured this was the best place to be. (I had, of course, no interest in selling candy or earning the six bucks a performance that the job paid.) "If possible, I would really like to work at the Majestic," said I. "We'll see," I was told.

A few days later I was called and told to show up tomorrow at 6:00 p.m. at the Shubert. *Promises, Promises* was, in my opinion, the funniest musical on Broadway. But it was already in its third year. I wanted a new show, like *Prettybelle*. That being the Gower Champion/Jule Styne/Bob Merrill/Alexander H. Cohen musical starring Angela Lansbury, which was just about to start its Boston tryout. "I was kind of hoping for the Majestic."

"*Prettybelle* doesn't come in until March," I was told. "Start at the Shubert, and we'll see if there's an opening at the Majestic." There was an opening at the Majestic, for sure; *Prettybelle* bombed, as I suspected, but so badly that it never left Boston and the Majestic remained empty.

Candyland

HOME AT THE SHUBERT

FORTUNATELY FOR ME—OR MOST FORTUNATELY FOR ME, CAREER-wise—I was safely at the Shubert. There I found a little old man named Louis Lapp; everyone called him "Lurkey." Why Lurkey? The big first act finale in *Promises* was called "Turkey Lurkey Time," but the nickname had apparently been in place thirty years before. Lurkey must have been sixty or more; the fact is, everyone in those days looked old to me. He had a wife named Dora; they had been at the Shubert since forever. (For what it's worth, they told me they liked *Whoop-Up!*—a laughably bad 1959 flop set on an Indian reservation in Montana that played there—and thought it would be a big hit.) But like many of the people working in the front of the house—which in theatre parlance means everyone not backstage—they seemed to have little interest whatsoever in anything theatrical. It was just a job, or in most cases a second job.

My routine, when I began in early February, started with entering the lobby and being "buzzed in" by the box office treasurer. There were two treasurers at the Shubert just then: a septuagenarian old-timer named Hughie something-or-other, who was nominally in charge; and a thirty-something up-and-comer named Phil Smith who did most of the work. I usually arrived at the theatre during Hughie's dinner break, so I quickly got to know Phil—who eventually became chair of the Shubert Organization.

I would start by setting up the candy stands in the orchestra, balcony, and lower lobby; then stand inside the entrance door—just next to the souvenir book man—when the house opened, trying to convince people to check their coats for a buck; then go up to the balcony fifteen minutes before the show to sell some candy; haul cases of orange drink and lemonade to the various stands, late in the first act; go up to the balcony for the intermission; pack up the leftovers after intermission; and count the money. The least enjoyable part was lugging those cases of twenty-four half-pint cartons up to the second balcony of the Shubert; the warmer the weather, the more cases of juice.

"That's all right," said Dora. "You know who used to sell drinks up there for us? Dustin Hoffman."

The best part, of course, was that I got to see the show. I had loved *Promises* when I saw it shortly after the opening; the score was fun and perfectly suitable, but the book by Neil Simon was hysterically funny. What's more, the show *moved*; the producer, David Merrick, had gambled on a young choreographer and a young set designer, who created a new, collaborative method of staging.

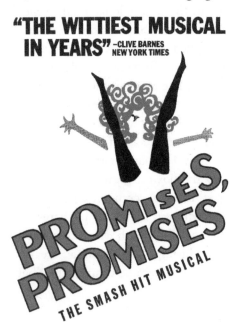

A nightly education in musical comedy, from professors Neil Simon and Michael Bennett. *Promises, Promises!* (1968).

It used to be: scene ends; blackout; scene change music; lights up on next set with actors entering. At *Promises*, the scene would end *without* a blackout. The "wagons"—winched platforms holding desks, props, or flats—would start to glide off, with actors upon them, while the elevator banks of the lobby set would fly in from above. Simultaneously, other actors would dance on, weaving their way through the exiting scenery and the flying walls, at the end of which the actors in the next scene would have already started their dialogue. All lit for viewing, all accompanied by music.

This sort of change had been pioneered in prior musicals, notably with a stunning sequence in *Hello, Dolly!* in and around the "Dancing" number. The innovative set designer Oliver Smith, whose stellar credits included such shows as *On the Town*, *My Fair Lady*, and *West Side Story*, had done a remarkably colorful job on *Dolly!* He had a gifted young assistant named Robin Wagner, who was interested in making scenery *move*, and who appears to have worked out the mechanics of the "Dancing" change.

Merrick's associate producer, a former stage manager named Samuel "Biff" Liff, had worked with Oliver on numerous shows (including *Gentlemen Prefer Blondes* and *My Fair Lady*). *Promises* was a new-style musical, though, with a pop score from Burt Bacharach and Hal David and a pop sound featuring recording-studio sound amplification; why not try something new, scenery-wise? Wagner had just designed his first Broadway musical, *Hair*—which had an adaptable unit set but didn't necessarily suggest a designer with a keen musical comedy mind. But Biff knew that it was Robin who had made *Dolly!* and *Baker Street*—another highly mechanized Oliver Smith musical—move.

Biff also found the choreographer. Merrick's prior big-budget, big-business musical—which opened almost exactly a year before *Promises*—was a somewhat cheesy affair called *How Now, Dow Jones*. During the tryout, they fired the director (Arthur Penn) and brought in George Abbott. They also fired the choreographer (Gillian Lynne), bringing in a kid to whom they didn't even bother giving credit. Michael Bennett was the name; while he certainly couldn't fix *How Now, Dow Jones*, his dances made it more watchable. (Like Wagner, Bennett had been an unheralded

Merrick employee several years earlier, dancing in the chorus of the 1961 musical *Subways Are for Sleeping*.) Impressed with Bennett's uncredited work on *How Now* plus another flop, *Henry, Sweet Henry*, Biff convinced Merrick to give the newcomer a chance on *Promises*.

Bennett and Wagner obliged by creating scenery that danced; further experimented when Bennett was brought in to try to fix *Seesaw*, another musical mess; created a legendary landmark with *A Chorus Line*; and revolutionized the entire concept of musical theatre movement in *Dreamgirls*. But this happened thirteen years after *Promises*. Me, I just sat there at the Shubert watching the choreographed scene changes and thought: this is wonderful, and it really does change the way musicals work.

Promises also gave me the opportunity to observe audiences respond to Neil Simon's jokes. While I tired of watching the entire show every night, I was always in the house just before intermission (setting up, quietly) and just after intermission (packing up), which meant that I saw Bennett's "Turkey Lurkey Time"—which remains one of the most outlandishly dazzling Broadway production numbers ever—at every performance, right before intermission.

And I saw the second act opener, a song called "A Fact Can Be a Beautiful Thing," featuring an amusing saloon dance featuring drunken Santa Clauses. More to the point, though, was the short scene that led to that song and the scene that followed immediately thereafter. Chuck, the hero, picks up a girl in an owl coat named Marge MacDougall—she picks him up, actually—and takes her home. This Marge is at the top of the list of funniest characters in the annals of the Broadway musical. It was a brief role with only two scenes; the actresses who played it in the original production (our friend Marian Mercer, from *A Place for Polly*) and in the 2010 revival (Katie Finneran) both walked away with easy wins in the Tony competition—which is a testament not only to the actors but to the guy who wrote the jokes.

By the time I reached *Promises*, replacements had long taken over the principal roles. My Madge MacDougall was Mary Louise Wilson. Folks, I saw Marian Mercer, I saw Katie Finneran, and they were excellent. But Mary Louise Wilson gave one of the funniest performances I have ever seen, anywhere. And I got to see her every performance, month after month. That's the kind of reward you get, standing at the back of the house every night.

INTERMISSION GAME

Not that I stood at the back of the house every night. I immediately found that my worn and tattered blue Golub Bros. blazer provided free access to all Broadway theatres. Any show that had a different playing schedule was fair game; soon after I started there was a show at the nearby Morosco called *And Miss Reardon Drinks a Little*, the first Broadway effort of Paul Zindel (who had won the 1971 Pulitzer for his off-Broadway play *The Effects of Gamma Rays on Man-in-the-Moon Marigolds*). *Miss Reardon* was a flop, with a three-month run.

But I was fascinated by it; you might have been, too, given the deft performances from Julie Harris (suffering a nervous breakdown), Estelle Parsons (who drank a little, continuously) and Nancy Marchand (as their disapproving sister). Plus, a Tony-winning featured performance by Rae Allen and a comic assist from Bill Macy, who was en route from the pits of show business—in the original cast of *Oh! Calcutta!*—to playing Bea Arthur's husband in the sitcom *Maude. Miss Reardon* contained a wonderful moment at the climax when Parsons gleefully tortured her vegetarian sister Julie by pulling a handful of raw hamburger meat out of a Fanny Farmer candy tin—wonderful and horrifying, regularly pulling a gasp from the audience. The candy man at the Morosco didn't need me to pitch in and help, as the small theatre was never crowded; but I was free to go back and watch whenever I wanted to, merely telling the doorman I was going to the checkroom.

The neighboring theatres often needed extra hands for intermission; with houses in close proximity and intermission times staggered, I could easily cover a show with three short acts (like *No, No, Nanette* at the 46th Street) or an overlong first act (like *1776*, which had added an intermission and moved to the St. James).

As an aside, I suppose I should mention a Broadway fixture of that time. There were two different violinists who were omnipresent on the streets, working the crowds for tips. One was old, punctuating his music with stale comic patter; he favored "Sunrise, Sunset" and "The Anniversary

Waltz." The other—Richie was his name—was in his twenties, with great charm, something of a Horatio Alger look, and a less ethnic, crowd-friendly repertoire. They would show up at half-hour, when the doors opened, at the theatre where they'd realized they'd do best. Not the finest show or the biggest hit, but musicals attracting innocent tourists most likely to respond. Thus, the older violinist was always outside *Promises*, where he could also catch patrons going to see the other shows on the Forty-Fourth Street block; the other, I believe, started his nights at *Nanette*.

Given that curtain times were staggered, they were able to work two "come-ins"—after which they followed intricately organized inter-mission schedules. These were especially lucrative; there were always enormous crowds of smokers—along with pretzel and roasted chestnut carts—under the marquee. The violinists then proceeded to other theatres for the "walk-out," as the various shows ended. This allowed them to hit perhaps eight or nine theatres in a night. Given that I was often dashing from place to place to work intermissions that didn't interfere with *Prom-ises*, I was amused to find them on various sidewalks waiting for the doors to open. They knew enough not to start playing while the curtain was up, so as not to interfere with the show and be shooed away.

I don't imagine they actually coordinated their schedules, because they were in every aspect quite different; but I never saw them on the same block at the same time. And then one day—in 1975, perhaps?—they both vanished forever.

OLD FOLKS

In April, a charmingly forlorn Kander & Ebb musical called *70, Girls, 70* moved into the Broadhurst, directly next to the Shubert. The tim-ing allowed me to do the intermissions for the entire run of six weeks (including previews)—and to observe, in detail, the struggles of an ill-fated show.

70, Girls, 70 was a kiss-of-death musical. Literally. The Philadelphia tryout, which was going along disastrously, ground to a halt when the lead-ing man died onstage. David Burns was one of the great Broadway come-dians, going back to his performance as Banjo (the Harpo Marx–inspired character) in Kaufman & Hart's 1939 comedy *The Man Who Came to Dinner*. He won a Tony in 1958 for his performance as the obstreperous Mayor Shinn in *The Music Man*, and another in 1963 as the henpecked husband and father Senex in *A Funny Thing Happened on the Way to the Forum*. He might well have won a third, for *Hello, Dolly!*; but when the show was successfully doctored during its tryout, Carol Channing's Dolly was embellished while Burns's Vandergelder lost most of his songs.

Burns had started the 1970–1971 season in *Lovely Ladies, Kind Gentlemen*, a musicalization of *The Teahouse of the August Moon* that quickly flopped at the Majestic (thus opening the way for the *Prettybelle* booking). Upon that show's demise, Burns was rushed into *70, Girls*. One of the high points of the second act was "Go Visit Your Grandmother," a frenetic challenge dance between the one youngster in the cast—twenty-five-year-old Tommy Breslin, as the bellhop at the old-age home—and the sixty-eight-year-old Burns. At the Saturday matinee at the Forrest on March 12, Burns finished the number, collapsed in the wings, and died.

70, Girls—which wasn't selling any tickets, anyway—closed early in Philadelphia and tried to recover, bringing in Hans Conried as replacement (and he was stridently charmless). But the show simply wasn't going to work; the die was cast early on, when librettist Joe Masteroff and director/choreographer Ron Field—both of whom had worked with Kander & Ebb on *Cabaret*—withdrew. Davey Burns, meanwhile, was remembered in April with a posthumous Tony nomination—the first ever for a performer?—for *Lovely Ladies*.

There are musicals that are hits that you love; others that are hits that you don't much like; and others that are just altogether poor. And then there are occasional musicals that you like a lot, even though you know as you're watching that they just aren't going to make it. Musicals that you're rooting for, at which you feel disappointed and disheartened every time they come to a scene or song that you know—from seeing the show previously—just doesn't work. "Don't do that!" you want to yell to the director and authors, almost cringing as you can feel the people sitting around you withdraw their interest and affection.

70, Girls was a prime example, as were later musicals like *The Robber Bridegroom* and *Baby*. I saw *70, Girls*—parts of it—many times. I went back to see *Robber Bridegroom* and *Baby* three times each; they were lingering on with poor houses, papering heavily. (Papering, for the uninitiated, is what you do when you have scads of unsold tickets and wish to fill the house—or at least keep it from looking empty to the hearty few who actually did buy tickets.) Watching the weak sections of these shows again and again, I would sit thinking, I *still* like this—but I can understand why most of the audience doesn't.

I stood there at the back of the house at *70, Girls, 70* through previews, hoping it would magically get better. (I would rush out of *Promises* as the overture began, arriving at the Broadhurst during the opening number.) This was my first chance to closely observe the production staff of a Broadway musical, watching them as they watched the audience, as they hastily consulted in muffled voices, as they darted in and out of the house. (Songwriters and choreographers typically leave for the book scenes, which they really don't care to sit through ever again. Bookwriters leave during the songs.) I always seemed to be standing next to composer John Kander, although I didn't get to know him until twenty-five years later. He seemed to be especially fond of *70, Girls*; after the opening, when he had no more work to do and the show was clearly expiring, he continued to stop in just to watch and offer support to the cast.

70, Girls was about an Upper West Side retirement home full of feisty old-timers who band together to steal furs. (Now *that* sounds like an exciting musical, doesn't it!) My favorite moments came whenever Lillian Hayman had anything to do. She was playing—well, it's hard to say just what she was playing. One of the retirees, I guess you could call it, although she certainly didn't look like any of the other residents. Lillian was teamed up with a little old Jewish lady to sing rousing numbers during scene changes, during costume changes, and when the show otherwise ground to a halt (which was often). There was a corny but delicious song that meant nothing plot-wise about "Coffee in a Cardboard Cup"; another, "Broadway, My Street," that was a grandly corny salute to the theatre; and yet another in which she danced like an elephant (called, in an act of inspiration, "The Elephant Song"). She also had a religioso hymn to sing while the old folks were cracking a safe in a cold storage room; it was that sort of show.

I had met Lillian back in 1967, when I saw *Hallelujah, Baby!* Playing Leslie Uggams's mother, she had a number called "I Don't Know Where She Got It," which she turned into a showstopper so grand that she won the best featured actress Tony Award. I went out of my way, at fourteen, to go backstage at the Martin Beck to meet her. Lillian was always a joy to watch onstage, a performer in full control.

Passing the Broadhurst stage door one Saturday after the *70, Girls* and *Promises* matinees, I found Lillian talking to a couple of twenty-somethings; one turned out to be an usherette, the other a candy boy from the St. James or someplace. I stopped to join them. Then Lillian said, "Anyone want to eat?" and led us—like a Pied Piperess—across the street not to Sardi's but to China Peace, a sprawling place just east of the loading docks of the *New York Times*. Without advance planning, we joined Lillian again on the next two (and final) Saturdays of the run. No glorified tales of show business, no profound observations. Just four mismatched people having a quiet, sociable dinner.

Why a sixty-year-old character lady with her own Tony Award should choose to dine between shows at a midtown Chinese restaurant with three white teenagers she didn't know, I can't tell you. In retrospect, I now realize that our half block of West Forty-Fourth Street—which just then had four shows running—employed about 120 actors, only three of whom I calculate were Black. That's what it was like on Broadway back then. We were of course thrilled to sit over chicken and broccoli with someone as accomplished as Lillian Hayman; as for her, it just might be that she was glad to have *anyone* to spend time with between shows. China Peace would have presumably seated an elderly Black woman, back in 1971, but—Tony Award or no—she certainly got better service in the company of middle-class white kids.

INSTANT CLASSIC, ALMOST

At the same time, a new show moved into the Winter Garden—too far from the Shubert to simply drop in, but easy to walk into when the playing schedules diverged. This musical was the bane of the concession-aire's existence: *no intermission*—which meant they could sell candy (and liquor) beforehand but nothing else. A waste of the liquor license, it was.

If the Winter Garden concessionaire hated *Follies*, I found it pretty interesting. But I couldn't help noticing, on my several visits, that the show seemed to antagonize its base audience.

That *Follies* is a good show (whatever the word *good* might connote), an important show, and an influential show is now generally accepted. So is the quality of the score, which at the time was attacked on several fronts—including by Clive Barnes from the *Times*, who called it "the kind of musical that should have its original cast album out on 78's." Clive, bless him, went on to say that Sondheim's "words are a joy to listen to, even when his music is sending shivers of indifference up your spine. The man is a Hart in search of a Rodgers, or even a Boito in search of a Verdi."

Shivers of indifference?

Follies was the tale of two fiftyish couples—one middle class, one upper class—living through tattered marriages, blindly yoked to partners from whom they were long estranged. In the course of the show, which takes place in the course of an evening, the blinders are pulled off, revealing the secret desolation they each feel and the lies that mask their lives. They are surrounded not only by ghosts of their past, who illuminate the choices they made and "The Road You Didn't Take," but by a veritable bevy of colleagues—mostly women, mostly older—who have led similarly dissatisfying lives.

The base audience for *Follies*—that is, the people who were buying the majority of tickets for Broadway musicals in those depressed days of 1971—consisted of couples in their fifties and above, of the middle and upper classes, who had lived through many of the bumps that the characters of *Follies* had. These were generations for whom self-examination and divorce were relatively rare, when aggrieved spouses had little recourse but to stay stuck in tattered marriages. (In 1970, as *Follies* was being written, the US divorce rate was 33 percent. By 1975, it had risen to 48 percent.) "Look in the mirror, examine your failings, face the truth," it seems like the creators were saying to their characters—all the while holding up that same mirror to their audiences.

Standing at the back railing during the long, long, long show—more than two hours, without a break (although later productions have inserted an intermission)—I could feel aggression coming from a good portion of the paying customers in the expensive seats. Perhaps because I was wearing a candy seller uniform and thus appeared to be an employee, the men felt free to grumble their complaints. They walked out of the show in a huff, or escaped to the restroom for overlong breaks with a visit to the bar at the Hawaii Kai restaurant next door. They came to the Winter Garden to be entertained by a musical about the *Follies*, and they were betrayed by—well, by the mirror with which they were confronted.

The so-called theatre folk in the audience mostly loved *Follies*, yes. And there was a not insignificant segment of the audience that was under thirty that embraced the show; these are the people who for decades have been loudly proclaiming the original production of *Follies* as the best and greatest piece of theatre in the history of the world. There is something to be said for this viewpoint. But it is my contention, based on the experience of standing there through four performances over the run, that the core audience that was needed to support the show—which I might have described at the time as our parents, our grandparents, and their friends—did not like it. Many were incensed by it. Not that it applies, but I can at the same time say that the people streaming out of the non-challenging *Promises* after every performance were bubbling over with musical comedy–infused joy.

This all took place during the first stages of a nostalgia boom. The early months of 1971 featured not one but three Broadway musicals built upon the talents of "old-time" performers, and duly promoted as such. *Follies*, by its very title, brought to mind the Ziegfeld era. The cast included Hollywood's Alexis Smith, Gene Nelson, and Yvonne de Carlo from the 1940s; Dorothy Collins from the *Hit Parade* of the 1950s; and as many 1920s performers as the casting directors could find (including Ethel Shutta—a bona fide "Broadway Baby" who worked for Ziegfeld—and even Ethel Barrymore Colt, daughter of the first lady of the American Theatre circa 1901–1942). The title itself led to an expectation of a Ziegfeldian celebration of the good old days, which *Follies* decidedly wasn't.

70, Girls, 70 sounded like—well, like an offshoot of the *Follies* of old, with a title borrowed from the typical ballyhoo used by Ziegfeld and his competitors. In this case, "70" referred not to the cast size but the age of the performers. (The opening number began with ensemble members stating their actual birthdates, the earliest being 1892.) The cast featured one more-or-less Broadway star in Mildred Natwick, along with former Ziegfeld singer Lillian Roth. Roth was a walking, authentic example of precisely what Stephen Sondheim addressed in his *Follies* anthem, "I'm Still Here." She made her Broadway debut in 1917 at the age of six; starred in early musical talkies; and became a household name courtesy of the best-selling 1954 autobiographical account of her descent to the skids of alcoholism, *I'll Cry Tomorrow*. Susan Hayward was nominated for an Oscar for her performance as Roth in the film version.

But *70, Girls* was otherwise cast with smaller fry with lesser careers; it almost seemed that it was peopled with leftovers who didn't make it to the *Follies* callbacks. Joey Faye, anyone? Both shows opened within a fortnight, and let me add that I did actually hear middle-aged ticket-buying ladies confuse the shows. (At *70, Girls*: "Isn't this the one about the *Follies*?")

Both musicals—one from Sondheim & Prince, the other from Kander & Ebb—were obliterated at the box office by the least likely of that season's nostalgic musicals. *No, No, Nanette*—not a new show, a rehash of a simplistic 1925 musical—sounded like a pure vanity production, so much so that the producer couldn't even get a New York booking until the pre-Broadway tryout proved an instant sellout. Ruby Keeler? Patsy Kelly? Staging by Busby Berkeley?? But *Nanette* was unstoppable, a major financial hit with SRO audiences and multiple companies while *70, Girls* crashed and *Follies* limped along, both en route to financial wipeout.

Which is not to say that *Follies* wasn't a better or more important show than *Nanette* or anything else on the boards that season. *Follies* wasn't, though, popular entertainment.

SHUBERT ALLEY SALUTE

Most of my time that spring, though, was spent at the Shubert and *Promises*, a long way from the world outside. Vietnam, rather astonishingly, did intrude on Shubert Alley one Monday evening. (The internet tells me it was March 29, 1971.) I slipped out to the Piccadilly coffee shop on an errand, wearing my blue blazer, prior to the opening of the house. As I was passing under the marquee, one of the patrons milling around stopped me—a crewcut soldier in full military uniform, with a chestful of medals. Young (though older than me), distraught or drunk or both, but immensely polite.

"Are you connected with the show?" he asked in an accent that must have come from the hills of Appalachia.

When I said I was, he took out a twenty-dollar bill and tried to stuff it in my palm.

"Take this," he said. (I didn't.)

"You need to help me," he said, it now being clear that he'd had a few. "Can you tell them to make an announcement about Lieutenant Calley? It's a disgrace of justice, good Americans gotta protest."

The months-long court-martial of Lt. William Calley—who opened fire on a crowd of South Vietnamese civilians in 1968, killing twenty-two in what was known as the My Lai Massacre—had ended that afternoon in a conviction. The controversy, with the increasingly unpopular President Nixon mixed up in the affair, was rife across the country—although not especially with musical comedy audiences.

"They need to say it," he slurred.

His girl, or likely his teenage wife, apologized to me. "He's all upset."

I gently said something along the lines that I was sorry but they were unable to make such an announcement; it would need to be approved by the producer, who was not in town.

"It's a disgrace," he cried as I made my way into the theatre.

I did, later, wonder whether he enjoyed Neil Simon's jokes, "Turkey Lurkey Time," and Marge MacDougall.

FOOT IN THE DOOR

Candy selling was not, needless to say, my area of interest. The Merrick business representative at the theatre—the company manager, who among other things was responsible for interacting with the cast and checking the treasurer's statement of receipts at each performance—was a fellow named Jay Kingwill. He was just about the only show employee I came into frequent contact with, other than nodding acquaintances with stage manager Charlie Blackwell and the so-called pit singers. These were four girls who were heard but not seen; since they didn't need makeup or costumes, they hung out before the show outside our checkroom in the lower lobby. Everyone else connected with the show remained backstage, on the other side of the curtain.

But Jay I knew well enough to talk to whenever he passed through. As my freshmen year at NYU was nearing its end, my question was always the same: "They don't by any chance need any help over at the office?" One night just as classes were ending, Jay changed his habitual answer to: "Come in tomorrow at 10:45 and talk to Jack."

And so I did.

"Jack" was Jack Schlissel, a decidedly strange duck. Merrick's general manager, Jack oversaw all aspects of Merrick's production. Each commercial theatrical presentation was a corporation in its own right; if the producer was the owner, in effect, the general manager ran the business. Merrick hired Jack when he produced his first show, *Fanny*, in 1954. Jack had been working for Kermit Bloomgarden, most recently on Arthur Miller's *The Crucible*. Kermit was one of the old-school producers Merrick was determined to displace, so I expect he was happy to steal Jack away; Kermit probably didn't even notice—until a few years later, when Merrick had all but taken over Broadway.

(When the British adaptation of the Parisien musical *Irma La Douce* opened in London in 1958, Bloomgarden had his lawyers negotiate for the US rights. Merrick meanwhile jumped a plane, showed up at the theatre with checkbook in hand, and—being a lawyer by trade—drew up a handwritten but binding agreement. Kermit was understandably furious. Merrick suggested that on the title page it should say "Kermit Bloomgarden *resents* the David Merrick production of *Irma La Douce*.")

With as many as a dozen shows simultaneously on the boards in New York and on tour, Merrick became a publicity-hungry public target. Jack, though, was satisfied to be one of the most powerful—if little-known—people in the business. Merrick was roundly hated for his ruthlessness by members of the profession. Those in the know, though, knew that it was Jack who wielded the axe and out-Merricked Merrick.

I arrived at the St. James Theatre building promptly, ringing the bell at the entrance on Forty-Fourth Street and being whisked to the top floor by a crotchety elevator man. Just opposite the elevator was a receptionist with a switchboard, sitting behind a sliding window in a narrow, rectangular, glassed-in space. On the wall was a large, framed painting of a trolley car bearing the destination "Yonkers," reproduced from one of Oliver Smith's backdrops for *Hello, Dolly!* Sylvia Schwartz slid open her window.

"I have an appointment to see Jack Schiss—Shlish—"

"Schlissel," she said. "Say it: Schlissel." I tried, but didn't quite get it. "Okay, just call him Jack. If you can't get Schlissel right, don't even try. Okay? Now, calm down, it'll be fine." She buzzed inside, told me to have a seat on the bench just outside her window.

Five minutes later, Jay came out. "Don't mess this up, we need someone. Just answer Jack, let him do the talking." He led me down a narrow hall with windows on one side, and opened a nondescript door. We entered a small room with two desks and two inner doors leading in each direction. "Sit."

Behind the desks was a wall bursting with filing cabinets and one window, revealing a bird's-eye view of the top of the Majestic across the street. But my eyes immediately went to the framed window cards lining the walls. I've always been fascinated by theatre art, and here was a wall of it; some—the hits—familiar, but most altogether new to my eyes.

I didn't have much time to look. Jay sat at his desk, across from an older woman at the other, and within a minute I heard a phone slam from behind the door on Jay's side of the room. His buzzer rang, he instantly picked up the phone, then pointed me through the door at his left.

I entered a small room, spartan, monopolized by a large, antique desk with a large wooden throne in which sat Jack Schlissel. Small, jet-black curly hair, in his late forties. The desk was filled with papers, the room otherwise void of decoration. On the back of the outer door was a dartboard, featuring the face of Gower Champion. (Jack had long-standing battles with Gower, director/choreographer of Merrick's hits *Carnival!*, *Hello, Dolly!* and *I Do! I Do!*, plus the more recent flop *The Happy Time*.) On the floor in the corner was a gruesome-looking, six-foot lumberjack's saw, a leftover prop from *The Happy Time*. "To protect Jack when Gower comes in," Jay later told me.

Jack gestured to one of the two chairs in front of his desk; I sat down—and down and down. Deep, deep cushions, which placed the visitor—no matter how tall—well below Jack's gaze. The classic short executive's office accoutrement.

"Jay tells me you work the concession at *Promises*. Lurkey still over there?" (Yes.) "How old are you?" (Eighteen.) "Okay. Start at ten every morning, stay till you're not needed, 6:30 or 7:00. You can leave in time to get to the Shubert. Need Wednesday matinees off? You can take lunch then. You work for Jay, do whatever he tells you. When d'you go back to school?" (September, but it's NYU so I can come in part time.) "We'll see. No salary, but every week submit a bill for make-believe expenses, $25. Cabs, theatre tickets, Jay will show you. Actual expenses we'll reimburse in addition, out of petty cash. Tomorrow, ten o'clock," he said, buzzing the intercom and barking at Sylvia, "Get me Floria."

The next morning at ten I went to work for David Merrick.

Chapter Four

Discovery

PETER'S FRIEND

BUT BEFORE WE TRAVERSE THE PORTALS AND ENTER THE RICH, BLOOD-red office of David Merrick, it might be well to step back some years. Why was I hell-bent for Broadway at a time when my peers were spread across the land at diverse campuses, with beads, Beatles albums, and other paraphernalia? What magical spark ignited, early on, to set me on course for a career in the glorious, glamorous, decaying world of the theatre? I was in that day and age an anomaly, nearly one of a kind; but then, the theatre has always grabbed off a small but dedicated fraction of the great American youth.

I began as a child; that is, as a child I determined that no other interest or profession would do. I came from a family with no theatre in its blood; my parents, with middle-class Depression-era roots in Brooklyn, were of the two-show-a-year variety. When I first made my way to the living room record player, the shelf contained a mere handful of cast albums. And yes, I remember the titles, as I immediately commandeered the LPs as soon as I could reach the turntable in the late-Eisenhower years: *South Pacific, Guys and Dolls, My Fair Lady, West Side Story*, and the just-opened *Gypsy*.

This story begins in the summer of 1959. My eight-year-old brother was being shipped off to sleepaway camp. "I'm going, too," I insisted. Yes, in two years when you're eight, I was told. "No, if he's going, *I'm* going."

Not that I had any desire to go *with* him; I didn't know what sleep-away camp was, but even so. My parents explained that the camp didn't take six-year-olds; but the camp owner, who had come to enlist my brother with slide projector and portable movie screen, said that while the youngest group was eight, they did have one bunk with younger kids. "That's me," said I.

My mother knew the place, Camp Greylock in the Berkshire Mountains of Massachusetts; her brother and various cousins had attended starting in the mid-1940s. And so one late-June morning I said goodbye to my father at the old Pennsylvania Station and boarded the train to Pittsfield, Massachusetts, there transferring to school buses for the ride to Becket. Once there, I did what six-year-old campers were supposed to do. Except that Greylock was known for all athletics all the time, and I was supremely nonathletic. Not a good fit, but no matter.

The counselors were mostly college kids, although at six every over-twelve seemed old to me. One of the counselors was very much unlike the others. He must have been in his thirties, and not collegiate at all. He played guitar at all the camp events—a good acoustic guitar player—and sang well, although with a strong accent. His name was Cesario; I learned, later, that he had been a refugee from the Cuban revolution. (Castro had taken control in January of that year.) He wore some kind of leather brace on his forearm, which I suppose might have had something with his escape.

One afternoon Cesario called us together to tell us about the camp play. What a play was I didn't know, but it sounded more interesting than another round of basketball. The play was going to be *Peter and the Wolf*, that story I did know. He started to assign parts, looking around at the group and picking out the most likely-looking kids. Typecasting, we call it.

Peter, his grandfather, the Wolf, and four or five speaking parts were quickly assigned. (Being two years younger than most of the kids, I was hanging on the outskirts of the group.) Then he came to the soldiers. The unpicked kids were eager to be selected; while I knew nothing about plays and soldiers and extras, something instinctively told me that this was *not* where I wanted to be. He picked the First and Second and Third

Soldier (namely, my brother). This led me to shrink away from the rest. He then assigned everybody else as generic soldiers, or chorus to you.

Cesario and his assistant took down everyone's name on a list and sent them over to the camp seamstress to get measured for costumes. (Costumes, that sounded good!) All went gleefully off, except me. "Well," said Cesario, "go with the rest now and get measured for your costume."

And I started crying. Hey, I was *six*.

"I'm not in the play. I didn't get picked."

"Yes, of course you are in the play." He looked at his clipboard, for help. Then he said, "I have a *special* role for you."

"Me?"

"Yes. You are Peter's Friend. I make this specially for you." And he proceeded, on the spot, to do so. Peter and his Friend are out in the woods. Peter's Grandfather calls to him (not on a cellphone, but from the wings) to come home because the wicked old wolf is on the prowl. Peter tells Peter's Friend he should go home, too. Peter's Friend says, "Ha ha, I'm not afraid." Peter exits stage right. Peter's Friend, who is thoroughly not afraid and refuses to take shelter, gets eaten by Wolf.

I knew a featured role when I heard one, and instantly decided I liked this show business.

How I learned whatever lines I had, I don't know. The other kids— mostly going into third grade—knew how to read, but I was just out of kindergarten. I learned my lines, by rote I suppose, and I was ready! The camp had an old wooden rec hall with a real (if small and 1920s vintage) stage, lights, wings, and everything.

Eventually came our first and only performance. My big scene, I turned and shouted: "The wolf!" I jumped off the stage—dead center, with an audible thud—and streamed up the center aisle, screaming as loud and running as fast as ever I did. The audience of eights and nines and tens, who had been sitting lethargically, were suddenly energized by this kid jumping *out* of the play and screaming his way through them. I ran right on out into the night, with greasepaint in my veins. And slathered on my face; in those days, they actually still used greasepaint.

Word of my triumph reached home. In December, my grandmother gave me a present: the cast album of *The Music Man*, which was just then finishing its second year on Broadway. A musical full of bouncy tunes and featuring a little kid with a lisp. As a little kid with a lisp, this hit home. I took over the family record player and played it nonstop, in rotation with *Guys and Dolls* and *Gypsy* and the other LPs on my shelf.

SMOKE IN THE SMOKESTACK

When I returned from my second summer at camp, my father had a surprise for me: tickets, right before the beginning of school, to actually see *The Music Man*. Off we went to the Saturday matinee, my father, my brother, and me. The Majestic Theatre, on West Forty-Fourth Street. Seats on the left center aisle, seven rows back. Sitting there eagerly waiting for the show to start, I searched the theatre in all directions; I'd been in movie houses, some of them ornate, but never a place like the 1,600-seat Majestic. I looked up at the mezzanine, which went way far back—a sea of people. I looked up at the dome of the theatre, where I saw a hole in the ceiling. Not a hole, but a rectangular slice of paneling on the rear curve was missing.

"Why is there a hole?" I asked my father.

"That's not a hole. There are special lights in there, spotlights for the stars."

"Okay," I said.

The house lights dimmed to half. I saw a head rise down front, the conductor; a smattering of applause. A whistle blew; a snare drum played the beginning of a march tempo, and the band swung into "Seventy-Six Trombones." Just like on the record. After a half minute or so they started playing music that wasn't on the record, other tunes from the show that weren't included in the overture used on the recording. Didn't bother me; I was fascinated hearing the sound, so much different from what came out of the speakers of my pre-stereo record player. Midway through the overture, the dimmed lights went off as the band started playing "Seventy-Six Trombones" again (just like on the record). As they came to the end of the tune and started playing train music, the big red curtain flew out, revealing another curtain. A painted one, with a life-sized (or bigger?) locomotive. Suddenly, a hiss of steam—*and smoke came out of the smokestack*!!! That is, the painted show curtain had a panel in the smokestack that slid open on cue, with a blast from a fire extinguisher simulating smoke—but the people in the audience didn't have time to figure it out. Within moments the show curtain flew out, revealing the train interior, with a bunch of traveling salesmen singing the opening number, "Rock Island." "Whattaya talk, whattaya talk, whattaya talk" they sang, bouncing up and down in their seats as if the train was in motion.

Enchantment? Yes. I was home where I belonged, on the aisle in row G at the Majestic.

Professor Harold Hill, onstage, wasn't the guy on the record; but what did I know from Bob Preston? Instead there was someone called Bert Parks, a popular game show host who was already famous as the emcee of the annual Miss America Pageant. He is best remembered—or remembered only?—for singing that "There She Is, Miss America" song every year from 1955 until he was dumped in 1979. They needed to liven up the ratings, and it didn't help to have the new Miss America serenaded by a sixty-five-year-old. In September 1960, though, Parks was young enough and seemed pretty good. Barbara Cook was long gone from the show as well; her role was being played by someone named Barbara Williams, who was never heard from since.

If this was Broadway, I wanted more Broadway.

ENCHANTMENT, WITH PUPPETS

My first show was a classic, albeit with a replacement cast. My next was what we might call a B+ musical, but an innovative and magical one with far-reaching effect. On me, at least. Gower Champion became the director/choreographer king of the era, courtesy of the sleeper hit *Bye Bye Birdie* in 1960 and the 1964 smash *Hello, Dolly!*, the latter one of two contenders for "musical of the decade." In between came *Carnival!*, a gentle and moody musical taking place within the world of a third-rate traveling circus in small-town France. This was based on the popular 1953 MGM film *Lili*, which featured Leslie Caron as a waif befriended by puppets. The setting—and the puppets—enabled Champion to do what is among his finest work; not with that trademark musical comedy pizzazz, no, but something tender, thoughtful, and immensely touching.

David Merrick's eighth musical came to town in April 1961, unheralded and unexpected—and following a season of eight consecutive big-budget disappointments (including Lerner & Loewe's *Camelot* and the Cy Coleman/Lucille Ball *Wildcat*). The *Carnival!* reviews were highly favorable, resulting in a run of almost two years. A sturdy hit, if not a blockbuster; and Merrick's most financially lucrative musical thus far, slightly ahead of *Gypsy*. But that's neither here nor there. My father got us tickets for May, when the show was new and the cast was still giving their all.

There we were at the Imperial, in the fourth row on the right-side aisle. At the end of the row were curtains, under the boxes.

"What's back there?" I asked as we awaited the overture.

"The dressing rooms," said my father. I pictured a table with a makeup mirror right on the other side of the curtain, just yards away from where we were sitting; this image fascinated me. (The curtains do not drape off the dressing rooms; they cover a short corridor leading to a heavy pass door, on the other side of which are a few steps up to the stage. The dressing rooms are further beyond, as I discovered five years later.)

That *Carnival!* was different was immediately apparent: there was no curtain. Just a bare stage. Or what seemed a bare stage; it would be many seasons before we started to see the actual back wall of the theatre as a design choice. The show opened on an empty field with a dreary gray sky, a scrawny tree painted on the backdrop. A scamp of a fellow—an adult, obviously, but not much taller than eight-year-old me—came out and sat on a stool just beside the proscenium arch. Almost directly in front of me. He started playing a plaintive tune on a small accordion. (This was to be the musical theme of the show, "Love Makes the World Go Round.") It sure didn't sound like *The Music Man*, with its overture of trumpets and trombones and drums. Wasn't this a musical? I looked across over the orchestra pit; no conductor in view, waving a baton. Just this short fellow sitting on the side of the stage.

Eight measures in, the house lights started to dim; the audience stopped talking and watched. Another eight measures and a celeste— that tinkly piano with a glass keyboard, which sounds like the heavens or perhaps sugar plum fairies—joined the onstage accordion. Then the trumpets and others started to sneak in. Four dancers—as carnival roustabouts—came on with a tent pole, inserted it center stage, and then began constructing a circus tent as the rest of the ensemble started to appear with props and banners. By the end of the sequence the stage was bright and colorful and alive, with the cast launching into a lively opening number. Theatrical magic, Gower Champion style.

The leading lady—Anna Maria Alberghetti, from the opera world—was a somewhat high-strung soprano from whom I didn't get much of a warm feeling. The leading man I instinctively understood and related to—a bitter and moody outsider who lashed out at the world to hide a tortured soul. Paul was an ex-dancer whose leg had been mangled fighting for the Resistance; he had a bad limp, but I didn't notice that when I was eight. What I did notice was the actor playing the role was an awkwardly conflicted but personable and highly believable fellow named Jerry Orbach.

Paul the Puppeteer's humanity was apparent when he operated his alter egos, the puppets (which were designed by Tom Tichenor). Carrot Top is a sweet and friendly lad, always looking to help others; Horrible Henry is a cuddly, and clumsy, walrus. At eight, I related to the lonely Paul and especially to the ungainly but lovable Horrible Henry. (On my twenty-fifth birthday I received a most precious present from Leo Herbert, who had been the prop man on *Carnival!*: Horrible Henry, accompanied by Carrot Top. Worn and faded, but real. Not necessarily the opening night originals—*Carnival!* sent out two touring companies while it continued on Broadway, so they must have eventually built six or eight sets of puppets—but authentic. Henry nowadays sits on the ledge over my shoulder as I write.)

The first act builds until Lili, with nowhere to turn, contemplates suicide by plunging from a trapeze platform. She starts to climb the rope ladder, straight up; the audience, as I remember, stopped breathing. Suddenly, Carrot Top—from the puppet booth—calls out to her, gets her talking, and compels her to sing about how "love makes the world go round." Hope, life, love, puppets, and magic: *Carnival!*

The magic of Broadway: Horrible Henry from *Carnival!* (1961), in retirement. Puppet by Tom Tichenor.

THERE'S ONLY ONE PARIS

My next trip to Broadway was another Merrick musical, just as magical and with a similarly far-reaching effect on my developing musical-comedy soul. My father's father was a charming, self-made man—the only one of my grandparents who was not American-born, having arrived at Ellis Island in 1903 at the age of six. (He came from Preluki, a Russian shtetl that was obliterated from the map at the same time as the fictional Anatevka in *Fiddler on the Roof.*) His wife, however, was altogether lacking in personality and—well, much sense. The day before Thanksgiving in 1962, my parents planned dinner in the city with my grandparents. Since my brother and I didn't have school, my father drove us in with him, took us for breakfast at a grand old place called Kass on Spring Street, and left us with his mother for the day. (My grandmother lived to be ninety-six; this was the one and only time—ever—I was handed over to her.)

She decided to take us to a matinee, and why not? With such child-friendly attractions on the boards as the original productions of *My Fair Lady*, *The Sound of Music*, *Camelot*, and *The Unsinkable Molly Brown*, what did she choose to take her eight- and ten-year-old grandsons to? *Irma La Douce*, a musical about a dazzling Parisienne *poule*—a girl who "helps all Paris to relax"—and her *mec* Nestor, who becomes so jealous of Irma's clientele that he masquerades as a customer named Monsieur Oscar and demands her exclusive services. Nestor then becomes so jealous of M. Oscar (i.e., himself) that he kills his rival in a remarkably staged scene. Nestor is convicted of murder and sent to Devil's Island; escapes; and returns to Paris as M. Oscar, trying to convince the corrupt justice system that he is alive and kicking, and Nestor is thus innocent. It all ends with Irma giving birth, on Christmas Day, to twins—one fathered by Nestor, the other by M. Oscar.

For an *eight-year-old*? Who takes an eight-year-old to see *Irma La Douce*? I can only think that my grandmother must have found a discount ticket, and—having heard that the show was a hit—figured it was a safe choice.

Which, as it turns out, it was: *Irma* was critical to my burgeoning theatrical development. The show was tart, wry, and—well, *douce*, which is to say sweet. This was the work of Peter Brook, who went on to become the most innovatively creative stage director of the latter half of the twentieth century. His handling of that onstage murder, behind a *pissoir*—one of those round outdoor urinals covered by advertising posters that used to be omnipresent on the streets of Paris—remains memorable: a battle to the death with one of Nestor's sleeved arms gripping one side of the *pissoir* while M. Oscar's arm impossibly grips the other. Brook also gave us Nestor's escape by raft from Devil's Island, crisscrossing the stage amid a surrealistically comical ballet in which all the dancers—dressed in black suits—wear the obviously phony orange beard of M. Oscar.

Irma was a big dance show, with a superlative singer-dancer-comedienne named Elisabeth Seal at the show's center. Choreographer Onna White—the same Onna White who staged the dances for *The Music Man*, including a "Marian the Librarian Ballet" with the boys and girls dancing on the tables that wowed me—provided Seal, the only woman in a cast of seventeen, with a dazzlingly good barroom tour-de-force called "Disc-Donc." I still recall her dancing with abandon on the bar in a simple dress, swinging her long, beaded necklace. (Seal took that season's Tony, besting Julie Andrews of *Camelot*.)

While mesmerized by the goings-on, I couldn't help but notice that one of the gang of pimps was an actor named Fred Gwynne, who was just then starring in my favorite new sitcom, *Car 54, Where Are You?* Imagine, the star of a TV show playing a small role in a Broadway musical! I was amazed; someone I "knew," up there on the Broadway stage. I suppose that the network tried to buy out Gwynne's contract but Merrick refused, figuring that if the series was a hit it could only help sell tickets to the musical. *Car 54*—which was shot in New York—overlapped with *Irma* by about three months.

SATIRE DELICIOUSLY SERVED

I discovered on my next jaunt that all shows were not as good as *The Music Man, Carnival!*, and *Irma La Douce*. I went into *The Sound of Music* near the end of its third year, knowing the cast album by heart. The show itself, to this nine-year-old, was syrupy and unconvincing. Shortly thereafter I was taken to see the brand-new *Milk and Honey*, the first Broadway musical by composer-lyricist Jerry Herman. We had neighbors two houses over, with kids the same ages as my brother and I, whose uncle was a ticket broker. (Whatever *that* was; a few years later, he was sent to jail in a ticket scalping scandal centering on *Man of La Mancha*.) One Saturday, the uncle apparently had more *Milk and Honey* than he could possibly scalp, so off the four boys went to the matinee. In one scene, the hero—an old, old man who fell in love with a medium-old lady and sang an awful lot—actually milked a goat onstage. That and the exuberant dance to the title song were the only lively parts of the deadly afternoon. Critical lesson learned: just because a musical is on Broadway, that doesn't mean that it's going to be any good, even if it ends up running more than a year.

The early shows I saw were musicals, with one exception; in January 1963 my father for some reason took me to see an absurdist comedy by S. J. Perelman called *The Beauty Part*. I remain glad he did, because it gave me the opportunity to see the great Bert Lahr playing two different millionaires; a judge; a smarmy Hollywood agent; and a daffy old dame in a dowdy wool dress. I didn't understand a word of the thing—blame it on my youth, or on the playwright—but it was memorable. *The Beauty Part* also offered two fine Broadway comediennes, Charlotte Rae and Alice Ghostley, whom I mixed up for the rest of their lives; plus the thirty-year-old son of Mary Martin, Larry Hagman.

Shortly before, my father's mother (of *Irma La Douce*) had gotten us—my brother and my two slightly older cousins—tickets to *Camelot* in its final week. I missed out, with a case of chicken pox. My father promised me a rain check. When it came time to collect, he suggested we see *Oliver!*, a new Merrick musical and a child friendly one.

I had just then been visiting a school friend whose father was the only person in my universe with a show biz connection: he was a music publisher, running one of Frank Loesser's several companies. That afternoon, my friend put on an advance copy of the not-yet-released cast album of Broadway's newest musical, the Loesser-published *Here's Love*: an adaptation of *Miracle on 34th Street* with songs by Meredith Willson of *The Music Man*. By the third song—the first being an altogether interesting stage rendition of Macy's Thanksgiving Day Parade—I determined that the show, about a department-store Santa Claus, belonged in the same bargain basement as *Milk and Honey*. So my friend quickly pivoted to the recording of Loesser's still-running, Pulitzer Prize–winning hit, *How to Succeed in Business Without Really Trying*. When I heard the singers having a nervous breakdown over a coffee pot, I knew that this was the show for me. *Oliver!*, no thanks; I want to see *How to Succeed*.

This puzzled my father, but he figured he'd likely prefer *How to Succeed* to *Oliver!*, so he was glad to oblige.

Arriving at the 46th Street Theatre before the show, I saw something I've never seen before or since. Rudy Vallee, one of the stars, was standing outside the stage door in pince-nez and full costume, gruffly giving out autographs. (From what I've heard about Vallee, I wonder if maybe he was *selling* autographs?)

How to Succeed took off like a shot and never slackened. Funny, funny, funny. The lines, the lyrics, and—yes—the music; the cast, and the dancing; even the costumes and sets. I had by then developed a keen sense of humor, but what I saw that afternoon was altogether different. Every joke seemed a wise and witty attack, designed to puncture its target. No, I didn't quite understand everything they were talking about in this deft satire of Madison Avenue; but I understood the way librettist/ director Abe Burrows and songwriter Frank Loesser used words as scalpels, the way they built jokes, and the way everything paid off to the point that there were laughs upon laughs upon laughs. We have occasionally seen this since, notably in *The Book of Mormon*; but there haven't been many musicals comparable to *Mormon* or *How to Succeed*.

The show was already in the third of four-plus years, by which point Vallee was the only one of the five original leads remaining. (Michelle Lee, who had taken over the female lead shortly after the opening, was still in the cast.) But the replacements didn't matter; *How to Succeed* was in exceptional shape. I recall sitting there—pulling on an extremely loose tooth, which refused through the afternoon to slip out—thinking that these jokes, both spoken and visual, had been written just for me. I was immediately struck by the way the humor spread across all elements. The scenery looked like it was drawn in illustrator's ink; not flimsy canvas, good sturdy sets and props, but with the lines seemingly "inked" in by a cartoonist. Even the costume designer contributed major laughs.

And the choreography was funny and good, and good-and-funny. The "Coffee Break" number, with the dancers crawling around in nicotine withdrawal to an ominous cha-cha; "A Secretary Is Not a Toy," in which the girls swung their hips across the stage accompanied by the percussive sounds of a typewriter tapping away from the orchestra pit; the mock-revivalist hymn "Brotherhood of Man," with a stage full of business execs leaping about not like dancers but like momentarily uninhibited business execs. This was different dancing than they had in *The Music Man* and the other musicals I'd seen; this choreographer, a man called Bob Fosse, seemed to be living and working in a different world.

This was the ninth Broadway show that I had seen in my eleven years. I long ago concluded, with considerable bemusement, that the afternoons I spent at *Irma La Douce* (with its sly humor and Peter Brook's extreme theatricality), *Carnival!* (with Gower's magical enchantment and those puppets), and *How to Succeed* (with rapid-fire humor and razor-sharp satire from Loesser and Burrows) set my theatrical sensibilities for life, making it impossible for me to consider an existence anywhere but on and around Broadway. *Irma* and *Carnival!* also made me a confirmed Francophile at eight, long before I ever set foot in the land of croissants and camembert.

The first show that I officially worked on—with a union paycheck—opened at the 46th Street nine years later. The house manager's office, where we did the box office count-up, had a news photo framed on the wall. It was taken one night in January 1962 at *How to Succeed*, during curtain calls. Heading up the aisle—his head turned back toward the stage—is President Kennedy, waving to the actors in their finale costumes. The cast stands in a single line, applauding the president; the audience is enraptured. Hope, joy, spirit, and freedom are all there, in that photo. When the theatre was sold in 1978, I tried to get that picture off the wall; by the time I reached the new manager, it was gone. I've been looking for a copy of it for years now; presumably, it exists somewhere. The promise of the Kennedy years in black and white, a time capsule of the happy night JFK saw the brilliant *How to Succeed*.

END OF A (GOLDEN) AGE

Then came 1964, with *Hello, Dolly!* and *Fiddler on the Roof.* These shows, it turned out, marked the end of the so-called Golden Age of Musicals and the beginning of—well, a not-so-golden age. There is no need to discuss every show I came across thereafter. Let us just say that *Dolly!*—in its second week—was dazzlingly good. Bright, alive and aswirl with color, all in support of the outrageously improbable Carol Channing. I saw Channing play Dolly many times—the *world* saw Channing play Dolly many times—but in the early months, before we all grew to know what to expect, the performance was dazzlingly larger than life. Walter Kerr, in his *Herald Tribune* review, referred to the old artwork for the gramophone maker His Master's Voice (which by the time of *Dolly!* had been folded into RCA Victor): "Miss Channing has gone back for another look at that advertisement labeled 'His Master's Voice,' and she has swallowed the records, the Victrola, and quite possibly the dog." He was right; that was Channing in *Dolly!*, back when the show and her performance were freshly and insanely minted.

As I sat there immensely enjoying myself, though, I was somehow aware that the material itself wasn't quite so good as the rest of the show. I was by this point intensely familiar with *Carousel, Guys and Dolls, My Fair Lady, Gypsy,* and other great scores. *Dolly* was clearly in a different league; bright and fresh and enjoyable, but with none of those musical moments that make great musicals great. Production numbers, yes; but great songs?

This was the case with *Fiddler on the Roof* as well; an admirable and more moving show than *Dolly,* but does the score approach *South Pacific* or *West Side Story*? But ah!, the staging. A revelatory moment from director Jerome Robbins: after Tevye and his family lit the candles and sang the first refrain of "Sabbath Prayer," other families joined in—not onstage, but in mid-air over Tevye and the house unit. I later learned that this was accomplished by bleeding through the scrim, with chorus members standing on strategically placed scaffolding, but back in 1964 my eleven-year-old jaw dropped.

In the summer of 1964, between the openings of *Dolly* and *Fiddler,* I finished my six summers at summer camp. Not that I liked it—it was all sports, all the time, and I was decidedly nonathletic—but I didn't have an alternative. The only thing that made it tolerable was the annual camp play, which at least kept me engaged. While this is peripheral to our tale, I have two stories to relate that are not without relevance.

Visiting day, summer 1962. All the kids, and all their fathers, thronged around one of the parents who happened to be the head coach of New York's only football team at the time, the conference-winning Giants: Allie Sherman, winner of the NFL "Coach of the Year" award in both 1961 and 1962. All the kids except me.

I was otherwise engaged. I didn't have any idea what an orchestrator or musical arranger was or did—although fifty years later, I would "write the book" on the subject—but Ronnie Ramin's father, Sid, was the orchestrator of both *West Side Story* and *Gypsy.* Two cast albums I knew by heart. So there were all the boys and dads crowding around Allie Sherman, asking him about Y. A. Tittle, Frank Gifford, and the rest. Sid, who later became a good friend, had me, gawking at him.

The other memorable event came the last weekend of my six years there. An annual highlight was the summer-ending awards dinner, in which just about everybody (present company excepted) got some kind of award for prominence in some sport or other (soccer, volleyball, archery?) or a catchall category like "best camp spirit." Given that my group—or at least those kids who were planning to return—was "graduating" from the junior side to the senior side, they had a rather grander assortment of awards—including, of all things, a best acting award. I was never much of an actor, but I was—at least—very much present. So much so that the powers decided that after six years, I should at least get *something*.

After the ceremony, the camp owner pulled me aside to show me the plaque. This had space for thirty summers of winners; he explained that they would ship it to me after my name was engraved and that I would have to return it the following spring.

"Look here," he said, pointing to the 1950 inscription. "This boy, he's going to be a big star. He's an understudy on Broadway now; but he's a great actor. *Remember this name.*"

I was able to look at the name, on the plaque on my wall, through the winter. But I quickly knew I would surely remember it, because he was the only person I ever heard of with the name "Dustin." And what do you know? By the time I was fourteen, he'd turned up in *The Graduate* and everyone did, indeed, know that name.

CHAPTER FIVE

Waiting in the Wing

MAN OF WASHINGTON SQUARE

IN JANUARY 1966, THERE WAS A TWELVE-DAY TRANSIT STRIKE IN NEW
York City. My father, who for thirty years commuted daily to his office
just below Houston Street in what was to become the heart of the Soho
neighborhood, was forced to stay over at his parent's apartment eight
blocks away, just above Washington Square. At that time, there was an
actual Broadway theatre in the neighborhood: the ANTA Washington
Square on West Fourth Street, one block east of the square. While
awaiting the completion of the Lincoln Center complex on the Upper
West Side, the newly formed Repertory Theatre of Lincoln Center presented their first season in a temporary theatre that was more or less a
quickly assembled version of what would become the Vivian Beaumont.
Even though it was way downtown, the ANTA Washington Square—
due to its seating capacity and union contracts—was deemed a full
Broadway house. This is not to be confused with the ANTA Theatre on
Fifty-Second Street, across from the Alvin. Or I suppose we should say
what became the Virginia and is now the August Wilson, across from
the present Neil Simon. ANTA was the American National Theatre
and Academy, a nonprofit group that operated on Broadway from 1950
through 1981.

The Lincoln Center people moved out of the ANTA Washington
Square in May 1965, with the place slated for eventual demolition to
make way for a new NYU building. Along came an unlikely musical

called *Man of La Mancha*. Having originated in summer stock at the then newly established Goodspeed Opera House in East Haddam, Connecticut, the show was unable to get a booking in a traditional Broadway theatre and too large to fit on an off-Broadway stage. The unexpected solution had them moving into the Tony Award–eligible ANTA Washington Square in November 1965—to good reviews, shortly followed by a devastating New Year's Day transit strike.

This almost killed *La Mancha*. Customers simply couldn't get down there. What turned out happening, though, was that people stranded in the lower Fifth Avenue area took advantage of the one Broadway theatre temporarily in their midst. They strolled over to this musical version of *Don Quixote* and loved it—including my father, stranded on Washington Square. The Saturday after the strike ended, he needed to go to his office for a few hours, so he got me a ticket for the matinee. (I went early enough in the run to see Richard Kiley and Joan Diener; the producers eventually hired matinee alternates so that the stars would only have to play six performances a week.) *La Mancha* was the first show I attended alone, at twelve.

It was quite a show, with the excitement of the written material enhanced by stage and staging. The ANTA was laid out identically to the present-day Beaumont, with five seating sections in a semicircular layout fanning out from the thrust stage. *La Mancha* was built to fit; there was a more or less circular deck downstage center, which served as the prison upon which the story was staged. The other main feature was a long drawbridge that descended from high in the back wall to bring Cervantes into and out of the prison. For much of the life of *La Mancha*—when it moved uptown to the Martin Beck to allow the ANTA Washington Square to be demolished, when it toured, when the original production was repeatedly revived—this prison set was placed onstage at the curtain line. At the ANTA, the deck was thrust into the lap of the audience, making the whole thing more immediate. Due to the semicircular layout, no seat in the house—which held about 1,100—was more than sixty-five feet away from the stage. Jo Mielziner, designer of both the ANTA and the Beaumont, said his goal was that "each member of the audience must be able to see the expression in the eyes of a face as small as Julie Harris."

The thrust added an extra layer of electrifying theatricality to the original *La Mancha*. Furthering the excitement was the placement of the orchestra, split on either side of the thrust: true stereophonic sound, with brass on one side and guitars and percussion on the other—not sitting in a covered pit, but live and vibrant.

As I left the matinee to walk back to my father's office on Wooster Street, I followed a party of two adults and three kids down the side alley leading from Fourth Street to Third. They stopped at a door in the wall—the stage door—and said they were there to see Mr. Kiley. The doorman said they should come in and wait. Naturally, I followed them. There were another five people already standing in the corridor, by the cast callboard, which kept me from being obtrusive. We were there just a few minutes when Irving Jacobson—the Yiddish theatre actor who played Sancho Panza—came from the dressing rooms and started happily chatting and signing. The other lesser stars, Ray Middleton and Robert Rounseville, appeared and seemed glad to be asked for autographs. Middleton had starred opposite Ethel Merman in the original *Annie Get Your Gun*, in 1946; Rounseville created the title role of Leonard Bernstein's *Candide* in 1956. Now they were playing the subsidiary roles of the Innkeeper and the Priest in *Man of La Mancha*, albeit with generous billing, and glad to have the work.

Then came Kiley, friendly but exhausted, with another show to do that evening. As Kiley said his goodbyes, out came Diener—Aldonza!—in worn blue terrycloth bathrobe but *full makeup*. Diener, in the role, looked not like a sexy woman but a cartoon of a sexy woman. She was staying in her dressing room between shows, rather than having to take off all that makeup; but I suppose that when she heard Kiley had guests waiting for him at the stage door, she figured she might as well come out and try to upstage him. (When we did the 1977 Broadway revival of *La Mancha*, Kiley agreed to appear on the express condition that Diener—who was the wife of the show's director, Albert Marre—not be hired to play opposite him.)

For me, this was a revelation: you can go to the stage door after the show and get to meet the actors. Hmmm.

Richard Kiley introduces Don Quixote's "Impossible Dream" in the original production of *Man of La Mancha* (1965).
PHOTOFEST

INTO THE DRESSING ROOM

One Wednesday a few months later, I went to see *Funny Girl*. Not Barbra Streisand in *Funny Girl* at the Winter Garden; Streisand had left and the show had moved to the Majestic. Mimi Hines, a singer/comedienne popular from her appearances on *The Tonight Show*, was now playing the lead. As I wandered through the nearly empty lobby before the show, a lonely concessionaire desperately peddled his wares. "Souvenir program here, get it signed by the star." This got my attention.

"How do you get it signed?" I asked.

"Just go back to her dressing room after the show, kid."

"Are you sure she'll sign it?"

"Yeah, kid." He was looking for more customers, but nobody was interested.

I handed him my dollar. "What do I do?"

"Just go down the aisle on the left. Out the last door, you'll see the stage door."

"Are you sure she'll sign it?"

"She knows, she knows."

Back in the Majestic, where I had seen *The Music Man* six years and thirteen shows earlier. This time I wasn't in the sixth row of the orchestra; I was three rows from the back of the rear mezzanine, in the cheap section, amid a sea of empty seats. As the house lights started to dim, half of the not-very-many people around me started moving down to empty rows in front of us. Seeing that the ushers didn't seem to care, I moved—all the way to the *first* row of the mezz, on the side. I didn't look up at the follow spot booth in the dome, this time. My eyes, during the overture, were glued to the curtain under the boxes, which was going to lead me—yes—to the star in her dressing room.

I sat through the matinee, moderately entertained. *Funny Girl* isn't a well-made show. When they had trouble out of town, they wisely concentrated on the one thing that *was* working—the singing of Barbra Streisand—and added song after song after song. The final version of the show features fifteen songs; Barbra sang twelve of them. (Julie Andrews in *My Fair Lady* sang six, Merman in *Gypsy* and Channing in *Dolly!* sang seven.) This made *Funny Girl* quite a show, when Streisand was singing it; Mimi Hines was able to keep the show afloat an additional year and a half, thanks to spillover from Streisand and the popularity of "People." But every time they try to revive *Funny Girl*, they are likely to run up against the same problem: it will work spectacularly well as long as you can find someone who can grab the audience as effectively as Barbra Streisand. Otherwise, good luck.

Having scoped out an empty seat in the orchestra from my mezz perch, I moved downstairs during intermission. All through the second act, I was less concerned about whether Fanny Brice would break up with ne'er-do-well husband Nicky Arnstein and more concerned about whether I would actually get backstage. As soon as the curtain fell, I dashed over to the fire door near the curtain under the box. This took me into a dark alley; no sunlight because it was indoors. Actually, this is an interior service entrance for what was originally the Hotel Lincoln—more recently known as the Milford Plaza, presently named Row NYC—which includes the stage doors of the Royale (now Jacobs) and Golden Theatres as well. The three theatres and hotel were built simultaneously by developer Irwin Chanin.

Up three steps to the entrance. The doorman said to stand by the callboard in the narrow hallway, beside the pay phone. I told him the man said I could go to Mimi Hines's dressing room.

"Just wait here until Miss Hines is ready."

Business was slow at the souvenir book stand that day, I guess; there were only four of us waiting when Mimi's dresser came and led us to the star dressing room. There she stood, in a vaguely Japanese-style dressing gown, smiling graciously, like she was greeting her next-door neighbor's in-laws.

"That was really a wonderful performance," I said, in the manner of a thirteen-year-old who wanted to offer praise without gushing.

"Thank you," said Mimi. "Jule Styne was in Monday night and said the same thing, the show works better now than he has ever seen it."

Jule Styne being the composer. Now, this could be construed as an actor bragging about how good she is; I expect, though, that Hines was accurately reporting Jule's words. Barbra Streisand created *Funny Girl*, and *Funny Girl* was written to fit Barbra Streisand, and nobody ever has or is likely to give a comparable performance of those songs ("Don't Rain on My Parade," "People," "The Music That Makes Me Dance," and more). But *playing* the role of Fanny Brice? Streisand didn't play Fanny Brice; she played Brice à la Barbra. This worked marvelously well for *Funny Girl*, at least until Streisand got bored with playing eight times a week and started to walk through the script until the songs began. You were getting a fictional Fanny with Streisandian attitude, which was not what the creators necessarily intended. (The show was conceived as homage to the legendary Fanny; Frances Arnstein, the real-life daughter of Fanny and Nicky, was the wife of *Funny Girl* producer Ray Stark.) But if *Funny Girl* had opened as the creators originally intended, without months' worth of fixing during the extended pre-Broadway tryout and doctoring by Jerome Robbins, the show would likely have folded.

Here was Mimi Hines, singing the songs perfectly well but also playing the role of the young, ugly duckling who storms from the small time to the *Ziegfeld Follies*. Funny, vulnerable, and uncomfortably struggling with her burgeoning success, both with audiences and with the gambling con man of a husband who was thrown into Leavenworth. So yes, maybe Hines was accurately quoting Jule; perhaps she was indeed giving a better performance of the actual material, as written, than Streisand.

Flush with my success backstage at the Majestic, I immediately tried it again the following Wednesday afternoon. I got to the Palace stage door—which was down a now-vanished alley, bordered by the back wall of a church—and was told to wait outside for Miss Verdon. I waited and waited and waited; the featured players and chorus of *Sweet Charity* came wandering out, but no Gwen. After more than an hour, the doorman—whom I kept bugging—finally said that she must have gone out a different way. It is not uncommon, I later learned, for a star to avoid fans by slipping out a side exit or the box office lobby.

Back home, I wrote a letter saying how much I enjoyed etc. etc. etc., which I did indeed, and how I'd waited for her after the show but she never came out. I quickly received a response—typed on an engraved notecard, hand-signed "Gwen" in red ink—apologizing, but she was tired and needed to rush home to see her three-year old daughter. I would, though, eventually get to meet and at one point tangle with her.

INAUSPICIOUS OPENINGS

Up until this time, I had been happy to see two or three Broadway shows a year, almost exclusively musicals. In the fall of 1968, I entered tenth grade. As a fifteen-year-old, I was allowed to take the train to and from Manhattan as often as schoolwork didn't intrude (and I made sure that schoolwork didn't intrude). Thus, in the 1968–1969 season—a not-very-good Broadway year, with *Promises, Promises* and *1776* the bright spots—I found my way to twenty plays and musicals. It need be added, I suppose, that in those days theatre tickets—especially balcony seats—were easily affordable. In the summer of 1969, I worked for my uncle down on Wall Street; when my grandparents went away for the summer, I was allowed to stay in their apartment on East Sixty-Second Street. A twenty-minute walk from Times Square, this enabled me to see eight shows in July alone.

(When my ninety-year-old grandparents moved to Florida in 1995, I took over the apartment with my soon-to-be wife. My tenth-floor office window overlooked two rows of townhouses. To my right I look down into the garden of the townhouse where George S. Kaufman wrote *You Can't Take It with You* and *The Man Who Came to Dinner*, at 162 East Sixty-Third Street. On my left—until it was demolished in 2019—was the former House of Simon, birthplace of *The Odd Couple* and *The Sunshine Boys*, at 165 East Sixty-Second.)

Among my adventures in the spring of 1969 were two opening nights. How, or why, did I think to get a ticket for *Come Summer*, at the Lunt-Fontanne? A musical comedy, in the post-*Hair* era, about itinerant peddlers in nineteenth-century New England? Now there's one that sounds dead on arrival. The star was Ray Bolger, who had been big in the 1930s and 1940s—best known as the Scarecrow in *The Wizard of Oz*—but who was now sixty-five and stodgy. Authors who'd hardly ever written anything, but a big-name director/choreographer in Agnes de Mille. Who had been big in the 1940s and 1950s. De Mille achieved fame in 1942 with the Aaron Copland ballet *Rodeo*, which nabbed her the job of choreographing the thematically related *Oklahoma!*, followed by *Carousel*, *Brigadoon*, and other Golden Age classics. So I suppose this—the great Agnes de Mille!—is what was in the mind of the producers, who were just then raking in a fortune from their first musical, *Man of La Mancha*.

Come Summer was drab, humorless, and flat. The only thing of interest was a big production number that closed the first act in which the dancers—as lumberjacks—rolled logs down the river. (Rather than loading cut and trimmed logs on nonexistent flatbed trucks, nineteenth-century loggers floated them down the river to the sawmill.) By using a backdrop that looped horizontally, set designer Oliver Smith gave us the impression of a forest rolling by while de Mille's dancers leaped the logs. One number, though, couldn't make up for a drowsy evening. The show opened on Tuesday night with me in attendance and closed on Saturday.

Eight weeks later I came in for the Saturday matinee of Nicol Williamson's *Hamlet*, which had displaced Bolger at the Lunt. After getting my ticket, I happened over to the Barrymore, where a revival of *The Front Page* was opening that night. Why not? I thought.

This was not just another revival. Pretty soon—within months, actually—there would come a parade of Broadway revivals. The 1966–1967 season had one "star" revival; 1967–1968 also had one. *The Front Page* opened in May 1969, the first and only revival of that season; 1969–1970 suddenly had *six* commercial revivals. The point being that as conditions along Broadway began to deteriorate in the mid-1960s, play production started to dry up. Meaning more available theatres. Take a pre-sold title, put in a star or two, raise considerably less money; this seemed like a viable business model, except audiences weren't quite so interested in art by viable business model.

The *Front Page* revival stemmed from a noble idea. Martha Scott began her career as a tryout replacement in the role of Emily Webb in Thornton Wilder's 1938 drama *Our Town*. Her success took her to Hollywood, where she repeated the role—opposite William Holden—in the 1940 screen version. Imagine receiving a Best Actress Oscar nomination for your first film, the competition consisting of Katharine Hepburn in *The Philadelphia Story*, Bette Davis in *The Letter*, Joan Fontaine in *Rebecca*, and Ginger Rogers (who won for *Kitty Foyle*).

Scott peaked then and there, although she continued to work onstage, screen, and television. As she neared the age of sixty, she came up with the idea of forming a nonprofit repertory company in which major stars could appear in great stage roles without committing to long-term runs. Two such stars—Henry Fonda and Robert Ryan—joined her in establishing what they called the Plumstead Playhouse, named after one of the first theatres in America (founded in Philadelphia in 1749). The Mineola Playhouse—a stock house in Nassau County, New York, that hosted low-cost touring companies and had recently produced their own disastrous rep season—agreed to finance Plumstead. First up in the fall of 1968 were productions of *Our Town*, starring Fonda as the Stage Manager with Ryan in the smaller role of Mr. Webb; and *The Front Page*, starring Ryan as Walter Burns with Fonda in the smaller role of McCue of the City Press. The rep company included the likes of Estelle Parsons, Anne Jackson, John McGiver, John Beal, and Jo Van Fleet. I saw Fonda's *Our Town* on a school field trip to Mineola but missed *The Front Page*.

The two revivals played their allotted month and that was that for the Plumstead idea of an ongoing rep company. Too bad, because one of the future productions Scott had tentatively announced was the intriguing notion of Godfrey Cambridge in *The Man Who Came to Dinner*. Some producers, meanwhile, broached the idea of bringing the Plumstead plays to Broadway. *Our Town* was impossible, given Fonda's Hollywood commitments. Ryan, though, was very much available, sitting in his living room at the Dakota. (He soon thereafter sublet and eventually sold his apartment to John Lennon.) So in came *The Front Page* to the Barrymore, with a supporting cast not quite so stellar as it had been in Mineola.

The 1928 classic about newspapermen in Chicago was written by two ex-newspapermen from Chicago, Ben Hecht and Charles MacArthur—both long deceased. As usual, I moved down to an orchestra seat during the first intermission. Sitting across the aisle was a little old lady. That, I deduced, must be the great Helen Hayes, widow of author MacArthur. I screwed up my courage and approached her.

"Miss Hayes?" I said.

The little old lady beamed.

"No, I'm not Miss Hayes. Helen's over there," she said, turning; but Helen was not over there, having left her seat.

"I'm so sorry," I said. I didn't say that to a teenager, one seventy-year-old looks like another.

"Oh, that happens all the time. Helen's husband wrote the play with my husband."

"Ben Hecht," I said, telling her something she obviously knew. Turned out this was Rose Caylor Hecht, a Russian immigrant who somehow or other managed to wangle a job as a reporter at the *Chicago Daily News* back in the early 1920s, when there was virtually no such thing as a woman reporter on a mainstream newspaper. She met fellow-reporter Hecht and moved to New York with him in 1924, serving as a novelist and playwright but mostly assisting her husband during his provocative career in New York and Hollywood.

I was telling her how much I liked the play—what else was there to say?—when Hayes came back down the aisle. This was, even to me, clearly and recognizably Helen Hayes.

"Oh, Helen, you should meet this young man," Caylor said.

Helen, with a twinkle in her eye, did meet me during the first intermission and we chatted during the second. I got to see her again a half-year later. Among the parade of movie star revivals on Broadway was a production of Mary Chase's *Harvey*, which was a 1,775-performance hit when it first opened in 1945. James Stewart had left the Broadway stage for Hollywood stardom in 1935 and never looked back, except for a brief 1947 replacement stint in the still-running *Harvey* while he was preparing to star in the 1950 motion picture version.

Here he was at the ANTA in 1970, a living Hollywood legend starring opposite the so-called First Lady of the Theatre, Helen Hayes. After the matinee, I naturally headed through the stage door and up to the dressing rooms. In those days, you could tell the stage doorman that you wanted to go up to see Miss Hayes or Mr. Stewart and they would likely as not let you in. Nowadays, security concerns have made backstage a fortress. It used to be that if you liked a show, you could just go back and visit friends in the cast. Now, you need to inform them in advance that you'll be there so you can get your name on the list—which leaves you in the lurch if you dislike the show and prefer not to face them.

Hayes was standing by the doorway of the star dressing room with a crowd, signing autographs as she chatted. I got my program signed, then headed further upstairs to Jimmy Stewart. He invited me in—he was alone, without the sort of entourage Hayes encouraged—and we had our own chat. I told him how much I enjoyed his performance (pretty much, I guess, though it was far from revelatory), and how much I enjoyed his many films (which I did). As I handed him my *Playbill* to sign, I thought, how rude! Give the man praise, sure; but to stand there, after the performance, and ask him to give you back something (i.e., his signature)? I was instantly cured; while I was thereafter glad to meet and talk to people of extraordinary talent or fame—actors, writers, sports icons, presidents—I never again considered asking anyone for an autograph.

LYCEUM BOX

Another in that string of revivals—and a typically slapdash, shoestring affair—was a production of the old George Abbott farce, *Three Men on a Horse*, directed by old George Abbott. This tale of a seasoned racetrack gambler who finds a milquetoast greeting card poet with an uncanny knack for picking winners had been bright and breezy when Sam Levene played it at the Playhouse in 1935, suitably and hilariously captured on the screen when Levene went with it to Hollywood in 1936. (This was a highly unusual case of a film being released while the show was still running. *Three Men on a Horse* played a full two years on Broadway, plus a long tour.)

The play—written by John Cecil Holm and Abbott—was already creaky when it was revived on Broadway in 1942; in 1969 it positively limped across the finish line. Here was the original and near-legendary Sam Levene, re-creating his part thirty-four years later. And thirty-four years older. Still the same Sam Levene of the bushy eyebrows and machine-gun timing, but this desperate gambler was now sixty-two instead of twenty-seven.

One can understand the gestation of the production. A couple of shoestring producers—Gaston and Goldberg, our friends from *A Place for Polly*—presumably heard that Sam Levene was available and would work cheap. What to put him in? *Guys and Dolls*, for which he was best known, was a big musical that would be too expensive to assemble—and the authors would surely not entrust the valuable rights to Broadway newcomers. Why not *Three Men on a Horse*? Why not call Mister Abbott, the legendary director/playwright, and ask him to direct it just like he did in 1935?

Abbott, who had done eight consecutive flops since 1962, was glad for the job. The producers presumably gave him carte blanche on casting, as long as everybody would work cheap. With an intimate knowledge of the script and a vast backlog of actors he had directed over the years, Abbott was probably able to cast the thing over the bridge table. For the costarring role of the naïf Erwin, why not get Jack Gilford? He had played similarly nervous characters to great acclaim in two Abbott musicals, *Once Upon a Mattress* and *A Funny Thing Happened on the Way to the Forum*. So what if Gilford—just out of *Cabaret*—was in his sixties? He was younger than Levene, anyway, if only by a year.

From there, it was a simple Rolodex job. Let's get that girl who was so good in my last show, the 1969 musical disaster, *The Fig Leaves Are Falling*. Let's get that guy who was so good in my show before that, the 1968 musical disaster *The Education of H*Y*M*A*N K*A*P*L*A*N*. Thus came two soon-to-be Tony-winning stars, Dorothy Loudon and Hal Linden—both of whom were presumably thrilled to get the roles, even at union scale. Abbott called on employees recent and employees past. Paul Ford, a comedy master, starred in what was to be Abbott's final success, the 1962 comedy *Never Too Late*. Butterfly McQueen, unforgettable as Vivien Leigh's maid Prissy in the 1939 classic *Gone with the Wind*, had been in two consecutive Abbott plays during the 1937–1938 season, *Brown Sugar* (which lasted a mere weekend) and *What a Life* (which ran over a year).

The revival, assembled on a proverbial shoestring with a set that must have cost $157, was pretty much a bust. But that's not the reason I mention this production. Looking down from the second balcony during the first act—after I picked out an empty orchestra seat to move to—my eyes wandered over to the mezzanine box on the left side of the house. The Lyceum has two glorious, old-fashioned boxes, the sort you see in the movies. (The sight lines are surely no good, but these boxes were designed for people who wished to be seen in a box.) This was an open box—no ceiling on it—so I could easily watch a distinguished-but-bald old man furiously scribbling on a legal pad.

Mister Abbott was easy to recognize even if you didn't know what he looked like. What he looked like was a famous director; or I should say, the only person you'd find gliding around the theatre district in 1969 who was bald, eighty-two-years old, and about seven feet tall.

At intermission, I rushed down to the box. There he was, going over copious notes on a yellow legal pad.

"Excuse me, Mr. Abbott."

He looked up, with a stern demeanor. Mind you, he always had a stern demeanor. Forbidding, although I would find out some years later that this was merely his public face.

"I just wanted to, uh—" Wanted to what? I didn't really want anything, just to meet him. And he was definitely not the type you'd feel safe to ask for an autograph.

"What do you want?" he barked.

"Well, I saw you from my seat—"

"What are you? An actor? A director?"

Pretty gruff. I was just a high school kid.

"I just wanted to tell you that I've read a lot of your plays, and they've really taught me a lot about comedy."

"All right, I've got to work on these notes."

He turned gruffly back to his legal pad, and I turned and rushed away from Abbott's box as quickly as I could.

I'd later get to work with Mr. A. twice, and get to know him well enough to call him—well, Mr. Abbott. But it's now time to cross over from the Lyceum to the St. James, from Mr. Abbott to Mr. Merrick.

CHAPTER SIX

A Man Called Merrick

THE FORMER MR. MARGULOIS

AND SO IT WAS THAT ONE BRIGHT THURSDAY MORNING IN JUNE 1971 I entered the elevator entrance of the St. James—just east of the exit doors—ascended the elevator to the top (and only) floor, and eagerly took my place as a lowly office drudge.

David Merrick was not only the most successful and most powerful Broadway producer of the time, he had in the past dozen years thoroughly revolutionized the business. While his name remains visible on cast recordings of his numerous hits, he is relatively forgotten. While a handful of latter-day producers have attained similar success, they've been working in a very different market—one where a blockbuster musical can run more than twenty-five years in New York and in London, with duplicate full-scale productions mounted across the world. When Merrick started, only one musical had ever made it to the five-year mark, and there were only limited commercial opportunities outside America, England, and sometimes Australia. While Merrick had several relatively long-run blockbusters, his empire was built on multiple and constant hits—with as many as eight Broadway productions in a single twelve-month season.

So who was David Merrick, and how did he create this brave new world?

Merrick was *not* born on November 27, 1911, in St. Louis. That was one David Margulois. The unwanted lad grew up in Dickensian poverty, shuttled from one unwilling relative to another—at least, according to interviews he gave out from time to time. Family life, he gleefully reported fifty years later, was "like growing up on the set of *Who's Afraid of Virginia Woolf?*" He also sent out word, via his press agents, that while he was prone to hop a jet at a moment's notice if he sniffed an opportunity—he at all times carried his passport—he refused to take a plane routed over St. Louis. Not even an emergency landing was going to make him set foot in the city of his birth, he professed.

Young Margulois won a scholarship to Washington University in St. Louis. He settled on studying law, but his heart was in theatricals. A forgotten play he wrote won second prize in a college contest; an also-ran in that contest was fellow student Tom Williams, who within a decade had sharpened his skills and started to turn out plays like *The Glass Menagerie* under the catchier moniker Tennessee. Or was this simply one of Merrick's many made-up tales to be fed to unsuspecting interviewers? Years later, after the written-out Williams had lost his magic touch, Merrick saw fit to produce no less than four unworkable Williams plays: *The Milk Train Doesn't Stop Here* (which had already failed on Broadway under different management, twelve months earlier), *The Seven Descents of Myrtle, Out Cry,* and *The Red Devil Battery Sign*—which ran for a combined forty-six performances on Broadway, the latter closing during its 1975 Boston tryout despite a cast headed by Anthony Quinn and Claire Bloom. When Merrick was asked if he was closing *The Red Devil Battery Sign* for good, he said, "It is not closing for good, it's closing for bad."

The future producer eventually transferred to the less hallowed and less costly Saint Louis University, where he received a law degree in 1937. Shortly thereafter he married Leonore Beck, who was an heiress—or an heiress by Depression standards, anyway. New York called (anything to get out of St. Louis) and in 1940, he brought his new wife to Manhattan, not to practice law; while his training was to prove a considerable asset over a half century of wheeling and dealing, he had spent a good half of his life daydreaming about the theatre. And not as Margulois. His fancy somehow landed on David Garrick, the eighteenth-century British actor/manager. David Margulois merged with David Garrick, and thus it was that "David Merrick" sprung to life fully formed—a dour, dyspeptic outsider, with the mien of an undertaker—at twenty-eight.

Ungainly Amateur

He had engaged in amateur theatricals during college years and had spent a summer as an observer at a stock theatre in Harrison, Maine. Arriving in New York with the first Mrs. Merrick's bankroll, he determined that his theatrical entry should be as an investor in a Broadway hit. Through canny perception or perhaps pure luck, he settled upon a winner: *The Male Animal*, a college football comedy with social significance by *New Yorker* humorist/cartoonist James Thurber and actor Elliott Nugent. *The Male Animal*—which remains a wise and pretty good play, if considerably dated—opened in January 1940 and ran for 243 performances. Factoring in income from the road tours, the 1942 motion picture version (with Henry Fonda playing the Nugent role, while Nugent directed), and stock and amateur productions, Merrick turned his $5,000 stake into a profit of more than $20,000. After a year of looking for a follow-up to his *Male Animal* investment, Merrick went to that play's producer/director, Herman Shumlin, and took a job as the office go-fer. As in, "go for this" and "go for that."

Shumlin was a keen man of the theatre, notable among his peers as an independent outsider with integrity. His breakthrough came in 1930 with *The Last Mile*, John Wexley's tragedy about a serial killer set on death row. The play was an instant hit, in part due to a star-making performance by Spencer Tracy in the lead. Shumlin gained a reputation for important plays, including Lillian Hellman's first five. *The Children's Hour* and *The Little Foxes* had already opened before Merrick crossed beneath Shumlin's transom, which was in the Selwyn Theatre building, a former legit stage that in 1934 was downgraded to a second-run movie house. (The Selwyn was thoroughly renovated and reopened in 2000 as the Roundabout's American Airlines Theatre. The surrounding office building, which fronted on Forty-Second Street and included a renowned hamburger counter on the ground floor, collapsed during the renovation and was replaced by the New Forty-Second Street Studios.)

The reborn thirty-year-old learned the business from the ground up, with important lessons from the forty-two-year-old Shumlin. The office presented at least two major and provocative dramas during Merrick's days in residence: Emlyn Williams's *The Corn Is Green*, starring Ethel Barrymore; and Hellman's *Watch on the Rhine*, a virulently anti-Nazi play produced just before the United States entered World War II. Merrick also looked for plays to produce on his own. During this period, he became a company manager (for Shumlin and others) and was a credited producer or associate producer on the unsuccessful *The Willow and I* (1942), *Bright Boy* (1944), and *Jeb* (1946). There was also a four-performance 1944 flop called *The Man Who Had All the Luck* by a first-time playwright, Arthur Miller. By decade's end, Merrick started to become more visible in his own right, as coproducer of a non-Shumlin marital farce.

David Merrick, caught off-guard with an unaccustomed smile.
PHOTOFEST

Clutterbuck was a 1946 English comedy by Benn W. Levy, a prolific playwright who was at the time a member of Parliament. He was also married to a noted American actress, Constance Cummings. The 1949 Broadway production of *Clutterbuck*—Levy's twelfth play to appear in New York—was indifferently received. Merrick, though, here began to reveal himself as a master manipulator. He devised a series of "teaser" ads—small-sized, inexpensive newspaper ads intended to entice the reader to find out more about the product in question. The ads featured a cartoon figure—not unlike a modern-day cartoon gecko—and suggested that *Clutterbuck* was absolutely loaded with sex. Merrick also found unconventional ways to publicize the show, among which was his ruse of calling major tourist hotels at the pre-theatre hour and asking them to page "Mr. Clutterbuck." Whether this spurred ticket sales or not we cannot say, but it was typical Merrick. *Clutterbuck* withstood mediocre reviews to run the season—at which point, after a decade of preparation, he started to plan his own intensive production slate.

Paging Pagnol

But it wasn't quite so easy. Merrick—as lead producer, rather than associate—announced his first play in 1949. *A Candle for St. Jude*, it was called, based on the novel by Rumer Godden and adapted by Godden and Dorothy Heyward (coauthor of the play *Porgy*). Coproducing and providing the startup backing was one Julia Clayburgh, the wife of a wealthy textile executive who had also worked for Shumlin. The project was abandoned after two years, with Clayburgh remaining a loyal backer of Merrick through his early career. (At the time they set up office in 1949, Clayburgh had a five-year-old daughter. Jill never worked on Broadway for Merrick, but in 1977 she costarred with Burt Reynolds and Kris Kristofferson in one of Merrick's big-budget movies, *Semi-Tough*.)

Merrick spent a couple of years tracking down the rights to Marcel Pagnol's so-called *Marseilles Trilogy*, consisting of the Frenchman's 1929 play *Marius* and two film sequels, *Fanny* (1932) and *César* (1936), collectively about a young man who loves the sea more than the girl who loves him while his strong-willed father looks on. Merrick finally got the uncooperative Pagnol to agree, apparently by waving an unconscionably large advance payment in front of him and announced what would become the musical *Fanny* in September 1951. A month later, Shumlin and Merrick announced that they would transfer intact *The Lyric Revue*, an intimate affair from London with songs by Noël Coward and others. Like *A Candle for St. Jude*, that would never happen.

By the fall of 1952 Merrick was able to schedule *Fanny* for the following spring, with book by the husband-and-wife Hollywood screenwriting team of Albert Goodrich and Frances Hackett (whose 1942 drama, *The Great Big Doorstep*, had been produced by Shumlin during Merrick's apprenticeship). The score, it was also announced, was to come from the *Wizard of Oz* team, Harold Arlen and Yip Harburg. Within months, all four had departed *Fanny*.

Upon the realization that he would be hard pressed to get the Pagnol project on at all, the unconnected novice determined he needed a partner with theatrical clout. Joshua Logan was among the top directors of musicals at the time, with the landmark *South Pacific* still enjoying a record-breaking run. But how to get to him? Jo Mielziner, whom Merrick knew from *Watch on the Rhine*, was the most important scenic designer in the business; his recent offerings included not only *South Pacific* but *The Glass Menagerie*, *A Streetcar Named Desire*, and *Death of a Salesman*. Merrick made a deal with Mielziner: Get me Josh Logan, and I'll take care of you. Mielziner, who was himself interested in moving up to the producer's circle, agreed.

At that point, early in 1953, producers Merrick and Mielziner announced that they had optioned the musical rights to Eugene O'Neill's comedy *Ah, Wilderness!* This production wouldn't materialize until 1959, when it opened as *Take Me Along*, produced by Merrick, with Mielziner as neither coproducer nor designer (although Jo designed Merrick's prior 1959 musical, *Gypsy*). The pair of never-to-be partners announced one other musical before *Fanny*: Walter Kerr's *Goldilocks*, a failure that ultimately opened in 1958 with the involvement of neither Merrick nor Mielziner. Jo did produce one musical on his own: the unhappy *Happy Hunting* in 1956, starring Ethel Merman.

Mielziner made the Logan connection, and Logan was intrigued by the Pagnol material. The Princeton grad had started his career in the spring of 1938 with a well-received play—Paul Osborn's *On Borrowed Time*—and the Rodgers & Hart musical hit, *I Married an Angel*. Logan's facility for musicals was immediately recognized by Rodgers, who used him on two of the final three Hart musicals (*Higher and Higher* and *By Jupiter*). When Rodgers started producing, following the success of *Oklahoma!* and *Carousel*, he and partner Oscar Hammerstein hired Logan for Irving Berlin's *Annie Get Your Gun*. (Logan already had a relationship with Berlin, as director of the World War II patriotic revue, *This Is the Army*.) *Annie Get Your Gun* was an enormous hit, as were the next two R & H productions, the comedies *Happy Birthday* (starring Helen Hayes) and *John Loves Mary*. Logan directed both, receiving associate producer credit on the latter. After this, Logan had a blockbuster on his own, the 1948 play *Mister Roberts*, which he directed and coauthored.

Then came the big one. Logan and agent/producer Leland Hayward brought James Michener's Pulitzer-winning collection of stories *Tales of the South Pacific* to Rodgers & Hammerstein, who agreed to do the show providing that Logan and Hayward downgrade themselves to associate producer billing. Logan worked with the songwriters as they were creating the play, eventually stepping in as coauthor of the book; he had served as a captain during the war, giving him practical experience which the States-bound Hammerstein decidedly lacked. *South Pacific* was one of Broadway's biggest hits ever, and everybody was suitably happy—except Logan. Rodgers—who controlled matters with an iron fist—finally and begrudgingly offered co-librettist credit, but refused to give Josh a share of the authors' royalties. This caused increasing frustration on Logan's part, one of the elements that resulted in the manic-depressive director's very public nervous breakdown in 1953. Merrick—deep in preparations for *Fanny* and serving as an observer on the New Orleans tryout of Logan's production *Kind Sir*—was apparently in the hotel room when Logan was restrained in a straitjacket and whisked away to a sanitarium.

Have You Seen Fanny?

Nevertheless, Logan was atop the Broadway world courtesy of *Annie Get Your Gun*, *South Pacific*, and *Mister Roberts*. Logan agreed to take on *Fanny*, as director and full coproducer, and under Merrick's prodding brought the material to Rodgers & Hammerstein. They had just written and produced *The King and I*, which turned out to be a hit despite severe tryout problems—caused in no small part by the lack of an adequate director on the show, to the extent that Hammerstein himself unofficially took over and finished the job. Logan likely would have done *The King and I* had he not been fighting with Rodgers at the time over *South Pacific* royalties.

Rodgers & Hammerstein liked the Pagnol material, especially Hammerstein. But Rodgers—once again—refused to allow anyone to share producer billing on a Rodgers & Hammerstein musical; what's more, his personal antipathy for this strange and dour Jewish lawyer from St. Louis ruled out any association. Merrick was ready to sacrifice almost anything to get R & H to write *Fanny*—but not producing credit. He refused to relinquish the rights, and Logan—sensitive after his own battles with Rodgers—agreed to go ahead with Merrick.

(For their next project, R & H chose a musicalization of John Steinbeck's novel *Sweet Thursday*. Similarly, this was a case in which the producers who approached them with the project were forced to bow out and leave R & H with sole credit. In this case, the producers were of a far higher echelon than beginner Merrick; Cy Feuer and Ernest Martin already had three hit musicals in a row, including the blockbuster *Guys and Dolls*. They agreed to step aside, in exchange for 10 percent of the profits of the resulting musical. The 1955 *Pipe Dream* was a thorough failure, though, leaving Feuer and Martin with 10 percent of nothing.)

Without R & H on board, Logan—who appears to have been getting close to dropping the whole thing—insisted that he must have a songwriter he knew. He had just directed *Wish You Were Here*—an indifferent musical that worked its way into a hit, in large part because of the Hit Parade popularity of the title song—and so it was that composer/lyricist Harold Rome was given the new show. Logan shared the book assignment with S. N. Behrman, a writer of sophisticated comedies like the 1927 hit *Biography*. An unlikely choice, writing his first and only musical, but there was no question in this case of Logan receiving full authorship credit and participation.

Even without the presence of R & H, *Fanny* retained numerous links to *South Pacific*. Logan and designer Mielziner were joined by two of the three leading actors from that show. Ezio Pinza, who created the role of Emile ("Some Enchanted Evening") de Becque, played César, the father of the lovers. William Tabbert, who created the role of Lieutenant ("Younger than Springtime") Cable, was brought over to play the young lover, Marius. Merrick and Logan planned, perhaps unreasonably, to entice Mary Martin to play the teenaged heroine; instead, the role went to a bit player from *Wish You Were Here*, Florence Henderson, who at twenty was a full twenty years younger than Martin.

Merrick and Logan set about producing and more or less promising a second *South Pacific*; unfortunately, the new show wasn't nearly as strong. Rome wrote a couple of song hits, including a title song that inundated the airwaves for a year, but the score was more atmospheric than exciting. Atmospheric—rather than exciting—was a fair description of the enterprise. The reviews were favorable though lukewarm. That didn't stop Merrick. He promoted *Fanny* in a manner previously unseen along Broadway. It was not highbrow stuff; for example, Merrick had his minions visit men's rooms across the city and paste stickers to the wall— over the urinals—asking "have you seen *Fanny*?"

The biggest publicity coup came when a nude statue of the show's resident belly dancer (Nejla Ates) turned up one morning in Central Park. It was quickly removed by the authorities, as Merrick knew it would be, but stories and photos flooded the newspapers and magazines for weeks, as Merrick knew they would. None of this made *Fanny* a better show, but it cajoled the public into thinking it was a must-see hit. And so it turned out, returning its entire $275,000 investment in only sixteen and a half weeks.

Other musicals might have done so as quickly, for all we know; show finances in those days were not generally discussed. Merrick, though, announced the quick payoff ("which is believed to be a record in musicals") in a flashy and boasting manner. The resulting press coverage in itself fed the image of the show as blockbuster. *Fanny* ran 888 performances, not nearly on the level of Rodgers & Hammerstein's *Oklahoma!* or *South Pacific* but just as long as *Carousel*. Good enough for Merrick, in what he thereafter touted as his first Broadway show—although, as we've seen, it wasn't.

Merrick Parkway

So here was David Merrick, self-created, self-made, and self-aggrandizing: a modern-day Barnum, the perfect showman/huckster for Broadway at mid-century. One show running was not enough; Merrick already had big plans, although it took a few seasons to put them into practice. *Fanny* was successful enough—it ultimately turned a profit of $856,858—but it was a musical for the undiscriminating masses, with little to interest sophisticated Broadway insiders. For his second offering, Merrick went highbrow with a British import featuring three distinguished names: Thornton Wilder, the three-time Pulitzer-winning playwright of *Our Town*; Ruth Gordon, one of Broadway's leading actresses; and English director Tyrone Guthrie.

Guthrie and Gordon, who had happily worked together on the 1936 Old Vic production of *The Country Wife*, decided in 1952 that they wanted to again join forces. Garson Kanin, the playwright who was by this point Gordon's second husband, suggested Wilder's 1938 play *The Merchant of Yonkers*, which was—if you follow me—a twentieth-century Broadway adaptation of a nineteenth-century Viennese farce based on an eighteenth-century English comedy. Wilder had originally intended it for Gordon, who was just then starring in Wilder's successful 1937 Broadway adaptation of *A Doll's House*. Gordon turned *The Merchant* down, Shumlin produced it—just before Merrick first arrived in New York—and it was a quick failure. A dozen years later, Kanin determined it would be suitable for Gordon and Guthrie, so they enlisted Wilder to revise his forgotten farce. Guthrie presented it in Scotland under the title *The Matchmaker* at the Edinburgh Festival (for which he was artistic director), and the delectable, fast-paced farce enjoyed great success in Edinburgh, on tour, and in London.

Merrick, on the prowl to find something to join *Fanny* on the boards, latched onto the project. Gar and Ruthie—sensing that this near-novice producer was overly eager for the rights—insisted that the play could be done only if the producer guaranteed a Broadway run and agreed to import Guthrie and the full London production—a complete transfer, albeit with American replacements in several key roles. Merrick acceded to the demands, and opened *The Matchmaker* on December 5, 1955, at the

Royale. (The Theatre Guild, which had a prior interest in the play, coproduced with Merrick and received top billing; Merrick received a second credit on the title page, "Production under the supervision of David Merrick.") Gordon and British actress Eileen Herlie (as Irene Molloy)—from the London production—were joined by Americans Loring Smith (as Vandergelder), Arthur Hill (as Cornelius Hackl), and Robert Morse (as Barnaby Tucker). *The Matchmaker* was an instant hit, running more than a year. But Merrick, it turned out, was not yet through with *The Matchmaker*.

Despite two long-running, financially successful hits, Merrick found himself without anything on Broadway in the winter of 1957. But the showman was now in high gear. While American playwrights and their agents looked askance at this undignified snake-oil salesman of a producer—did we mention that he had a man in a monkey suit drive a Rolls around town, with a sign saying "I'm driving my master to see *The Matchmaker!*"—Merrick found that his money was most welcome in London.

He staked his claim to Broadway in the fall of 1957, opening not one but three shows in October: John Osborne's *Look Back in Anger*, which originated Britain's "angry young men" movement; Peter Ustinov in his comedy, *Romanoff and Juliet*; and the Harold Arlen/E. Y. Harburg musical *Jamaica*, starring Lena Horne. All hits. He added a fourth success of the 1957–1958 season in the spring, Osborne's *The Entertainer* starring Laurence Olivier. At that point, Merrick shows were playing in four of the seven theatres on Forty-Fifth Street between Broadway and Eighth Avenue. He had his press agents dub the block "Merrick Parkway."

During the 1958–1959 season he would produce six shows, including three major hits (*The World of Suzie Wong*, *La Plume de Ma Tante*, and Ethel Merman in *Gypsy*). In the fall of 1960, he opened three hits *within six days*—*Irma La Douce*, *A Taste of Honey*, and *Becket* (starring Olivier and Anthony Quinn). Yes, Merrick surely planned it that way; he knew he would look even more all-powerful by producing back-to-back hits. This left the competition—established producers including Kermit Bloomgarden, Robert Whitehead, Roger L. Stevens, Alfred de Liagre, Fred Coe, and the teams of Feuer & Martin and Robert E. Griffith & Harold S. Prince—looking decidedly lesser. And yes; Merrick *surely* planned it that way.

Man for All Seasons: David Merrick touts three simultaneous hits (1960).
PHILLIP HARRINGTON / ALAMY STOCK PHOTO

He was so successful that a *Saturday Evening Post* article—published just under seven years from the opening of *Fanny*—offered the breathless calculation that only four of the twenty-one Merrick shows thus far had lost money. I don't know that these statistics were actually correct, but they're close enough. This article came two years before *Hello, Dolly!*, Merrick's record-shattering 1964 musicalization of *The Matchmaker*.

From the opening night of *Look Back in Anger*, Merrick always had one or more productions on Broadway for a stretch of seventeen years. (Nowadays, a single musical can run more than seventeen years, but this was unheard of in Merrick's era.) Additionally, he had as many as five touring companies at a time, making him Broadway's biggest employer by far. These shows included the Bob Merrill musicals *Take Me Along* and *Carnival!*; Anthony Newley's *Stop the World—I Want to Get Off!* and *The Roar of the Greasepaint—The Smell of the Crowd*; Lionel Bart's *Oliver!*; and Harvey Schmidt and Tom Jones's *110 in the Shade* and *I Do! I Do!* Plays included Osborne's *Luther* (starring Albert Finney) and *Inadmissible Evidence*; Abe Burrows's *Cactus Flower* (starring Lauren Bacall) and *Forty Carats* (starring Julie Harris); *One Flew over the Cuckoo's Nest* (starring Kirk Douglas); *Marat/Sade*; Brian Friel's *Philadelphia, Here I Come!*; Woody Allen's *Don't Drink the Water* and *Play It Again, Sam*; Tom Stoppard's *Rosencrantz and Guildenstern Are Dead*; *Child's Play*; and the legendary Peter Brook production of *A Midsummer Night's Dream*.

Plus *Promises, Promises*, the hit of the moment, in its third year at the Shubert. The London production had opened in October 1969 and run 560 performances; there was presently a first-class touring company on the road in its second year; and a smaller-scale bus-and-truck production was scheduled to open in September. But for Merrick, it wasn't like the old days; with the closing of *Dolly!* and *Child's Play* in December 1970, the producer was down to a single Broadway show for the first time since 1957—albeit with four new productions scheduled for the 1971–1972 season.

Merrick, that summer, was back and forth between New York and Hollywood, where he was trying to wedge himself into the film industry with a big budget film version of F. Scott Fitzgerald's *The Great Gatsby*. Left to keep things running smoothly—or combatively, which was the Merrick method—was Jack Schlissel.

Chapter Seven

Lieutenants

Follow the Money

Jack Schlissel was born in the Bronx in 1922. A graduate of City College of New York, he started as an accountant working for Price Waterhouse. He moved into theatre accounting in the mid-1940s and was soon serving as business manager of established out-of-town spots like the Bucks County Playhouse (in New Hope, Pennsylvania) and the Pittsburgh Civic Light Opera. He returned to New York in 1950, managing four shows for producer Kermit Bloomgarden, ending with Arthur Miller's *The Crucible* in 1953. Merrick, at that point in the midst of assembling *Fanny*, presumably heard that Jack handled his rival Kermit's shows with canny efficiency and started turning to him for advice.

As 1954 approached, Jack told me he had two simultaneous offers from novice producers: Merrick's first musical, which was eventually pushed off to summer rehearsals, and a spring musical with no stars from first-time songwriters and first-time producers about a strike in a Midwest pajama factory. *Fanny*, with the director/coauthor, designer, and two stars from *South Pacific*, sounded a more likely prospect than what turned out to be *The Pajama Game*, so Jack cast his lot with Merrick instead of novice producer Harold Prince. Schlissel remained with Merrick for fifty-odd shows, over twenty seasons; he was probably far too hard-headed to have lasted long with Prince, anyway.

As general manager, Jack ran the business end. Merrick, certainly, expected things to run on a severe economic model; what's the point of having eight or more productions running simultaneously if you can't demand steep savings and discounts? Jack got the savings and discounts Merrick required, which went to lower costs and boost profits. Jack's nature, though, was to negotiate the lowest possible price—and then apply pressure with the thumbs (as they used to say in *Dolly!*) to demand more (as they used to say in *Oliver!*).

This, obviously, allowed for kickbacks; these, I suppose, went directly into Jack's pocket. This seems to have been okay with Merrick, so long as they were not overly rapacious. My understanding is that Jack's overall deal did not include a share of the profits. Rather, he got incidental perks that enabled him to amass an untold but substantial sum. An important part of this was the souvenir book, those oversized programs for sale in the lobby of the theatre. Figure a thousand or so captive customers a performance; figure a price of $1, at a time when an orchestra seat cost $8 or $10; figure minimal cost. Figure all those road companies of all those hits—the flops had books, too, though with smaller audiences to sell to—and you come up with a substantial fiefdom, which was all Jack's own.

While working *Promises* I had a close view of the book seller, not incidentally the grown son of Jack's chief bookman. Before the house opened and during lulls in the crowd, he would make stacks of singles, folding them lengthwise. Buy one $1 book with a ten, you'd get back seven singles; buy two books with a twenty, you'd get back fourteen singles. "These big spenders on a date, they're not going to stop in front of the girl and count the change," he bragged to me. "If they do, sorry, my mistake."

GET YOUR SEATS HERE

Jack also had control of house seats. These were and are prime tickets contractually set aside for the producer, creators, stars, and theatre owners. Not free tickets, they are sold at the regular box office price. If you are an author or director or star of a hit, you are unavoidably pestered for seats by family—close and distant—along with your dentist, dry cleaner, and people you went to school or war with. Hence, house seats. For a smash hit these are a hot commodity; ticket brokers and scalpers, since time immemorial, have gouged well-heeled customers and expense account businessmen for locations of this caliber—although you might wonder just how brokers and scalpers got their hands on so many prime seats they could sell at a markup.

Ticketing was (and remains) under the control of the theatre owner, with the producer (via the general manager) negotiating for the most house seats, in the most prime locations, they can obtain. The producer (via the general manager) simultaneously negotiates to assign to the authors et al. the *lowest* number of house seats they'll accept. The rest stay with the producer and general manager to accommodate celebrities, business associates, agents/lawyers/stars with whom they are negotiating for other shows, and company members who do not rate house seats of their own—plus miscellaneous requests.

The house seat game has changed since Merrick & Schlissel ruled their own slice of Broadway. At the time, it was technically illegal for anyone to resell tickets except for licensed brokers, with strict markup limits. "Maximum resale premium for Orch., Mezz., Balc. or Box tickets resold (unless resale restricted) $1.50 plus 10 percent lawful tax," said a small-print disclaimer printed on every ticket, adding "Retain stub to support any claim for overcharge." As if. Laws of that sort were so rarely enforced that the government, busy trying to stop *real* crime and corruption, eventually let the rules lapse.

In 2001, the producers of *The Producers*—the *Dolly!* equivalent of the day, and the biggest hit to play the St. James since Carol Channing first descended that iconic red staircase—came up with a bold and novel idea. Those slimy ticket scalpers were cornering seats at the regular box office price (which was a then-record $100) and easily reselling them for $500 apiece or more. Why can't *we*—legitimately, at the box office—charge, say, $480? This way, the added $380 will go into the pockets of our investors (and *us*). The royalty recipients would benefit, too, with their share of the increased gross; even the taxman. Everybody wins.

Even the scalpers won, it turned out; they immediately discovered that they could buy the $480 premium seats and resell them for $700 or more. Everybody won, except the average non-expense-account theatergoer. The seats offered at the "official" non-premium price were usually in the back, on the side, and decidedly non-premium, unless the show was a soft ticket, in which case the nigh-unsellable premium seats were sold at list price or less—or not sold at all.

But this is a twenty-first-century policy. Back during the Merrick years, the official box office price—plus that laughably small $1.50 premium—was the maximum that could be legally charged. Hence, the system of ice. I.C.E. was a political term, originally, meaning "incidental campaign expense." That is, unregulated cash flowing around to allow operatives or ward heelers to buy votes or line their pockets, either or both.

Each theatre had a head treasurer, who oversaw his own personal inventory. That is, virtually the entire seating capacity. The house seat allotments of the producer and theatre owner removed a chunk of the best seats, yes; but this still left the treasurer plenty to play with. Would you rather sell prime locations to Joe Public for the regular price, or to some broker/scalper buddy for three or five times the price? Tax free? What's more, house seats—other than on the most massive of hits—are only used occasionally. A playwright with a four-seat allotment is entitled to thirty-two a week, 130 a month; how many friends do you think he or she has? These are not free seats, after all.

Unused house seats used to expire a day or two before the performance; nowadays it is usually a ninety-six-hour expiration, and in Jack's day it was twenty-four hours. At that point, the unused prime tickets were released—*into the hands of the treasurer.* If the show was a hot ticket and a scalper had a good client demanding prime seats, cost be damned, the treasurer could demand an exorbitant bounty for these unused house seats. None of this happens anymore, or not nearly to the same extent; with computerized ticketing overseen by the theatre owner and the advent of premium seats, opportunities for treasurer chicanery are some-what minimized. In the good old days before business went bad in the early 1970s, though, you never saw a head treasurer wearing a dime-store watch or "a respectable Republican cloth coat" (look it up if you must).

This ticket tangent is simply to illustrate the meaning of what I was told by more than one Merrick company manager. With big hits and likely-to-be hits, Jack would turn up in the tryout city a few days prior to the first performance; check in with the director and the stars; then disappear into the box office with an empty briefcase. He'd leave with a smile and a full briefcase, return in the late afternoon with a bigger smile, wait around till after the dinner break, and take the late train—with, now, a cash-filled briefcase—back to New York. The local scalpers, suddenly, had great seats available at great prices.

Jack also controlled theatre party buys. Theatre parties—organizations that bought large blocks of seats (at regular prices) and sold the tickets to donors (at high prices, legally, with the difference going to the charity in question)—were an enormous force at the time. It was not uncommon for big new musicals to come to town with a hundred or more fully sold-out dates. A flop, in fact, could run for several months solely on the strength of the presold and theoretically nonrefundable parties. The organizations got their tickets from one of a group of cutthroat theatre party brokers, each of whom demanded the "best" dates for their most lucrative clients.

Merrick produced more shows with more stars and more "star" creators than other producers, meaning he had the most desirable shows for the theatre party trade. Jack would field requests and disburse dates like a modern-day Solomon, gleefully lording over an overstuffed binder full of ticket broker letters. Many of these charities were spearheaded by the most important and richest socialites and businessmen (and businessmen's wives) of the day, none of whom were accustomed to taking no for an answer. The brokers needed to accommodate their most powerful clients, who were otherwise quick to find a *different* broker who could provide tickets for *that* show on *that* date—which put Jack in what they used to call the catbird seat; he could call up party agents Gertrude or Lenny or their main competitors and say, simply, "So you *really* need October eighteenth? How much do you need it?"

Jack was clever, smart, and devious in Machiavellian fashion. I kind of liked him, actually; he was at least consistent. A man of many secrets, it turned out that he had a big one that might have helped fuel his ruthlessness. In 1979 or so, several years after the Merrick Empire disbanded, a twenty-year-old composer moved into the fifty-seven-year-old Schlissel's apartment in the Hotel des Artistes. (Jack immediately hired him to conduct his next Broadway musical; he did a fine job, as it turned out.) Through a quarter century on Broadway, it seems, Jack had been living a secret life and apparently loathing himself for it.

How long this had been going on we don't know, but Leo Herbert—Merrick's propman from day one, who had worked with Jack even before *Fanny*—told me that one afternoon in the early 1960s he was walking on West Fifty-Fourth Street, seeking props for the next in the steady stream of Merrick shows. The door of an all-male pornographic movie theatre opened and out slithered Jack, practically bumping into Leo. Schlissel stood there, frozen. Leo, who lasted thirty-six years with Merrick because he always knew how to adapt to any eventuality, simply said "Hello, Jack" and walked on by.

BLONDES AND FAIR LADIES

More interesting—creative, knowledgeable, personable, supportive, and altogether friendly—was Samuel "Biff" Liff, who went under the title associate producer. Hailing from Boston, he began his career as a stage manager at the Nantucket Playhouse in 1940 and moved to the Bucks County Playhouse in 1941 (long before Jack got there). The stay was brief; Biff went into the Signal Corps after Pearl Harbor and remained through the war, winding up as a captain. He went back to work in 1946 at Tamiment, the summer camp in the Poconos that bred numerous talents (including, some years earlier, the likes of Danny Kaye and Jerome Robbins). That fall, he got his first important job, as replacement stage manager of producer Herman Levin's postwar revue hit, *Call Me Mister*.

In the fall of 1949, Levin hired Biff for his upcoming *Gentlemen Prefer Blondes*, starring newcomer Carol Channing as Lorelei Lee. *Blondes* was a smash hit, keeping Biff occupied for almost four seasons. He was to remain with Levin, on and off, for eighteen years. During the off periods he did various shows, including two that are relevant to our story. In early 1954 he was hired for a flop musical—the Shirley Booth vehicle, *By the Beautiful Sea*—which Jack managed immediately before joining Merrick for *Fanny*. In 1955, Biff did Merrick's second production, *The Matchmaker*.

Biff left the play about Dolly the matchmaker at year's end to go into rehearsal with Levin's next show, the Lerner & Loewe musical about Eliza Doolittle and Henry Higgins. *My Fair Lady* kept him busy until 1962, remounting various companies for director Moss Hart and himself directing productions in Australia, Russia, Israel, and the United

States. Levin and Biff, though, were left out of the *Fair Lady* team's next musical: Lerner, Loewe, and Moss Hart decided to produce it themselves. *Camelot* was one show that, as things turned out, was in desperate need of a real producer.

Levin countered his loss of Lerner & Loewe by turning to Noël Coward for the 1963 *The Girl Who Came to Supper*. Biff stage managed this outright dud, which closed shortly after *Hello, Dolly!* opened in January 1964. When Neil Hartley—Merrick's production supervisor since *Jamaica* in 1957—left the firm to join director Tony Richardson in filmland, Biff was the obvious choice to oversee the upcoming multiple companies of *Dolly!* and the rest of Merrick's burgeoning slate. Thus he entered the firm in the spring of 1964, in time for the September opening of the British import *Oh, What a Lovely War!*

RUNNING INTERFERENCE, GENTLY

Biff's title was associate producer. In practice, he more or less produced the shows. Merrick would choose the properties; assemble the writers and directors (with Biff's input); and raise the money, which after *Dolly!* became a question of mostly choosing which investors *not* to accept. (In 1966 he arranged an unprecedented financing deal with RCA Victor, which was making a continuing fortune from the best-selling original cast album of *Dolly!* The label put up a cool $2 million, in a day when you could produce a new musical for $400,000. What they got were 75 percent investments in the flops *How Now, Dow Jones* and *The Happy Time* plus the legendary fiascos *Mata Hari* and *Breakfast at Tiffany's*.)

Merrick showed little interest in preproduction and rehearsals; his modus operandi was to arrive just in time for the out-of-town tryout; stir up everybody and everything; threaten to fire everyone; and play with his employees like a wily cat with a forlornly sleep-deprived mouse.

Biff's chores fell in three areas: assembling the shows; maintaining the ones that ran long enough; and remounting the touring companies. On the new shows, he would work with the writers, select the directors and choreographers (where they were not part of the initial package), and assemble the design team. Biff had his own in-house casting department to find the actors, and a team of head stagehands who would oversee each production and then move onto the next. Biff would launch the shows into rehearsal, putting out the various fires that arose, until the show was ready to hit the road. Once Merrick turned up, Biff's job was to attempt to implement the producer's often argumentative demands while keeping the show from imploding.

Sometimes, privately, he would try to talk down the producer. Biff was standing with Merrick at the back of the Colonial in Boston at the first tryout performance of the two-character Mary Martin/Robert Preston/Gower Champion musical *I Do! I Do!* "Where's the orchestra?" Merrick whispered harshly. "I don't see the orchestra!"

"Upstage, behind the backdrop. We discussed that," Biff said. "We only have two actors, so Gower moved the playing area as close to the audience as possible."

"I'm paying for a full orchestra, people will think the whole thing is recorded. Tear it out and put them back in the pit," Merrick demanded and stalked away.

This would have meant totally restaging the show, resetting the scenery, and redesigning the lights. Gower, Biff, and designer Oliver Smith came up with a solution. They replaced the back curtain with a painted scrim. Lit from the front, with a blackout curtain behind it, it appeared solid throughout the performance. During curtain calls, Bob and Mary gestured upstage center. The blackout drop was raised and lights came up behind the scrim; there, suddenly, was the conductor with his full orchestra, playing away. Gower's choice to place the show down front worked perfectly for the show, but Merrick's insistence paid off; the sight of the band brought a collective gasp from the audience, followed by a roar of appreciation. Every night.

Two years later, the pre-Broadway tryout of *Promises, Promises*: same theatre, same issue. Merrick found Biff backstage and pulled him out front. "What's that?" he snarled, pointing at the orchestra pit.

"The orchestra pit," said Biff.

"Why is it covered?" There was a black fabric covering over the stage right side of the pit.

"The sound man"—he pointed to a large console board at the back of the side orchestra—"needs the brass and percussion covered, so he can re-create the recording studio sound."

"This is theatre; I don't want it to sound like a record. Open up the pit—and get rid of that thing [i.e., the sound console]. This is live theatre."

"But David, that's the whole reason we hired Burt Bacharach! So the show would sound contemporary, like on the radio. That's what we're paying for."

"Well," said Merrick, sensing that this was not something to fight about, "we'll see how they like it tonight." They liked the first Boston performance of *Promises*, so the sound man and the pit covering stayed.

After the out-of-town openings of pre-Broadway tryouts, there would always be a staff postmortem. At these, Merrick was always at his best, which meant he was at his worst. He would demand that songs be thrown out, dialogue rewritten, dances restaged, and occasionally directors, choreographers, designers, or actors fired. After that, he would disappear—often with a surreptitious chuckle—and leave Biff to clean up the mess. Part of Merrick's style was to cower everyone into submission. This didn't work with Gower and a few other self-assured souls like Neil Simon (bookwriter of *Promises*), but everyone else jumped. Merrick *enjoyed* stirring people up and getting the authors and directors fighting with each other; for him, it was part of the fun. During tryouts, he had a habit of flying in other writers or directors to see the show, "for advice." He would carefully instruct the company manager to seat them away from the writers or directors of record. Not too close, but *close enough to be seen*.

It was left to Biff to implement whatever changes Merrick demanded—which meant getting an understanding of what Merrick actually meant. Merrick knew what didn't seem right to him—that was one of his strengths; but he wasn't the sort of producer who had an artistic sense of what to do about it. Given Biff's strong theatrical instincts, practical understanding, and soothing demeanor, he was typically able to put out the fires Merrick stoked and smooth things over—at which point the people involved were more likely to get the work done, in the hopes that Merrick would leave them alone.

Once the shows opened on Broadway, be they hits or flops, Merrick seemed to have little interest in the already-birthed baby. He didn't even care to spend time basking in success, unless his competitors or the press were watching. (There were three exceptions to this, for various reasons: *Fanny, Dolly!* and the 1980 blockbuster *42nd Street*.) For Merrick, yesterday's show was old business. His attention immediately shifted to the next project, with the next set of battles.

After leaving the production side of the business in 1972, Biff went over to run the theatre department of the William Morris Agency, where he continued for almost forty years—and where he represented many of the people and estates whom he had helped facilitate during their tussles with Merrick.

Over the years, I considered Biff as sort of a favorite great-uncle—infrequently present but always instantly available, thrilled to hear from you, and sincerely interested in hearing about your current progress both inside and outside the theatre. (As he was dying, he sent me a framed, three-dimensional model of the first act set—Vandergelder's parlor—from *The Matchmaker*. This was presented to Biff by Tanya Moiseiwitsch, the famed designer of that production, when he left the play to begin rehearsals of his next show. The engraved and by this point hopelessly tarnished plaque on the picture frame says: "*Biff.* Anglo-American: *The Matchmaker*. American-Anglo: *My Fair Lady*.") What I discovered, when he died in 2015 at the age of ninety-six, was that there were at least a dozen of us "favorite nephews" and nieces whom Biff had nurtured over his seventy years in the business.

Also on Call

There was a third member of the upper staff floating around. Alan DeLynn was his name. What he did, precisely, none of us knew. I didn't know, either, why his nickname among the lowly go-fers was "Stinky." Alan worked from a three-page list of names of celebrities, creative types, and money people that we called "the flimsy." (The lists were typed on onion-skin paper, which would curl when you held them.) His job seemed to be to call everyone on the flimsy over the course of the month, then circle back and do it again. "David is thinking of you," he would tell them, and then get them talking about what they were doing, what they wanted to do, and more. The point of this exercise? At such time that an important writer had a new script, or a bankable star wanted to do a new show, they would think—"I have a direct line to David Merrick." "Stinky" sat in his office off the back hallway, a door over from Biff, with a secretary perpetually making phone calls from the "flimsy." DeLynn was decidedly nontheatrical—he dressed like a junior partner at an ad agency—and I don't think I ever saw him talking to anyone other than his secretary. Not even Sylvia, and certainly not Jack.

There were two other longtime office employees, both of whom in those days would be described as middle-aged ladies. They couldn't have been more different, though. The aforementioned Sylvia Schwartz was the gatekeeper of the office since 1959, sitting at her switchboard just outside the elevator. (It is said that she safeguarded Jack; if someone stormed in whom she knew Schlissel didn't want to see or was actually afraid of, she would signal him so that as soon as he heard them entering his outer office he could escape via the side door.) Sylvia screened all the incoming calls; made all Jack's outgoing calls; and was keeper of the all-important house seats for all the shows. She signed all the ticket orders, although Jack was firmly and protectively in charge.

Jack had a full-time assistant camped outside his door—by this point, it was Jay Kingwill, handling all the business details—but it was Sylvia who was his confidential confederate. If ever there was an attorney general investigation into the illegal ticket trade, it was Sylvia who knew all the secrets; and she would clearly go to any lengths to protect Jack.

She was like a Jewish mother from Brooklyn—a mother with a warm but steely core. When Jack and Merrick parted ways, Sylvia left as well. She landed not with Jack but with Biff, at the William Morris Agency, where she controlled all of the house seats for the Morris stable of theatrical actors, writers, and directors. For years thereafter when I didn't have a direct contact for house seats, I would just call Sylvia. Given the clientele of the Morris office at the time, she had access to anything you might need.

Sitting directly opposite Jay, outside Merrick's door, was Helen Nickerson. Helen Livingston Nickerson, that is. A divorcee from San

Francisco high society, she joined the firm in 1963 as Merrick's secretary and assistant. Helen was all business, and so dry as to seem humorless. (Perhaps this was because unlike Merrick, Jack, Biff, and Sylvia, Helen was not Jewish.) She took her work very seriously and expected us all to do so as well. When she was in earshot, anyway.

Helen conscientiously and jealously guarded Merrick's door, his schedule, and his checkbook. I was especially fascinated by the day-by-day calendar on her desk. Merrick's appointments were carefully noted, in Helen's meticulously neat, rounded handwriting. Sorted into the proper dates were numerous checks written on Merrick's personal account, handwritten by Helen but unsigned until it was time to send them out: alimony checks, in different amounts and with different frequency, to Merrick's then three ex-wives. The third ex-wife, Etan, was around that summer, stopping in to check on the office renovations. He was to remarry her in 1983, for a while at least.

Otherwise, there were six staff assistants—like me—and two workers toiling in Biff's casting office. Numerous other people drifted in and out; stage managers, stagehands, and others turned up when necessary or when Jack so commanded. He would have Sylvia track them down—early or late, at home, a backstage pay phone, or a local bar—and say simply: "Jack wants you." And they would leap to action.

Journeyman

THE BOY AND THE BABE

TWO OF THESE MERRICK VETERANS WILL BE A CONSTANT PRESENCE IN these pages, and thus deserve a more detailed introduction—not only by virtue of my adventures with them, but as representative examples of life in the Broadway theatre during the latter half of the twentieth century. In addition to their knowledge and experience, they were wonderful raconteurs with story after story; hence, I hereby record some of their most memorable anecdotes. Both, in 1971, were about fifty—just older than my father, in fact—while I was still only eighteen; but each were in their own way ageless, and to me more like older brothers. They generously shared everything they knew about the theatre crafts, and within a few years I was enlightening them on the sometimes-puzzling aspects of the business end of show business. I also had the opportunity and pleasure, over the years, to employ them on occasion.

Leo Herbert, Merrick's head property man, was by any description a character. By the time I met him, he was a walrus of a man; find a photo of Victor Herbert—Broadway's top operetta composer in the early years of the twentieth century, and a distant cousin—and you'll see Leo. He also looked enough like Walter Slezak—the Austrian-born actor who starred opposite Ezio Pinza in *Fanny*—that the two of them formed a kinship.

Leo was a man of a thousand stories, most of them rooted in truth; or at least, partial truth. For example, he told a tale of one summer's day in 1932, the heart of the Depression. Leo's father, who had lost the family

Leo Herbert, man of a thousand stories.
COURTESY CHERI HERBERT

brush factory in the Crash, was working as a taxi driver in their home-town of Kingston, New York. On sultry days like this, he would drop Leo off along Esopus Creek for an afternoon of fly fishing. On this particular afternoon, the fish were jumpin'—so much so that Leo quickly caught the legal limit of trout. Being a virtuous twelve-year-old, he sat on a big rock in the sun, along the waterside, and unwrapped his sandwich.

Just then, a barrel-chested bruiser in waders came splashing down the creek. Looking over, Leo spotted a large fish under the rock just in front of the man. He waved his arms to attract his attention (the fisher-man, not the fish), then pointed to the trout's location. The burly fellow quickly scooped it up—it was indeed a large fish, as it always is in these stories—then headed over to little Leo. Leo started to shake; even from a distance, this fellow—America's biggest celebrity, more famous even than President Hoover—was clearly identifiable.

The fisherman approached. "Thanks, kid." Leo was frozen.

"Yeah, I'm shy, too," said the fisherman, offering his hand. "You can call me Babe."

"You can call me Leo," said Leo. "I already caught my quota."

"So did I," said the Babe.

They sat on the rock, sharing Leo's sandwich and chatting.

"I'm staying up at Mrs. Coots's Boarding House. Why don't you come for supper?"

"Gee, I can't," said the wide-eyed Leo with sorrow. "My dad is going to get me later; he won't know where to find me."

"We'll take care of that. Come on."

Leo and the Babe went walking up the road, chatting. Leo had a system whereby he would make a pile of small rocks by the road near where he was fishing, so his father would know where to look for him. Babe explained the situation to the landlady; she sent her son—also about twelve—off to sit along the road and wait for Leo's father, by the rocks.

Leo had a wonderful afternoon, one of the thrills of his life, culminating in supper with Babe Ruth (who, like Leo even then, was a prodigious eater). Young Coots eventually intercepted Leo's father, took him over to the boarding house, and then the two Herberts drove home.

As was typical with Leo's stories, this one had a postscript. One night in 1955 during a performance of *Fanny*, Edna Preston—the character lady who played Honorine, the fishmonger mother of beautiful young Fanny—asked Leo to stop by her dressing room after the show; she wanted him to meet her son-in-law. He did so and was introduced to a countryish fellow in his thirties named Bob Coots.

"Say, did your mother used to have a boarding house up outside Kingston?" asked Leo.

"Yes."

"Great fishing," said Leo, sizing him up. "Say, I bet some famous people must have stopped there."

"If they liked fly fishing."

"Do you remember one summer when Babe Ruth stayed there?"

"Do I?" said the stranger, with the dawn of suspicion.

"He must have fished at that bend in that river, with the deep fishing hole. *Beside that pile of rocks?*"

Coots looked at Leo with long-simmering annoyance. "So you're the sonofabitch who took my chance at dinner with Babe Ruth."

"Nice to see you," said Leo, slipping out the door. "'Night, Edna."

That Babe Ruth fishing hole remained one of Leo's favorite spots. Upon his death in 1993, he instructed his wife Janice to contact his friends at the Rhinebeck Aerodrome Museum, in upstate New York; have them take her up in a World War I–era Sopwith Camel biplane; fly along Esopus Creek; and swoop her down so she could empty his ashes right there. Which she did.

NORMANDY

As a teenager, Leo started working summers at the local playhouse in Woodstock, New York. He would play small roles and build scenery. One of the Woodstock Playhouse plays moved to Broadway in November 1938, so Leo went along. (He remembered that he got some big laughs.) *Ringside Seat* quickly closed, but for Leo seven performances at the Guild Theatre (which became the ANTA, which became the Virginia, which is now the August Wilson) was enough to set a new course. He instantly decided not to return home for his senior year in high school and stayed in New York. He married the pianist from the Woodstock Playhouse—who was considerably older than he—and did occasional acting while supporting himself as a stagehand.

The war came, and Leo took a job in a munitions factory. Being Leo, he soon worked himself into a position of authority as a floor manager. His strategically important occupation—plus the fact that he was married with an infant, born in 1942—left him exempt from the draft. Leo continued at the factory in New York, but his heart was on the battlefield, so much so that he enlisted in 1944, arriving in France in the first wave of reinforcements after the D-Day invasion. His division had a terrible time of it. They were assigned to search the countryside for Allied corpses and body parts. And while doing so, fighting off the occasional German sniper.

Years later, Leo played Paris with the 1976 international tour of *Porgy and Bess*. When they had a weekend off between engagements, he drove up to Normandy with Janice and twelve-year-old daughter Heather. Going through a nondescript village, he suddenly stopped; bolted from the car; and froze. When he finally spoke, he pointed to an old building with stone steps leading from the street down to the cellar.

"We were ambushed, we had to dive down those steps." He pointed to the wall above. "See the bullet holes?"

The soldier he was with died in the attack. In fact, Leo and a staff sergeant were the only members of his unit who survived.

The battle and the gruesome aftermath were too much for Leo; he suffered a nervous breakdown, unable to speak and (as he later described it) walking around "like a zombie." When he finally returned stateside in 1945, he was emaciated like a scarecrow, withdrawn, and with a stutter so torturous that he all but stopped talking. With three children to feed—there would be five by 1953—he needed to find a job, which turned out to be as a goatherd outside Woodstock. Yes, they had goatherds in upstate New York in the late 1940s. He also found work as a movie projectionist and stagehand at the Woodstock Playhouse. After three years of treatment he started recovering his voice, although the damage was deep-rooted: despite his outgoing personality and sense of universal cheer, Leo was ever after haunted by severe nightmares.

Noted dramatic actress Eva Le Gallienne and equally noted English director Margaret Webster lived together on a farm near Woodstock. In September 1948, the latter formed the Margaret Webster Shakespeare Co., sending out *Hamlet* and *Macbeth* on a cross-country tour. Badly in need of a job to support his growing family, Leo went along as electrician. As he adjusted to full-time life in the theatre world, the stutter disappeared. And he never stopped talking thereafter.

LORD OF THE BAR

As a stage electrician, he could pretty much do his job and keep to himself. In early 1952, he was working on the Broadway-bound import of playwright Christopher Fry's London hit, *Venus Observed*. During rehearsals, the director—who had directed, produced, and starred in the London production but was merely directing here—called for an antique secretary. Not an old lady who takes dictation, but a piece of furniture with a built-in bookcase and fold-out desk. The propman got him some piece of furniture or other. "No," said the director, "I need a *secretary*." A new desk appeared in time for the tryout at the Shubert in Philadelphia. "No, no, no!" he yelled impatiently, in perfectly rounded tones. "Doesn't anyone here know *anything* about furniture?"

With the propman oblivious, Leo stepped over and said, "I know what you're looking for." And Olivier—for the director was Laurence Olivier—said, "then, *please*—get it!" This was not Leo's department, but he went scouring the local antique stores, rented an authentic secretary for the Philadelphia and Broadway engagements of the show, and had it onstage when Olivier returned after the dinner break.

That midnight, Olivier wandered into the bar across the stage door alley. Stranded in Philadelphia—with wife Vivien Leigh back in London, and with no interest in socializing with Rex Harrison (who was playing the Olivier role) and Rex's wife/costar Lilli Palmer—he spotted Leo, walked over, and started talking. Leo, as always, was able to converse with anyone on any and all subjects. After a couple of nights of this, Olivier asked "Why are you wasting your time as an electrician? You should be a propman. You work directly with the director, you're *part of the process.*"

Thus it was that Leo became a propman; the uncontested dean of Broadway propmen. And he *did* work closely with his directors. Some directors left everything to the designers and were happy with whatever they turned up. Others—especially on musicals—*needed* help, conversation, the ability to work out ideas and try them.

He worked especially closely with Gower Champion: when he was pondering ideas for a dance number, Gower would talk it out with Leo. Leo would go off and return with sample props to try out. When Gower decided he wanted to stage one of the duets in *Carnival!* with the suave James Mitchell—a noted dancer who was playing a seductive magician—performing a magic trick with his leading lady, Leo disappeared into the shop and constructed a "sword box." This was a raised, square contraption that the actress would step into; the outside included precut slots for the swords, each of which had a metal sheath through the interior. The sheaths were so arranged that there was just enough room for the actress (Kaye Ballard, originally) to slip in among them. When I lived in a large loft in Soho in the early 1980s, I had the *Carnival!* sword box on display as a conversation piece—and it was, indeed, a conversation piece.

For *Mack & Mabel* Gower wanted a whimsical prop for a short dancer (Don Percassi) on the beach. Leo eventually came up with a cute, easy-to-dance-with hot dog cart. In *42nd Street*, there were all those "silver dollar" boxes that the multitudinous chorus danced upon in the "We're in the Money" number. Leo set up a small factory in his garage in New Jersey, turning out silver dollars by the hundreds, for each of the several productions of the show, and then continually replacing/repairing the heavily battered props. Charging a fee, naturally, for each and every one.

During the tryout of *42nd Street*, Leo told me several times that Gower was tired and worn out. Struggling to come up with ideas for numbers, he was asking Leo for props that they'd already used in *The Happy Time*, *I Do! I Do!*, and other musicals. As we later learned, Gower had reason to struggle: he was undergoing blood transfusions for a fatal disease that killed him on the day the show opened in New York. At Gower's memorial service at the Winter Garden, one of the scheduled speakers didn't turn up. They found Leo in the lobby and drafted him. He ambled on in the penultimate slot—traditionally the featured spot, in vaudeville—and regaled the audience with an impromptu eulogy. The *New York Times* reported that "the warmest applause" of the star-studded event went to Leo, who capped his speech with an anecdote about Gower the perfectionist and the aforementioned hot dog cart. The punch line: "I wound up auditioning *twenty* pushcarts for him."

Man at the Diner

Jack knew Leo from the Pittsburgh Civic Light Opera; Leo didn't work the shows, but would be brought out to build special props. Jack put Leo on some of the Bloomgarden plays and then *By the Beautiful Sea*. When Jack was hired by Merrick for *Fanny* in 1954, he assembled a trio of head stagehands (Leo, carpenter Teddy Van Bemmel, and electrician Mitch Miller, who was an assistant on *Fanny* but soon moved up). Leo remained with the producer until his death in 1993—doing all eighty-five Merrick shows from first to last, plus setting up one hundred or so touring productions of Merrick hits. No one, not even Schlissel, remained with Merrick nearly so long—not that Leo wasn't fired occasionally; he would be axed by Merrick (or Jack) now and then, only to get a phone call a day or so later from Jack (or Merrick) asking where he was. In the busy years, Leo would open a show and move on to prepare the next. Once the pace at the Merrick office died down, Leo was in high demand for other people's shows. Whenever Merrick started up again, it was understood that he had first call on Leo's services. And Jack—who had a long post-Merrick career—came next.

Leo had a strangely close relationship with the reclusive Merrick, possibly because he was so very easy to talk to. Leo, that is, not Merrick. Leo always knew when to speak and when to just listen. This could be seen early on. In October 1960, Merrick called Leo into his office; he had just had his "three hits in a week" week. That is, *Irma La Douce* and—on consecutive days—the award-winning *A Taste of Honey* (starring Joan Plowright and Angela Lansbury) and *Becket* (starring Laurence Olivier and Anthony Quinn). During the run of the latter two, Olivier finalized his divorce from Vivien Leigh and married Plowright on a Friday afternoon in the office of a justice of the peace in Connecticut. In true "show must go on" fashion, neither of them missed a performance.

"Leo," said Merrick, "some lady reporter from the *New York Post* is doing a five-part story on me. We've tried everything to stop it, but we can't. What I want you to do, take this reporter around. Backstage, rehearsals, any of the shows, wherever she wants to go. Jack'll arrange total access for you, replace you if you have to miss performances. Answer all her questions, tell her everything she wants to know. Only, *don't tell her the truth.*" Accurate in places and fanciful in others, that series by Helen Duda—which ran in December 1960—has served as one of the primary sources for supposedly factual information about Merrick's origins and early career.

When Merrick's second daughter, Marguerita, was born in 1972, he asked Leo to come up with an extra-special present. Leo built a child-size replica of Noah's Ark and spent an inordinate amount of time carving animals, two by two, to fill it. Several years later, in a fit of anger with Merrick over their divorce, Etan Merrick—Marguerita's mother—had the ark and animals destroyed, to Leo's everlasting dismay.

While I ran into Merrick occasionally following my time at the office, I only rarely saw him with his guard down. Leo had a widely extended clan, anchored by two wives and six children, all of whom formed into one happy group of which I was an honorary member. In 1980, they planned a surprise party for Leo's sixtieth birthday in typically Herbertian manner. On a Sunday night, they took over the River Diner, a long-since-demolished working-class dive in the no-man's-land of the far West Side on Eleventh Avenue at Thirty-Seventh Street. Here they threw a big party, featuring chili—a family specialty—cooked up by Leo's elder son, Liam.

Also memorable was an unearthly Sacher torte, the diameter of a bicycle wheel, sheathed in delectable chocolate. This was made by Laura, the new wife of Leo's younger son, Kim. The summer before, Kim was working as an actor at the American Stratford Festival in Connecticut. At a cast meal from a local caterer, he was so amazed by the lemon bar dessert that he asked to meet the baker. She turned out to be the younger sister of the caterer, who would soon transcend Connecticut and create a cooking, publishing, and merchandising empire of her own. Included in Martha Stewart's first glossy coffee table book was a photo spread of the wedding she threw for Laura and Kim—this complete with shots of Leo and the bohemian Herberts, who decidedly did not fit in with the Westport crowd.

The diner was packed with family and assorted stagehands, including quite a few from the heyday of the Merrick office—a casual and friendly group, fueled by chili and beer. At about 9:00 p.m., Merrick—dressed, as always, in a funereal black suit—walked in, accompanied by a little girl who turned out to be Marguerita. (Janice had invited Helen Nickerson, who as a matter of course mentioned it to Merrick.)

Merrick, with no shows on the boards for the first time since 1954, held little sway over the blue-collar crowd; he was pretty much ignored. Except by me, naturally. He worked his way along the narrow aisle between counter seats and window booths, and slid with Marguerita into the banquette where I was sitting with Charlie Blackwell. Merrick had very little to say; he was so shy, in all but business pursuits, that he merely mumbled. I talked mostly to the little girl, who was naturally shy but not pathologically so.

What I remember most is the image of Merrick, *so* uncomfortable and *so* out of place in the real world. What on earth could have brought him on a Sunday night down to a rough stagehands' party in a rough dive of a diner? And with eight-year-old Marguerita, in a pretty party dress?

Leo, of course; Merrick was unquestionably fond of him. But celebrating birthdays, or celebrating anything, was not typical of Merrick. There at the party, he hardly spoke to any of his longtime employees there assembled other than Leo. He barely said a word at all to anyone, even Marguerita.

Another Journeyman

IT'S MITCH

AMONG THOSE PASSING THROUGH THE OFFICE WAS MITCHELL ERICK-
son, Merrick's preferred stage manager for nonmusicals. His most recent
play—Christopher Hampton's *The Philanthropist*, starring Alec McCowen,
the latest of the Merrick imports from London, had closed in May. (All
I remember about this one, which seemed interminably talky, was a stunning piece of stagecraft. One of the actors—sitting in a chair center stage,
facing the audience—stuck a gun in his mouth, pulled the trigger, and
a burst of blood violently splattered across the wall behind him.) Mitch
stopped by the office early in July, en route to London to familiarize himself with the next import, Robert Bolt's *Vivat! Vivat Regina!*

Mitch, like many stage managers, had started his career as an
underutilized actor. He was born in Duluth, Minnesota, in 1921. The son
of a blacksmith, he was interested in theatre from the start. Mitch said
his mother always used to say she didn't remember a time when Mitch
didn't want to go to a show, although I wonder just how many shows
there were to see in Duluth in the Roaring Twenties and the Depressed
Thirties. This was to become a running joke among Mitch's friends;
when he wasn't working on a play of his own, he would go *anywhere* to
see any show. His letters from London would carefully list everything he
saw, which—given the varied playing schedules—would regularly reach
twelve or thirteen shows a week. I know that when I would invite him
to come along to see something, it would not be uncommon for him to

say, "I saw that Thursday, the direction wasn't very good, the actors were unprepared, what time should I meet you?"

While he was a student at Duluth Junior College, the war started. Mitch enlisted and was sent to both Notre Dame and Cornell to pick up credits for Officer Training School. He served as a lieutenant (junior grade), stationed in Hawaii. He remained in Honolulu after the war, attending the University of Hawaii on the G.I. Bill before making his way to New York. In 1949, he answered a newspaper ad looking for an actor to perform in a touring program of scenes from Shakespeare, Rostand, and other classics; at the time, there were many such professional acts taking "live theatre" to small-town schools, colleges, ladies' clubs, and the like. The actor/manager running the tour was a fellow named Richard Corson, who had already established a reputation as an expert in stage makeup and other related areas. His 1942 book, *Stage Makeup*, is the authoritative text—"the bible of stage makeup," they call it—and is presently in its eleventh edition, albeit edited by others following his death in 1999.

"It's Mitch." Mitchell Erickson at the Eisenhower Theatre (1985).
PHOTO BY JOAN MARCUS

Mitch toured with Corson and moved into his apartment on Prince Street, one of those third-floor tub-in-kitchen walkups. Rent was so unconscionably low—$28 a month, initially—that it was never possible to convince Mitch to move to a place with an actual shower. He only gave up the apartment after sixty-two years in 2011, having turned ninety—by which point, thanks to New York City rent-control laws, the cost had increased to $550 for the two-bedroom in the heart of what had become trendy Soho.

Mitch spent his time looking for acting roles, holding a permanent side job as copy boy at *Time* magazine with a flexible schedule that allowed him to take time off for auditions and other activities. He—like so many actors who couldn't find work on Broadway—took off summers to act in summer stock. The "straw-hat circuit" was in full swing at the time, a leftover from the days when Broadway theatres were not air-conditioned. New York shows (other than hit musicals) typically closed for the summer, from Memorial Day through Labor Day. This, mind you, is why the official theatrical season still ends the last day in May (although award deadlines fluctuate).

Broadway stars—those who wanted (or needed) to keep salary checks coming in over the break—would set up mini-tours that filled the dark months with a string of one-week engagements in the numerous small-town stock theatres spread through the Northeast. So would underoccupied movie stars. In the days before television, air conditioning, and a proliferation of movie theatres, a night of live theatre was prime entertainment—especially in small towns. What's more, these towns drew a large number of city dwellers escaping the heat for the summer, prime customers for "Broadway hits" with stars.

Rather than touring complete productions, a system developed wherein the star and two or three major supporting actors would travel from town to town. Each local theatre would provide the balance of the cast, the scenery, and a local director of sorts. The traveling cast would finish in one town on Saturday, drive to the next on Sunday, run through the play with the local actors on Monday (at which point the star would often redirect the cast so as not to interfere with his or her own "stage business"), and open that night. The local cast would have spent the prior week performing a different play—with a different traveling star—at night while learning their parts in the new play during the day. And so it went, all summer every summer.

The local theatres would hire a nucleus of a company for the season, under the heading of types: a character man, a character comedian, a juvenile, an ingénue, and more. They would take the corresponding role in each play, if any, or fill in some other role. In 1949, Mitch found himself hired as the juvenile—that is, the actor playing the young male adult roles—at the Kennebunkport Playhouse in Kennebunkport, Maine, just outside Portland. Mitch went back to Kennebunkport—"Maine's Most Beautiful Summer Theatre," it said on the window cards—for eight seasons, always with the hope that by the following season he would be unavailable for stock. That is what eventually happened.

SUMMER STOCK

It made for a grueling summer vacation, with little money; but then, he was acting onstage and getting paid for it. Things were kept collegial by working—season after season—with many of the same actors. Mitch was especially close to his female counterparts at Kennebunkport; in 1949, the ingénue was a twenty-year-old named Marian Seldes. He was even more ideally matched with the ingénue for the next several seasons; so much so that on weeks when they had bigger roles, they were billed in the local press as "Maine's Favorite Romantic Couple." This was the only context in which Mitch and the young Canadian Colleen Dewhurst were linked romantically, but they remained good friends through long parallel careers. As did Mitch and Marian.

Among the roles Colleen and Mitch played at Kennebunkport were the ingénue (Alice) and her beau (Tony) in a production of George S. Kaufman & Moss Hart's *You Can't Take It with You*. Some thirty years later in 1983, Mitch (as stage manager) was instrumental in lining up producers to move a regional production of *You Can't Take It with You*—starring Jason Robards and Colleen—to Kennedy Center and on to Broadway.

Colleen got her big break at Kennebunkport. The traveling attraction that week was a British farce called *Springtime for Henry* by Benn Levy (author of Merrick's *Clutterbuck*). The star was Edward Everett Horton, a beloved Hollywood character man who, among myriad roles, served as Fred's comic foil in the Astaire-Rogers *Top Hat* and *Shall We Dance*. His film career died down in 1946, but he continued to work until his death in 1970 at the age of eighty-four. (His instantly recognizable voice can be heard narrating the "Fractured Fairy Tales" on reruns of the old *Rocky and Bullwinkle Show*.) In 1951, Horton did a short-lived Broadway revival of Benn Levy's creaky old trifle, which ran a mere seven weeks. No matter; he took it out on the summer stock circuit and kept playing it for years. He traveled with a full cast because this was a four-character play, giving the local actors a week of nights off while they rehearsed the next scheduled play during the day.

Horton was unhappy with the young actress in his touring cast, or she had to leave unexpectedly, or both; Mitch didn't remember which. But the call came to Kennebunkport: they needed a replacement to play the role that week. Colleen, the local ingénue, did so. Horton was so taken by the way she could hold her own against such an inveterate scene stealer as himself that he asked Kennebunkport to release her so she could play the rest of the summer with him. That was the end of Colleen in summer stock, and she never looked back. Her winter job, Mitch said, had been answering the switchboard at the Screen Actors' Guild. She was thrilled not to ever have to go back to SAG—although she later served as president of Actors' Equity.

In between summers at Kennebunkport, Mitch continued his day job at *Time* and spent his remaining hours at the HB Studios. HB was the acting school run by Uta Hagen and her husband, actor/director Herbert Berghof. During Mitch's first summer of stock, the character woman mentioned that Uta was starting to give acting classes. "Let's all go study with Uta when we get back to New York," she said, which sounded like a good idea to everyone. Nobody did, though, except Mitch. He went to see her in the Clifford Odets play *The Country Girl* and was thunderstruck. "I thought, anything this woman knows, I want to learn." Mitch auditioned and got right in. He remained with Uta as student, teacher, advisor, and friend, soon becoming part of the family. After Herbert's death in 1990, Mitch would spend his summers—when not working—

out at Uta's place in Montauk. Uta would garden and cook, Mitch would drive, serve as sous-chef, and socialize.

Mitch often compared himself to the character Bobby in Sondheim's *Company*, surrounded by "those good and crazy people my friends" who were always trying to get him to settle down. Uta and Herbert were one of four couples who "shared" Mitch; Biff and his first wife, Arline, were another. His California home was with the acting couple Kent Smith (who starred in Mitch's first national tour) and Edith Atwater. In Washington, it was Jean Getlein, an editor from his days at *Time*, and her husband Frank, an arts and food critic. When you called him on the phone, it was always an energetic "It's Mitch." "It's Mitch at Uta's." "It's Mitch at Biff's."

The HB connection led to Mitch's Broadway debut in 1956, playing a hospital attendant in a play that Berghof directed. *Protective Custody*, a Cold War drama starring movie star Faye Emerson, opened the Friday after Christmas and closed the Saturday after Christmas. The following summer, Mitch was back at Kennebunkport.

A DIRECTOR COMMANDS

Mitch's stage-managing career began in 1960. Gore Vidal's political drama *The Best Man* was the play, starring two grand old leading men—Melvyn Douglas and Lee Tracy—surrounded by a cast of twenty. During the Boston tryout, the play looked so promising that the producers called New York looking to add a clutch of reporters and people-in-the-crowd. Mitch was offered one of these nonspeaking roles, with a small understudy assignment. Early in the run, the stage manager approached him. "We need a second assistant stage manager, can you do it? It means an extra $25."

Instead of eagerly accepting, Mitch asked "Can I still act in the play?" He kept his (nonspeaking) role and became one of the stage managers. When *The Best Man* closed after a successful fifteen months, Mitch was promoted to become the nonacting first assistant stage manager on the tour. Marty Fried, the production stage manager, was an aspiring director and more than happy to let the eager Mitch do most of the work.

Mitch's fourth Broadway show, in 1963, ran only four weeks but turned out to have long-term ramifications. William Inge—who with *Picnic* and *Bus Stop* was third only to Tennessee Williams and Arthur Miller on the list of important new American playwrights of the postwar era—found his career run aground. *Natural Affection* opened during a newspaper strike and quickly closed, despite the presence of Kim Stanley in the leading role. But the director was Tony Richardson, who had already staged three influential British plays that Merrick successfully imported to Broadway: *Look Back in Anger* and *The Entertainer*, by John Osborne, and Shelagh Delaney's *A Taste of Honey*. Richardson, after ten years of directing in London and New York, instantly recognized that this assistant stage manager was excellent. Tony went off after the January opening of *Natural Affection* to finish postproduction of his soon-to-be-released film, but told Mitch to be available in July for rehearsals of his next play—for David Merrick.

Mitch waited and waited. No call ever came. He assumed Tony had just mentioned the job in passing, to be nice; he didn't care to embarrass him by bringing it up. When he heard that another stage manager was hired for the job, he figured that was that. But it wasn't.

The play in question was Osborne's third major London hit, the 1961 *Luther*. The Broadway production, with a mostly American cast, was delayed until 1963 while Richardson, Osborne, and *Luther*-star Albert Finney filmed *Tom Jones*. When setting the schedule for the Broadway run of *Luther*, Richardson told Schlissel that Mitch was his stage manager and to hire him. Jack—typically—figured this was a big-budget, major play with a major star, and that there was no way some director was going to force him to hire a stage manager who had never done a Broadway show on his own. Rather than call Mitch, who would have surely agreed with Jack and happily accepted the assistant job, Schlissel ignored the situation and hired one of his regulars.

Tony arrived in New York for the first day of rehearsals, walked in, and found no Mitch. He called Jack on his first break. Jack said he had offered the show to Mitch, who was unavailable. Tony reached Mitch late that night. No, he wasn't working. No, he'd never heard from the Merrick office.

The next day, Tony didn't show for rehearsal. The frantic stage manager called the office, and it took Jack hours to track down Tony. "Why aren't you at rehearsal?" Schlissel barked in a voice as polite as he ever got.

"My stage manager isn't there, so I naturally can't rehearse," said Tony just as politely.

The next morning, Mitch was the production stage manager of *Luther*. Jack, who didn't like to lose, knew when it was time to fold, especially because word was already out that the *Tom Jones* movie—scheduled to premiere two weeks after the New York opening of *Luther*—was going to be a massive hit, bringing international stardom to Finney and Best Director and Best Producer Oscars to Richardson.

As for Jack, he somehow managed not to hold the matter against Mitch; or perhaps he simply realized that Mitch was a perfect stage manager for dramatic plays. In any event, Mitch worked for Merrick and Jack on another ten significant shows.

THE MAN IN THE TRASH

Mitch did *Luther* in New York and then directed the national tour. On a visit to Hawaii, he helped the local producer assemble a sit-down Honolulu production. When the actor cast as Luther was forced to leave during rehearsals, the role was taken over by: Mitch! It would be his last performing job until 2001, when he stepped in to replace an ailing actor in the Broadway production of *Judgment at Nuremberg*.

After *Luther*, Mitch returned in the fall of 1965 for Osborne's *Inadmissible Evidence*. (Unlike *Look Back in Anger*, *The Entertainer*, *A Taste of Honey*, and *Luther*, this was not directed by Richardson, whose career had been overtaken by film.) One night during the tryout in Philadelphia, Merrick was pulling his usual tricks and threatened to fire director Anthony Page. The star—the volatile Nicol Williamson—stormed off to his dressing room. The production staff calmed Merrick down, convincing him that there was no practical way he could fire Page without jeopardizing the show.

Williamson didn't hear this, however. Merrick was standing in the stage door alley behind the Locust Street Theatre when Nicol—in an emotionally overwrought state—came storming out. He ran over to

Merrick and slugged him; Merrick fell back into a garbage bin. Instantly horrified by his actions, Williamson ran off down the alley. Mitch, the dutiful stage manager, went running after his star. (Leo Herbert, hearing the commotion from the pay phone inside the stage door, ran to Merrick's aid and literally lifted him out of the trash.)

Nicol's dresser Billy and Mitch combed the neighboring bars, looking for the vanished star. They finally found him at 3:00 a.m. in Thirtieth Street Station, cowering in a corner; he was afraid he was going to be arrested. They took him back to his hotel and deposited him in his room. Merrick, meanwhile, had gleefully alerted his press agent to spread the news. What wonderful, ticket-selling headlines!

Mitch followed *Inadmissible Evidence* with two provocative Merrick imports by Irish playwright Brian Friel, *Philadelphia, Here I Come!* (which ran a successful eight months) and *The Loves of Cass McGuire* (which ran a mere two weeks). Then came a landmark of the modern theatre, Tom Stoppard's *Rosencrantz and Guildenstern Are Dead*. Mitch tended to develop long, loyal friendships with people on his shows. In this case, he became lifelong friends with both the playwright and actor John Wood, who played Guildenstern.

He next did a very American comedy, Woody Allen's *Play It Again, Sam*. Mitch, who often pitched in on casting for upcoming Merrick productions, was running the Equity Open Call. An Equity rule provided that before the producer can hire any actors other than "stars" for a new production, they must first allow any card-carrying Equity members to be seen—not actually audition, but someone from the production staff must hold at least a quick interview. Open Calls are usually academic; plays are generally cast from actors submitted by agents. In this case, though, Mitch knew that Biff was having trouble finding someone to play the kooky ingénue.

Into the Open Call walked a nondescript actress whom Mitch dutifully chatted with. Her experience was not exactly promising: a role in the ensemble of *Hair*, then in its sixth month. But there was something arresting about her, and refreshing. "Maybe *this* is what Woody is looking for?" he thought, and set up an audition with the director/playwright/star. There turned out to be a great deal of chemistry between Woody Allen and Diane Keaton, which was not of Mitch's doing. Without Mitch, though, would Woody have ever crossed paths with the actress from the chorus of *Hair*?

Opening night, Woody gave Mitch a fancy, gold-plated traveling alarm clock. Handsome, but as Mitch was quick to point out, it never quite kept time accurately.

STAR TURN

Mitch came to be known as a prime example of an "actor's stage manager." Stage managers are often chosen by the director; alternatively, the producer's office will have preferred stage managers who work on their shows (as with Mitch at the Merrick office) unless the director intercedes (as with Mitch on *Luther*). Mitch quickly became the preferred stage manager of certain directors, including Tony Richardson and José Quintero. He was also, from *Luther* on, the stage manager of choice for Merrick plays (as opposed to musicals); and writers like Tom Stoppard, who felt especially safe with Mitch on board. But he was to become known for his position as the preferred choice of a wide array of stage actors.

While performers did not necessarily have a choice, major stars could—if the producers wanted them badly enough—hold out for "their" stage manager. Thus, Mitch worked repeatedly with Jason Robards, Colleen Dewhurst, Uta Hagen, John Wood, Maggie Smith, Ian McKellen, Julie Harris, Deborah Kerr, Eileen Atkins, and more. Even when he only worked with them on one show, he would form a quick bond. Meet them years later at a play, or backstage, or on the street, they would take up right where they left off. Zoe Caldwell, Rosemary Harris, Vanessa Redgrave (Tony Richardson's wife, and the mother of his children). It was always an instant family reunion.

The first time I witnessed this was impressive: as we walked along West Eighth Street one afternoon toward Broadway in 1972, Mitch was instantly in a bear hug with a shaggy-haired man with a smileful of teeth, emerging from the subway, who turned out to be Stoppard. "You remember Steven from *Rosencrantz*?" Mitch asked Tom, who didn't. After Tom headed up Broadway, I said, "Mitch, when you did *Rosencrantz* I was only fourteen!" For the next ten years, Mitch called me "the teenager."

Mitchell Erickson and
Ian McKellen barn-
storming the country
with *Acting Shakespeare*
(1984).
COURTESY JOHN HANDY

Mitch was noted for keeping his stars happy; or, for those who were fated to never be happy, at least content. Many were long established and did not especially need to take on plays, which typically paid far less than they could get with a briefer and easier film job. This was especially the case with tours, or Broadway visits by Brits with children overseas. These performers, too, might have personal issues—family dysfunction or alcohol dependence, for starters. Having an understanding and trusted friend as stage manager, offering counsel and protection on a round-the-clock basis, could make the difference.

A typical instance: Mitch was touring with Deborah Kerr in *The Day After the Fair*, an underattended import from London. In the limo from the airport to downtown Chicago, Deborah noticed that there was not a single billboard or sign suggesting that she was coming to town. After settling her into her hotel, Mitch went over to the theatre and found a stack of window cards (posters) piled in the manager's office. They had been duly imprinted with the theatre info and dates and dispatched to the theatre, but nobody had bothered to distribute them. So Mitch went out overnight with fifty posters and a staple gun, and "sniped" them all the way from Deborah's hotel to the Blackstone Theatre—so that when she made the trip the next day and every day, she would see that Chicago "knew" she was there.

Typical Mitch. His job, as he saw it, was to make sure that the stars would be at their best—and as undistracted as possible—every time they stepped out onstage. If that meant taking them out to dinner after the show and sitting in their hotel room while they called their spouse and waiting until they were ready to go to sleep, and escorting them to early morning press events, then that was what Mitch would do—which indeed made him indispensable.

Woody Allen's *Play It Again, Sam* was followed by the Robert Marasco thriller *Child's Play* and the aforementioned *Philanthropist*, which takes us to the summer of 1971, when Mitch stopped into the office during my third week there.

CHAPTER TEN

Above the St. James

AT MERRICK'S

AS I ENTERED THE AERIE ABOVE THE ST. JAMES ON THAT JUNE MORNING
in 1971, my first official assignment—in typical go-fer fashion—was to go
to the Act One deli on the corner of Forty-Fourth and Eighth fer Jack's
standing breakfast order: Sanka (an instant coffee that, at the time, was
the only readily available form of decaf) and a dry bialy (an onion-studded
variety of bagel, toasted but with no butter and hence "dry").

There were four Merrick productions under way at the time: *Promises*
at the Shubert; the first national tour of *Promises*, on the road; a touring
company of *Forty Carats*, the Abe Burrows comedy (originally starring
Julie Harris) that had closed in New York in November; and a special
summer tour of Pearl Bailey in *Hello, Dolly!* The Broadway production of
Dolly! had closed on December 27, 1970, as the longest-running show in
Broadway history; it broke the record set by *My Fair Lady*, a title it held
until surpassed by *Fiddler on the Roof* eight months later. These were on
the boards, with three plays and one big musical scheduled for the 1971–
1972 season. As it turned out, the still-powerful office was at the end of
its dominance. Merrick was still to offer another eighteen productions.
Four would make a little money; thirteen would quickly fold, including
three star vehicles that collapsed during the pre-Broadway tryouts; and
there was to be one last smash hit, *42nd Street*.

There were six of us so-called staff associates at the time, two of
whom I remained friends long past our joint time at Merrick's; one, who

was barely a year older than I, was to remain an important colleague of Merrick for the rest of the producer's life. He had talked his way into the office in the spring of 1970, doing a work-study program while attending Emerson College in Boston. Jack took a shine to the lad, as they say, and said that he'd hold a full-time job for him after graduation. He finished at Emerson as I entered the office, packed up his things, and moved to New York.

Mark Bramble hailed from the Eastern Shore of Maryland. His family owned an extensive farm on the Chesapeake Bay. From the picture window in the living room, you could actually see Baltimore across the water, although it was a drive of more than two hours. The land was adjacent to the site of Tolchester Beach, which until 1962 had been a prime Chesapeake entertainment resort linked to Baltimore by six ferry lines.

Mark's father and brothers were outdoorsy types. Bramble senior—a well-connected industrial contractor specializing in building county highways—had bought the land from a hunting companion; the pair used to regularly go to the latter's hunting lodge on the property. When Mark, after a career of theatrical activity, finally saw fit to move back down to the farm, he initially lived—quite incongruously—in the old hunting lodge on the shore of what Google maps, nowadays, calls Bramble Lake.

Mark was anything but an outdoorsman. In an effort to "toughen him up," as overbearing fathers of the time put it, he was sent off to the McDonogh School in Owings Mills, Maryland. Just outside Baltimore, it was a long drive around the expanse of the Chesapeake. Boarding school had rather the opposite effect on Mark. The resulting pressures led the teenager to what he described as a full-scale nervous breakdown. He spent his recovery, under the sheltering protection of his loyally supportive mother, constructing Victorian toy theatre kits.

School placed him close enough to Baltimore and Washington to attend touring shows and pre-Broadway tryouts. Later, at college in Boston, he regularly studied not his schoolwork but the new musicals trying out there. This far more useful education built a love, and a vast knowledge, of musical theatre.

Within months of his return to the office, he had moved in with another one of the staff assistants. Kim Sellon, too, hailed from

Maryland—Chevy Chase, to be specific. Being a New Yorker, I always assumed that the Washington suburbs and the Chesapeake Shore were more or less the same; I didn't understand the difference until I had visited both homes, which were worlds apart. Kim's father was the business editor of *U.S. News & World Report*, at the time the highly respected DC-based competitor of *Time* and *Newsweek*. Kim was more than out of place in this junior debutante world, taking refuge in the theatre. During high school she served as an usher at her local playhouse, the National Theatre in Washington, seating patrons along with similarly out-of-place-in-the-sixties teenagers including one named Frank Rich.

I quickly recognized Bramble and Kim as sympathetic souls, all of us having grown up in what seemed to be the wrong world. (Protest? Drugs?? The Beatles???) We would become increasingly close for much of the decade, until unforeseen circumstances intervened.

OFFICE AFFAIRS

I was mostly assigned, at the office, to Jay Kingwill. In addition to being Jack's all-round assistant, he was the company manager of *Promises*. In actuality, Jay was not the manager but Jack's intern, nearing the end of his three-year apprenticeship with ATPAM (the Association of Theatrical Press Agents and Managers). Company managers were allowed to hold only one contract at a time, while general managers—unregulated by any union—could collect from multiple shows. Thus, Jack himself held the union contract and collected the benefits for *Promises*, while Jay did all the work. Or, rather, Jay did the real work as well as whatever Jack needed on other shows, and assigned the rest to me.

This was a time before the advent of computers; a couple of forward-looking general managers were already using computerized payrolls, but not the Merrick office. This meant that the weekly payroll had to be written out on a ledger; the taxes calculated by the accountants; union dues and other items (ticket charges, etc.) deducted; and the whole thing checked and double-checked on bulky non-electronic adding machines until the numbers came out right. Royalties had to be calculated as well. These were easier, simple percentages without taxes. All the checks had to be typed, with pay envelopes listing the withholding taxes and deductions. The latter we could hand write, and luckily so; most of us, in those days, were hunt-and-peck typists. We used a white correction tape—and a couple of years later, a fast-drying white liquid—to cover our errors. The salmon-pink *Promises* paychecks that summer were riddled with black-on-white corrections.

The bane of our existence were the union forms: we had to pay pension and welfare benefits each week for perhaps eighty actors, stagehands, and musicians at *Promises*—with each report containing everyone's social security number. By my next musical, we would simply type these forms once and Xerox them each week; but in 1971 we were still using an old, "wet" copier, with grayish paper that smelled like chemicals and tended to curl unless you held it down. The union forms needed to be typed on a sheet that included five color-coded reports generated by interior slips of carbon paper. When you corrected an error on the top copy, you created duplicate smudges on all the rest that then had to be individually corrected.

In addition to office work we served as messengers, with constant trips—in the days before fax machines, let alone the internet—to Merrick's lawyers on Fifth Avenue; the accountants on Broadway; the William Morris Agency on Fifty-Fifth Street; press agent Harvey Sabinson on Forty-Fifth Street; the Blaine-Thompson advertising agency, next door in the Sardi building; and the various theatres and rehearsal halls where Merrick shows were playing or rehearsing. Plus frequent trips across the street to Jack's favorite "bank": the Shubert box office, where Phil Smith would cash checks on any of the show accounts (or for Merrick or Jack personally) when quick money was needed.

At that point in time, Merrick was renovating a separate suite of offices off the back hallway for his movie operation. He had for several years been dabbling in Hollywood, building up a large stake in Twentieth Century Fox. Not coincidentally, he had made a somewhat treacherous *Dolly!* deal with Fox, whose $2 million payment for the film rights included the traditional prohibition from releasing the film while the show was still running on Broadway. This seemed a safe bet in 1964, but nobody expected Pearl Bailey to take over at the St. James in 1967—three years into the run—and turn *Dolly!* back into a hot ticket. Fox finished filming in mid-1968, while the show ran on and on. With an expensive, star-laden film on the shelf, the studio—struggling with numerous other financial problems—pleaded with Merrick to allow a December 1969 holiday opening. He finally agreed, in exchange for an additional, early-release payment of $1.8 million.

Merrick had already begun hatching what was to be his biggest film venture, the 1974 version of *The Great Gatsby* starring Robert Redford and Mia Farrow. In the meantime, though, he started his movie career with a motion picture version of his 1970 Broadway thriller, *Child's Play*, starring Marlon Brando and James Mason. But Brando quit during rehearsals—driven out by the incessantly hectoring Merrick—with Robert Preston stepping in to take over the role. Filming on *Child's Play* had not yet begun, but director Sidney Lumet was ensconced in the film office. I went in to visit him a couple of times; the office still had that smell of new carpet. Sidney was quiet, polite, and very short.

Among my chores was typing royalty checks for the *Dolly!* tour. Sitting there week after week, I was puzzled. I knew full well that Jerry Herman had written the music and lyrics. So why I was sending weekly checks to Lee Adams and Charles Strouse (Gower and Mike Stewart's songwriters on *Bye Bye Birdie*), and also Bob Merrill (Gower and Mike's songwriter on *Carnival!*)?

As an inquisitive teenager, I of course asked Jay, who said "Just do it." I asked Jack, who waved his hand and walked away. I finally asked Helen, who as Merrick's secretary was not involved on the financial side. She said "I don't know, they wrote some songs. Ask Jack."

I let it go at that, for then at least, although I would uncork the mystery in my first book. Jerry, in fury, threatened to sue me for revealing the details, although he later gratefully greeted me as his savior, freeing him from living under the cloud of *Dolly's* mysteriously rumored authorship.

Reception

I spent much of my time hidden away in one of the back offices, although we assistants would occasionally be called to cover Sylvia at the switchboard. This meant sitting in her glass-walled cubicle in the hallway near the elevator, guarding the inner sanctum. This also meant seeing whomever came past. Like a spry, athletic, and suntanned man who came bounding out of the elevator one day with his bicycle, wearing trouser clips on his ankles. Why did they let him bring his bicycle up in the elevator? I wondered, until I realized that it was Gower himself. Leaving his bicycle by my side, he nodded and went in (unannounced).

A more memorable encounter with him came a few weeks later, when Biff sent me to deliver the new draft script of the next Merrick musical. "You need to get it there before Gower leaves at three," he said, so I rushed across town. Gower was subletting a townhouse on Sutton Place, a ritzy enclave overlooking the East River. I rang the bell. No answer. I knocked, loudly, on the door. No answer. I stepped back to the curbside, looking up at the four-story brownstone. All quiet.

Now, what do I do? Hike over to First Avenue, find a phone booth and call Biff?

I heard the heavy sound of a window opening, three flights up. Out came Gower's head.

"What?" he shouted down.

"I've got a script from Biff."

"One minute."

I waited, not very long considering he was three flights up. The door opened, revealing Gower dripping wet, clutching a towel.

"Thanks," he said, snatching the envelope and shutting the door.

Among my other reception visitors was Pearlie Mae herself, just back from the summer tour of *Dolly*.

"Hello, darlin,'" she brayed at me, assuming that whoever I was, I was surely overwhelmed by seeing her in person.

"Tell David to watch out, I'm comin' in."

"Sorry, Miss Bailey, but he's in California."

"Hmmph. Well, tell darlin' Jack I'm here."

"He's at the lawyers'."

"Nobody home?" she said. Then she changed gears and opened the manila envelope she was clutching like a rare treasure. With a suddenly warmer and more sociable tone, she said, "Well, look at this, darlin'!"

"This" was her new autobiography, *Talking to Myself.*

"Just got the first copy. Look!"

She eagerly showed me, a thorough stranger who enjoyed her Dolly but was otherwise not enthused.

SOME LIKE IT NOT SO HOT

Activities were more interesting when I was borrowed by Biff, for whom I would sit in on casting discussions; sort the hundreds of pictures and resumes that came in from actors and agents each week; shuttle scripts, ground plans, and sketches to various members of the creative team; and sometimes assist at auditions. Casting was in full swing that summer for Merrick's next surefire hit, the inevitable successor to *Dolly!* and *Promises*: the Jule Styne/Bob Merrill/George Axelrod *Sugar*, to be directed and choreographed by Gower. (One of my messenger assignments, after they brought in replacement librettist Peter Stone—of the then-current hit *1776*—was to hand-deliver the letter firing Axelrod from the show.) Like our current musical, this was an adaptation of a hit Billy Wilder movie comedy: *Promises* was adapted from the 1960 classic *The Apartment*, while *Sugar* was based on the equally excellent 1959 classic *Some Like It Hot*.

Axelrod, who was best known for the 1952 comedy hit *The Seven Year Itch*, was not the first librettist. The show had started with the team of Jerry Herman and Michael Stewart, reuniting with Merrick for the first time since *Dolly!* in 1964. *One of the Girls*, they called it. The adaptation was hampered by legal issues. Wilder's *Some Like It Hot* had been a remake of a 1951 German film *Fanfare of Love*, which itself was a remake of a 1935 French comedy. Merrick had obtained the rights to the original films, but not to the 1959 screenplay. Any material specifically created by Wilder and his screenwriting partner I. A. L. Diamond, including the Chicago/Miami locales and the gangster subplot, was off limits. Mike wrote his script—multiple scripts, in fact—under these strictures, placing the action in Germany during the 1930s.

When Merrick eventually cleared the rights to use the Wilder screenplay, Mike and Jerry—understandably annoyed—declined to go back and start over. Merrick turned to composer Styne, who had a decided feel for the period. He had been a Chicago bandleader during the Roaring Twenties, and had once been forced to turn over his baton so Al Capone himself could lead Jule's band in the *Rhapsody in*

Blue. According to Jule, anyway. Styne had written three musicals for Merrick—*Gypsy, Do Re Mi,* and *Subways Are for Sleeping*; lyricist Merrill had done three as well, *Take Me Along, Carnival!* and *Breakfast at Tiffany's.* Merrick had also hired Styne and Merrill to write what would become one of their biggest successes, *Funny Girl*—although Merrick withdrew from that show during rehearsals.

Sugar turned out to be not so sweet; *you* try to improve on the perfect *Some Like It Hot,* without Marilyn Monroe, and see what you get. The only thing they got right was the successor to Jack Lemmon in the role of the bass-playing Jerry, who dons a dress to become Daphne. Robert Morse had started his career with two major roles for Merrick, in the 1955 *Matchmaker* and—with full star billing, albeit under Jackie Gleason—in the 1959 musical *Take Me Along.* Morse, as it turned out, was a joy in *Sugar,* the one element that lived up to the source material. I was gone from the Merrick office when the show finally opened, but I would walk over to the Majestic at least twice a week, in my candyland blazer, to watch Bobby do a deliciously pert first act duet with his leading lady called "We Could Be Close."

The other major role—Joe/Josephine, the saxophonist played on screen by Tony Curtis—could have and should have been just as winning. One August afternoon, Hal Linden, the 1970 Best Actor Tony winner for his performance in *The Rothschilds,* arrived at the Shubert to audition. He shooed off the Merrick-provided rehearsal pianist and brought on his own combo: trumpet, trombone, drums, and string bass. Hal started singing an upbeat, Roaring Twenties tune and then pulled out a sax and let it wail. Linden, it turns out, started his career as a reed player with the Sammy Kaye Orchestra. Hal and his combo rocked the Shubert; perhaps the best audition I've ever seen. And what did it get him? Not even a callback.

The part went to Tony Roberts, a reliably competent comedian—best known as Woody Allen's sidekick in a series of films—but not the sort of spotlight-stealing star who could have sparked *Sugar* and stood his own against Morse. Roberts had been a Merrick regular since 1966, with a featured role in Allen's comedy *Don't Drink the Water*; the male lead in the musical *How Now, Dow Jones*; a costarring role opposite Woody in the stage version of *Play It Again, Sam*; and the lead in the

1969 London company of *Promises*. Just then, he was playing the role in the Broadway company.

Tony was a thoroughly respectable light comedian, but without the dynamism Hal would have brought to *Sugar*. I expect this had to do with Linden's physical appearance. Tony Curtis, Tony Roberts, and Larry Kert (who played Joe in the road tour of *Sugar*) were all Jewish; but Linden—born Harold Lipshitz, from the Bronx—*looked* Jewish. This was accentuated in his audition by the full beard he grew to play Mayer Rothschild. Even without the beard, the creators knew from his prior appearances—he started his career as understudy to and eventual replacement for the male lead in Styne's *Bells Are Ringing*—that Linden looked Jewish in a way that Curtis, Roberts, and Kert didn't. I expect that settled the matter. Hal's presence would not have solved the problems with *Sugar*, but he would have made a difference. What's more, he might might have spurred the writers to give him better songs than the mediocre ones provided for Roberts. The show also ended up with a leading lady named Elaine Joyce, who—quite obviously—was not the equivalent of Marilyn Monroe. Who could have been?

Sugar underwent a typically tortured tryout, but it was clearly ill-fated from the moment the idea was broached. The show is a perfect example of what should be the guiding dictum of screen-to-stage adaptations: If you can't make it better—or at least as entertaining as the original—why do it at all?

Also casting at the time was the bus-and-truck company of *Promises*, scheduled to open in September. National tours played multi-week engagements in major cities (Boston, Philadelphia, Chicago, Detroit, Washington, Los Angeles, San Francisco). Bus-and-truck tours hit the smaller spots; one-week towns (Indianapolis, Buffalo, Louisville) plus places that can only provide audiences for a half (split) week or one night. Dayton, anyone? The physical production was cut down significantly; after the performance, they would quickly disassemble the set and load it onto a couple of trucks, while the cast (though not necessarily the stars) would board a charter bus and sleep through the night. Hence, bus-and-truck.

Stars were usually enlisted for national tours, which generated enough income to pay them. (Mary Martin, Ginger Rogers, Eve Arden,

Betty Grable, Dorothy Lamour, and Carol Channing herself headed the national and international touring companies of *Dolly!*; Barbara Rush played *Forty Carats*, while comedian Red Buttons starred in the tour of *Play It Again, Sam.*) Bus-and-trucks were low budget, drawing upon a less exalted acting pool. One afternoon I was sitting in the darkened Shubert when a fellow named Fred Rogers came in to audition. (*Mister Rogers' Neighborhood* had recently moved to PBS but was not yet the institution it eventually became.) Rogers came onstage and started to sing some up-tempo song or other, pleasantly but innocuously. He quickly got everyone's attention when he stepped out onto the aforementioned pit cover, over the brass section, and slowly sunk through as if he was in quicksand. He did not get a call back, but his audition was almost as memorable as Hal Linden's.

ANY CASTING TODAY

A more enduring, and pathetically wrenching, memory concerns a trio of occasional visitors to the office. There was a short bench along the wall, just outside the sliding-glass reception window. Once a week, in would walk three aged-and-worn actors looking like they came out of a Depression-era show biz movie.

"Any casting today?" one of them would ask in a wavering, pretend-brave voice.

"No, sorry" was the perennial answer. While Biff did have a casting department along the back hallway, casting was done through agents, open calls, and the mails. By 1970, I don't expect there were any theatrical offices where you'd have a stable of actors, wearily waiting for someone to storm out of the office, see them, and shout "*You*" as if they'd found gold. By this point, casting was on a production-by-production basis, with no sudden need for actors who might walk in through the door.

Yet these three did walk in through the door, or rather off the elevator, once a week. "Any casting today?"

Even if there had been casting, it is unlikely that they would have ever been hired. The woman—Edna Thayer was her name, I well remember—was ancient. She had thinning-to-the-point-of translucent but impossibly blonde hair, against skin the shade of a painted bisque doll. Despite her fireplug-like short-and-wide shape, she looked altogether ready to disintegrate into the ozone. Think *Whatever Happened to Baby Jane?* Not as a horror film, though. A real-life Baby Jane striving to look young, alive, *castable*.

Always with her was a man named Leon Belasco, who had a long career as one of those vaguely recognizable comedic character men of stage and screen. I had actually heard of him, not by virtue of his theatrical name (he was unrelated to the legendary David Belasco, born Leonid Berladsky in Odessa) but from my collection of cast albums. He had a featured role, as a bumbling Soviet commissar on the loose in Paris, in Cole Porter's 1955 musical, *Silk Stockings*, and a year later as an eccentric quasi-European hotel manager in Monaco in Ethel Merman's *Happy Hunting*.

Belasco was hopefully dressed in a dark, threadbare suit—same suit, same tie every time. His shirt (his *only* presentable dress shirt?) was frayed at cuffs and collar; his shoes shined but worn. Thayer was in a light, little-girl dress that you might imagine Mary Pickford running around the garden in. The third actor who always accompanied them, I'm afraid, I don't remember.

There they'd sit, ramrod straight, for an hour. Were they waiting for the casting call from Merrick's minions that would never come? Or was it simply a hospitable place to sit down, as a break from their hopeless rounds? Where did they live? How did they pay their rent? How did they afford food? When was the last time they had a paying job? What impelled them to get dressed up one day a week—I assume they did this only one day a week—"walking off their tired feet" (to quote Mr. Sondheim), "pounding Forty-Second Street to be in a show."

That was 1971, and the image and futility of Edna Thayer—who I suppose must have died several lifetimes ago—still depresses me.

CHAPTER ELEVEN

Merrick Parkway

PAPER CHASE

I WAS INITIALLY HIRED FOR THE SUMMER BREAK BETWEEN MY FIRST and second year of college, fully intending to wangle my way to an extension. Jack, though—seeing how production activity was dying down precipitously—determined that I was expendable, and Jack always got his way. So I glumly returned to Washington Square in September. Through this all, mind you, I kept working the Shubert selling candy; with my magic jacket I could slip into any Broadway theatre at will, and why would I give that up?

Two weeks later, Nickerson called. Could I come up to talk to her? I did, and fast. Turned out there was a situation she needed to resolve. *Dolly!* had run at the St. James from the beginning of 1964 through the end of 1970. In fact, with the exception of an eight-month stretch starting in late 1962, the St. James had only seen Merrick productions since the fall of 1960 (the others being *Do-Re-Mi*, *Subways Are for Sleeping*, and *Luther*). Merrick had been ensconced in the offices above the theatre since 1954; there's a wonderful photo of the producer sticking his head out the window, looking at the electric lights above the Majestic during the run of *Fanny*. Over the course of time, Jack had slowly converted the top two floors of dressing rooms into wall-to-wall filing cabinets.

During my first months at Merrick, Joe Papp's Shakespeare in the Park offered a grand, new-style, pop-themed musicalization of Shakespeare's *Two Gentlemen of Verona*. The music was by Galt MacDermot (of the still-running *Hair*), the book and lyrics by John Guare (of the recent *House of Blue Leaves*). The show was an instant hit at the Delacorte, and quicker than you could say Raul Julia a Broadway transfer was announced. *Two Gents* was booked to move into the St. James in mid-October.

Sammy Schwartz, who as general manager for Jujamcyn Theatres ran the two Broadway houses they then owned (the other being the Martin Beck, now the Al Hirschfeld), had lost a long battle with Merrick over some *Dolly*-related expenses and was now in battle mode. So when the *Verona* general managers—two former Merrick company managers, as it happened, named Gene Wolsk and Manny Azenberg—asked why they couldn't have the top floors of dressing rooms, Sammy told Jack: get out.

That was Nickerson's special situation. She needed to clear four dressing rooms crammed with filing cabinets, with no apparent space to move them. Could I come in and take care of it?

Could I dig through the files of fifteen years of Merrick shows, from *Fanny* to *Dolly!*—and get paid for it? I was ready to start before Helen finished asking. My immediate questions, though, were: What do we keep? Where do we put it? And what do we do with the rest of it?

Helen handed me a letter from Merrick's lawyer determining what records we legally needed to retain. The answer was, basically, partnership papers; contracts with what Jack used to call the Big Staff (creators, mainly the authors and directors)—as opposed to the Little Staff (designers and the rest); and financial papers. What about actor contracts? *Out!* What about scripts and programs, and publicity materials? *Out!* The daily stage manager's reports, which chronicled the inside goings-on of the production in often laconically amusing style? Helen shook her head. "That's all, Ben Aslan says, and that's what Jack wants."

"Maybe we can give it to a library or someplace?" I pleaded.

"Neil Hartley sent files on the early shows to the University of Wisconsin, before I started here. But Jack said that takes too much time. He wants everything thrown out, now."

I've spent much of my time in the intervening years digging through material just like this—savoring every research discovery I made, with a knack for recognizing what's important or astonishing. But at eighteen, I was a novice; I shudder to think of all the material we piled into the dumpster in the stage door alley behind the St. James. A golden history of the Broadway theatre of the era, gone to some incinerator in Jersey.

I did know enough to save at least some items consigned to the dumpster and take them safely home. Scripts and programs, naturally. Interesting correspondence, certainly. Various contractual items that didn't fit in with the lawyers' edict? Sure. I amassed a considerable selection of documents, ephemera, and miscellanea, sharing the spoils with Mark and Kim. Items like unused tickets for *Dolly!* and *Breakfast at Tiffany's*; the divorce papers when Merrick rescinded his coproducer's share of *Funny Girl*; and a clutch of eyebrow-raising *Gypsy* missives from Jerome Robbins, Arthur Laurents, and Gypsy Rose Lee herself.

And the September 5, 1961, letter reproduced on page 140, which is self-explanatory except to say that the "David" in question is Merrick; "Jerry" is Robbins; and *The Roman Comedy* is the musical that became *A Funny Thing Happened on the Way to the Forum*. If you don't know who "Steve" is, you're reading the wrong book.

Also among the documents was a rare copy of a full-page advertisement from the early edition of the January 4, 1962, *Herald-Tribune*: the infamous *Subways Are for Sleeping* ad. Foreseeing that this musical would receive dismissive reviews, Merrick had press agent Harvey Sabinson assemble a group of motley New Yorkers with the same names as the first-string critics; regally ply them with food and drink; and compose a series of quotes about just how good *Subways Are for Sleeping* was. ("One of the few great musical comedies of the last thirty years," said Merrick's ersatz Howard Taubman, namesake of the critic who had recently replaced Brooks Atkinson at the *Times*.)

When the show opened to the expected chorus of critical slams, Harvey put the plot in motion. He sent the ad copy to the major papers past deadline; the various editors caught the hoax in time. Except for the *Herald-Tribune*, which ran the ad in its early edition before pulling it. The hoax itself became the story, with excessive coverage in all the papers, *Time* magazine, and elsewhere.

Stunned to find an actual, folded-up copy of the full-page ad, I went to Nickerson. "Surely, we want to keep *this!*"

"Contracts and financials only," she said.

September 5, 1961

Dear David —

I am embarrassed by the turn of events on "The Roman Comedy." As you predicted, Jerry slithered away, much to my shocked surprise (he asked for another year's postponement), but only after we had committed a deal with Milton Berle. This, plus George Abbott's interest (and Berle's desire for him) makes the whole position impossible.

I apologize, David. But I hope to make it up to you. As you may know, Arthur and I are starting on a new show and we both think highly of you as a producer.

Abashedly,

Steve

Stephen Sondheim letter of September 5, 1961, to David Merrick.

And so the *Subways* ad sits framed on my wall. I included it as an illustration in my 1990 book *Opening Night on Broadway*; every time I've since come across it in other books or on the internet, it is apparent from blemishes in the newsprint that it has been reproduced from my original—which is to say that rescuing it from the dumpster behind the St. James has managed to keep it in circulation.

My own personal Merrick collection has contributed inside information to my various books and articles over the years. But I lament the invaluable documents which did not make the cut, due to space concerns or my sheer teenaged ignorance. I further lament that following Merrick's death in 2000, the files that I so carefully compiled seem to have disappeared; at this point, the only Merrick business papers from the pre-1971 period that exist are apparently those in my possession.

The attorney-sanctioned material was moved into an unfinished crawl space in the St. James attic, which provided access to the follow spot booth atop the second balcony. (The offices above the theatre were off four hallways, in the middle of which was a dingy, square asphalt courtyard over what was the actual dome of the theatre interior.) Over a couple of months, I consolidated thirty filing cabinets into seven. Yes, I could have done it quicker; but wanting to remain as long as possible, I used "my class schedule" as an excuse.

CRITICAL MATTER

One of said classes that semester—and one of only three professionally relevant subjects I took over my entire time at NYU—was a course on theatre criticism taught by Clive Barnes, the all-powerful drama critic of the *New York Times*. This was NYU in the harsh and rough early 1970s, when the campus green—or at least Washington Square Park, the asphalt of which was as close as there was to a campus green—was typically filled with scraggly students strumming guitars and, to use the parlance, studiously inhaling.

That being the case, most of my Barnes classmates were not so much interested in Clive or criticism; rather, they needed English credits that were unlikely to be time intensive. I, naturally, stood out as someone who was interested in and knowledgeable about Broadway, and—with my penchant for seeing new shows in previews—spoke the same language as the professor. I was surely the only person there, Clive included, who appreciated that our classroom was in a modernistic new building on the site of what had been the ANTA Washington Square Theatre.

That October, I was vocally upset about Clive's handling of an unconventional musical called *Ain't Supposed to Die a Natural Death*, a slice-of-life picture of uptown life written by Melvin Van Peebles. I realized that I had a certain predisposition for the show, in that my friend Charlie Blackwell, the production stage manager of *Promises*, was one of the lead producers. Even so, I recognized *Ain't Supposed to Die* as exciting and vibrant, bringing subject matter, style, and a vital truth to a Broadway that had never seen anything so grittily contemporary.

Clive's review mostly agreed, offering significant praise. But he managed to slam the show along the way, complaining that "Peebles's ghetto has no sweetness, and no light. It is a tough place to spend an evening even on a tourist jaunt." What's more, in the all-important final paragraph, he threw in that the show was "sometimes clumsy, sometimes mawkish."

This, of course, was Clive's prerogative; far be it from me to blame a critic for offering an honest opinion. But a careful reading of the review made it clear that he recognized and sincerely appreciated the work. Why did he have to accentuate his disclaimers, which were likely enough to steer potential viewers away?

And so I asked him why. He admitted that, yes, perhaps he came across a bit more negative than intended. Fair enough; but highly damaging to the producers, who knew that for survival they needed traditional playgoers (which in those days, meant *Times* readers) to give the show a chance.

Two months later, in his review of a far inferior but somewhat similar inner city musical revue called *Inner City*, Clive referred to *Ain't Supposed to Die a Natural Death* as "brilliantly innovative, both musically and structurally."

I happened to see Charlie at the office that morning. Yes, we both agreed, Clive was *absolutely* right. But why couldn't he have said so back in October, when his opening night review clearly dissuaded a significant number of customers? As if to make it better—or worse—Clive followed up with his downbeat end-of-year roundup, calling *Ain't Supposed to Die* "one of the best things on Broadway. It has power, honesty, and brilliance."

By this point—in actuality, after only four weeks—the Shuberts had tossed the show out of the Barrymore, sending it to exile at the infrequently booked Ambassador on Forty-Ninth Street. (The show they ejected *Ain't Supposed to Die* for? The short-lived *Inner City*.) The combined power of the changing opinions of the Man from the *Times* did help somewhat, with the Van Peebles show managing a significantly discounted but impressive-under-the-circumstances 325-performance run.

Meanwhile back at the office, I was very much aware that while this was still the irascible David Merrick of legend, he was distracted and tired. While *Dolly!* ran and ran and ran, he remained engaged. The simple act of keeping it open, and surpassing what was then the all-time longest running musical mark held by *My Fair Lady*, kept him challenged. Once he reached that plateau on September 9, 1970—celebrated by a matinee-day, between-shows dinner at Sardi's—he was ready to let the no-longer-lucrative production close after the Thanksgiving/Christmas season.

While Merrick still maintained a small backlog of stage projects in the works, it wasn't like the old days when he outmaneuvered the competition in the race for hits. During my summer at the office, there was only one big musical in preproduction: the aforementioned *Sugar*, which was less surefire than problematic. *Promises*, yes, managed to more or less match the quality of its source material, Billy Wilder's *The Apartment*. But the question that loomed unanswered, and ultimately unanswerable, was: How do you do Billy Wilder's *Some Like It Hot* without Marilyn Monroe?

The rest of Merrick's slate—perhaps as a reflection of the ignominious failure of what was meant to be his big hit of the prior season, Carol Channing and Sid Caesar in the Abe Burrows set of unfunny one-acts, *Four on a Garden*—was inauspicious, consisting of plays transferring from other locales. He was also at the time occupied by his ultimately unsuccessful quest to storm the movie world.

From my position—slowly finishing my foray into the files—I saw my days at Merrick's dwindling away. Given that Jack was determined to cut half the staff assistants from the office payroll and Bramble and Kim were clearly favorites, I asked Biff—who was in charge of all production elements—whether there might be anything for me to do backstage at one of the new plays. "Mitch'll be back from London next week," he said; "we'll ask if he can use you on *Vivat.*"

By this point in time, Mitch had worked out a pattern on such British imports as *Rosencrantz and Guildenstern Are Dead, Inadmissible Evidence,* and *Philadelphia, Here I Come!* He'd go to England to see the plays during their initial run and consult with the directors, who wouldn't be slated to come stateside until rehearsals. He would then return to New York and work with Biff on the casting, consult with the local designers to adapt the UK physical production, and more. He returned to London for the closing week, personally supervising the packing and shipping of the scenery and costumes.

Mitch turned up the following Monday, full of energetic enthusiasm. When I asked whether there was a place for me during rehearsals, and at that point I had only met him once and barely said a word, he responded with energetic enthusiasm:

"That would be *wonderful.*"

Backstage Pass

Vivat! Vivat Regina! was a retelling of the decades-long duel between Elizabeth I and Mary, Queen of Scots. Bolt, whose 1960 *A Man for All Seasons* had been anointed an instant modern-day classic, created a swirling and somewhat talky court drama (as opposed to courtroom drama) moored by two flamboyantly flashy star roles. He wrote the role of Mary for his then-wife, Sarah Miles; *Vivat* was first produced in 1970 at the Chichester Festival, in West Sussex, immediately followed the filming of David Lean's epic drama *Ryan's Daughter*—also written by Bolt and starring Miles. Playing the ultimately victorious Elizabeth opposite Miles's sultry Mary was Eileen Atkins.

When the play moved to Broadway, Miles stayed in London, as did Bolt, who only turned up for the opening. Stepping into Mary's slippers—and the revealingly diaphanous nightgown she wears in the final scene as she descends into the orchestra pit toward the executioner's block—was Claire Bloom. While Miles had made a couple of prominent films, Bloom was stage and screen royalty, starting with her 1952 starring role opposite Charles Chaplin in *Limelight*. She had returned to New York the past spring in celebrated twin revivals of Ibsen's *A Doll's House* and *Hedda Gabler*.

The only imported person, besides Eileen, was director Peter Dews, who had spearheaded the play in Chichester. Dews had one prior Broadway credit, but it earned him a Tony Award: Peter Luke's *Hadrian VII*, a 1969 hit starring Alec McCowen. I had been properly impressed when I saw it at the Helen Hayes on what turned out to be my first two-show day, spending that evening at Hal Prince's problematic *Zorbá*.

Rehearsals began in mid-October at the Plymouth Theatre (now the Schoenfeld). There was a Boston tryout, starting Thanksgiving week, after which we would move into the Broadhurst after New Year's for a January 20 opening.

The first day of rehearsal, John Handy—Mitch's preferred assistant stage manager, since *Rosencrantz*—and I set dozens of chairs on the stage, and we all sat around for a first reading of the play. It was quite a crowd, with a cast of twenty-four; this was no intimately economic undertaking. And there was I, on the Plymouth stage. Not as an interloper stealing a moment by the ghost light. This time, because I *belonged*.

Mitch introduced Dews, who welcomed the cast, and then Claire and Eileen. He then went across the stage, asking the actors to introduce themselves by name and character. Mitch then turned to me, sitting unobtrusively on the far side of the stage. "And this is Steven. He's a college student, he's agreed to stay and help us out." The cast smiled warmly.

I had agreed to help *them*? Rather, they—Mitch and Biff—had agreed to let me join their family.

The *Vivat* company, as is any theatrical company, was a family of sorts. This group wasn't an especially warm one, though; Eileen was (and, at this writing, remains) a reserved but naturally friendly person with high humor. Claire was a cold sort, keeping to herself. Given her detailed descriptions of three abusive marriages—to actor Rod Steiger, agent/producer Hilly Elkins, and writer Philip Roth—one might wonder about her inner temperament.

With the exception of two "ladies-in-waiting," who were in actuality the stars' understudies, the cast was all male. Some younger, mostly older

"Not—enough—jokes," says Mr. Merrick. Eileen Atkins portrays Mary Queen of Scots in *Vivat! Vivat Regina!* (1972). PHOTOFEST

character men; and from my vantage point, not a collegial one among the group. No matter, with Mitch and Johnny and to some extent Eileen on hand.

After four weeks of rehearsal, the company prepared to decamp to Boston. Mitch and Biff invited me to go along. My first pre-Broadway try-out! Yes, I was taking a full course load at NYU; but I managed to attend rehearsals without letting them interfere with my theatrical activities, although I did temporarily retire from the candy-selling trade that month.

During the final week of rehearsals, Mitch sent me to JFK in a limousine to retrieve Ann Dews, who flew in to join her husband. I brought her back to the Meurice Hotel on West Fifty-Eighth Street as Peter was returning from rehearsal. There and then it was that, as they say in *Gigi* (or is it *The Sound of Music?*), I tasted my first champagne. From a chilled bucket, in flutes of fine crystal.

Two days before decamping for Boston, Jack sent word that I couldn't go. I wouldn't be covered by the show's insurance policies, he explained sternly. (That has never stopped anyone from doing anything, in my experience.)

So I was done with *Vivat*, and done at the office. For a couple of weeks, until St. James landlord Sammy Schwartz stormed into the office, furious that the dressing room files had been moved into the unused and otherwise unusable attic space that was not part of Merrick's lease. Another call from Helen and I was brought back to winnow down the material even further. Leo installed a set of horizontal file cabinets in the space behind Merrick's inner office, leading to his private toilet overlooking Forty-Fourth Street, and I crammed in whatever I could fit.

The Turkey and the Crab

Next up at the office was *There's One in Every Marriage*, an English-language translation of the Feydeau farce *Le Dindon*. *Dindon* is French for *turkey*, and this one was. It had been a popular hit at Canada's Stratford Festival the prior summer. When the American stage manager assigned to the transfer—a former Broadway dancer named Bob Bernard—came through, I explained I was a gofer on *Vivat!* and asked if he perhaps would like me to help out.

"No," he said, turning away.

The other Merrick play was something else again. Michael Weller's *Cancer* had opened in 1970 at London's Royal Court in London—being, presumably, too provocative and antipatriotic to find a US hearing. Alan Schneider, an incisive director whose work included the Broadway premieres of Albee's *Who's Afraid of Virginia Woolf?*, *Tiny Alice*, and *A Delicate Balance* as well as Harold Pinter's *The Birthday Party*, saw the Weller play in London. He immediately agreed to direct his own production at Arena Stage in Washington, DC, in November 1971. The explosive drama—retitled *Moonchildren*—created a wave of excitement, meriting an immediate Broadway transfer.

Weller's first play was about a diverse group of disillusioned college students living communally in a crowded apartment. The action took place in 1966, providing a cross-section of the boomer generation long before anyone ever used the word "boomer." In those Vietnam War days, all male American teenagers lived in fear of being drafted. Unless, I suppose, you had bone spurs. My number, pulled from something like a large bingo lottery machine, was 311 (of 365), so I was safely out of range.

The Broadway audience of the time—upper middle class and well heeled—was appalled by the (true-to-life) attitudes, language, and sex emanating from the stage of the Royale. The reviews were good. Clive Barnes of the *Times* called *Moonchildren* a rare play that "manages to provide an epitaph for its time," comparing it to *The Cherry Orchard*, *Awake and Sing*, and *Look Back in Anger*. He also called it "bitterly funny and funnily bitter"—which was, indeed, a good description.

But the audience reaction was violent, with the countercultural *Moonchildren* collapsing after only sixteen performances. I was there for several of them; but not backstage. The stage manager handling the transfer was a transplanted Brit named Alan Hall. Ten years earlier, he served as young stage manager for a quartet of collegiate intellectuals from Cambridge and Oxford doing an unconventional topical revue at the Edinburgh Festival. The quartet consisted of Peter Cook, Dudley Moore, Jonathan Miller, and Alan Bennett. *Beyond the Fringe* quickly moved on to the West End and Broadway. When the show finally ended its life following a return New York engagement, Alan remained and—given his high professionalism and mild demeanor—joined the ranks of prime Broadway stage managers.

When I asked if I could help out, he said that he was sorry but no; they were doing only one week of brush-up rehearsals, and Schneider, who was famously difficult, was adamant that nobody observe him work. But Alan said so apologetically, unlike Bob Bernard, and hoped that I would see the play and let him know what I thought.

Moonchildren was riveting, and so was the young-and-unknown cast. The male students were played by Kevin Conway (in a staggeringly powerful performance that remains unforgettable), James Woods, Stephen Collins, Edward Herrmann, and Christopher Guest. The girls were Maureen Anderman, Jill Eikenberry, and Cara Duff-MacCormick, who went on to a lesser career than the others but received the play's only Tony nomination. Among the "adults" were Louis Zorich, Robert Prosky, and

Michael Tucker, the latter of whom was to marry Eikenberry. All this, and off to the warehouse after only two weeks.

Given the times, *Moonchildren* clearly belonged off-Broadway. It was in fact revived at the Theatre de Lys in Greenwich Village a year later, with a different director and cast, and enjoyed a year's run. At that time Clive—who was sometimes very perceptive and sometimes not—redoubled his praise, calling it one of the best American plays of recent years and referring to the Broadway run: "Its inexplicable failure there, in an admittedly good production, was possibly the most formidable condemnation yet of Broadway as a viable arena for the serious business of the nation's theater." While Walter Kerr, also in the *Times*, noted that "its initial run was inexplicably, not to say, disgracefully, short." Inexplicable, yes; but Broadway audiences in 1971 were simply not interested in paying to see virulently outspoken contemporary comedy.

Not Enough Jokes

Just after Christmas week, *Vivat* returned from Boston and set up in the Broadhurst. Back I went with them for ten further days of rehearsal, but it was different. If I was part of the group before, now—after they had played the show for five weeks—I was merely an expendable outsider. I was happy, though, to become acquainted with the Broadhurst, yet another theatre to add to my collection.

Vivat played three previews; then came opening night on January 20, 1972. The final image of the play was Claire, in that oh-so-flimsy nightgown, rushing off to be beheaded to the sound of drums and the cast chanting "Vivat! Vivat Regina!" At that point I rushed backstage, so I could watch the calls from the wings.

As I traversed the short hallway between the stage door and the stage, I practically crashed into Merrick, who was rushing from backstage to the front of the house.

He stopped, held up his index finger, and said in dramatically funereal tones: "Not—enough—jokes." And then he loped out to the front of the house.

Intermission

BACK IN THE BLUE COAT

MY TIME AT THE MERRICK OFFICE ENDED WITH *VIVAT*, AND IT WAS back to the candy stand. I had now graduated from hired hand to what they called chargeman, the person in control of an individual theatre. This could be relatively lucrative in the bigger houses, where a hit musical could rack up liquor sales. (*No, No, Nanette*, with its particular demographic, was an alcohol blockbuster.) The smaller theatres didn't have liquor licenses in those days, so opportunity was limited. They didn't have steady bookings either, with the industry in a severe slump, so I wandered from house to house for such brief runs as David Rabe's *Sticks and Bones*, which had transferred from Joe Papp's Public Theater to the Golden. This was followed by a negligible play called *Promenade, All!* starring Hume Cronyn, Eli Wallach, and Anne Jackson, which followed *Company* into the Alvin. This was, already, a homecoming of sorts for me; I would come in early, through the stage door, and sneak over to that same spot I'd discovered the night at *The Great White Hope* with James Earl Jones.

Other houses I ran included the Morosco (now demolished), where Alan Bates was playing a limited engagement in Simon Gray's *Butley*. This was a remarkable, acclaimed performance. More remarkable to me, though, was the steady stream of customers coming to the check room/candy stand—at the rear of the orchestra—complaining that they couldn't understand much of what Bates was saying. There were many dozens of complaints per performance, at a time prior to the use of infra-red hearing devices. I then went up to the ANTA (now the August Wilson) for two shows.

First was a series of modern ballets from independent troupes under the banner American Dance Marathon, memorable for two reasons. Not being a dance aficionado, the only item on the program that excited me—and that I would bother to go upstairs repeatedly to watch—was *District Storyville*, a ballet by Donald McKayle. His name was somewhat familiar to me, in that he had a few minor Broadway credits. The work was altogether refreshing. I also got my first up-close view of a general manager at work other than the enigmatic Jack Schlissel. R. Tyler Gatchell Jr. and Peter Neufeld were the new hot team, circa 1971, having taken over the Broadway-bound *Nanette* (with a famously tempestuous producer) and immediately followed it up with the controversial *Jesus Christ Superstar*. Tyler would appear several nights a week and plant himself at my little circular lobby bar, nursing himself through four scotches. ("Wouldn't you rather go across the street to Gallagher's and get a *real* drink," I would ask him repeatedly.) While Neufeld had a cold and forbidding personality, Tyler was likable and friendly.

The dance marathon was followed by *The Last of Mrs. Lincoln*, by James Prideaux (known to me for *Postcards*, which shared the bill with the quickly forgotten nudist comedy *Grin and Bare It!* at the Belasco). Julie Harris won her fourth Tony, but this story about crazy old Mary Todd Lincoln was exceedingly dull. During the Christmas holiday, with empty houses, I got tickets for my parents to bring my eight-year-old brother Jimmy—who was the *only* person I ever found who liked the play.

I remained in the candy trade about two years. It served its purpose, getting me my place at the Merrick office—which in turn set up contacts that led to many years of activity. At the time, I was thrilled to have virtually total access to all the Broadway theatres. The company I worked for ran concessions in all of them, so I could put on my worn, dark blue candy blazer and get "buzzed in" to any theatre at will, either to work or simply to "visit." Over these couple of years, I calculate that I filled in—or did intermissions—at more than half the then-operating houses, plus Carnegie Hall, where the biggest seller at the nonalcoholic candy bar was fresh-brewed coffee.

AND THE WINNER IS . . .

I also found my way into two very special "special events." As the Twenty-Sixth Annual Tony Awards approached on April 23, 1972, I determined that I ought to find a way to work it. Surely they needed extra help at the ceremony? As it turned out, there were no concessions at the Tonys, so all that was required was someone to check coats. Fine with me. The concessionaire sent me off to a dingy tuxedo rental place up a steep and very narrow stairway on Forty-Second Street off Times Square, so I was ready on the appointed Sunday.

It was a lovely day; no coats. Even so, I took my place in the inner lobby of the Broadway Theatre, offering checkroom services. Nary a customer, which as far as I was concerned was all to the good, until the entire audience was seated. Then in came Joe Papp, wearing a full-length white mink. (I guess if you are Joe Papp and you have a full-length white mink, you are eager to find places to wear it even in late April.) This was Papp's biggest night thus far, in the course of which he won the awards for both Best Musical and Best Play. There were no revival awards in those days; if so, Joe would likely have found a way to win those, too.

I took Papp's mink downstairs to the checkroom, where the charge-man babysat it, and returned to the house. I had heard tell during my days at Merrick of what were mysteriously called Tony seat-fillers: people who lined the side aisles, in evening clothes, so that as soon as anyone left their seat—either to present an award, perform on the telecast, or just go to the restroom—they could be siphoned into the empty space. (Alex Cohen, who produced the telecast, didn't want the TV audience to ever see an empty seat.) I found the harried person in charge of seat fillers, told her I worked in the checkroom, and asked if she might have a place for me. I apparently came along at just the right moment, because she said, "You? Good! L-102. Franny Sternhagen came alone." She marked it off on her clipboard and sent an assistant to seat me.

Frances Sternhagen was in L-101, nominated for Best Supporting Actress in the revival of Lorraine Hansberry's *The Sign in Sidney Brustein's Window*. I took my seat next to Franny, introducing myself. ("My husband," she apologized, "had to stay home with the children.") The telecast had not begun; the TV director was onstage, instructing the audience how to behave. I turned around in my seat to survey the terrain. Nominee Alexis Smith, from *Follies*, was behind me; her castmate and fellow nominee Dorothy Collins was across the aisle, behind Best Actor nominees Raul Julia from *Two Gents* and Barry Bostwick from *Grease*. More familiar names in front and behind us. I settled down to watch the Tonys.

When the time came for Franny's on-screen moment as they announced her nomination, I was more than sharing the screen with the diminutive Ms. Sternhagen. They went on to announce the winner, Elizabeth Wilson from *Sticks and Bones*, and that was that. Franny won her first Tony two years later, for Neil Simon's *The Good Doctor*.

(Some years ago, the 1972 Tony telecast inevitably turned up on the internet. There I am, in the ninety-sixth minute, a nineteen-year-old with long sideburns that make my kids snicker and do look pretty ridiculous, in profile with Franny as if we were the Lunts while they announce her nomination.)

This was a night of considerable excitement. There was a star-studded salute to Richard Rodgers, ending with the composer—looking ill, pale, and ancient—seated at a piano as it winched across the stage. He didn't play or speak. He didn't even walk; just stood there accepting an honorary Tony Award from Deborah Kerr, looking startled as the crowd rose in a standing ovation.

This was followed by a second salute, to Ethel Merman. The star looked similarly ancient but gave a highly energetic performance, going through an assortment of her hits ("I Got Rhythm," "I Get a Kick Out of You," "You Can't Get a Man with a Gun," "Anything Goes," "Everything's Coming Up Roses").

The evening culminated in one of the major upsets in Tony Award history. The Stephen Sondheim/Hal Prince musical *Follies* won seven awards, for score, direction, choreography, star Alexis Smith, and more. But not the Best Musical award, which went to *Two Gentlemen of Verona*. There was an audible gasp from the audience when this was announced; people, especially people who did not see both productions, to this day claim that *Follies* was robbed.

I had a more practical view of the matter. *Follies* was artistically the best musical of the year, no doubt, and it has proven its worth over the decades. But that original production had a mixed reception, closing after a disappointing run and a loss of its entire investment. Hal Prince has made the distinction between flops (bad shows) and failures (shows that might be excellent but lose money). *Follies* was a failure, in good part because it challenged a large segment of the 1971 audience. *Two Gents* was admirable, though not nearly so much as *Follies*; but it was a hip, contemporary musical, with actors gleefully cavorting through the audience. (At one memorable moment, cast members climbed up to the boxes and threw Frisbees across the house.) Audiences left the St. James enchanted, while they left the Winter Garden frustrated. So I thoroughly understood why *Two Gents* took the Best Musical Award on that Sunday night at the Broadway, even though I expect most people—even the creators of *Two Gents*—would agree that *Follies* was surely the season's best.

Thirty-odd years later, at some forgotten play at the Barrymore (or was it the Music Box?), I happened to find myself sitting across the aisle from Franny and her son, the actor Tony Carlin; he was one of the children Franny's husband had to stay home with, making my seat available. While waiting for the show to begin, I reminded her of our night, such as it was, at the Tonys. She said, "Oh."

POURING FOR THE STARS
An even bigger event came later that year. The rapid, Roaring Twenties expansion of the Broadway theatre district had ended, with a thud, in 1931, when producer Earl Carroll opened a palatial art deco playhouse—Broadway's largest ever, with almost three thousand seats—intended to out-Ziegfeld Ziegfeld. The Depression almost immediately took its toll, forcing Carroll and his Earl Carroll Theatre into bankruptcy within six months. (Ziegfeld himself took it over, producing his 1932 revival of *Show Boat* at the renamed Casino; but he, too, was insolvent and died shortly thereafter.) The Depression knocked about half the existing playhouses out of business, being converted into movie houses or radio studios, or simply demolished. By the time I arrived on Broadway, about a dozen former legit theatres were showing films. The remains of the palatial Earl Carroll Theatre were a ghostly presence on West Fiftieth

Street until 1990, sitting empty with a Woolworth's—fronting on Seventh Avenue—carved out of the theatre's ground floor.

Now, forty years after the opening of the Earl Carroll, came the first new Broadway theatre in the Times Square area. The Uris family included their own Uris Theatre in an office tower on the site of the old Capitol Theatre, directly across from the Winter Garden. The theatre part of the building itself was on the far section of the plot, near Eighth Avenue; the landlords also built a smaller, basement theatre for the nonprofit Circle in the Square company, no doubt earning all sorts of tax credits in the process.

The Uris opened with a rock musical from Galt MacDermot, the temporarily high-flying composer of *Hair* and *Two Gentlemen of Verona*. *Via Galactica*, it was called; the initial title of the show was *Up!*, until the ad agency came in with a marquee design that said—simply—"Up! Uris." That was all too fitting, as it turned out. The theatre itself changed names a decade later, to the Gershwin.

Via Galactica had pedigree; it was directed by Peter Hall, founder of the Royal Shakespeare Company and by that time artistic director of the National Theatre. While specializing in the drama, Hall had already demonstrated a visionary musical hand with a series of operas. *Via Galactica*, though, was his Waterloo. The incoherent plot was about an inter-stellar garbage collector (Raul Julia) on an asteroid in 2972. Little Irene Cara, from *The Me Nobody Knows* but now thirteen, costarred along with Keene Curtis, who played a disembodied head in a tin box that slid along on a track near the top of the proscenium. Yes, a disembodied head. The stage floor consisted of thousands of ping-pong balls. Yes, ping-pong balls.

Jimmy Nederlander—operator of the Uris, Broadway's largest barn of a theatre albeit a thousand seats smaller than the Earl Carroll—decided to "decorate" the massive lobby rotundas by establishing what was called the Theater Hall of Fame. This was not a museum or a public space. Rather, they simply engraved the walls with names of theatre celebrities. The originally announced plan was to include displays of related memorabilia, but nobody ever came forward to assemble, maintain, or insure said displays. In order to see this Hall of Fame, you had to buy a ticket to

Via Galactica or whatever was playing at the theatre. (The *New York Times* noted at the time that the venture was under attack by theatre industry executives as a publicity gimmick to bring attention to the Uris and to Nederlander.)

The theatre, and the Hall of Fame, opened with 123 gold-leaf names on the wall. They elected another eighteen in 1974 but ran out of money and didn't engrave them until 1979. The Hall of Fame remains in place today, although you can see the names on the wall only by buying a ticket to whatever is playing at Nederlander's Gershwin.

To celebrate the opening of their so-called Hall of Fame, the Nederlanders announced a black-tie gala at which the recipients—as many of the living legends as they could get in attendance—were to be inducted. The evening consisted of a cocktail party, a preview performance of the musical, and a champagne supper for the honorees at the new restaurant in the Uris Building.

This sounded like the Broadway event of the season, to me anyway, and it might well have been highly successful, except that the show that the assembled Broadway royalty had to sit through was—*Via Galactica*. At any rate, I applied to work concessions. The Uris lobby had four separate, double-sized concession counters; the event would be open-bar, with eight of us dispensing the drinks.

I momentarily hesitated as I signed on, knowing full well that nineteen-year-old me didn't actually know anything about serving liquor. At that point, I didn't even drink. I had recently started as chargeman at the Alvin, which means that I did in fact run the bar there. But few people bothered to attend *Promenade, All!*, and those who did weren't drinkers; I expect that I never served more than twenty drinks a night. An open bar in a 1,900-seat theatre sounded like it would be busy. But I wasn't about to pass up the chance of being at the gala and maybe even meet Fred Astaire.

I went back to the tuxedo rental place, and then to the Uris on November 19, 1972. (I had already seen a preview of *Via Galactica*, the prior weekend. At that point, there were temporary panels covering the Hall of Fame names.) I took my spot behind one of the bars and waited. We were alerted when the lower lobby doors opened, and up they came on the escalators. Broadway theatre royalty, in hordes. There's something magical about the conjunction of the two phrases, "show folk" and "open bar," perhaps harkening back to olden times when strolling players were seen as cutthroats and vagabonds; stake them to a bottle and you were safe. This held true, even in dinner clothes. They stormed the bars. Some helped themselves to boxes of free candy, but it was liquor they were after.

Fifteen minutes in, we were mobbed; arms outstretched, clamoring for service. Initially I carefully measured my pours with a shot glass, as taught. The concession company had a primitive but strict inventory system; the bottles were measured every night, ounce by ounce. Tonight, though, there would be no inventory check; because the drinks were free, no calculations need be made. The practiced bartender next to me, on loan from the 46th Street, indicated I should just pour. So pour I did, with so many people shouting multiple orders at me that I served with what you might call a free hand.

As I put back whatever bottle I had just served, I heard a clarion voice bark out for a vodka. "Clarion voice" gives it away, doesn't it? "Vodka on the rocks!" "Sing out, Louise!" I hadn't had time to stop to identify my patrons thus far, but hey—this was Ethel Merman.

Sure, I said, handing her a generously poured glassful. And she was gone. But she must have liked the stiffness of the drink: With eight bartenders spread across the lobby, she was back ten minutes later for another, and once more after they unveiled her name on the wall of fame. And back again, during intermission. I can't rightfully attest, these years later, that it was vodka on the rocks; but whatever it was, it was most decidedly Ethel Merman.

The evening itself was a bust. It didn't take long for the less patient honorees to head for the lobby, complaining about the irredeemably lousy—and loud—rock musical they were forced to endure. Intermission came, and a good quarter of the house seemed to sit out the second act. They couldn't leave, though; they were the honored guests at the dinner afterward.

Opening night of the quasi–Theater Hall of Fame at the new Uris Theatre (1972), featuring Ethel Merman at the bar.

OLD MAN WITH ROAST BEEF

The party was in the Pub Theatrical, a new restaurant owned by the Stouffer's Company. This group ran two other then-popular midtown restaurants, Top of the Sixes—in the penthouse of the office building at 666 Fifth Avenue—and Act I in Times Square. They also were celebrated with a lyric in Frank Loesser's *How to Succeed*: "There's a yummy Friday special at Stouffer's ..."

Pub Theatrical never caught on, in part because it was located in the windowless basement of the office tower. Uris had built two plazas in front of their building, with curving cement staircases descending from the Broadway sidewalk; one served as a subway entrance. These subterranean plazas were presumably intended to bring in business. Instead, it was dreary, dark, and dangerous down there. Stouffer's Pub Theatrical was soon gone, with various restaurants coming and going over the decades. (When my children were little, circa 2010, they attended several parties in the space, which had become a dark and dismal theme restaurant called Mars 2112.)

The night of the opening of the Hall of Fame was itself dark and dismal, outside the theatre as well as in. The honorees were escorted to the restaurant through the inner basement of the Uris Building so they wouldn't have to brave the weather and negotiate that outdoor staircase. Reasoning that I couldn't get in the front door of Pub Theatrical without a party ticket, I simply attached myself to a mass of anonymous theatre royalty and followed them through the basement labyrinth and the unattended back door of the restaurant.

This was my first grand Broadway party, so I was unprepared for what I found. Basically, throngs of people lined up to check their heavy winter coats, and even thicker lines at the buffet tables. (See above, re "show folk" and "open bar"; only more so, with added "free food.") So I stood in that new but darkly sprawling restaurant, waiting in line with all the celebrities and hangers-on. Successful after a long half-hour, I took my heaping plate and went to find a table. In room after room after room—the place seemed to have endless small rooms—all of the seats taken. I finally reached the last room. In the back was a high table with four bar stools, one little old man sitting there eating his roast beef from the carving table.

"Do you mind—?" I asked.

"Please, do join me," he said.

He was not a little old man, actually; he was old, but not little. We sat in silence, eating from equally overloaded dishes. I found it perfectly natural for a teenager—me—to be at this gala alone, but this fellow was older than my grandparents. Sitting all alone, late at night at this show biz party, he looking like a retired country practitioner in an ill-fitting tuxedo. Wasn't someone there to take care of him?

"I suppose you saw the show upstairs," I said. "What brings you here?"

"The induction ceremony," he said pleasantly. "Do you work in the theatre?"

"I'm a student, at NYU," I said.

"Oh, I used to teach, up at Yale."

After a while, I asked whether he was there with someone.

"No, they invited me so I came down from Connecticut."

"Oh," I said.

"I'm one of the—"

"The—people—?" I asked.

"The names on the wall. I'm a writer." He then dropped his fork and offered his hand, "Call me Thornton."

But of course, I realized: the author of *Our Town* and *The Skin of Our Teeth*, a three-time Pulitzer winner, this old man in the basement of the Uris. He seemed more interested in who I was, and who I hoped to be. So we sat there pleasantly, in our own little island of the loud, crowded party, and held each other's place when we went to visit the dessert spread.

And that's the story of the night I had roast beef with Thornton Wilder.

TRICKS OF THE TRADE

Meanwhile, I kept putting in my time at NYU. In October, Mitch told me he was starting a new show, would I like to come to rehearsals and help out? This was not at Merrick's; the days of multiple productions up there were finished, with only *Sugar* still on the boards. Mitch left the office when *Vivat!* closed in April. Biff, too, was gone. Merrick produced four shows during the 1971–1972 season, with only *Sugar* running more than three months; this was followed by only one in the 1972–1973 season, the Tennessee Williams twelve-performance flop *Out Cry*.

As previously mentioned, Biff had started his career as stage manager for producer Herman Levin, principally on the major hit *Gentlemen Prefer Blondes* and the smash hit *My Fair Lady*. Herman found a new show called *Tricks*, a rock version of Molière's *Les Fourberies de Scapin* that originated at the Actors Theatre of Louisville. The resident artistic director, Jon Jory, had written the book and directed; the score came from a pair of understandably little-known songwriters, Jerry Blatt (music) and Lonnie

Burstein (lyrics). After Louisville, there had been a second production at the Arena Stage in Washington, where it was hailed as something fresh, unpretentious, and new. Herman, seeing it there, decided to spiff up the musical and bring it to Broadway. With Biff having departed Merrick, Herman signed him on as associate producer. Biff, naturally, called on Mitch.

Yes, Herman had produced *My Fair Lady*; but that was back in 1956. In the interim he had produced a parade of negligible shows with one notable exception: *The Great White Hope*. (This had also been a transfer from the Arena Stage, which is presumably why Levin was called down to see *Tricks*.) More recently, he had produced what was to be his final large-scale new musical, an adaptation of the Pulitzer Prize–winning 1953 play *The Teahouse of the August Moon*. It opened at the Majestic in 1970—the Shuberts forced *Fiddler on the Roof* to move to the Broadway, to make room—and lasted a mere two weeks. The lede in Clive Barnes's review in the *Times*: "I come to bury *Lovely Ladies, Kind Gentlemen*, not to praise it."

Herman immediately sent a furious complaint to the *Times*, vowing to keep the show running (which he couldn't). While fighting, he sent the cast to picket the *Times* Building. They brought along Lady Astor, the goat used in the show, wearing a sign that proclaimed, "Clive gets my goat." Two years later, Levin was still enraged over the matter.

Herman hired a fabled design team, at least by my standards: set designer Oliver Smith (*Gentlemen Prefer Blondes, My Fair Lady, West Side Story, The Sound of Music, Hello, Dolly!*) and costume designer Miles White (from the original *Oklahoma!* and *Carousel, Gentlemen Prefer Blondes, Bye Bye Birdie*). But Oliver was from the era of painted flats and canvas; the Broadway musical had moved in different directions. As for Miles, he still had a fanciful flair, but had spent most of his later career working on the Ringling Bros. Circus, the *Ice Capades*, and the like.

So there I was for rehearsals, back again at the Alvin (which had been empty since *Promenade, All*). I was thrilled to be sitting in on a real, new Broadway musical. What's more, I could go—during breaks or after rehearsal—and stand on that same spot from which I'd surveyed the house just four years earlier, and which in the interim had been filled mostly by Sondheim's *Company*.

From the start, though, *Tricks* looked mighty flimsy. The score was pallid, trying to be simultaneously contemporary, witty, and *commedia dell'arte*, and failing in all aspects. The overall effect was washed-out, watered-down Molière. The main selling point—the only selling point, really—was the presence of René Auberjonois, in his first starring role. René had made a major splash in the 1969 Alan Jay Lerner musical *Coco*, as an over-the-top dress designer who schemes to defeat Katharine Hepburn as his boss Chanel. He had a solo called "Fiasco" in which he worked himself into such a frenzy that he almost levitated from the stage, earning a Tony Award in the process. Here he was, three years later, attempting an awkward Scapin.

The cast was mostly new to Broadway, with several holdovers from the prior productions. Christopher Murney, as Scapin's sidekick Sylvestre, had been with *Tricks* since Louisville and was the best element of the show by far. (Murney had a four-year-old at the time named Julia, who has gone on to a more auspicious career. Chris, himself, was an accomplished and immensely likable actor.) The music came from what in those days was a small-for-Broadway combo of eleven pieces, with a quartet of onstage rock singers called "The Commedia." Three of them—Joe Morton, Ernestine Jackson, and Shezwae Powell—will quickly reappear in our story. The insipid juvenile—the role was insipid, not the actor—was a young fellow named Walter Bobbie, who went on to better things. I still picture him walking about in a trance singing a pallid love song called "Who Was I?" and remind him so every time I bump into him.

Despite the frailty of the enterprise, I was happy to observe it. The typically interminable waits when nothing was happening gave me time to talk with the professionals on hand: musical arranger Peter Howard— another Merrick veteran, from *Carnival!*, *Dolly!*, and other musicals— and the two designers. One day, Oliver and Miles walked in grumbling because a new version of *Gentlemen Prefer Blondes* starring Carol Channing had just been announced, with neither of them offered the job. The show, under the title *Lorelei*, turned out to be a lumberingly pale version of the original—with a hideous-looking unit set and garish costumes.

I took advantage of the down time at the theatre to ask Miles about the two Rodgers & Hammerstein classics. He was still a beginner at the time, so much so that the morning after the New Haven opening of *Oklahoma!* he jumped on a train and returned to New York. It took all day for the stage manager to track him down. He said that he thought that after the first performance, he was finished; he had no idea that frequent changes would be needed until the show reached Broadway. He also mournfully told me that when the cash-starved producers offered him a small percentage royalty, he adamantly insisted on $25 a week.

As for *Carousel*, I happened to mention the color photo on the then-newest reissue of the original cast album—the only full color shot I'd seen, which demonstrated just how vibrant the costumes originally were. He explained to me that he created the checked trousers of Billy Bigelow—the carnival barker, played by John Raitt—by having the shop stitch colored ribbons on black fabric. You couldn't actually discern this from the audience, but the costume—enhanced by lights bouncing off the ribbons—made Billy Bigelow stand out whenever he was onstage.

From that point forward, I would pepper any Broadway veterans I came across with questions. Not long afterward, I realized that there was as much or more to be learned from people who worked on flops. I have written about many shows over the years, whenever possible including first-person details I picked up along the way.

This was a time when most Broadway musicals—even small, low-budget musicals—prepared for New York with an out-of-town tryout rather than weeks of previews. *Tricks* packed up the week before Thanksgiving and departed for five weeks at the Fisher in Detroit. (I have been in this business since 1971, and have thus far never set foot in Detroit.) As was to be expected, things went poorly; a modernized *commedia dell'arte* comedy needs to have a spark, which *Tricks* didn't. As it happens, director Frank Dunlop and actor Jim Dale had developed their own version of the same Molière play, which *did* have the requisite spark. *Scapino* was the opening attraction at the Young Vic in London in 1970. It was an eye-opening delight when it reached Broadway in 1974, transforming Dale into a star.

GREAT VIVACITY BUT LESS LIFE

With *Tricks* in severe trouble in Detroit, Herman and Jory chose not to address the score, the book, or the direction; they simply fired the choreographer. John Sharpe was a veteran dancer, having worked on various Bob Fosse and Michael Kidd shows. He was a pleasant enough guy and his work was adequate, as *Tricks* wasn't much of a dance show. When the company limped back to New York on New Year's Day, there was a new choreographer in place: Donald Saddler. Donald, too, started out as a dancer; he was partnered with the equally unknown Helen Gallagher in the 1948 George Abbott/Jerome Robbins *High Button Shoes*, a musical in which the most inspiring feature was Robbins's "Bathing Beauty Ballet." When Robbins—after a long period of procrastination—finally turned down the choreography job on the 1953 Abbott/Bernstein/Comden & Green musical *Wonderful Town*, Saddler was given the job.

Wonderful Town and its star Rosalind Russell appeared strong in its tryout, but Abbott wasn't totally satisfied with the dances, so he called Robbins to come in and improve them. A fair amount of Saddler's work remained; he retained full credit and walked away with a Tony Award. Donald went on to a string of secondary musicals, including the *Milk and Honey* that bored me in 1961; it reached the point that when you couldn't hire Robbins or Fosse or Kidd or Champion, you could always get Saddler. In 1971, he had his biggest hit: nobody expected much from the aforementioned Busby Berkeley/Ruby Keeler revival of *No, No, Nanette*, but it was a major success sparked by a half-dozen showstopping, cheer-garnering dance numbers. Donald won a second Tony. Once again, he had significant help from two assistant choreographers (one of whom, Mary Ann Niles, was the first Mrs. Fosse).

With *Nanette* still a major hit in New York and on tour, Donald came to try to fix *Tricks*. I spent two days at Broadway Arts—a popular rehearsal hall, then located above a car dealership on Broadway at Fifty-Fifth Street—watching him restage the title song. It was about tricks, so he filled it with vaudeville steps and gags. It made the number better, yes, but not the show. There wasn't much he could do, anyway; he only had a week of rehearsals and five previews before we opened.

Back at the Alvin during tech rehearsals, I witnessed my first big Broadway meltdown. René clearly realized that the show, which was built around him and could potentially carry him to stardom, was a sure turkey. He was working with a rehearsal prop while the real one was off being repainted, a string of lanterns or something of the sort. As he was doing some cross-the-stage blocking, the thing snagged, twisted, and broke. He stopped the run-through, screaming—and he could sure scream—about the cheap props, the cheap show, and the cheap producer.

"*Cheap*," Levin boomed from the darkened house. "Nobody ever called me cheap! I produced *My Fair Lady!*"

"Well, this isn't *My Fair Lady*," cried René, storming off to his dressing room—the same one formerly occupied by James Earl Jones.

Tricks opened on Monday night, January 8, 1973. For the first time, I experienced the Broadway tunnel effect. You are in rehearsals, in previews, and the outside world stops; all you concentrate on is the opening.

"This isn't *My Fair Lady!*"
René Auberjonois in *Tricks*
(1973).
PHOTO BY BILL YOSCARY

You walk around on the big day excited and a bit disconcerted; people on the street—people you know, strangers, everybody—seem to think it's just another day. I suppose this tunnel view only affects beginners; after several shows, you realize that this one will open, it will eventually close, and there will be another. But at the time, you wonder: Doesn't everybody know tonight is *opening night*?

The opening went as expected, which is to say it was not any better than the previews had been. The highlights, for me, were offstage. As the audience was settling in before the show, Herman took me down the side aisle and pointed to an ancient man standing at his seat, third row center.

"Do you see that man? That's Max Gordon."

I knew all about Max Gordon, producer of the legendary *Band Wagon*, Jerome Kern's *Roberta*, Robert E. Sherwood's *Abe Lincoln in Illinois*, Garson Kanin's *Born Yesterday*, and other hits. A few years earlier, I had eagerly read his eye-opening autobiography *Max Gordon Presents*. He relates how during the 1932 Philadelphia tryout of his revue *Flying Colors*, matters were so dire that during the dress rehearsal he tried to commit suicide by jumping from the balcony of the Forrest Theatre. (His general manager, realizing what was happening, grabbed him. Which I suppose is as good a job description of a general manager as any.) They hustled him off to a sanitarium. As he lay there a couple of weeks later, in a state of shame, desperation, and financial failure, Noël Coward—a virtual stranger—walked into the hospital room and insisted that Max produce his new play. *Design for Living* was a surefire hit, written as a vehicle for Coward to star in opposite his pals Alfred Lunt and Lynn Fontanne. Now, in 1973, Gordon was old and infirm, so Herman asked me to get him after the show and bring him backstage—which I did.

Tricks being exceedingly cheap (to quote René, who was correct), there was no money for an opening night party. We milled around backstage for an hour, then a couple dozen of us went to Sardi's—my first time there. We were seated on the main floor, in one long group down the center of the main room consisting of ten tables pieced together. After ordering drinks and food—it was now a couple of hours after the final curtain—I spotted Clive Barnes entering. I went over to the entrance, where he was waiting to check his coat.

"Were you over at *Tricks* tonight?" I asked, knowing that he was.

He reached into his jacket pocket, pulled out some folded sheets of paper. "Do you want to read it? Just return it when you're done, I'll be at the upstairs bar," he said, mounting the staircase.

I couldn't very well stand in the entrance and read the review, so I went back to the table. Everyone was chatting, waiting for food. Clive's copy was burning a hole in my pocket, as they say. While I wouldn't dream of taking out a newspaper at an opening night party—unless I knew the review was good—I reasoned that nobody would suspect if I just read some typed pages. It was a carbon copy, on three leaves of onion skin. Double-spaced, just like Clive told us to prepare our assignments. So I held the review on my lap, under the table, and read it.

He liked *Tricks* slightly more than *Lovely Ladies, Kind Gentlemen*, which he had more or less embalmed with his review. "There was a great deal of vivacity at the Alvin Theatre last night," it said, "but rather less life." Mitch saw me reading surreptitiously, gave me a glance. "You don't want to see it," I told him.

After the next evening's performance, Herman called everyone onstage for a company meeting and gave us the expected news. "I'm going to fight this! I've been on the phones all day, and I'm close to raising enough money to combat the *Times*. We have to post notice, as a precaution. But we *will* play on."

Herman wasn't even offstage when one of the jaded character men, who had weathered such flops as *Darling of the Day*, said (*sotto voce*), "Sure we will."

The one-week run of *Tricks* was eventful for me, at least. At the Wednesday matinee, Mitch asked if I'd like to "call" part of the second act. That is, sit with the prompt book, announce the electric-set-and-sound cues over the intercom, and operate cue lights for the conductor and actors waiting to make their entrances. I said sure, Biff gave permission, and Mitch handed over the controls for a relatively noncomplex section of the show. That evening, I called it again; on Thursday Mitch doubled my portion; and at the closing on Saturday night, I—two weeks shy of twenty—called more than half of a performance of a real, if terminal, Broadway musical.

CHAPTER THIRTEEN

Enchantment

RENÉ THREW A CLOSING NIGHT PARTY AT HIS APARTMENT ON THE Upper West Side. Herman wasn't there, or Biff for that matter. Mitch pulled me aside to say that he'd just gotten word that his next job was starting immediately. Jean Giraudoux's *The Enchanted*, starring Elizabeth Ashley, was an in-house production at the Kennedy Center, for Washington only. But they were rehearsing in New York, was I interested in helping?

Of course I was.

I spent non-classroom time over the next two weeks at the Whitehead/ Stevens office helping with casting and logistics. This was atop the Palace Theatre building. The Palace had been the flagship of the Keith-Albee circuit from its opening in 1913, and as such was the prime venue for vaudeville in the country (as in "you haven't lived until you've played the Palace"). The house fell on hard times during the Depression, as did many Broadway theatres, although there was something of a rebound in the 1950s. It converted to stage attractions in 1966, opening with Gwen Verdon in the Bob Fosse musical *Sweet Charity*.

Just north of the box office lobby was a narrow entrance with three grand old elevators, two of which seemed to be permanently out of order. By 1972, most of the offices were empty, although Whitehead-Stevens remained on the top floor. While the Palace itself remains in place today, the office building originally containing it was demolished in 1988 to make way for a forty-three-story DoubleTree Hotel—which itself has since been razed for a grand Broadway shopping mall, which is intended to envelope the fabled Palace.

The long, slow, attendant-operated elevator took you up to the aerie that had originally served as the office of E. F. Albee, president of the Keith-Albee-Orpheum circuit. Yes, the father of the playwright, whom the vaudeville magnate adopted (and what a happy family *that* was). The elder Albee was a walrus of a man; the master bathroom, still extant, featured a built-into-the-floor-and-wall scale capable of bearing his girth. Legend has it that when Sarah Bernhardt played the Palace in 1913—at a daily rate of $1,000 in gold—she would take the narrow backstage "cage" elevator up to Albee's office and watch as the gold was weighed. Personal observation: Albee's meat-market scale registered within a pound of the Detecto on my bathroom floor, Divine Sarah or no.

I spent little time in Whitehead's bathroom, only sneaking in after hours to look at the Albee scale. Rather, I worked with Mitch and with Whitehead's casting director, a pixieish woman of indeterminate age named Terry Fay who was married to Oscar Oleson, Whitehead's longtime general manager. It was Terry who, while casting Carson McCullers's 1950 play *The Member of the Wedding*, visited stage manager Frederic de Wilde at home, was captivated by his wide-eyed seven-year-old, and convinced Fritz to allow the boy onstage. Brandon de Wilde managed to hold his own against the play's two powerhouse stars, Ethel Waters and Julie Harris. He repeated his role in the film version, soon thereafter becoming the youngest person ever to receive an Oscar nomination for his iconic performance in the 1953 *Shane*. But destiny can play funny tricks on former child stars, and de Wilde died just after turning thirty.

Whitehead had long since formed a partnership with Roger L. Stevens, the patrician producer and real estate man who at one point owned the Empire State Building. Roger was founding Chairman of the Kennedy Center and undertook to keep the two legit theatres within the complex booked with touring shows. When there was "open" time at the smaller venue, the 1,100-seat Eisenhower, Whitehead-Stevens produced in-house plays to fill the gaps. Mitch, who had close friends with a charming townhouse in Alexandria and thus a local abode, was to become their preferred stage manager for these years.

Several of the plays moved on to Broadway, including Preston Jones's *A Texas Trilogy* and the Zoe Caldwell/Judith Anderson *Medea*. Another item, a 1975 production of Coward's *Present Laughter* starring Douglas Fairbanks Jr., Ilka Chase, and Jane Alexander, did not make it north but provided one of Mitch's stories.

Hollywood star Fairbanks—son of swashbuckling silent film icon Douglas Fairbanks Sr., stepson of Mary Pickford, teenaged husband of Joan Crawford, war hero, etc.—was also noted for being in the International Best Dressed Hall of Fame. When Mitch stopped by Fairbanks's New York apartment to take him to a photo shoot, the star showed him his well-stocked and impeccably neat closet.

"How do you keep everything looking so fresh and new?" asked Mitch.

"The secret is that you mustn't ever send your suits out to the cleaners," said the star. "Just have your man sponge them off."

DISENCHANTED

The Enchanted, an early offering at the Eisenhower, was not likely Broadway fare. Actress Elizabeth Ashley was on one of the Kennedy Center advisory boards, she wanted to do the play (unsuited as she was to it), so Roger took it on. They hired an accomplished director: Stephen Porter, who in 1971 had staged an exceptional production of Moliere's *School for Wives* starring Brian Bedford. Brian was nominated for the Best Actor Tony against John Gielgud, Alec McCowen, and Ralph Richardson. When his name was unexpectedly announced, he went up to the podium and—love him—started his acceptance speech with "Very wise choice."

The Giraudoux play was one of those dreary French fantasies, a 1933 work by the dramatist best known for his 1945 play *The Madwoman of Chaillot*. *The Enchanted* finally reached Broadway in 1950 in an adaptation by Maurice Valency, who had done the same for *Chaillot*; lasted a fortnight; and disappeared. The story tells of a bright young heroine who goes off into a magic forest and ponders life, death, and other matters.

Elizabeth Ashley as Giraudoux's gamine in the green forest. *The Enchanted* (1973).
MAX A. WOODWARD COLLECTION, MUSIC DIVISION, LIBRARY OF CONGRESS

The production was built around Liz, who by this point was anything but a fantastical young heroine. She was surrounded by a brace of character men; her costar was Fred Gwynne, whom I had last seen onstage in *Irma La Douce* but was now a major television star, courtesy of his series *The Munsters*. Fred was craggy, and not especially chatty. If Liz and Fred didn't come off well in *The Enchanted*, they were both smashingly good the following year when reunited for a revival of Tennessee Williams's *Cat on a Hot Tin Roof* at the ANTA. The pairing of stars—both of whom gave extraordinary performances, as Maggie and Big Daddy—was something of a direct offshoot of *The Enchanted*, as this *Cat* was also produced by Whitehead.

Rehearsals were not all that interesting. There was a cast of sixteen, including six "young" girls to play Liz's students. These were mostly in the cute French gamine category, although one was strikingly odd: a twenty-year-old named Carol Kane. She had already made her film debut in 1971 in a small but noticeable role as middle-aged Art Garfunkel's teenaged girlfriend in Mike Nichols's *Carnal Knowledge*, and within two years would have a Best Actress Oscar nomination for *Hester Street*. Liz and Carol actually did make an eccentrically watchable pair of young French maidens.

For me, there was plenty of running around during New York rehearsals, searching for props, taking actors to costume fittings, and the like. With limited rehearsal time and an enormous amount for Liz to memorize, I was sometimes dispatched to the star's hotel room to cue her. One night, a child ran in to share some important information, only to be met with a stern "Not now, darling. Mommy—is—*running—lines*" through clenched teeth. The five-year-old stealthily backed out of the room, clearly used to high-voltage parenting.

The Green Forest

The Enchanted moved to the Kennedy Center. I went along; the onstage production period more or less coincided with my spring break. It was my first visit to Washington; Mitch drove us over to the Tidal Basin late at night, after rehearsal, to show us the blooming cherry blossoms.

During the take-in, we ran into a grand delay: Robert O'Hearn's set was a luscious green forest overrun with willows and such, but the green of the stage deck—under the lights—didn't quite match the green of the scenery. This called for a special in-theatre paint job that refused to dry. (For years thereafter, Mitch wore sneakers tinged with forest green.) We filled the time by running unnecessary rehearsals in the upstairs rehearsal hall. This gave me plenty of opportunity to talk to the actors; I immediately discovered that I tended to be keenly interested in hearing old-timers talk about shows they had done.

The most renowned of the group, playing one of the two old biddy schoolteachers, was Eugenia Rawls. She was well known for her many years as protégé to Tallulah Bankhead, beginning when she played Regina

Gidden's daughter, Alexandra, in Lillian Hellman's *The Little Foxes*. Rawls was semiretired, having long since wed Donald Sewell, at the time attorney to Bankhead and the Lunts, and more recently a Broadway producer who eventually founded the Denver Center for the Performing Arts.

I didn't have much interest in Bankhead or Eugenia. I had never heard of the other character lady, but Margot Stevenson turned out to be most interesting. One night, in the darkened theatre while we were supposed to be doing a run-through but were stuck interminably focusing lights, I overheard the conversation in the row ahead of me. Margot, who was married to character actor Val Avery, mentioned her first husband, screenwriter Robert Russell. "Is that the Robert Russell who wrote *Take Me Along*?" I surprised her by asking. (*Take Me Along* was the David Merrick adaptation of Eugene O'Neill's *Ah, Wilderness!*, best known not for the script but for Merrick's publicized battles with star Jackie Gleason.) Yes, this was the same Robert Russell; he also wrote, with Mr. Abbott, the Kander-Ebb-Prince-Minnelli musical, *Flora, the Red Menace*.

But then Stevenson started talking about her early career. As a twenty-four-year-old ingénue back in 1936, she was playing the small role of one of the aspiring actresses in the George S. Kaufman/Edna Ferber hit *Stage Door*. Four weeks into the run, she was summoned to producer Sam Harris's office on a Monday afternoon and handed a script and a train ticket to Philadelphia, where Kaufman was trying out his new play. "Read this on the train," Kaufman's producing partner Harris told Stevenson. "George will see you during a rehearsal break tomorrow. Only, don't tell anyone."

Margot dutifully appeared in Philadelphia, read for Kaufman, and got the part. They hid her in a nontheatrical hotel for two days, away from the company. She learned the role on her own and watched the Wednesday night performance from up in the mezzanine where she wouldn't be spotted. The actress playing the part—the second one they had tried, as it happened—was fired Thursday night; Margot performed Friday and Saturday, and the following week opened on Broadway as Alice Sycamore in what was to be one of the biggest hits of the decade, the Kaufman/Hart Pulitzer winner *You Can't Take It with You*.

Stevenson was presumably fine in the role of Alice Sycamore, the "normal" daughter in an unconventional family—good enough for

Kaufman, anyway—but that was to be the high point of her career. (For the film version, they placed movie star Jean Arthur in the role.) Here Stevenson was, almost forty years later, playing an unimportant role in a negligible production.

I stumbled across an even more startling case talking to one of the assistant stage managers. John Handy, Mitch's assistant on *Tricks* and other shows, wasn't on this one; Terry Fay gave Mitch two longtime Whitehead-Stevens employees as assistants. This other stage manager named Johnny was a wispy, mild-mannered family man from Brooklyn of about forty. Picking up stray hints from Mitch, I discovered that he had not only been a child actor but a full-fledged Broadway star. Johnny Stewart started in 1947, at thirteen, as Nanette Fabray's son in the Jule Styne/Jerry Robbins musical *High Button Shoes*; moved on to a more major role—again as Fabray's son—in the Kurt Weill/Alan Jay Lerner/ Elia Kazan *Love Life*; starred, at the age of fifteen, in the Rodgers & Hammerstein–produced comedy hit *The Happy Time*; played Yul Brynner's number-one son, Prince Chulalongkorn, in the original production of *The King and I*; and starred in two more Broadway comedies before he turned twenty. And then—small roles, understudy roles, and assistant stage manager work. Unlike Brandon de Wilde, who never was able to adjust to the end of stardom, Johnny Stewart managed a long and happy, if near-anonymous, post-limelight existence.

Breakfast at the Waldorf
Back in New York, I checked in with musical arranger Peter Howard, whom I'd gotten to know on *Tricks*. He mentioned that he was just then assembling the score for that spring's Milliken Show.

The Milliken Breakfast Show was an annual extravaganza produced each May in the grand ballroom of the Waldorf-Astoria. This was in the genre of what they used to call "industrial shows," glossy entertainments produced not for paying audiences but for buyers, salespeople, and high-volume customers. Major brands used industrials to introduce their new product lines, an event that provided said customers—those lucky enough to be favored with a coveted invitation—with a trip to New York City or a similar mecca.

The classiest industrial of them all was the Milliken Show. (The largest and most expensive industrials were thrown by automobile manufacturers in Detroit, introducing new model cars.) No, you likely never heard of Milliken; they were not a clothing manufacturer, but a maker of the fabrics used by top fashion designers. This was their twentieth annual production, scheduled for thirteen performances before something like 25,000 buyers from department stores and the like. The Milliken Show had an unheard of—for show folk—"early" curtain: 7:50 a.m. The buyers were fed a Waldorf breakfast at 7:00, enthralled by the seventy-minute performance, and then whisked off to Garment District showrooms to place orders for the fall line. The script and lyrics—using mostly show tunes with parody lyrics—were stoked with plugs for hundreds of products made from Milliken fabrics. That, of course, was the point.

This was no shoestring affair; rather, they had top Broadway talent on hand. This edition was directed by Robert Moore, of *Promises, Promises.* The budget was massive; about $1.6 million, I was told. (Hal Prince's lavish production of *Follies* was capitalized at $800,000.) Unlike a commercial production, there were no ticket sales and no potential income; Peter explained to me that the producer—a fellow named Myron Sanft, a former adman who specialized in industrials—had no interest in or need to cut corners. Quite the opposite—if he wound up spending less than anticipated, Milliken might ponder cutting next year's budget. I seem to recall that Sanft's nickname was "Tiny," which he wasn't. Alas, I can find no way at this point to verify this.

For Broadway professionals—directors, designers, arrangers, stage managers—industrials were pure gold. Hard work, yes; but paying far more over a three-week span than they might earn from months of regular work. Peter, for one, arranged his schedule so that he could participate every year. The stars were paid regally. For the dancers—and there was a cast of sixty-four—this was a much sought-after job; the rehearsal and performances were arranged so as not to interfere with the Broadway playing schedule. Thus, the Milliken Show attracted the very best chorus people on Broadway, not only for the money but because at the end of the strenuous run they would go home with the twelve to fifteen costumes— the newest fashions, designer labels, made from Milliken fabrics—they wore in the show. Even shoes were taken home; what were they going to do with all those used shoes?

When Peter mentioned the Milliken Show, I immediately asked how I could get in to "help" with it. Peter said, "Call Alan Hall. He's very nice."

This was Alan Hall of *Moonchildren*. As in that case, he apologized that there was no room for helpers; Milliken gave him a full complement of paid assistant stage managers, which he sometimes struggled to keep looking busy. But he invited me to attend the full-day, break-in dress rehearsal at the Waldorf.

And so it was that I went uptown early one Sunday, prepared for a day of surprises. Alan left my name in the lobby, with a badge waiting for me. When I located him, he just waved me aside and continued dealing with myriad tech issues. I never did get to talk to him that day, although I would eventually enjoy working with him on two large-scale Broadway productions.

REDHEAD

A vast section of the ballroom floor was filled with dancers going through their individual warm-up routines. (I was quite used to this, from innumerable evenings spent in the orchestra section of the Shubert before half-hour at *Promises*.) I sat quietly observing the tech rehearsal and dancers for a couple of hours, until it came time for the stars to start arriving for their call. Not having considered who might be in the cast, I was altogether stunned when in came—wearing black dancer togs, with a shock of brilliant red hair—the legendary Gwen Verdon.

I had first discovered Verdon via the cast recording of the 1955 musical *Damn Yankees*, which opened when I was two. Most fortunately, this was one of the rare Broadway musicals to be filmed using much of the stage production. George Abbott re-created his direction; Bob Fosse did the same with his choreography, in fact performing one of the dance specialties himself; and Verdon played her original role of Lola (as in "Whatever Lola Wants . . ."). While the Broadway musical is one of the most ephemeral of art forms, you can even now watch Gwen at her best and see precisely what all the fuss was about.

When it was announced in 1965 that Verdon was returning to Broadway in her first new show since 1959, I was ready to go; and when it was further announced that it would be opening on the night of my thirteenth birthday, I decided that I was old enough to go to a Broadway show at night alone and take the late train back home. I wrote away for a seat, enclosing a check and what we used to call an SASE (self-addressed stamped envelope). In those days, they held the orchestra floor on opening night for the investors, cast, and important guests; but the mezzanine and balcony went on sale to the public. Back came my ticket for the opening night of *Sweet Charity*, my first chance to see Gwen Verdon.

Unfortunately, the Palace Theatre—which was just then being converted to a legit house—was not quite ready for occupancy, with the opening pushed off three days. I sorrowfully returned my ticket, getting in exchange a ticket for a matinee a couple of months into the run. Still, I looked forward to the show, and to standing at the stage door afterward to meet the great Gwen Verdon.

I did indeed do just that, except Verdon never appeared. Seven years later, biding my time in the Waldorf ballroom, there she was; and would be for the next eight hours!

Rather than pouncing, I waited until she was sitting around unoccupied, after lunch. (They served a plated, hotel-banquet meal, given that budget was no concern.) I went over for a chat, careful not to put her on the defensive; since this was a rehearsal situation, she likely assumed that whoever I might be, I belonged there. Even so, I was unsettled enough that I practically ignored Robert Morse—another favorite performer of mine, whose presence otherwise would have impressed me—who was sitting beside Verdon while I talked to (or rather at) her.

I would have another conversation with Gwen fifteen years later, one in which her fiery temper was, initially, mistakenly directed—full throttle—at the altogether innocent me.

ASSISTANT STAGE MANAGER

As I was moving through the second half of my second year of college, I realized that by cramming my schedule full of courses I could amass enough credits to graduate after only three years. Which is to say, in the spring of 1973. While I was by this point intent on working in a producer's office and becoming a company manager, it would take three to five

years—with luck—to be accepted in the apprenticeship program and ful-
fill the requirements for a full union card. My experience with Mitch on
Vivat, Tricks, and *The Enchanted*—along with the knowledge that Equity
membership didn't require an apprenticeship but merely the offer of an
Equity job—led to the realization that I could get to Broadway quicker
as an assistant stage manager.

It was standard practice for the assistant stage manager of a play to
also understudy and/or play a small role. Mitch had started as an actor/
stage manager in *The Best Man*; John Handy had started as actor/stage
manager in *Rosencrantz and Guildenstern Are Dead*. Even Hal Prince
started as an assistant stage manager, understudying a small role. As it
turned out, Mitch—needing a female ASM a couple of years later for
the Maggie Smith *Private Lives*—gave the job to my college girlfriend
Nancy, who had some stage training (having studied with Stella Adler).

Before I left the Washington tryout of *The Enchanted*, I asked Mitch
to keep me in mind if an assistant job came along. He called a few weeks
later to say that he heard that Jerry Brigham was looking for an assistant.
He mentioned me to Jerry, who asked that I give him a call.

Jerry (not his real name, as he might still be alive and I wouldn't want
to embarrass him) was a highly respected stage manager, currently on a
long-running hit. *Sea Change* (as we'll call it) would begin a two-city tryout after Labor Day and open that fall. A five-character play from a top
writer and top producer with the likelihood of a strong advance sale, it had
all the earmarks of an assured success. What a wonderful place to start!

I called Jerry, who told me the dates and explained that I'd have to
understudy one of the roles. He would leave a script for me that night
at the stage door of the theatre where his current show was still playing;
I should come by between shows on the following Wednesday to read
for him.

I was already packing my bags for the Wilmington tryout, figura-
tively, before picking up the script. When I read it I was taken aback,
and not only because it wasn't very good. The part that I needed to
understudy was a *major* role. Most small-cast plays try to get away with
two or three understudies; the age ranges here were so disparate, though,
that they would need four understudies. By using the ASM as the fourth

understudy, the producer could save a full salary. I dutifully studied the pages Jerry asked me to prepare. And my, it was a *strange* play.

The Audition

Wednesday, I arrived at the theatre as directed at 5:30. "Jerry's in dressing room six, two flights, taking a nap," said the stage doorman. "He said you should wake him." I went up to dressing room six; the door was closed, so I knocked. I knocked again. Not wanting to barge in but not about to miss this opportunity, I opened the door.

The lights were out, although there was enough late-afternoon daylight creeping in from around the air conditioner that I could see clearly. What I saw was Jerry Brigham—whom I had never met—asleep on a flat mattress in the middle of the room, wearing almost nothing. Beside him was a hand towel, and a bottle of what looked to be Johnson & Johnson's baby oil.

I was an innocent lad at the time, but knew enough to stay out of the dressing room. I called to him, from the doorway.

"Oh, I fell asleep, come on in," he said.

I said, "That's okay. Take your time." I kept the door open but moved down the hall, out of sight. He soon emerged (dressed), as nice as can be.

"Mitch says you're just finishing at NYU," he said as we headed downstairs. He took me out on the stage—one of Broadway's most revered houses, steeped in fifty years of Broadway history—and said, "Let's see what you can do." He stepped off the apron and sat on the arm of a seat on the aisle, starting to feed me the lines. I proceeded to act the scene, lit by the ghost light on the set of a Broadway hit.

Now let me say, I am not an actor. The same can be said for many assistant stage managers; this was for an emergency cover, and the likelihood of an emergency was not great. In those days, circa 1973, the work ethic was such that actors rarely missed a performance unless they were deathly ill—unlike today, when days off are actually written into the Actors' Equity contract. I can get by; and if I happened to be suited for the role, I suppose I'd have been adequate.

But in this case, I was woefully *not* suited for the role. The character was a psychotic basket case, with an Italian accent. My emergency performance in this opus—against two Tony Award–winning stars, as it happened—would have been unfathomably indecipherable. ("What is he saying? What is he doing??") Imagine Nathan Lane playing the young boy in *Equus*. He'd no doubt give a performance, and it would be memorable; but what would come across might not be just what the author had in mind. And I'm no Nathan Lane.

My reading was clearly unsuccessful, so much so that I suggested to Jerry what was evident; while I could cover a small role, this was far beyond me. He thanked me for coming in, and that was the end of that. I'm left wondering though; what if I had passed the first part of the audition, up in the dressing room? Not that I had any interest in trying; but if I had, how could Jerry *possibly* have given me the job? Surely, the director would have taken one look and (rightfully) insisted on replacing me. Although the director in question, given his reputation, would likely have first wanted to audition me himself.

Let it be said that Jerry was as nice as can be. Years later, he worked for me: a true gentleman of the theatre and a genuine pleasure to have around. When he came in to sign his contract, I can't imagine that he remembered my audition, or recalled our meeting. And I was certainly not going to remind him.

As I was writing this passage, I mentioned the anecdote to a colleague who had entered the business around the same time. He surprised me by identifying Jerry Brigham and the play despite the cloaked names. When he noticed my astonishment, he explained that he had gone to Wilmington for the tryout of *Sea Change*—and slept with Jerry.

"You have to understand," he explained. "In those days, if you were young and gay and finally away from home, that's what we did."

CHAPTER FOURTEEN

Fried Chicken and Shoe Polish

CROSSING THE TAPPAN ZEE

MITCH CALLED IN MAY WITH ANOTHER SUGGESTION. HE WAS UP AT Arthur Cantor's office, starting work on *The Day After the Fair*, a British import based on a story by Thomas Hardy. Cantor, who had coproduced *Vivat* with Merrick, had originated this production in London the prior October. It clearly wasn't strong enough for Broadway, but Arthur decided that movie star Deborah Kerr would sell tickets on the road.

"Arthur and Bob Fishko have taken over the Tappan Zee Playhouse and are doing a season there. They need an assistant. Do you want to call them?"

Cantor, it turned out, had nothing to do with the operation; I never saw him at the theatre that summer. The season was being produced by Fishko (a manager) and John Prescott (a press agent). Fishko had been general manager of *Promenade, All!*, for which I sold candy at the Alvin, although I didn't recall meeting him. Prescott hired me to handle the press for Tappan Zee, under his supervision, and otherwise assist them both.

I had never done press work, but John instantly sent me off to write a press release and there I was. Prescott was the friendly one, so I dealt mostly with him; Fishko was a quieter sort, with whom I never quite connected. The two were longtime friends and business associates from Florida.

The Tappan Zee Playhouse was a historic theatre on South Broadway in Nyack, New York, about an hour north of Manhattan. The Dutch explorer Henry Hudson, heading up the river that now bears his name, found a place where the river widened into a sea. This was the neighborhood of the Tappan Indians, so it became known as the Tappan Zee (Tappan Sea). Since 1955, the area has been best known for the Tappan Zee Bridge, a three-mile cantilever bridge from Tarrytown (on the east of the Hudson) to Nyack (on the west). The outmoded original bridge, which would periodically need to close in stormy weather due to waves crashing across the span, was replaced in 2017.

The Playhouse—built in 1911, converted from an old stable—had seen better days. By 1970, with competition from films and television readily available, many summer stock houses had gone out of business unless they had a special niche or a supportive local audience of summer residents. Cantor and Fishko tried to revive the Playhouse, but to no avail; after a season or two, they let it go and it languished until being demolished.

As was typical of summer stock theatres at the time, our season was built on one-week engagements from late June through Labor Day. Unlike in former days when the theatre would have self-produced some of the shows, these were all touring packages. Each theatre on the circuit—Westport and Candlewood in Connecticut, Falmouth in New Hampshire, the Pocono Playhouse in Pennsylvania—paid the operating costs for their week plus an overhead fee. The fee, multiplied by ten bookings, covered the startup costs and included a guaranteed profit for the producers. At least, that was the theory.

Our season was a hodgepodge of mid-level attractions, and cheap; I recall they paid the stars $1,000 and nothing much to anyone else. While some stock theatres aspired to classy entertainment, at Tappan Zee they just wanted to eke out enough ticket sales to cover costs.

SHOWCARD

Heading the 1973 list was Broadway's newest musical, *Follies*. But *Follies*—as previously mentioned—was pretty much a bust. After a disappointing run, Hal Prince took his production—with the original cast—to Los Angeles as the opening attraction at the Shubert Theatre. The show quickly closed there, and that was that.

With no interest from bookers for a full-scale national tour, the rights were immediately released to bargain basement promoters, in this case the aforementioned Ken Gaston of *A Place for Polly*. He put together a dirt-cheap tour, the cast headed by Robert Alda and Vivian Blaine—the original stars of *Guys and Dolls* in 1950 but more lately altogether underemployed. Jane Kean and Don Liberto—I can hear you saying, who?—played Sally and Buddy. Lillian Roth, a true former star who had a brief comeback with *70, Girls, 70*, was Hattie, the "Broadway Baby"; also on hand were half-forgotten names of the 1950s like Mary Small and Lynn Bari, and even "the Incomparable Hildegarde" as Solange. The producers provided a small band, and I expect gave the aging actors only ten days of rehearsal—and it showed. This production made the acclaimed and influential *Follies* look flimsy and underwritten.

Far more intriguing, on paper anyway, was a four-person revue called *The Gershwin Years*. Broadway's favorite musical comedy heroine, Barbara Cook! Cabaret star Julie Wilson! Two-time Tony winner Helen Gallagher! Three swell dames, plus Harold Lang of *Kiss Me, Kate* and *Pal Joey*. This quartet in an evening of Gershwin, how could it be anything but exciting? But it wasn't. The four of them—including the washed-up Cook, two years after her final musical comedy appearance and a year before the beginning of her phoenix-like rebirth as a cabaret singer—sat on bar stools like overstuffed pigeons, waiting their turn.

How about *A Song for Cyrano*? There were not one but two musical versions of *Cyrano de Bergerac* on the boards that summer. Christopher Plummer had just opened at the Palace in *Cyrano*, winning a Best Actor Tony Award in the process. Meanwhile, José Ferrer—America's most famous Cyrano, having won a 1947 Tony and a 1950 Oscar for the role—decided that he, too, would star in a musical adaptation. He got songwriters Robert Wright and George "Chet" Forrest, of *Kismet*, to write the score. The book duties were assigned to one J. Vincent Smith, AKA José Vincente Ferrer. *A Song for Cyrano* played the 1973 stock circuit, with Tappan Zee the fifth stop, and fittingly disappeared.

Most of the other offerings were even more negligible. *A Shot in the Dark*, starring Patty Duke and John Astin? Patty—who had mesmerized audiences as Helen Keller in the stage and screen versions of *The Miracle*

Worker and starred for three seasons in her popular sitcom, *The Patty Duke Show*—was washed up and something of a joke, her career all but destroyed by her notably awful performance in the 1967 film *Valley of the Dolls*. She discovered a decade later, and publicly revealed, that she had long been suffering from manic depression.

In 1970, in something of a daze, she had a very public affair with Desi Arnaz Jr.—she was twenty-three, he was seventeen—which was terminated due to vociferous opposition from Desi's mother, Lucille Ball. She also had an affair with the thirty-nine-year-old John Astin, star of the television series *The Addams Family*. She *also* married a rock promoter, for thirteen days. All of this, mind you, within a one-year stretch. So when she gave birth in 1971, she was reportedly unsure which of the three was the father.

Duke married Astin in the summer of 1972, had a second son in May 1973, and turned up that July in Nyack with the two-year-old (now an actor in his own right, under the name Sean Astin) and infant in tow. She played the Julie Harris role in *A Shot in the Dark*, opposite her husband and billed as Patty Duke Astin.

This was not a distinguished theatrical event, by a long shot; rather, it was a chance for local folk to see just what had become of little Anna Marie Duke from Elmhurst. The fact that she was on her feet, even, was a victory. The most memorable moment came offstage: sitting stuck in a limo with the Astins and the two boys for seventy-five minutes on the Major Deegan Highway while transporting them from Nyack to Manhattan for an interview on the WNEW-TV talk show *Midday Live*. Sean slept, the baby cried, Patty and John stared glazed-eyed out opposite windows at the bumper-to-bumper traffic.

FRIED CHICKEN AND SHOE POLISH

And then there was Uncle Miltie.

Like Duke, Milton Berle was a child star who transitioned into film. He moved on to the small screen just as the popularity of television exploded in 1948, instantly becoming a household name. "Mr. Television," they called him. His show, *The Texaco Star Theatre*, was so popular that it achieved as much as an 80 percent share of the nationwide audience; it is said that movie theatres would schedule their showings around Berle's Tuesday night time slot. In 1951, NBC—concerned about losing their first and biggest television star—signed him to a thirty-year contract at a million dollars a year, which needless to say was enormous at the time. As it turned out, Berle's reign was over by 1956, supplanted by younger funnymen Sid Caesar, Jackie Gleason, and Phil Silvers. The NBC stipend kept rolling in, though, while Berle continued working whenever he was asked. By 1973, he was a sad old man: over the hill at sixty-five, irrelevant, and as washed up as Patty Duke.

Norman, Is That You? was a crass comedy that briefly stopped at the Lyceum in 1970. Lou Jacobi played a middle-class dry cleaner from the Midwest who visits his son, Norman, in New York, only to find Norman living with a *boy*friend. This was a novel situation for the stage at that time, written so crassly by a pair of television writers that it crumpled up and closed after twelve performances. But it was a Broadway comedy, the sort of thing that schlock summer stock operators could cast with a star and find enough bookings to pay their costs. So here was the great Milton Berle, relegated to playing tripe—and he knew how subpar it was—for a thousand bucks a week, and altogether miserable about it. Not for the money, as the NBC deal was a bust for the network but a bonanza for him; what he needed, and couldn't breathe without, was the roar of the audience—even a small, summer stock audience.

My first glimpse of Berle came while he was dressing for the opening performance on Monday night. He traveled with an old retainer who served as assistant, valet, dresser, and confidante/cheerleader. Milton was sitting before the dressing room mirror in a worn terrycloth robe. "Hiya, kid," he said wearily. The dresser was applying black shoe polish to Milton's hair; yes, Johnson's shoe polish in the hair, to make him look anything but ancient.

Thursday night I stopped by the dressing room to give him his cash per diem. "Whatchya doing, kid?" Milton asked. "Kid" not only because I was forty-five years younger, but because he surely had no idea who I was. "Did'ya eat dinner? Come after the show." Now, Berle was—to me—a relic, a dinosaur. His period of fame ended when I was about three; all that I had ever seen from him were sad, desperate, sometimes nasty

Milton Berle in happier times (1943), sans shoe polish.
WIKIMEDIA COMMMONS

performances. But he was still Milton Berle; to the middle-aged audiences coming to see him in *Norman, Is That You?* on the summer stock circuit, he was still Uncle Miltie, Mr. Television.

I followed his limo back to his motel, across the river in Tarrytown. It was a Howard Johnson's, with an ice cream shop in the front and rooms out back, parking by the door. I followed Berle—already puffing away on a cigar—and the assistant into the motel room. Waiting inside was a bucket of fried chicken from a pre–Kentucky Fried Chicken chain called Chicken Delight ("don't cook tonight," went the jingle, "call Chicken Delight"), along with mashed potatoes, corn on the cob, and cups of pink lemonade.

Over greasy chicken, Milton expounded on comedy. It turned out that he was writing an autobiography—which eventually came out in 1975—and wanted to try a chapter on me. I listened politely, although his pontificating didn't amount to much; Milton's comedy was something to be experienced, not explained. At one point, the phone rang and he went into the other room for a long, pleading call with his wife out in California. He returned deflated; I soon departed. But the image of the one-time king, an old man with a cigar and shoe-polish hair, stuck in the middle of nowhere in search of an audience—any audience—remains with me.

DRIVING MISS SADA

The high point of the summer arrived when Sada Thompson came to town.

Sada was one of those character actors who spend their careers years in anonymity, toiling away at regional theatres with little chance of fame. Along the way, though, she was cast in an unlikely off-Broadway play with the unwieldy title *The Effect of Gamma Rays on Man-in-the-Moon Marigolds*. This family drama followed in the footsteps of Tennessee Williams's *The Glass Menagerie*, but did it so well that it became a Pulitzer Prize–winning hit in its own right. Paul Zindel's play—and Sada's performance as a troubled mother very much in the mold of the *Menagerie*'s Amanda Wingfeld—garnered immediate acclaim when it opened in 1970, even though it was playing in a hole in the wall on Mercer Street—so much a hole in the wall, in the basement of the derelict Broadway-Mercer Hotel (which had opened in 1870 as the Grand Central Hotel, at the time the finest and largest hotel in the United States), that the play was forced to move when the hotel collapsed in August 1972. By that point *Marigolds* had run for more than two years, with Sada having been supplanted by a parade of replacements.

I saw *Marigolds* early in the run—just before I started at NYU—and Thompson was astonishing; not unlike Maureen Stapleton, but without the overly grand theatricality, which had by that point overtaken Maureen. (Stapleton, incidentally, starred in Zindel's 1972 comedy, *The Secret Affairs of Mildred Wild*, a three-week flop that was altogether fanciful and unjustly neglected. While it might sound misguided to praise the scenery all these years later, the timeworn Greenwich Village candy store—with what appeared to be actual cobwebs strung along the top shelves—remains vibrant and made me an instant fan of designer Santo Loquasto.)

Sada left *Marigolds* to star in a comedy called *Twigs*; actually, four one-act comedies in which she played three sisters and—in the final piece—their mother. This was a piece with pedigree, coming from author George Furth (of *Company*) and director Michael Bennett (of *Company*). With a song, even, contributed by Stephen Sondheim.

In fact, there were direct vestigial ties to *Company*. Furth had written an evening of eleven short plays about marriage, tied together as a vehicle for the revered Kim Stanley. This had been announced, as a three-character comedy encompassing seven of the plays, for a March 1969 opening. When the producers couldn't raise the capitalization for *A Husband, A Wife and a Friend* (as the play was called), Furth's friend Sondheim sent the plays to Hal Prince. Excited by the episodic notion of Furth's piece, Prince conceived the musical and incorporated three of the one-acts into *Company*. Following the musical's success, Furth built *Twigs* on four of the remaining one-acts.

The first three pieces (branches?) of *Twigs* were decidedly funny, but the fourth—with Sada as the ferociously funny mother of the women she played in the other plays—was outlandishly hysterical, one of the wildest performances I've ever seen.

Twigs opened at the Broadhurst in the fall of 1971, moving to the Plymouth in January to make way for *Vivat! Vivat Regina!* Sada won the Tony for Best Actress the following spring, her competition including Colleen Dewhurst, Rosemary Harris, and *Vivat*'s Eileen Atkins. (Claire Bloom was not nominated.) Sada, having spent twenty years as a sturdily dependable character actress, was the correct choice and a highly popular one.

Following her Tony, Sada and fellow 1972 Tony winner Vincent Gardenia (of Neil Simon's *The Prisoner of Second Avenue*) were signed to play recurring roles as Archie Bunker's neighbors on *All in the Family*. While taping her first episode, the third season opener, Sada disagreed with director Norman Lear so severely about the interpretation that they scrapped the footage and replaced her with Betty Garrett. Sada was supremely pleasant and well-mannered, but strong as a rock when it came to integrity. This left her suddenly and unexpectedly available, hence a summer stock tour of *Twigs*. Thompson eventually did get a series of her own—*Family*—which earned her a Best Actress Emmy to go with her Tony.

As the Tappan Zee week of *Twigs* approached, Prescott told me that Sada didn't wish to stay in a hotel; she wanted to commute from her apartment in Forest Hills, Queens, which was about an hour from Nyack. She would make her way to the theatre on her own, but could I drive her home every night after the performance? Of course I could.

Eight viewings of Sada's performance in *Twigs* made my summer of dubious stock worthwhile, but it was the car rides—Driving Miss Sada?—that were most magical. Sada was warm, lovely, and humane. My favorite author at the time was Booth Tarkington, a now-forgotten Hoosier novelist/playwright who won two of the first four Pulitzers for Fiction (for *The Magnificent Ambersons* and *Alice Adams*). During our very first drive, I discovered that Sada was a Tarkington enthusiast as well. When we realized that we also shared a fondness for George Barr McCutcheon, a far less-highbrow Graustarkian novelist also from Indiana, our friendship was sealed. Our invigorating late-night talks were clearly the highlight of my time at Tappan Zee. We would have a happy reunion in 1981 when I set up a tour of *On Golden Pond* starring Sada and James Whitmore.

SAFECRACKER

The most memorable afternoon of the long hot summer occurred in early August. I spent half my time in Nyack and the rest at the Fishko-Prescott office on Broadway. Literally on Broadway, one flight up from the box office of the Broadway Theatre. This was a highly theatrical space, just over the marquee, with seven large windows looking out on a sweeping view of Broadway. (The office space disappeared when a skyscraper was built above the house sometime around 1990.)

The staircase—hidden to the side of the theatre lobby—took you up to one big room split in two. Fishko and Prescott had one side, the other was occupied by Earl Wilson, the gossip columnist for the *New York Post*. We never saw Earl there; he was a night owl, working the streets and headquartering at Toots Shor's. The office was occupied by his long-suffering secretary, Julie, with constant drop-ins by ghostwriter/ photographer Tim Boxer.

On one of those steamy summer afternoons, I climbed up to the office. I was surprised to find the door locked; we always kept both the street entrance and the upstairs door unlocked, because there was an endless stream of press agents and messengers dropping off photos and releases in hope of getting mentions in Earl's column.

The Broadway Theatre (1970), with office windows above the marquee.
BILL MORRISON COLLECTION, THE SHUBERT ARCHIVE

I knocked. The door was opened—by a fellow with a gun. He took me in, tied my hands behind my back, and pushed me down onto the couch next to the similarly tied-up Julie. He had two compatriots. They slowly ransacked the place, searching for valuables.

Not five minutes later, another knock. They warned us not to stir, although there wasn't much noise we could make with packing tape covering our mouths. They brought in Prescott and tied him up as well.

Now, Julie—who presumably had seen everything over the years—was relatively calm. I, oddly, was altogether calm; I was unimpressed by these amateur burglars and felt like I was watching a bad movie. Even with the gun, the intruders seemed more desperate than threatening; most likely addicts looking for drug money. Prescott, though, was altogether panicky, so much so that I feared he might set off our visitors. There wasn't much of value to find.

As they were about to leave, they suddenly commanded us into Earl's office. Hidden behind faux-wood office paneling, they had found an old floor safe. When I say old, I mean old; dirty, rusted, and with what looked like pneumatic tubes built in. This had presumably been installed for the theatre manager when the Broadway first opened, in 1924, as the Colony (a prime movie house). When the Shuberts bought the building in 1939, the decrepit safe was presumably too expensive to remove.

It had clearly been untouched for years. But the brigands, eagerly discovering the safe, demanded that we open it. This was a theatre, wasn't it? There must be money.

We explained to them that this was a deserted safe, more than fifty years old. And we explained that the theatre (and the box office) had been empty since October, with no tickets to sell.

The brunt of the demand fell on Prescott, who despite being relatively young with curly blond hair and beard was clearly the responsible party. He practically passed out. We finally convinced them that we didn't have the safe combination, and they decided to hightail it with a few typewriters, a camera, and a couple hundred dollars from our collective pockets.

Julie worked her hands free and called the police, who finally arrived and said, in effect: this was New York, what did we expect?

We did keep the doors locked thereafter, though.

With the Tappan Zee season ending, I started looking for my first "real" job. I stopped by Arthur Cantor's office in the Sardi Building, where Mitch was getting ready to finally leave town with *The Day After the Fair*. I then went two doors down to the St. James and up to the Merrick office, visiting Mark and Jay and reinforming Schlissel that I was out of college and ready to work for real. Two days later, I picked up the phone to find Sylvia Schwartz, from the Merrick switchboard.

"Jack says call Helen Richards," Sylvia said. "She's looking for someone."

CHAPTER FIFTEEN

Up on Fifty-Seventh Street

CHERRY BLOSSOM

I HAD NEVER HEARD OF HELEN RICHARDS.

"General manager of *Purlie*. She has two musicals this fall. Call her."
Sylvia gave me the number; I called within minutes and went in the next
day. Not in the theatre district but across from the Russian Tea Room at
157 West Fifty-Seventh Street, a building that was torn down thirty-five
years later. (The plot of land now holds the One57 apartment building,
already memorable for the construction crane on the roof that collapsed
during Hurricane Sandy, dangling over the street and forcing the evacu-
ation of the area.)

This was a converted apartment building, Helen's office a former
one-bedroom with kitchen and bathtub removed. I was led down the
hallway to what had been the bedroom in the back, holding a non-
office-like white table and a large white wicker chaise. Sitting behind
the table—on a chair with an oversized circular white wicker backrest, in
the shape of peacock feathers—was a slight and petite blonde woman of
indeterminate years, puffing away while on the phone. She was fifty-six
at the time, but you couldn't quite tell.

Helen offered her small hand and introduced herself, in a southern
accent. She was from Texas—Wichita Falls, to be precise—and spoke
with a drawl that ranged from deep to deeper to nonexistent, depending
on the situation and the audience. Helen Stern Richards was the name
she used, although at times she would expand it to incorporate the several

married names accumulated over the years. She referred to herself as the Jewish Scarlett O'Hara (a nickname that fit) and sometimes as Cherry Blossom (which also, oddly enough, fit). Her conversation was marked by a hacking cough that shook her frail body like a freight train rumbling past, and the click-click-click of a round, gold-plated cigarette lighter. She also had an ever-present ashtray with a plated-gold cog in the shape of a thimble, which she was convinced obliterated the harsh odor of her never-ending chain of cigarettes. It didn't.

She had married at twenty-one or so, to get away from Wichita Falls and the Depression, and by 1939 was living in Oklahoma City, Oklahoma. Her first husband, Bert Stern (not the photographer), operated the Municipal Auditorium there, back in a day when stage stars like Katharine Cornell and the Lunts would bring their Broadway shows to places like Oklahoma City. Thus, Helen was hosting the show folk who passed through. By 1945 she had moved to New York—and away from her husband—and took a job as "advance man" for operetta-composer Sigmund Romberg (of *The Student Prince* and *The Desert Song*). Romberg and his orchestra would annually embark on a route of seventy-five or so one-night stands around the country. The advance man—it was unheard of to have an advance *woman*, which made Helen instantly memorable on the road—would travel the itinerary a couple of weeks ahead, arranging local housing and making sure that the local promoter had everything set up properly when Siggy and his musicians came to town.

In 1948 she moved to Manhattan and married an ex-serviceman named Dick Richards, whom she said looked good in uniform but "was not a nice man." She had a child in 1949; Little Jeffrey she called him, although he was at the moment working in the next room and four years older than I. Helen's second husband had a volatile temper; when he became angry at the baby ("holding a loud transistor radio up to his ear," Helen reported), she threw him out. The husband, not the baby.

LEARNING THE ROPES

Stranded—a thirty-year-old two-time divorcee with a toddler—she left Jeffrey in New York with her mother and went back on the road as a press agent, working for a touring producer named Paul Gregory. *Don Juan in*

Hell—four classy actors in evening dress on stools, with no sets or props, giving a rendition of the third act of George Bernard Shaw's overlong *Man and Superman*—was an enormous hit, due mostly to the presence of movie stars Charles Laughton (who also directed), Charles Boyer, Cedric Hardwicke, and Agnes Moorehead. The tour was so successful that a one-night appearance at Carnegie Hall in the fall of 1951 resulted in two Broadway engagements the following year. Next came Stephen Vincent Benét's *John Brown's Body*, which visited Broadway in 1953. This one had Laughton directing Judith Anderson, Raymond Massey, and Tyrone Power.

At that point, Helen decided she needed to stay in New York with Jeffrey. She took a job in the press office of one Reuben Rabinovitch, whose new clients were the fledgling producing team of Robert E. Griffith and Harold S. Prince. Thus, Helen worked as press agent on *The Pajama Game, Damn Yankees, New Girl in Town,* and *West Side Story.* (Among the artwork on Helen's office wall was the 1958 play, *A Swim in the Sea,* Griffith & Prince's fifth venture following the four above-named hits—a two-week flop at the Walnut Street in Philadelphia.) She also banded investors together to take small positions in these—as well as subsequent—Prince productions, including *A Funny Thing Happened on the Way to the Forum* and *Fiddler on the Roof.* During my years with Helen, she routinely received profit distributions from these shows, meticulously worked up a spreadsheet, and hand-wrote checks to her numerous contributing angels.

In 1960, Richards turned company manager as a replacement on Griffith & Prince's *Fiorello!*; press agents and company managers are related via union, the Association of Theatrical Press Agents and Managers, or ATPAM. While there were had been a handful of female press agents going back to the 1930s, Helen was—as far as I can tell—the first woman company manager on Broadway and remained the only one for most of the decade. She was a replacement company manager on Lorraine Hansberry's *A Raisin in the Sun,* which she followed with Ossie Davis's 1961 satirical comedy, *Purlie Victorious*; both were produced by a man named Philip Rose. Following the latter, she was a replacement manager on Neil Simon's first comedy, *Come Blow Your Horn.* She then got a long-running hit, the 1962 George Abbott farce *Never Too Late*—about a middle-aged husband (Paul Ford) and wife (Maureen O'Sullivan) who discover to the horror of their grown children that they are expecting a child. This was a flimsy comedy, for sure, but unaccountably topped one thousand performances. Helen then moved over to general manager Eddie Knill, working on a string of Neil Simon plays including *Barefoot in the Park, The Star-Spangled Girl,* and *The Odd Couple.*

Helen's general manager resumé, when I walked in the door just after Labor Day of 1973, was limited to the previously mentioned *Three Men on a Horse* revival (where I annoyed George Abbott) and that same *Purlie* that opens this chronicle. She also, although I discovered it only when I was writing these pages, happened to be general manager of *A Place for Polly.* We can't say that Helen was the very first female general manager on Broadway; I can find a couple who had minor credits on limited runs. But she was apparently the first to be hired to handle a mainstream commercial production, on her own, from inception.

The long, albeit financially unsuccessful run of *Purlie* was enough to land Helen jobs on two "Black" musicals for the fall of 1973, which was why I was there. Additionally, she had another two musicals for later in the season under the aegis of *Purlie* producer Rose, although as it turned out both would be delayed. While the fall shows were not Phil's, he was closely linked to the first.

WAITRESS

Phil, whose office was two floors above us, was a distinctive-looking character. Five-foot-five with receding hair, and so thickly bespectacled that a caricature might bare a resemblance to Mister Magoo, Phil was like a squat sparkplug firing off energy. His character was set as a poor, Depression-era teenager from Delancey Street on the Lower East Side. Just out of high school, he got a job in Washington as a bill collector for a downtown department store catering to the poor. Sent to collect unpaid money and threaten to repossess purchases, he quickly found himself befriending and championing the families his employer was victimizing. By the late 1940s, he was back in New York, working as a singer with a sideline as a salesman for a manufacturer of "race" records.

During the summer of 1949, Phil worked as an entertainer at a camp for adults and families in upstate New York; unlike better-known spots such as Green Mansions or Tamiment, Camp Unity allowed—and positively encouraged—integrated families and was known for its intellectual/philosophical/socialistic bent. At the dining hall, he was served by a nineteen-year-old waitress—a Black teenager from Chicago—who turned out to have similarly progressive views of civil rights. They became quick friends, remaining so as they both moved back to New York. Phil became distributor for a new label featuring Black artists—Atlantic Records—and by 1954 was producing recordings for his own company.

While Phil had started his professional career singing Gilbert & Sullivan operettas, he had no experience in or affinity for the theatre. Working in the music industry, complimentary tickets were frequently available. Phil would invite the ex-waitress, who turned out to be remarkably well-rounded; together they would dissect the plays and she would instruct him on Shakespeare, Williams, Miller, and more. Phil also began to move in Black theatrical circles, befriending the distinguished actor William Marshall (of *The Green Pastures*). Marshall introduced the enthusiastic young white man to many of his colleagues, including two significant ones: The great and celebrated Paul Robeson, and a young actor looking for a break named Sidney Poitier. Phil and Sidney shared the same likes, dislikes, and civil rights views; they and their families would remain close for life.

Having met the acclaimed poet and activist Langston Hughes through Marshall, Phil decided in 1955 to produce a recording of poetry by Hughes and other writers including Paul Laurence Dunbar and James Weldon Johnson. The selling point was that the poems would be read by Sidney—who had just had his film breakthrough, with *The Blackboard Jungle*—and Phil's wife, actress Doris Belack. *Poetry of the Negro* it was called, the initial recording from Phil's new label Glory Records. The former waitress, now twenty-five, helped select the poems and wrote especially cogent liner notes. The pair continued attending theatre together. After one community-theatre play about Black people, she said: "If I were going to write a play about a Black family, I could do better than that." Phil said, "Why don't you try?"

Several months later, she invited Phil and Doris to her flat on Bleecker Street and read several scenes from her play-in-progress. Phil spent a sleepless night and finally woke the playwright at 6:30 in the morning to tell her that he was going to produce her play on Broadway. Never mind that Phil had never produced a play, let alone on Broadway. Never mind that there had never been a play by a Black woman on Broadway.

At that point, in 1955, there had been hardly any Broadway plays by Black men, either. *Take a Giant Step*, by Louis Peterson, had a favorable reception in 1953. The only others I can discover before that—and we're not talking about musicals or revues—were Langston Hughes's *Mulatto* in 1935; Richard Wright's *Native Son* in 1941, which was coauthored by white Pulitzer-winner Paul Green and directed by Orson Welles; and Theodore Ward's *Our Lan'* in 1947. When Phil told his friend Sidney that he was producing a play, the latter helpfully connected him with his entertainment lawyer. Phil did not tell Sidney, or the lawyer, that he had already determined that Sidney would play the leading role.

The odds, thus, were stacked against Phil and his new play. Who would invest in a Broadway play about a Black family, by a Black woman? Who would invest in an admittedly controversial play from a novice producer? Who would even want to see it? And what theatre owner would book this unlikely-sounding project into a Broadway house? But Phil and his playwright, Lorraine Hansberry, were blissfully ignorant of the realities. Hansberry later relayed that she figured, at the time, that maybe the play would get done in some church basement somewhere.

The pair fought through several years of discouragement; the presence in the cast of Poitier, who by the time the play was produced in 1959 was a bona fide movie star, helped Phil and coproducer David J. Cogan, raise the money; and the play itself was so well received in its pre-Broadway tryout that the Shuberts—who had ignored Rose until seeing the Philadelphia reviews—quickly made the Barrymore available.

The success of *A Raisin in the Sun*, though, turned out to be Phil's downfall. Everyone had repeatedly told him that he would never get the show on. Thereafter, he produced another fourteen plays and musicals. One play, *The Owl and the Pussycat*, was a considerable hit; one musical—the one that I would be working on—turned a negligibly small profit;

Striking artwork for a groundbreaking classic, Lorraine Hansberry's *A Raisin in the Sun* (1959).
MAX A. WOODWARD COLLECTION, MUSIC DIVISION, LIBRARY OF CONGRESS

and all the rest failed. "I'm sure it's good, Phil, really, but it ain't gonna work," he was told again and again by friends and colleagues. He just smiled and nodded; that's what everybody had told him about *A Raisin in the Sun*, wasn't it?

HUSBAND
And now there was a musical version of *A Raisin in the Sun* on the way to Broadway. Phil wasn't officially involved, but he and his original investors had a contractual share of the royalties. (According to the then-standard formula, the Raisin in the Sun company received 40 percent of the 2 percent royalty received by Lorraine's estate from the upcoming musical.) Thus, Phil had a financial reason to aid and support the project, as well as a personal reason: he knew *A Raisin in the Sun* better than anyone alive, having guided Lorraine (who died in 1965) through the writing, formation, and creation of the play. What's more, he sincerely cared about

the integrity of the work. Countering this, though, was his long-standing anathema to the producer of the musical *Raisin*: Robert Nemiroff.

Nemiroff was a small-time book editor and full-time protester when he met Hansberry on a picket line at NYU in Greenwich Village. They married in 1953. While Lorraine worked as a reporter for the left-wing magazine *Freedom* (founded by Robeson) and as a waitress, Nemiroff—who called himself a writer, with little to show for it—was mostly unemployed. In 1955, when Hansberry was working with Phil on the *Poetry of the Negro* recording, she pleaded with him to give Bobby some kind of job at his new recording company. Rose did so, out of friendship for Lorraine. Nemiroff was not much of an employee. Phil's partner at the time explained that Bob would badmouth Rose when he wasn't around; the partner eventually left the business after a fight with Nemiroff. Bob remained in the office for about five years, with little to show for it.

His one accomplishment during this time—and seemingly his only concrete credit ever, apart from the Hansberry connection—came in 1956. Phil had several folk singing groups under contract. One day, Nemiroff and Burt d'Lugoff—a mutual friend of Bob and Phil, whose brother Art ran the Greenwich Village jazz-and-comedy haunt, the Village Gate—walked in with a song they'd written. Or rewritten; it was a new lyric for "Pay Me My Money Down," a stevedore song from the Sea Islands along the coast of South Carolina. Phil recorded it with Vince Martin and a folk trio called the Tarriers. "Cindy, Oh Cindy"—published under the pseudonyms Robert Barron (as in Robert Barron Nemiroff) and Burt Long (d'Lugoff)—was a top ten hit, offering Nemiroff and Hansberry their first taste of solvency.

One of these "Tarriers" was a twenty-year-old guitarist named Alan Arkin. The group had another hit two months later, this one written by Arkin and his partners based on a Jamaican folk song. "The Banana Boat Song" they called it, although it's better known for its opening cry ("Day-o!") and the repeated plaint "daylight come and I wanna go home." "Cindy, Oh Cindy" and "The Banana Boat Song" were Phil's biggest hits as a record producer.

Bob was very much around during the creation of *A Raisin in the Sun*, even though at some point along the way he and Lorraine separated. The marriage was surely complicated, not only racially but otherwise; Hansberry's archives include self-revelatory letters she wrote in 1957 for publication in the just-established lesbian magazine *The Ladder*, published under the initials "L. H. N." Lorraine and Bob quietly divorced, although this remained a secret until after her death.

Following the success of *A Raisin in the Sun*, Nemiroff—with a now rich, famous, and justly celebrated wife by his side, produced a musical comedy with d'Lugoff in 1961. *Kicks & Co.* it was called, a mostly Black musical written by jazz composer and activist Oscar Brown Jr. Mr. Kicks, a Satanesque character in this Faustian tale set on a segregated college campus, was played by Burgess Meredith. Phil, sensing disaster, chose not to participate.

Word from rehearsal was dire, with director Vinnette Carroll fired and replaced by the star. Nemiroff rewrote the book, adding himself a shared credit with Brown. As things further disintegrated, Bob prevailed on Hansberry to step in as director in lieu of Meredith. When Lorraine—who had never done any directing—called for advice, Phil was firmly against the idea, suggesting that Bob was using her fame to try to salvage his surefire flop. Hansberry nevertheless was impelled to take over; perhaps she felt guilty about the state of their non-marriage, and Bob—from my experience with him—was certainly a great, wheedling manipulator. *Kicks & Co.* was savaged upon its opening in Chicago: "A $400,000 fiasco," said *Variety*, "lacking in interest, involvement, purpose, and point." The show died there, after four performances.

The strange relationship between Hansberry and her husband—and her ongoing struggle with the ovarian cancer she developed in 1963—resulted in Lorraine's decision that Bob should supplant Phil as producer of her second Broadway play, *The Sign in Sidney Brustein's Window*. As her health seriously disintegrated, Bob "helped" with the writing, but the play came across as underdeveloped and unfinished. *Sidney Brustein* received mixed-to-poor reviews when it opened at the Longacre in October 1964 and struggled on for 101 performances. On January 12, 1965, a week before the closing, Hansberry died at the age of thirty-four.

Nemiroff was named executor of her estate and spent the rest of his life overseeing her work. And living off it, as well. The most constructive of his efforts was *To Be Young, Gifted and Black*, a 1969 off-Broadway revue that consisted of excerpts from Hansberry's writings as adapted by Nemiroff. This ran successfully for almost a year and helped permanently establish Hansberry's legacy. Next, Bob took an unfinished play of hers, *Les Blancs*, and completed it. It ran five weeks in 1970 at the Longacre—a hard-to-book "flop house" of last resort, at the time—and to me was all but unfathomable. Two years later, Bob rewrote *The Sign in Sidney Brustein's Window*; this one lasted a mere five performances, also at the Longacre. The revival's one Tony nomination went to Franny Sternhagen, which is why I was seated next to her at the 1972 Awards.

ADAPTATION

And then came *Raisin*. The musical had been in the works for almost a decade. Composer Judd Woldin was a member of the original 1961 class of budding musical theatre writers assembled by Lehman Engel for the BMI Workshop. As a class project, he and lyricist Robert Brittan started experimenting with *A Raisin in the Sun* in 1965. Without the rights to the material, naturally. Woldin was pit pianist for *Hello, Dolly!* and remained with the show for many years; his work on the 1967 Pearl Bailey/Cab Calloway version seems to have enhanced his affinity for the Hansberry play.

Nemiroff, being naturally obstructive, refused to let the valuable rights go to these unknown, first-time songwriters. Over time, he couldn't avoid hearing recommendations from people who had heard the score-in-progress. Bob finally agreed to the musicalization of *A Raisin in the Sun*, provided that he serve as producer and librettist. He had never done either on such a scale, unless you want to count *Kicks & Co.*, but Woldin and Brittan—having already expended years of creative effort on the project—were happy to agree to any conditions. A sense of urgency set in for Bob as income from *To Be Young, Gifted and Black* started to dry up in 1970, followed by the immediate failures of *Les Blancs* and the revival of *Sidney Brustein*. With no other Hansberry properties to commercialize, Nemiroff turned his full attention to the musical.

A key element in what was to become *Raisin* was the choice of Donald McKayle as director/choreographer. McKayle had attracted acclaim in the 1960s with his own modern ballet company; I had been duly impressed by *District Storyville*, which I saw only because it was performed as part of that ballet season at the ANTA. Donny had some minor Broadway credits: Sammy Davis's long-running failure *Golden Boy*, plus the quick failures *A Time for Singing* (about a mining disaster in Wales) and *I'm Solomon* (about King Solomon in old Jerusalem). Before that, it might be noted, he served as choreographer of the ignominious Chicago tryout of Nemiroff's *Kicks & Co.* But modern dance seemed a good fit for *Raisin*. As it turned out, McKayle was an almost perfect choice for the show. His selection, in itself, was notable: as far as I can tell, he was the first Black man to serve as director/choreographer of a Broadway musical. (Lloyd Richards, director of *A Raisin in the Sun*, had been hired to direct the 1965 musical *The Yearling*, although he was replaced during the tryout.)

At some point in the process, Biff became involved; immediately after the opening and closing of *Tricks* in January 1973, he had moved to the William Morris Agency as head of the theatrical department, and the Hansberry Estate was among his clients. I would guess that Biff helped arrange *Raisin*'s regional theatre tryout at Arena Stage that spring, following the same path as *Tricks*. Also from *Tricks*, and surely at the instigation of Biff, were the singers who sang those ineffective rock songs from the onstage platform. The trio took three of the four leading roles in *Raisin*: Joe Morton as Walter Lee Younger (the Sidney Poitier role), Ernestine Jackson as his wife, Ruth (the Ruby Dee role), and Shezwae Powell as his sister, Beneatha (the Diana Sands role). In the costarring role of the mother, Lena, was Virginia Capers, whose only Broadway appearances had been understudying featured roles in the Harold Arlen musicals *Jamaica* (1957) and *Saratoga* (1959). And yes, she had been the intended star of the unproduced *Sister Sadie*, with which I had been tangentially involved over the summer of 1970.

The several links between the new show and *Purlie* resulted in a sizable contingent moving from one to the other. The earlier musical's comic character lady, Helen Martin (as the cook Idella), took on the comic character lady role in *Raisin*, Mrs. Johnson; Ted Ross, Sherman Hemsley's understudy as Purlie's brother-in-law Gitlow, was cast as Bobo, one of the men who leads Walter Lee astray; and the chorus was peppered with people who did time in the Broadway or touring casts. Joyce Brown, the scene-stealing conductor of *Purlie*, was on hand initially but did not retain the job when *Raisin* moved to Broadway.

As Nemiroff started planning the musical, he turned to *Purlie* general manager Helen Richards. My guess is that he did so on Phil's strong recommendation, and because Helen likely agreed to provide budgets for free until the show got produced, if ever.

The two musicals were even further intertwined. Ossie Davis, husband of *A Raisin in the Sun* costar Ruby Dee, had replaced Sidney in the Broadway company. Determined to become a writer, he pounded away at a play in his dressing room. Phil read *Purlie Victorious* and agreed to produce it, with Davis and Dee in the title roles. A decade later, the success—or near-success—of the musical *Purlie* helped develop a new nonwhite Broadway audience that was key to the potential success of *Raisin*.

TRYOUT

Bob, meanwhile, coauthored the book of *Raisin* with Charlotte Zaltzberg, who was, not coincidentally, the sister-in-law of librettist Joseph Stein of *Fiddler on the Roof*. (Knowing Bob, he expected—and most probably received—unpaid input and counsel from Stein.) The show opened at Arena Stage in May 1973 to strong reviews, including an important nod from Clive Barnes in the *New York Times*. Clive, who started his career as a dance critic and remained proudly dance savvy, was a strong and immediate champion of Donny's work on the show. Bob quickly raised the money for Broadway, booked the 46th Street Theatre for an October opening, and moved ahead. The Broadway-bound version premiered at the Walnut Street Theatre in Philadelphia, where *A Raisin in the Sun* had played during its pre-Broadway tryout in 1959.

Raisin opened in Philadelphia on September 19, 1973, so I drove down to see that week's Saturday matinee. Mark and Kim came along; Merrick's play *The One-Night Stand* was folding that night at the Forrest. This Bruce Jay Friedman comedy, formerly titled *Turtlenecks*, starred Tony Curtis and had been a disaster altogether. Merrick battled with the author and the director, Jacques Levy, throughout the Detroit tryout.

Given that the show wasn't selling any tickets anyway, he decided to cancel the Plymouth Theatre opening and close after only two weeks in Philly. The day this was announced, he instructed Leo Herbert to go out to the house boards in front of the Forrest with a can of red paint and paint out the phrase "David Merrick presents."

We saw the final performance of the Tony Curtis play that night. The show—as mirthless as reported—was about a fellow who designed football half-time shows, forming marching band routines with three-foot-tall prop "musicians." Seeing that we were there following the positively final performance ever, Leo gave us each one of the musicians. The trumpeter remains, covered in house dust, next to *Carnival!*'s Horrible Henry on a ledge in my office.

Raisin at the Walnut Street was vibrantly exciting, with McKayle's opening dance prologue getting things off to a dynamic start. There was something about the show that didn't quite click and never would, although it took numerous viewings to figure out just what that was. Four weeks later, we started previews at the 46th Street Theatre, where I had so enjoyed *How to Succeed*—pulling on a loose tooth—nine years earlier.

Between Washington and Philadelphia, *Raisin* had undergone one major change. Shezwae Powell, a distinctive singer, was perhaps too distinctive for the role of Beneatha. There are moments where we see just how vibrant she can be—Hansberry acknowledged that the character was semi-autobiographical—but at other points she must be part of the group, and Shezwae was not one to fade into the background.

She was replaced by one of the girls in the chorus, who had made her debut as a dancer in *Purlie*. Deborah Allen, for me, was the finest element in *Raisin*. She was bright, young, and believable, with an intensity in her performance that I suppose was similar to that of Lorraine. Five years later, I went back to Philadelphia to see Debbie in what was intended to be her star-making role, as the title character in *Alice* (as in Wonderland). This was sure to be Broadway's next blockbuster musical; Mike Nichols produced *Alice* just after he did *Annie*. It was thoroughly devoid of interest, though, and died ignominiously at the Forrest. Allen went on to a major career as an actress and choreographer, but I forever see her in the guise of the idealistic and vibrant Beneatha Younger.

THREE IN ONE

We started New York previews of *Raisin* at the 46th Street Theatre on October 10. I had already spent several years working on Broadway, either as an unpaid assistant or a lowly and inconsequential concessionaire. Now, though, I was part of the show, with my name in the program and a spot on the payroll. I was no longer an occasional visitor backstage and in the dressing rooms; I was now there officially, doing my job as apprentice company manager. This gained me entry to a previously forbidden zone of the house: the box office. I had until then been on a nodding acquaintance with treasurers; at many theatres they would "buzz" concessionaires into the house. Now I could perch on the other side of the window and look out at the customers.

Given excellent word-of-mouth from Philadelphia, boosted by Clive's highly enthusiastic Arena Stage review in the *Times*, business started off at a strong pace. The reaction at the nine previews was pretty much dynamic. Dynamic, yes, but there was something lacking. We opened on the eighteenth to very good reviews, with a hitch; almost everybody praised the show, the staging, the performers, and the dancers. The score, though, was generally described as exciting but merely okay. Which was accurate. The *musical* sound of the show, and the overlay of modern dance, was exciting and vibrant and—for the Broadway musical—new. But the actual songs, despite a few high spots, mostly ranged from adequate to merely functional.

Raisin can be looked at as three shows in one. You had a Donny McKayle musical, with inventive staging built on pantomime (on the one hand) and much-welcomed modern dance (on the other). Yes, Broadway was accustomed to dance-heavy musicals from Robbins, Gower, Fosse, and even de Mille. Still in the wings were Michael Bennett, who was soon to step to the forefront; and Tommy Tune, then still dancing onstage. But McKayle gave us something else again. His predecessors regularly based their movement on the songs, while Donny seemed to infuse the entire evening (other than the book scenes and the traditional musical comedy sections) with a *pulse*. This was to be his only major Broadway achievement, though. His final director/choreographer work was an ignominious 1975 venture titled *Doctor Jazz*, which stumbled through five performances at the Winter Garden. He later conceived the long-running 1981 revue *Sophisticated Ladies* but was replaced as director during the tryout.

Raisin took place in a big-city ghetto—Chicago, circa 1956—with the street energy pretty much bubbling upstairs into the Younger family's rundown tenement apartment. Hansberry's original play was somewhat cut down to allow room for musical elements, but the text remained remarkably strong. The score, meanwhile, alternated between street music for McKayle and his dancers; a few heavy dramatic songs, with phrases often lifted from the script; and damaging musical comedy filler.

The overall result was that while *Raisin* was uplifting and exciting, especially in Donny's work with the ensemble, the piece was at its most compelling when the characters were playing actual scenes from *A Raisin in the Sun*. All too often there was a letdown when they started singing, which is the opposite of what one wants to happen in a musical. Not poor songs, exactly; but you'd sit there at times wishing they'd just stick to Hansberry's play. It was like you were simultaneously watching two different tennis matches on two adjacent television sets. *Look over here!* No, look over *here!*

Post-opening business got off to a good start. There was some audience resistance; this was a time when a substantial segment of the middle-class audience was not interested in a "Black" show, unless it was full of tap dancing; and the Black audience—greatly encouraged by the Pearl Bailey *Hello, Dolly!* and *Purlie*—was only beginning to feel comfortable traveling to Times Square and sitting in a legit theatre. (While New York theatres had long been integrated, the only Broadway-caliber playhouse in the nation's capital—the National Theatre—had not started admitting all audiences until they were forced to do so in 1952 after a four-year closure due to a boycott by Actors' Equity.)

In our first season, business at *Raisin* was relatively strong—rarely a sellout except on weekends, but steadily profitable. This was helped, to a large extent, by the lack of competition. The only other new musicals of the season were *Molly*, a clumsy show based on characters from Gertrude Berg's radio-and-television series, *The Goldbergs*; *Rainbow Jones*, an amateurishly flimsy fantasy that played three previews and closed opening night at the Music Box; *Over Here!*, a pastiche musical starring the two still-living Andrews Sisters of World War II fame; and the long-running *The Magic Show*, which featured Canadian magician Doug Henning performing tricks in a nightclub setting while the cast sang a string of negligible songs by Stephen Schwartz. There were also two star-laden but poorly executed revisions of classics, the previously mentioned *Lorelei* (derived from *Gentlemen Prefer Blondes*, starring Carol Channing) and the first-ever stage production of Lerner & Loewe's *Gigi* (starring Alfred Drake).

But even as *Raisin* settled into its run, we were head deep in another musical.

CHAPTER SIXTEEN

Not Quite Classic

7½ CENTS

As I sat interviewing with Helen Richards in early September, *Raisin* was two weeks away from the start of its Philadelphia tryout. The next show on the schedule—a revival of the 1954 musical, *The Pajama Game*—was going into rehearsal the following week, prior to an October tryout at the Kennedy Center Opera House. Helen's plan was to serve as general manager on both and—once they were both playing in New York—hold the union-sanctioned company manager contract on one, enabling her to collect three salaries (out of which I would be paid); a company manager could only collect one union salary at a time, but the general manager position wasn't unionized. I would begin officially working for Helen when *Pajama Game* went into rehearsal the following week, but would it be okay if I started right away helping out Little Jeffrey?

Jeffrey Richards—growing up with a single mother who worked in Broadway offices when she wasn't on the road with a show—seemed to have spent his entire life preparing for a career in the theatre. Helen had a knack for calling gruff theatrical managers, putting on her little-old-southern-me voice, and getting free tickets so Jeffrey had full-time access to Broadway from the time he was old enough to climb into a seat. When he later became a prolific producer, he mixed provocative new shows—like *August: Osage County* and *Spring Awakening*—with revivals of plays that he'd seen as a child, including Herb Gardner's *A Thousand*

Clowns, Harold Pinter's *The Birthday Party*, and Gore Vidal's *The Best Man*.

Jeffrey was about to embark on his first job as a theatrical press agent; Helen had talked the producers of *The Pajama Game* into hiring him, even though he had little actual Broadway experience. (Helen had handled press on the original production in 1954, which helped smooth the way.) Jeffrey had experience in publicity, though. Helen's nephew Jay Bernstein—later famous as a flamboyant personal manager of Hollywood stars—was already a powerful publicist, and Jeffrey took care of events that Jay's office set up in New York. One of the events I worked on for Jeffrey, that week, was a press luncheon at 21 for Muhammad Ali, who was trying to rehabilitate his image following the broad public condemnation and his ban from boxing for his refusal to be inducted in 1966. I nodded to Ali—who was still known to many as Cassius Clay—and he nodded back.

Jeffrey's lack of Broadway experience was not a problem, as it turned out; he was a natural, and his work on *The Pajama Game* almost immediately propelled him directly into shows of far more prominence than Helen would ever manage.

Back in 1973, revivals of Broadway musicals were not as prevalent as they would quickly become. The prior seasons had brought two nostalgic new productions of forty-odd-year-old shows headed by bona fide former movie stars: *No, No, Nanette*, from 1925, a smash hit starring Ruby Keeler; and *Irene*, from 1919, a box office bonanza (initially) starring Debbie Reynolds that wound up losing a fortune due to inefficient producing. *The Pajama Game*, however, was a relatively recent show, having ended its original Broadway run a mere seventeen years earlier.

With a farfetched plot about Midwest factory workers fighting for a 7½-cent raise, *The Pajama Game* had seemed unlikely when it first came along. Richard Bissell was one of those wry, homespun midwestern writers out of Dubuque, Iowa, only with a Harvard education; he wrote like a witty sophisticate with a Mark Twain drawl. Like Twain, he had served time as a riverboat captain on the Mississippi. Bissell's 1953 novel *7½ Cents* was a Book of the Month Club selection and a best seller. Two novice Broadway producers read the book and decided to turn it into a musical.

One of the pair was no newcomer; Robert E. Griffith had been George Abbott's preferred stage manager since 1936. Griffith's young partner, Harold S. Prince, joined the Abbott office in 1949 as a twenty-one-year-old casting director of the Irving Berlin musical, *Miss Liberty*. After service in Korea, Prince returned to the firm and served as Griffith's assistant stage manager (and as an understudy) on the 1953 musical, *Wonderful Town*. This was directed by Abbott, with music by Leonard Bernstein and lyrics by Betty Comden and Adolph Green. While it turned out to be highly successful, it went through a bloodbath of a production period. The original songwriters, Leroy Anderson and Arnold Horwitt, were fired and replaced by the long-haired Lenny and the satirical Betty and Adolph. The librettists—Joseph A. Fields and Jerome Chodorov, who had written the underlying 1940 comedy hit *My Sister Eileen*, derived from stories by Ruth McKenney—waged an extended battle over the nature of the show: Was it a nostalgic comedy, or a brash satire of the 1930s? Abbott remembered *Wonderful Town* for "more hysterical debate, more acrimony, more tension, and more screaming than any other show I was ever involved with." And Mr. A., whose active Broadway career spanned an astounding seventy-four years, was involved with very many shows.

Griffith and Prince optioned the novel knowing full well that they could count on the involvement of Mr. A., assuming he liked the material. (After many years of producing his own shows, Abbott had decided at sixty-five that he was ready to leave the producing to others.) Griffith had technical expertise and the enthusiastic Prince had artistic tendencies; what they didn't have was money. Fortunately for them, Rosalind Russell—the invaluable star of *Wonderful Town*—had a husband in tow, Frederick Brisson. His nickname was "the lizard of Roz," which might give you an idea of his character. The Copenhagen-born Brisson, looking to establish an American career apart from his wife, joined the two stage managers for their first three musicals, all hits: *The Pajama Game, Damn Yankees,* and *New Girl in Town*. Griffith and Prince did the work; Brisson got top billing.

Rags to Riches to Rags
It was quickly decided that Bissell and Abbott should collaborate on the book, the one contributing his refreshingly tongue-in-cheek voice and the other crafting it into a well-oiled machine of a musical. Bissell's folksy vernacular naturally suggested songwriter Frank Loesser, whose *Guys and Dolls* was the reigning hit of the time. Abbott had guided Loesser through his 1948 Broadway debut on the hit musical, *Where's Charley?*

But Frank was careful not to repeat himself; he chose to follow his fable of tinhorn Runyonesque gamblers with a Pucciniesque Broadway operetta, *The Most Happy Fella*. Loesser, though, was also a canny businessman; taking the lead from Irving Berlin, he had formed his own publishing company that—thanks to the song hits from *Guys and Dolls*—was an instant powerhouse. (If Irving Berlin can do it, Loesser figured, I can too. And he did.) Among his newly signed songwriters were Richard Adler and Jerry Ross, who immediately gave Frank Music Corp. the pop hit "Rags to Riches." Loesser sent Adler and Ross over to Abbott to audition for *The Pajama Game*. Abbott invited them to write songs on spec; they did so, and were hired to write the score.

Richard Adler was a conflicted fellow, demonstrating brash eagerness—or some might say conceit—on the outside with unsurmountable conflicts within. He was the son of noted piano teacher Clarence Adler, whose students included Aaron Copland. Richard, being stubborn, refused to learn the piano; during his composing career, he devised his tunes on a toy xylophone. Richard's choice of becoming a pop songwriter, too, was in part calculated to annoy his father.

Richard was a not-very-successful fellow of twenty-nine, when—in the summer of 1950—he met the twenty-four-year-old Jerry Ross on the street outside the Brill Building at 1619 Broadway, the Tin Pan Alley of the day. Ross had been a child actor in the Yiddish theatre. They both wrote music as well as lyrics; both had been collaborating with other writers; both had little to show for their efforts. They started working together and were quickly discovered by Loesser, who was happy to add some nontheatrical pop writers to the firm. (If Irving Berlin can do it, Loesser figured, I can too.) In the fall of 1953, "Rags to Riches" topped the Billboard charts for eight weeks. Loesser quickly got them a show—the revue *John Murray Anderson's Almanac*—which opened in December 1953 to moderate success; it also, parenthetically, included an interpolation from newcomer Cy Coleman and another from the young Sheldon Harnick. And then came *The Pajama Game*, which opened on May 13, 1954.

Rags to Tin Pan Alley Riches. Richard Adler (moody, in tie) with the photo-friendly Jerry Ross contemplating *The Pajama Game* (1954).
PHOTOFEST

Adler & Ross—Ross was the nice one, Adler the sonofabitch—won a Tony Award for Best Score; the songs included "Hey There," "Steam Heat," and "Hernando's Hideaway." A week shy of a year later, on May 5, 1955, they opened their second musical: *Damn Yankees*. Here came another Tony, rewarding them for songs such as "Whatever Lola Wants" and "(You Gotta Have) Heart." They were the first writers to win back-to-back Tonys. And then, in November of that year, Jerry Ross—who had always been frail—died of a lung ailment at the age of twenty-nine.

Adler went on; he went on for another fifty-six years, never able to equal or even distantly approach his early success. Ross was a close partner; unlike other composer/lyricist collaborators who mostly wrote independently, they worked together on each song. In the eighteen years between *Damn Yankees* and our revival of *Pajama Game*, Richard had written two produced musicals: the 1961 flop *Kwamina* and the 1968 flop *A Mother's Kisses*.

Kwamina, which starred Adler's second wife, Sally Ann Howes, had an interesting score—not interesting enough to make the misguided show work, though. It was a brave try in that it took place in modern-day Africa and offered an interracial romance between an English doctor (Howes) and an African medical student (Terry Carter) newly returned from school in England. Matters weren't helped by giving Sally Ann—who had just entertained Broadway audiences as the first replacement for Julie Andrews in *My Fair Lady*—a clone of "Just You Wait, Henry Higgins." Nor were they helped when Richard found his wife, during the Toronto tryout, in bed with her leading man. There was plenty of show-fixing by Adler, by director Bobby Lewis (of *Brigadoon*), and by choreographer Agnes de Mille (of *Oklahoma!* and *Brigadoon*), but to no avail. Lost in the turmoil was the decidedly intriguing score that Adler wrote on his own, without Ross.

As it turned out, Richard would have only one song hit after Jerry's death. This came before *Kwamina*, back in 1958. Enmeshed in a bitter divorce, Adler's first wife, Marion—who knew all about Sally Ann, having been informed by her two young sons—discovered that he had already moved the singer into his apartment. Incensed, she threatened to sabotage Howes, who was just about to step into *My Fair Lady*, by exposing the affair. Richard sheepishly went to producer Herman Levin to warn him about the potential scandal. Herman philosophically mused that it would probably only help sell tickets, with Herman's lawyer quoting the proverb "all the world loves a lover." Richard left the meeting with the phrase—which seems to originate with Ralph Waldo Emerson, although oft attributed to Shakespeare—spinning through his brain. "Everybody Loves a Lover," with lyric by Adler and music by Robert Allen, was an immediate hit for Doris Day, who had just starred in the 1957 film version of *The Pajama Game.*

Adler also embarked on a lucrative career in the advertising world, his work including the immortal "Let Hertz Put You in the Driver's Seat." But this was a far cry from back-to-back Tony Awards and back-to-back Broadway smashes, which at the time were Broadway's ninth and tenth longest-running musicals ever.

Half a Team

While at loose ends, Richard found himself drafted to produce a fundraiser to celebrate President John F. Kennedy's forty-fifth birthday. (One of Adler's college friends from the University of North Carolina–Chapel Hill, recommended him to the president.) This was the now-legendary bash at Madison Square Garden on May 19, 1962. With no restraints on the talent Adler could amass—JFK was highly popular, most every star in the country was thrilled to be invited to appear, for free—Adler came up with the idea of bringing on Marilyn Monroe to breathlessly sing "Happy Birthday" to the president, along with Adler's parody lyric to "Thanks for the Memory." Eleven weeks later, Marilyn was dead.

Adler continued staging events for JFK and carried over into the Johnson administration. Kennedy had asked Adler to participate in the arts center that was being built on the Potomac; Johnson followed through and named him a trustee of the Kennedy Center, which in part is why the *Pajama Game* revival was able to arrange a tryout there. But Richard's political work ended when Johnson left office and Nixon came in. He—Adler, not Nixon—went to work on *A Mother's Kisses* and got married a third time (of five). That marriage worked out better than the show, but not much.

A Mother's Kisses was one of those "Jewish mother" musicals designed to be gobbled up by theatre party ladies and their customers. Based on Bruce Jay Friedman's 1964 comic novel of the same title, it was as poor as it might sound, shuttering after a week in New Haven and two in Baltimore. Bea Arthur—following her featured role of Yente the Matchmaker in *Fiddler on the Roof* and her Tony-winning turn as Vera the Lush in *Mame*—here starred as the overbearingly abrasive Jewish mama.

(From an interview with our friend Mr. Merrick: "Richard Adler played the score for me. I told him to start a new project the next hour. I told him not to wait till the next day.")

If you wish to play Broadway genealogy, Bea Arthur was married to Gene Saks, director of *A Mother's Kisses* as well as the 1966 *Mame*. Her first husband, from whom she derived her stage name, was Robert Alan Aurthur—who wrote the book for *Kwamina*.

Meanwhile, a fellow named Bert Wood approached Richard with an idea: Why not try an interracial version of *The Pajama Game?* The Broadway musical had seen mixed romances in the 1961 *Kwamina*, Richard Rodgers's 1962 *No Strings*, and the 1964 Sammy Davis vehicle *Golden Boy*. How about a mixed-cast production in which race was not a plot point but merely incidental, presented without comment?

Bert had been an assistant stage manager on several Abbott/Prince shows, starting as a replacement on the original *Pajama Game*. Abbott had been a friend of his father; Bert mentioned that as a teenager he sometimes played tennis with Mr. Abbott, which led to his first theatre job. More recently, Bert had been working as a stage manager for industrials and at theme parks.

George Abbott, a mere octogenarian at the time, was bored and eager to join in. Unexpectedly, Richard latched on to the notion of coproducing the show with Bert.

It quickly became apparent that while Bert might have been a proficient assistant stage manager, he was altogether ineffectual as the man in charge. One of the decisions he did make was to bring in Helen—who was a longtime friend from their days on *Fiorello!*, and who had more recently given him a replacement stage manager job on *Purlie*—as general manager. Richard oversaw the creative side and—when it became clear that Bert couldn't raise a nickel, either—put together the financing. To that end, he enlisted an ambitious thirty-year-old to align investors in exchange for associate producer credit. Nelson Peltz ran a wholesale food-distribution company at the time, although within twenty-five years he was a fearsome hedge fund manager and activist investor. His *Pajama Game* investment, though, was a bust.

THE ASTONISHING MR. A

The added racial element aside, the plan was to closely replicate the original. Abbott, of course, led the team as director. He had always been the most workmanlike, no-nonsense director around, and therein lies the key to his long reign as Broadway's most successful director of the century. Not the most influential or innovative—Elia Kazan, with *Streetcar* and *Death of a Salesman*, offered an altogether different variety of direction— but Abbott kept pounding them out over the years. Starting in 1913 as an actor, he began writing plays in 1925 and directing them in 1926. In the fall of that year, he wrote and directed the groundbreaking melodrama *Broadway* and—three months later—directed the original play version of *Chicago*. The hardworking and industrious Abbott was happy to undertake as many as five Broadway shows a season. No, they weren't all hits; but no matter what might happen with this one or the next, there were always three or four in the works.

By 1932, he had tired of ineffectual producers and started producing on his own with the comedy hit *Twentieth Century*. This was the first of a string of six lucrative farces of the thirties that he directed and produced (and in some cases wrote), the others being *Three Men on a Horse, Boy Meets Girl, Brother Rat, Room Service*, and *What a Life*.

Abbott's most canny talent, though, turned out to be with musicals. It wasn't until he turned forty-eight that he gained entry to the field. Richard Rodgers was keen to create a new, more substantial form of musical comedy than those he and Lorenz Hart—and other practitioners such as Jerome Kern, Cole Porter, and Oscar Hammerstein—had been writing. Rodgers invited celebrated hitmaker Abbott to join him on a string of Rodgers & Hart musicals starting with *Jumbo* in 1935 and culminating with *Pal Joey* in 1940. From 1938—when Abbott produced, directed, and wrote the book for Rodgers & Hart's *The Boys from Syracuse*—till 1951, he was perhaps Broadway's preeminent producer of musicals. At that point he turned sixty-five and decided to restrict his future efforts to writing and directing. Given that he was understandably in high demand, producers were happy to reward director Abbott with a sizable slice—usually 10 percent—of the profits as well as guaranteeing him the opportunity to make a substantial investment.

Much has been made of Abbott's work with young songwriters early in their careers. The list starts with Hugh Martin & Ralph Blane on *Best Foot Forward* in 1940 and continues with Leonard Bernstein, Betty Comden & Adolph Green (*On the Town*); Jule Styne (*High Button Shoes*); Frank Loesser (*Where's Charley?*); Adler & Ross (*The Pajama Game*); Bock & Harnick (*Fiorello!*); Stephen Sondheim (*A Funny Thing Happened on the Way to the Forum*); and Kander & Ebb (*Flora, the Red Menace*). And these are only some of them.

Paradoxically, Abbott wasn't especially musical (although his favorite offstage pastime was to go out dancing). Rather, he was a well-rounded, practical man of the theatre with a well-tuned stage sense and a keen appreciation for what would translate to the audience. If it worked, don't touch it; if it didn't work, if the audience were sitting back in their seats uninvolved, throw it out.

This is illustrated by a discussion I had with Prince years later, in which he explained that back in the 1950s you went into a tryout *expecting* to replace songs. In the days before rehearsal costs and overtime construction of new scenery and costumes became prohibitive, you would regularly budget for the probability of a few such changes.

He cited a song from *The Pajama Game*. Listening to Adler and Ross demonstrate "Her Is," a comedy duet for the second female lead and a union official who is trying to seduce her, Prince thought: "This song is awful." Over the weeks, it didn't get any better. As the tryout neared, Hal—who was in the rehearsal hall as assistant stage manager (for the salary) but also as novice producer—went to Mr. Abbott. "This song is awful," he said. "Aren't we going to cut it?" Abbott replied, "Probably, but we've got bigger things to fix. Leave it be, we'll see how it plays in New Haven."

They did indeed have bigger things to fix; they cut out a subplot— along with featured comedienne Charlotte Rae—and replaced several songs. But "Her Is," thanks to the adorably impish performance of dancer/comedienne Carol Haney, landed; it got a big hand, actually. So "Her Is" stayed in, even though Prince admitted fifty years later that he still found the song embarrassing.

To further illustrate the character of the unshowy and noneffusive Abbott, consider the case of Stanley Prager, the actor who sang "Her Is" with Haney. Early in the run of *The Pajama Game*, Prager was branded a Communist by the House Un-American Activities Committee. At that point in time, the HUAC blacklist was all but lethal. That evening, he found a note at the stage door asking him to stop in to see Abbott the next morning. Fearing the worst, Prager turned up at the Abbott office in Rockefeller Center.

"I think," Mr. Abbott said in his blunt and no-nonsense manner, "we need to give you a raise."

MENTOR

A key component of Abbott's success—musical theatre–wise, at least— was his ability to recognize budding geniuses and entrust them to demonstrate their talent. The choreographer of his first book musical, Rodgers & Hart's *On Your Toes* in 1936, was a Russian émigré named George Balanchine. Abbott didn't himself select Balanchine, but he saw fit to incorporate two full-scale Balanchine ballets into the libretto and entrust the choreographer—who, like Abbott, was working on his first full-scale book musical—to pull it off. The notion of culminating a Broadway musical with a plot-related ballet appears to have never before been done or even contemplated. It turned out to be the making of the show; the climactic *Slaughter on Tenth Avenue* is still performed, apart from the show, by ballet companies worldwide.

After several more musicals with Rodgers, Hart, and Abbott, Balanchine went back to his preferred world of ballet. Not long after, in 1944, Abbott signed on to direct *On the Town*, which was derived from Leonard Bernstein's ballet *Fancy Free* and devised as a musical by that ballet's choreographer, Jerome Robbins. Abbott immediately recognized

Robbins for the talent he was, inviting him to choreograph four additional shows in six years, in later cases as codirector.

By 1954, Robbins was too busy to choreograph someone else's show. He had just entered the world of TV with great success, staging the legendary Ethel Merman/Mary Martin duet on the *Ford Fiftieth Anniversary Show*. He was now attempting to direct, choreograph, and write a musical version of *Peter Pan*; this began its West Coast tryout several months after *The Pajama Game* opened, with Martin in the title role. In the meantime, Abbott offered Robbins codirector credit on *Pajama Game* on the understanding that he would unofficially back up the novice choreographer whom Abbott and the producers had selected.

This new choreographer had never done a stage show. He was a creature of night clubs, but Joan McCracken—the star of Abbott's then-current musical, Rodgers & Hammerstein's *Me and Juliet*—vouched for him. She had to; she had recently married him. Bob Fosse thus entered the Broadway world, and after three successive musicals with Abbott (and Griffith and Prince), moved on to become a director/choreographer in his own right. Along with Robbins and Fosse, we can add Prince to the mix. As has been seen, he joined Abbott's office as casting director and assistant stage manager. Prince then produced nine Abbott shows, after which he began directing his own musicals. So in addition to all Abbott's hit musicals over the years—and all those legendary songwriters whom he successfully launched—he is also in large part responsible for the seasoning of perhaps the three most influential Broadway directors of the latter half of the twentieth century: Robbins, Fosse, and Prince.

The list of young writers nurtured by Abbott belies another truth. He jumpstarted the careers of many of Broadway's finest songwriters, yes; but this was early in their careers, when they were eager for the opportunity and willing to bend their work to follow the suggestions of the master. Once established, they rarely chose to return to Abbott. He launched the careers of Bernstein, Sondheim, Bock, and Kander, yes; but his traditional, workmanlike form of showmaking would arguably have stunted the creation of such artistic musicals as *West Side Story*, *Follies*, *Fiddler on the Roof*, and *Cabaret*. At the same time, each of those musicals were directed by one of those aforementioned Abbott protégés, who had worked with the songwriters in question on prior Abbott musicals.

Star Quality

By 1973, Fosse was one of the most powerful men on Broadway, with *Pippin* just starting its second year. He wasn't about to come back and re-create the choreography for his first show. He instead sent his dance assistant from the original *Pajama Game* and *Damn Yankees*, Zoya Leporska, who had restaged Fosse's dances for the original London productions of those two musicals. When she got the call for our revival, Zoya was working as a waitress at Serendipity III, an Upper East Side ice cream parlor. Restaurant work was the lot of out-of-work dancers and ex-dancers; one of the founders of Serendipity, in fact, was a former chorus dancer. Zoya temporarily put down her apron and restaged the show, with Fosse taking the time to stop in at the rehearsal hall two or three times to look things over (while taking most of the choreographer money as well).

As for the cast, I suppose Richard intended to go with a Tony-winning leading lady on the level of Diahann Carroll or Leslie Uggams. And why wouldn't they be just dying to do a second-rate revival of *The Pajama Game*? He ended up with Barbara McNair, a popular recording artist with frequent TV exposure as well as a 1968 appearance in *Playboy* magazine. She also had experience carrying a Broadway musical, having replaced Carroll in *No Strings*. But excitement? Not quite. When Richard complained about Barbara's bland performance during the tryout, Abbott matter-of-factly said, "It was your idea, Dick, we'll just do the best we can."

In August, the *Times* announced that *The Pajama Game* would star Barbara McNair as the heroine Babe and television comedian Nipsey Russell as the efficiency expert Hines. While Russell was very much interested and long negotiations seemed close to a successful conclusion, a last-minute big-money television opportunity intervened. The good-natured warmth and contemporary feeling he might have brought turned out to be sorely missed.

Playing opposite Barbara was Hal Linden, a journeyman song-and-dance man who had been star understudy to Sydney Chaplin in *Bells Are*

Ringing and John Cullum in *On a Clear Day*. He never got a leading role of his own until he achieved "overnight" stardom in 1970 in *The Rothschilds*. Hal came to *The Pajama Game* from Mr. A.'s inner casting file; he had more or less stopped the show in a small role in Abbott's 1968 *The Education of H*Y*M*A*N K*A*P*L*A*N*, where he also understudied star Tom Bosley. (That musical had the misfortune to open the night that Martin Luther King Jr. was assassinated, with New York's Mayor John Lindsay pulled out of the house during intermission to deal with race riots in Harlem.) Hal also filled in as one of the comic crew in Abbott's 1969 revival of *Three Men on a Horse* at the Lyceum.

Where do you go for a star comic in an interracial *Pajama Game* once Nipsey Russell has dropped out? Especially once you've settled on two non-ticket-selling stars for the romantic leads? Cab Calloway was the solution, although it turned out that he was a triple letdown: he didn't sell tickets, he gave an ineffective performance, and he prided himself on being "difficult."

Cab had long been a headliner. Primarily a bandleader and jazz singer, he had built a widespread following, not only with his orchestra at the Cotton Club in Harlem, but as a larger-than-life personality. His 1931 hit "Minnie the Moocher" provided his scat catchphrase—"Hi-de-hi-de-hi"—and his penchant for high-shouldered zoot suits made him something of a self-caricature. His fame was multiplied by a series of Hollywood short subjects, both in person and as an animated-cartoon version of himself. While Calloway was never as big a star as Mickey Rooney, their career trajectories were similar; once red hot, they spent later decades trapped in their earlier personas with one last hit late in the day. Rooney's came with the 1979 Broadway musical, *Sugar Babies*; Cab's in the 1980 film, *The Blues Brothers*.

Cab did have a couple of successful Broadway appearances on his resume. First came the role of Sportin' Life in the 1952 international tour of *Porgy and Bess*, starring Leontyne Price and William Warfield. This visited the Ziegfeld in 1953, and Calloway—not surprisingly—was well suited to the role. Fourteen years later came *Hello, Dolly!* Merrick, as previously discussed, cannily brought Pearl Bailey and Cab into the already long-running New York company, moving the show back into the SRO column.

Merrick had cast Cab because his name still meant a great deal, especially to the people who were expected to make up a large portion of the audience. It was immediately clear, though, that Bailey was the main draw. It no doubt rankled Cab to be outranked by Pearl, who had never been the star he was; I expect that he restrained himself mightily when Pearl acted up, knowing that his paycheck depended on it. But it couldn't have been fun or ego-salving. Since the end of their run in *Dolly!* in 1969, Pearl had been in high demand, but not Cab. He was presumably hungry for dollars and applause. Enter Richard Adler and *The Pajama Game*.

As soon as we got onstage at the Kennedy Center Opera House, it became apparent that Cab was a serious detriment to the show. Adler and Abbott took one look at him and sent out an emergency call to Eddie Foy Jr., the veteran song-and-dance man who had created the role of Hines on stage and film. But Foy was even older, and more decrepit, than Cab. Richard reported back to us that as they rode up in the elevator to the rehearsal room in the Opera House, Foy dropped his hearing aid battery. As he crawled around the elevator floor frantically searching for the battery, Richard knew we were stuck with Cab.

CHAPTER SEVENTEEN

Offstage Left

HEARD THAT SONG BEFORE

THE MAIN PROBLEM WITH THE SHOW, THOUGH, WAS NOT CAB, THE
nineteen-year-old material, or the eighty-six-year-old director. It was
simply an uninspired production with no spark from the romantic leads,
regardless of the interracial aspect. What's more, it was a cheap—and
excessively cheap-looking—production. The show retained its tuneful,
good-natured flavor, and "Steam Heat"—the dance number that put Bob
Fosse in the spotlight—was still superb. But in 1973, *The Pajama Game*
seemed awfully tired.

We started previews at the Lunt-Fontanne on December 5. Yes, the
production was clearly not so good; but here I was on Broadway with
not one but two musicals, directly opposite each other on Forty-Sixth
Street. I could cross from *Raisin*—at the time a budding hit, in its second month—to *The Pajama Game*, a foot firmly planted on each side of
the street. I distinctly recall repeatedly dashing from one to other, in the
snow, through traffic, without a coat.

We opened Sunday night, December 9, 1973, to deservedly lukewarm reviews. This left Richard angry at the world, and angry at me as
well. After seeing the show at Kennedy Center, I told him how much I
liked the way he had taken a promising-but-lost song from *Kwamina*
("What's Wrong with Me?") and rewritten it into something called
"Watch Your Heart, Old Girl." This replaced the leading lady's reprise of
the ballad "Small Talk," a song that worked well as a duet for the stars in

the first act but seemed stranded in the second. Richard was, of course, glad for the praise and glad that someone remembered *Kwamina*. I didn't see *Kwamina*; in 1961 I was attending only a couple of shows a year. That was the year of *Irma La Douce* and *Carnival!* But I knew the score from the original cast album, which until compact discs came along was out of print and high on the list of rarities.

The week after the opening, Richard walked in with a copy of *Penny-Saver*, one of those giveaway newspapers that were distributed in supermarkets at the time. The amateur critic not only gave us a bad review; he pointed out that Adler was so washed up that instead of writing a new song, he borrowed an old one and made it worse. Why Richard—with bigger problems to deal with—was reading the *PennySaver*, I can't tell you. He decided, however, that I must have somehow told this amateur critic that "Watch Your Heart" was from *Kwamina*; anyway, it gave him someone to lash out at—for a day or two, anyway.

TANTRUM

The most extraordinary event of *The Pajama Game*, for me, occurred during previews. Hal Prince, after all these years, still shared an office with the not-quite-retired Mr. A.; rather, he had more or less taken over the office to run his *Fiddler on the Roof* empire but kept Abbott's name on the door. Hal came to the second preview and offered a positive assessment; when the die is cast and changes are not possible, it is unseemly to be unduly negative. The next night, a Friday, in came Robbins. Yes, he had codirector credit on the original production, but he hadn't actually done much of the direction. He did stage two of the musical numbers—"There Once Was a Man" and "7½ Cents"—while Fosse was busy with the rest of the show.

After the show, Robbins angrily stormed backstage as soon as the house lights came on. This was not my first glimpse of him. One day in 1971 back at Merrick's, I spotted an engraved invitation on Helen Nickerson's desk: a reception at the New York Public Library to celebrate publication of the Richard Rodgers autobiography, *Musical Stages*. "Is he going?" I asked. "God no," said Helen; the long-running battle between the two, stemming from the time Rodgers tried to push Merrick out of *Fanny*, was still in effect.

"You want to go? I'll tell them we're sending someone from the office."

And so I went to the reception. There was Rodgers, a sickly old man with a mechanical smile receiving colleagues and well-wishers. I stood on a short line, shook hands with him, and said something complimentary. We didn't talk; he simply nodded mechanically.

The crowd—and it was a big crowd, up at the Lincoln Center library—milled around with wine and hors d'oeuvres, looking at the exhibits. The walls and display cases were stocked with original theatre art—posters, designs, music manuscripts—and since this was from the composer/producer's own collection, a lot of it was fascinating. Eventually spoon was clinked to wineglass and the room hushed for speeches.

I was standing with my back to the wall. Directly to my right—and under my very nose, as the fellow was considerably shorter—was a gleaming bald head with a silver fringe of hair, a silver beard, and a big smile. Jerry Robbins on his best behavior, I recognized, even with the uncharacteristic grin. The speaker made a joke and directly to my left there was a familiar-sounding gurgle, one I'd heard many times on my stereo: it's Peter Pan! There I was at eighteen, an impostor who'd crashed the party using David Merrick's name, standing between the real Jerome Robbins and the real Mary Martin.

This night at the Lunt, though, J. R. wasn't smiling. I was standing at the stage manager's desk, just behind the stage right proscenium and up a few steps from the pass door, when Robbins flew past. The cast was still onstage, following the curtain call; the orchestra was playing the exit music.

"Terrible! This is terrible!" he raged at the actors. "There aren't more than three of you who care what you're doing!"

The cast was in shock. Several of them knew Robbins from the past; his reputation for artistic tantrums was well established, so this behavior wasn't all that unusual. Most of the dancers were young, though, and understandably in awe of the genius from *West Side*, *Gypsy*, *Fiddler*, and the New York City Ballet.

Abbott, who had calmly followed Robbins through the stage door, appeared in the wing. Because he was George Abbott, eighty-six years old and the tallest person in the building, everyone—including Robbins—stopped and watched as he authoritatively loped to stage center.

"Everybody go change," he said calmly. "Notes in the house, fifteen minutes."

The cast exited; rather, they quickly and quietly slinked off. Stagehands came on to clear the set. I finished what I was doing at the stage manager's desk, then quietly stole upstage to see what the two Broadway geniuses were up to. The pajama factory unit—which given the cheap nature of the production, was something like a flimsy jungle gym of wood—was stored against the back wall. My eyes picked out the pair in the shadows. There was Mr. Abbott, stern, ramrod straight, and towering over Robbins, well more than a foot taller. And there was Robbins, head tucked and eyes lowered to the floor, like a naughty child being scolded by the solemn kindergarten teacher for dipping the braids of the girl at the desk in front of him in ink. Jerry Robbins, the most feared man on Broadway, whimpering in the corner. Abbott did what he had to do and said what he had to say; unlike Robbins, though, he saw that it was done in private. Or what he thought was in private. Quite a sight, although I'm the only one who saw it; as Sondheim might have noted, I was "someone in a tree"—thus puncturing any remaining notions I had of Great Men of the Theatre.

CUE LIGHTS

An unforeseen opportunity resulted from the stage manager setup on the show. Coproducer Bert Wood held the production stage manager contract even though he was incapable of doing the job. Producers did not receive a salary; other than a small royalty, their money came from a share of the profits after the show recouped. By allowing Bert—who needed an income to support his family—to hold the stage manager contract, Richard was in effect paying him to be the producer.

Simply put, the job of production stage manager—like Mitch, or Biff on *My Fair Lady*—has several components. He (or she) sets up the show in the rehearsal hall, with the director and the actors. They move into the theatre for the put-in; when the set is assembled, lights and sound equipment are installed by the stagehands. The production stage manager runs the "techs" (technical rehearsals) when the director and designers work through the show and set the cues; and then the dress rehearsals, when the actors, wardrobe, and orchestra—in the case of musicals—are added and everything is synchronized into one, smooth performance.

The PSM will then "call" the show during previews, while working with director et al. by day to incorporate necessary changes into the show. Once the director leaves after opening, the PSM's job is to make sure everything is kept the way the director set it. This means giving notes to the actors and crew about performance or technical issues. In order to do so, the PSM often roams the theatre—both backstage and out front—during the performance. Thus, the first assistant stage manager also runs the show. There are often some complex cues when a stage manager might be needed to be on deck (in the dark), away from the stage manager's desk, to make sure things run properly. This is part of the first ASM's nightly routine. When the latter is calling the show, the PSM handles these moments. The second ASM—back then, at least—was typically a chorus member. (Equity rules for a musical allowed the second ASM to also handle acting duties; on a noncomplex nonmusical, the first ASM was allowed to act or understudy—as on that play for which I "auditioned" the prior spring.) The second ASM handles organizational matters, mostly, like collecting the cast's valuables (wallets and jewelry) before the performance and locking them up safely. When the PSM watches the show out front or is otherwise occupied, the first ASM calls the show and the second ASM performs the necessary duties, even if it means pulling the latter out of chorus numbers.

Bert managed to get through rehearsals in good shape; after all, he had been ASM on the original *Pajama Game*. Once the company arrived at the Kennedy Center, everything stopped. Bert had no idea how to set up the hundred-odd cues, as dozens of stagehands stood around on steep hourly rates. He looked to his first ASM for help. Jerry Laws was a former singer who had played a small role in the 1942 and 1953 productions of *Porgy and Bess* and had most recently been a second ASM on *Purlie*. He was nice, and Black—an important consideration, given the production's interracial setup—but without the training to do what Bert needed to be doing.

The no-nonsense Abbott had little patience; after a day of tech rehearsals, he said, "get someone here tomorrow" and went back to work with the actors. Abbott's assistant made a call and got a fellow named Bob Bernard to drop what he was doing and get on a plane to Washington.

Bernard was a PSM, although not on the highest level. He was, in fact, the fellow who brushed me off when I volunteered to help backstage at Merrick's *There's One in Every Marriage*. He had been a dancer in many musicals—including *Fiorello!*, as it happened—who proved capable and eventually moved into stage managing; most recently, he was replacement PSM on the Pearl Bailey/Cab Calloway production of *Dolly!* Bob didn't need or want the *Pajama Game* job; he had a big-money industrial coming up in five weeks, and in any event you are setting yourself up for trouble when you step in to tech a show you haven't rehearsed. But when Mr. Abbott calls, you go. He also magnanimously agreed to take the assistant contract—and protect Bert's job, on paper—although it was understood that Bob would get the full PSM salary, and under the circumstances was well worth it.

Bob took us through the New York preview week; he could stay till opening night but no longer. This meant that we needed to find a new ASM—and one who would similarly cover for Bert, but work for the lesser ASM salary. Who could we get?

I had by this point firmly decided to become a company manager. This required acceptance into the three-year apprentice program for ATPAM. I had started at Helen's after the 1973–1974 apprentices had been selected, which meant that I'd have to wait until June 1974 to apply. I saw the *Pajama Game* ASM job as a quick advance, career-wise; and given my experience on *Tricks*, I considered myself qualified. I also knew full well that the ASM job came with more than twice the salary I was receiving as Helen's assistant.

So I said to Bert, I can do it; if you want a reference, call Biff (whom I knew would back me up). Bert didn't call, perhaps because it would be embarrassing to explain why they had to bring in Bob Bernard. I told Helen not to worry, I would still do my assistant company manager work. As for Richard, I explained that while Equity would insist that I receive ASM scale, I would waive my other salary so he'd save money. And so

I signed on as the official ASM of *The Pajama Game*, presumably the youngest Broadway stage manager ever, as I was a mere twenty. I was also to become the youngest ATPAM member in history, at twenty-three; but that was the last time I was the youngest anything.

I started as ASM with the first preview, so I'd know the show when Bob left after opening night. Thus, I was calling the bows the night of the Jerry Robbins tantrum.

Abbott also provided my other strong visual image of the production. The star dressing room at the Lunt—at the time, anyway—was a big suite with grand windows that can be glimpsed over the marquee, just above the stage door. Barbara McNair was ensconced there, and Hal didn't much care where he was put. Cab, however, did. There was a large prop storage room along the rear wall backstage, just inside the loading doors and about twenty feet above the deck. At some point, this had been converted into a dressing room, oversized but accessible only by a steep, industrial grade staircase with unusually high stairs. I marveled at the time—and still marvel at the memory of—the long-limbed, eighty-six-year-old Abbott bounding up to Cab's dressing room, three steep steps at a time.

SEARCHING FOR POOPSIE

The Pajama Game is a fine, sturdily constructed show. There is a top rank of Broadway musicals, consisting of titles such as *My Fair Lady*, *West Side Story*, *Gypsy*, *Fiddler on the Roof*, *A Chorus Line*, and four Rodgers & Hammerstein masterworks. In my estimation, *The Pajama Game* falls within the upper reaches of the "B" list. Nobody ever considered it high art; but when done well, it is a delight. Our revival was not done well; what might have been provocative with Diahann Carroll or Leslie Uggams or Lena Horne was simply bland with Barbara McNair. Hal—returning to the same theatre in which he'd played *The Rothschilds*—was good in his role, most probably acting it better than John Raitt (who originated the part). The pairing wasn't enough to create fireworks, though, and Cab detracted from the proceedings by playing it like—well, like Cab Calloway. Besides, Richard assembled the show on the cheap, and it showed.

Director George Abbott—at a young 86—trying to re-create a magical *Pajama Game* with Cab Calloway, Barbara McNair, and Hal Linden (1973).
PHOTOFEST

What worked best were the reconstructed Fosse numbers. "Steam Heat"—for Gladys, the second female lead and two "boys"—was and remains Fosse at his best. By the time the revival opened, he had moved onto an earthier, sexier, starker style and I believe was somewhat embar-

234

rassed by his early "musical comedy" work on *Pajama Game, Damn Yankees*, and *How to Succeed in Business Without Really Trying*. I personally find the best of the earlier numbers superior to the icy-cold late-Fosse style of *Pippin* and *Dancin'*.

Our "Steam Heat" dancers were good, although without the crackle of the originals: Carol Haney, who had earlier danced with Fosse in the film version of *Kiss Me, Kate*; Buzz Miller, Robbins's lover at the time; and Peter Gennaro, who was a featured dancer in the next Robbins-Fosse musical, *Bells Are Ringing* and then co-choreographer of Robbins's *West Side Story*. These dancers, of course, had the steps sculpted on them by Fosse. A respectable performance by our trio was enough to make the number a highlight, watchable night after night.

The most ingenious—and, for the stage manager, most fun—number was "Hernando's Hideaway." (The presence of both "Steam Heat" and "Hernando's" in the second act helped give the show a much stronger finish than was the norm.) The plot revolved around a union strike at a pajama factory. The new foreman, Sid—a loner from out of town—realizes that the owner is feigning his losses; there's a second set of books. The sexy bookkeeper keeps the key to the hidden ledger on a chain around her neck. Sid tries to get her to cooperate, but she'd rather have him take her out for a drink. Where? "I know a dark, secluded place," she sings, "it's called Hernando's Hideaway, olé!" They do an exaggerated tango in the office; at the end of the bridge, she notes "you may take my heart, you may take my soul, but not my key!" The key to the second set of books—that's the plot point, you see.

This continues into a full production number. In those days before mechanized scenery, you first needed a cross-over; that is, you'd lower a drop and bring in a blackout drop, so the work lights behind the drop could go on and the stagehands could remove what in this case was the office set and assemble the restaurant set. In order to hold the audience, though, you would continue the number downstage "in one." That is, in the sliver of stage before the first portal. Here, the drop was painted as a street, with a (functioning) doorway representing a small-town dive—Hernando's Hideaway—leading to the stage left exit. The music continued as various cast members entered from stage right, danced across the apron, and exited into the wing, presumably entering Hernando's. This stream included Gladys and Sid. At the end of the cross came a Spanish fanfare leading into a mariachi-like trumpet solo. This is how the number was devised in 1954. By 1973, stagecraft would allow you to get from one place to another without the cross-over; but we performed the song as originally staged.

The interlude ended with the curtain rising on a totally dark stage. (You'd have trouble replicating this today, due to exit light rules.) The third and final section of the number begins with "haunted house" music. There is dialogue in the dark; one girl says, "It's dark in here!" while a fellow with a high-pitched voice calls out looking for "Poopsie," one of the factory girls.

Then we return to the refrain. A girl lights a match that shines on her face, and sings the first line ("I know a dark secluded place"); a second girl lights a match, sings the next line, followed by a third. They sing, together, "It's called Hernando's Hideaway" and simultaneously blow out their matches. There is another mysterioso section in the dark as more choristers arrive, everybody knocking three times and giving the password ("Joe sent us"), while the high-pitched fellow keeps looking for Poopsie. (He is ultimately answered by a blustery man saying, "Hey, buddy, dis ain't Poopsie!")

Next comes the bridge, with a girl lighting a match and singing "at the Golden Fingerbowl or anyplace you go." Match out. During two measures of dance, two lights intertwine as if a couple is dancing; for this we used pin-sized flashlights, because matches would be extinguished from the movement. Then a boy sings the next line; another short "dance" from two flashlights; then come three more separate solo lines, each with their own match.

For the grand finale, the entire chorus—lined across the stage, midway up from the front—strike matches ("and talk of love!"). They work their way downstage to the apron, to music, lit only by the matches on their faces while singing the final stanza ("Just knock three times and whisper low"). After "then strike a match and you will know," they blow out their matches and sing "you're in" [full stage lights] "Hernando's Hideaway, olé!" Fosse presumably didn't care much for the number, whereas it is all musical staging without much choreography; but it was brilliantly conceived and executed, and always effective.

The number called for old-fashioned wooden stick matches. Between 1954 and 1973, safety standards had changed so that the wooden matches you'd find in the store no longer lit on a simple surface; you had to strike them against the side of the "safety match" box. Leo—who was our propman on the show—found old-fashioned matches someplace in the wilds of Pennsylvania and ordered them by the case full. After the opening, Actors' Equity came to us demanding hazard pay for the actors, $15 a week. Richard went to the union board and screamed "What do you mean, unsafe? A child of five can light a match!" And what do you know? Equity backed down, more likely because we pointed out that they had not previously demanded risk pay for the actors who did this number in the 1954 production.

Sidelight on Poopsie: I have come across correspondence between cast members of the original *Pajama Game* national tour, which traversed the country for more than two years. They regularly referred to their dilettante producer, who would occasionally breeze into assorted towns to bask in the excitement of local opening nights, as "Poopsie Prince."

SING OUT

Equally effective was the soft shoe dance to the duet "I'll Never Be Jealous Again." Corny as all hell, with a leg-crossing step that propelled Hines (Cab's character) and his secretary across the stage and back; and another where they slapped their chests, slapped their knees, then leaned over to pound the floor. This was pure, old-fashioned delight, supremely delectable even with Cab doing it. He played opposite Mary Jo Catlett, who replaced an actress we fired in Washington and was the best of the principals next to Linden.

If there was little musical comedy talent among the principals and the singers, aside from Hal, the fourteen dancers included some people of note. One, Hank Brunjes, went way back with Fosse; when Bob understudied Harold Lang in the 1952 revival of *Pal Joey*, Brunjes was in the chorus. In 1957, he worked for Robbins in *West Side Story* as one of the original Jets (Diesel, who sings the "Judge" section of "Gee, Officer

Krupke"). He also understudied one of the leads, Mickey Callan as Riff, and later took over the role.

A handful of the dancers were to reappear later in notable guises, so much so that I wonder whether Fosse himself—rather than Zoya, the choreographer in name—made the final selections. These included Ben Harney, who went on to win a Best Leading Actor Tony as Curtis in *Dreamgirls*. Ben's first big role was as replacement to Tiger Haynes as the Tinman in *The Wiz*. Haynes, well-remembered for a showstopping duet with Carol Burnett in Abbott's 1964 musical, *Fade Out—Fade In*, was also in our revival, playing a small role while serving as Cab's standby. At the same time, Ted Ross—who was to win a Tony as the Cowardly Lion in *The Wiz*—was across the street with us in *Raisin*. Cameron Mason was to be one of the *Chorus Line* originals: Vicki Frederick—who had also been in *Tricks*—was a replacement Cassie in *A Chorus Line*, after which she was in the original cast of *Dancin'*. Finally, Chester (later Chet) Walker went on to become a replacement in *Dancin'*, a swing dancer in the 1986 revival of *Sweet Charity*, and choreographer of *Fosse* and the 2013 revival of *Pippin*.

Let it be added that some sections of the choreography were, indeed, disposable; at least, if you were Bob Fosse you might want to dispose of them. The big "Once a Year Day" number, featuring an endless dance as the entire cast frolics at the annual company picnic, is not very good; the end features everyone "comically" collapsing in a heap, and I think the audience might have understandably collapsed as well. The 1954 show built to a climactic dream ballet—"The Jealousy Ballet," in which Hines pictured marriage to the flirtatious Gladys—which was cut from our revival altogether, and being extraneous went unmissed.

My favorite nightly moment in the show—along with calling the "Hernando's Hideaway" number—came early in the first act. The leading lady's opening number is a swinging waltz called "I'm Not at All in Love." This was within the factory set; after Babe sings the first refrain (with assorted lines from her coworkers), the full female chorus joins in for the second, putting her on a factory dolly and wheeling her around the stage to the choreography. The number ends with Babe center, on a crowded stage. Blackout.

Barbara McNair—unable to see in the dark—needed help getting off, so the ASM was assigned to slip onstage as soon as the lights went down, grab her by the elbow, and escort her safely into the wing. I started the number on the other side of the stage, crossing behind the backdrop during the second refrain—the one sung, loudly and in unison, by all the girls. And what did I do, being alone in the dark on the stage of a Broadway theatre with the band blaring? I sang along, at the top of my lungs. With a full orchestra, fifteen girls and—in those days—no microphones, my voice did no harm to the mix. But it was as exhilarating as skiing down a black diamond, or more—for me, at least. Hey, I was only twenty, and got any desire to sing on a Broadway stage out of my system then and there.

A couple of weeks after the opening, we ran into a near catastrophe; that is, a catastrophe in terms of that night's performance. The song hit of the show was "Hey There." Prince once told me that of all the songwriters he worked with—and I daresay I needn't list Bernstein, Bock, Sondheim, Kander, Lloyd Webber, and more—Adler & Ross were uncanny in their ability to devise how the songs should be staged, and they were usually right. The song slot had the new-to-town factory manager Sid rebuffed in his advances to Babe; clearly, she was labor and he was management. He sits at his desk, depressed, then shakes it off and switches on the Dictaphone—an early machine that transcribed messages, like a tape recorder, for his secretary to type—and starts to dictate a business memo. His heart isn't in it, so he continues: "Memo to Sid Sorokin" [i.e., himself]. . . . "Hey there, you with the stars in your eyes—" And there it is, the biggest song hit of 1954.

But there's more. After the applause, Sid in disgust switches the Dictaphone to playback. "Hey there," comes his taped voice (without orchestra), "you with the stars in your eyes." "Who, me?" he asks. The band steals in and the song continues as he sings a duet with his prerecorded voice about how he'd better forget her. Thus you have a romantic ballad—and a mighty good one—serving as a strong and inventively canny musical scene.

Technology is technology, though. One item on the stage manager's nightly list was to have someone nearby at the start of "Hey there," in case the tape failed. The tape never failed, until one January night when it did. I was calling the show. Bert, who should have been standing by, was nowhere to be found. Hal flipped on the Dictaphone for the repeat, and nothing came out. He did an involuntary take, and waited. Conductor Joyce Brown, in the pit, waited. I immediately thought: if nobody is going to sing, I'd better. But how do I sing while also calling light cues within the song? Nevertheless—and it all happened in an instant—I moved to the wing, a few feet behind where Hal sat at his office desk, to start to sing. (From all those years of listening to the original cast album, I knew the words, the tempo, and even John Raitt's vocal interpretation perfectly.)

Just as I was about to make what likely would have been a disastrous solo singing debut, from far across the stage came "Hey there." Stan Page, the second ASM and a cast member of the original *Pajama Game*, had been doing a costume change for the picnic scene in the corridor off stage left. As soon as he heard the silence, he dashed over—half-dressed—to sing what should have been coming from the speakers. Far better than I would have, too.

Hi-De-Hi-De-Hi

In a cast full of people acting professionally, Cab stood out by omission. He was always polite to me but was our biggest problem in performance. There is a scene in which he winds up with his pants off. (This was high-class stuff.) There is a slowdown in the pajama factory, resulting in complaints from distributors about defective product. Being the efficiency expert, he tries on a pair of pajamas and they fall down; it turns out the button affixers are sabotaging the bottoms. He puts the pants back on, and blackout. Drop flies in, we move on.

At least two shows a week, though, Cab was apparently drunk. After falling down on cue, he'd be unable to get up. Since he was rolling and weaving around, it was impossible to give the cue for the blackout and curtain; I didn't want to hit Cab on the head with the drop, which was weighted with a wooden batten across the bottom. There was Cab flailing around, while poor Hal was forced to stand there, waiting to start the next scene, in disgust. After repeated occurrences, Hal took Cab up on charges at Equity. Cab filed countercharges but ended up with an official reprimand from the union. When a show is a hit, you are more likely to live with these things. When the show is clearly a flop, your annoyance level is higher.

Cab Calloway in happier, and younger, days (1943).
PHOTOFEST/TWENTIETH CENTURY-FOX FILM CORPORATION

Hal's contract gave him an out for additional filming on a TV pilot he'd made before rehearsals. (You occasionally give a star such an out, especially if you know he will give a high-quality performance and he doesn't sell tickets anyway.) After New Year's, he went off to Hollywood for two weeks to do retakes on his pilot, about a New York City cop. No, not *Barney Miller*, that came two years later. This was a crime drama called *Mr. Inside/Mr. Outside*, which was not picked up (although the pilot was aired).

Business, meanwhile, went from poor—with a small pickup during the holidays—to dire. The Tuesday after Hal left, we posted a provisional closing notice. Union-wise, you need to give a full eight-performance notice; by posting it on Tuesday before the first performance, we could pay everyone for the week and close on Sunday. But at the preperformance meeting, Richard informed everyone that if business picked up— or if he could raise additional money—he would rescind the notice and go on another week.

Ticket sales did not pick up, and Richard could not raise money, so that seemed like the end. On Saturday afternoon, after the matinee, Cab called Richard aside and said *he'd* provide the necessary funds. We were saved!

After the curtain went down on what would have been our closing performance, Cab made a speech to the company, telling them how much the show meant to him and how glad he was to help out any way he can. And, he said, wasn't Hal's temporary replacement—a little-known actor named Jay Stuart—wonderful? He was glad to help keep the show open, and also to keep Stuart in the role. That is, Cab was in—as long as Hal was out.

As it turned out, Cab didn't come through with a nickel. We played the second week with Stuart, and then one final week with Hal (and things were especially frosty between the two stars). We closed February 3, after an eight-week run and the loss of the entire $300,000 investment.

At the final Sunday matinee, Cab had a surprise—an unwelcome surprise—for us. Hines, who served as narrator, had a final transition into the closing scene. This was staged way downstage, in a spotlight, while the finale scenery was being assembled behind the blackout drop. That afternoon, Cab—in his spotlight—stepped down to the apron. Instead of his short speech, he launched into an a cappella rendition of his 1931 hit, "Minnie the Moocher."

"Hi-de-hi-de-hi," he sang, expecting the audience to echo the phrase like they used to do when he was an enormous star. Not much echo; the audience, or at least most of them, had no idea what this was. It sure didn't sound like *The Pajama Game.* Joyce Brown stood in the pit waiting to start the scene change music, not knowing what to do. While I had a backstage intercom to call cues, it wasn't strong enough to reach the follow spot booth atop the theatre so I couldn't tell them to just kill Cab's light. So I waited, and the cast waited, and the audience waited while Cab indulged himself to no reaction. He finally finished, stepped upstage, and allowed us to proceed. That was the last I saw of Cab, and more than enough.

DRIFT AWAY

I enjoyed being a stage manager. Unlike the company manager, press agent, or general manager, you are part of the performance—literally so; nothing goes into motion without the stage manager giving the cue. You are also a member of the performing company. The company manager is in close contact with the cast daily and is—or was in the predigital age—the person who usually signed and distributed the paychecks as well as dealing with ticket issues and the like. (The company manager on a touring show also dealt with transportation and hotels, which required endless interaction.)

But the company manager is always something of a temporary visitor backstage. Once the curtain is up and the show is on, the company manager is usually gone. Understandably so—the actors and stage managers might arrive at the theatre between six and seven, for an eight o'clock performance; the company manager's day starts at ten or eleven in the morning. While the company manager is involved in backstage temperament and problems—and is often the problem solver—it is the stage manager who actually lives with said problems.

Over the course of my two months as stage manager, I found myself dealing with a work-related problem of my own. Parts of the performance—specifically musical numbers—are fun to call; other sections are technically tricky to handle and require close attention, especially when you have moving sets and equipment that can injure actors. Some cues are dependent on other cues; you are watching for something, or listening for something, then rushing to the next cue and the next. (Nowadays many aspects are automated, but in 1973 every signal and cue light came from the stage manager's desk.)

I didn't mind the complicated parts; they were challenging and could be invigorating. But these were countered by quiet patches in book scenes. I'd come to a stretch with no cues at all, perhaps three or four script-pages worth. I would look ahead to the next cue and wait—and wait, and wait. Every once in a while, while listening through those intervening pages of dialogue, I would drift off. Thinking of something else, or making a note about something performance-related, we'd be three pages later and I'd have to scramble to give the cue. I don't remember ever missing anything, exactly; but I would come close, repeatedly. Recognizing my tendency to drift, I tried various methods of keeping on top of the script, but as the run ended it was very clear. I had the makings of a stage manager; but I would likely always have a problem sitting there paying rapt attention through those dialogue scenes I'd heard over and over.

When *The Pajama Game* came to an end on February 3, 1974, so did my career as a stage manager. I went back across the street, to *Raisin*.

Chapter Eighteen

Toiling in the Vineyards

We Don't Do That Anymore

The major problem with *Raisin*, which despite a healthy first year wound up a financial failure, stemmed from Bob Nemiroff. Helen's business instincts were good; her advice was usually proper, and she sternly and repeatedly advised him against actions that were ill-advised or bordering on the questionable. Bob, though, wouldn't listen.

He *would* listen, actually; he would sit there, puffing his pipe, listening and talking and going on and on, running the conversation into the ground. Sample dialogue: "Well . . . [puff] [puff] I think tha . . . [puff] [puff] [puff] don't you think [puff] what I—wait [sound of lighter] well—"

Despite Bob's seeming patience as he listened, he always did precisely what he intended in the first place. He had a Machiavellian press agent named Max Eisen, an old-timer who had done a good job bringing nontraditional (i.e., Black) audiences to the Hansberry/Nemiroff *To Be Young, Gifted and Black*. Max had done a less successful job attracting people to *Les Blancs*, but there was no way to get anyone to want to see *Les Blancs*. Max seemed to sit on Bob's shoulder with a pitchfork, egging him on. Bob, at least, always tried to cloak himself in a bland-but-insincere professorial politeness.

Opening night, Bob gave me a book of African American poetry, with the handwritten inscription: "To Steven—whose unsung toiling in the vineyards brings projects like this to fruition."

Joe Morton, Deborah Allen, Ernestine Jackson, and Virginia Capers in a moment of levity in *Raisin* (1973).
PHOTOFEST

TOILING IN THE VINEYARDS?

Shortly after the opening, we had something of a windfall. *Raisin* included strong performances from just about all the principals, but Ralph Carter stood out with one of the most endearingly charming performances on Broadway. At twelve, he was already a veteran; he made his Broadway debut two years earlier, replacing Douglas Grant as the littlest kid in *The Me Nobody Knows* for the final months of the run.

In the fall of 1972, he had the distinction of being featured in two of the biggest disasters in memory. First, he played the child version of the title role in *Dude*, from the *Hair* team of Galt MacDermot and Gerome Ragni. This was memorable in part because they tore the seating out of the Broadway Theatre, reconfiguring it into an environmental theatre-in-the-round. People in the valleys—the top price seats, at $15—sat on uncomfortable stools on the playing area in the middle (and bottom) of the amphitheater setup. Then came the foothills, the mountains, the trees, and the cheap seats in the "treetops."

Dude had an especially tortured life. It started previews on September 11, with dire results. Ragni, given the success of *Hair*, was able to get whatever he wanted from his producers—including the appointment of a friend with little theatre experience, one Rocco Bufano, as director. Ragni's demands also included actual dirt covering the floor of the valleys. At the first performance, the cast started dancing, the dirt started flying, and the actors and valley-dwellers started choking. The next night—which I attended—they wet down the dirt, turning the floor into mud and ruining the costumes. Out went the dirt. The producer—Adela Holzer, a prodigious con-woman who wound up serving multiple prison terms, including one for swindling Elvis Presley (I'm not making this stuff up)—held the line by refusing Ragni's request to release one hundred butterflies in the treetops at each performance.

The first performance revealed that *Dude* was an incoherent shambles, so much so that after five previews they fired director Bufano and closed down while new director Tom O'Horgan (of *Hair*) came in to try to fix the thing. (They retained the cast lineup, divided—for no discernable reason—into "The Theatre Stars," "The Shubert Angels," and "The Theatre Wings.") They regrouped for more previews, opened on October 9, and closed for good two weeks later. Having seen the show in both incarnations, I can say that Tom's version was marginally better but still unfathomable; Gerry Ragni, at that point, was indecipherable.

Galt, meanwhile, was already in rehearsal with *Via Galactica*, the show that opened the Uris Theatre with the aforementioned Hall of Fame celebration. *Dude* closed on October 21; *Via Galactica* previewed on November 6, with Ralph Carter already added to the cast. The two shows, combined, didn't give him more than sixteen weeks of work. Of course, he was in grade school at the time.

Several weeks after *Raisin* opened, Bob called excitedly. Excitedly for him, that is—he was never one to sound enthusiastic. But he had big news, he said between puff after puff on his pipe: television producer Norman Lear had just *bought* Ralph, for $75,000. *Raisin* had been capitalized at $350,000, so this was a significant sum.

"What do you mean, you're selling Ralph?" (There was a sardonic song in *Raisin* in which Joe, Ernestine, and Debby—mimicking the folks from the Clybourne Park Improvement Association who wanted to prevent them from moving into their white neighborhood—sang "no, we don't do that anymore.")

Lear was the most successful sitcom producer of the day. *All in the Family*, in 1971, had spun off characters into *The Jeffersons*—starring Sherman Hemsley, of *Purlie*—in 1972. Now, a character was moving from *The Jeffersons* and starting a third series, *Good Times*. (Two years later there was yet another *All in the Family* spinoff, *Maude*.) *Good Times* was a Black family comedy, and Lear wanted the most adorable-but-savvy child actor he could find.

Would Bob release Ralph—the biggest crowd-pleaser in *Raisin*—from his newly opened, still-building Broadway show? Of course he wouldn't. But then Lear started offering cash in exchange for Ralph's release, and when he reached $75,000 Bob acquiesced. Even so, he drove a hard bargain, insisting that Ralph temporarily return for the weeks when the Tony voters would be seeing the show. *Good Times* went on the air in February, and Ralph was suddenly a celebrity.

WINNER OF NINE TONY AWARD NOMINATIONS
As we passed the profitable holiday weeks and entered cold January, our grosses started to fall; we were still making money every week, but not the sort of profits that signified long-term success. And so we set our sights on the Tonys.

In the meantime, Bob and his press agent Max—anxious to make whatever deals they could—devised what Helen referred to as the "green sock" policy: if you came up to the box office wearing a green sock and a red sock, you got a big discount; if you came up wearing a red sock and a green sock, you got an even lower price.

This drove the box office treasurers to distraction; they had an easier time when people just paid the list price, rather than having to collect all these scraps of paper—documenting the different discounts—and doing the requisite paperwork. Conversely, numerous discounts gave treasurers ample room for chicanery, such as selling full-price tickets but manufacturing backup to "prove" that they had been discounted and pocketing the difference.

The nominations were announced on March 28, the official season ending earlier than it does nowadays. The news was excellent: we led the pack with nine nominations, in every eligible area except the design categories. (*Raisin* had a skeletal set, with much of the action artfully pantomimed.) "Winner of Nine Tony Nominations including Best Musical" sounded good—and was good—but it was deceptive. Close on our heels was Hal Prince's revival of *Candide*, with eight. But *Candide* earned its eight nominations without being eligible for Best Musical or Best Score. In any case, Bob and Max plastered "Winner of Nine Tony Nominations including Best Musical" in paid ads and posted on building sites across town.

Best Musical and Best Score were complicated categories that year. *Candide* and *Lorelei* were rewritten, thoroughly overhauled versions of the 1956 Leonard Bernstein/Richard Wilbur *Candide* and the 1949 Jule Styne-Leo Robin *Gentlemen Prefer Blondes*. Could they be considered new musicals? How could the scores—both of which had some new material but both of which were built upon the well-known songs from the originals—compete with a brand-new score written specifically for a new show?

And what about *Gigi*, the stage version of the Oscar-winning 1957 motion picture? This had never before appeared onstage, and thus— unlike *Candide* and *Lorelei/Gentlemen Prefer Blondes*—had never actually been eligible for a Tony Award. Still, how could you consider the renowned hits to comprise a new score, even if authors Frederick Loewe and Alan Jay Lerner had added four new songs for the occasion?

The Tony administrators have always had a difficult time coming up with rulings; as soon as they take a definitive stance, something else comes along to challenge it. They determined that *Candide* and *Lorelei* (but not *Gigi*) were indeed eligible for Best Musical. After protests from the producers of the season's few original musicals, the committee changed their collective mind and ruled that *Candide* and *Lorelei*—on second thought—would not be eligible.

This left *Raisin* with a relatively easy field. *Seesaw*, the Cy Coleman/ Dorothy Fields musical, had a calamitous tryout in Detroit, during which they fired the director, choreographer, librettist, orchestrator, and leading lady along with a few other actors. Michael Bennett was called in to salvage the show—his first musical directing job on his own—and did a good job of turning a dismal embarrassment into something mildly palatable. But mildly palatable, and passably entertaining, was not enough. What's more, it reached Broadway in March 1973—just after the 1972–1973 cutoff date—and closed in December, so that it was gone three months before the 1974 nominations were announced. The other nominee was *Over Here!*, a flimsy piece of World War II nostalgia that starred the two then-surviving Andrews Sisters. *Raisin* was the only one of the three that received highly favorable reviews, and the only one that did decent business.

BACK AT THE TONYS

On April 21, 1974, I returned for my second Tony Award ceremony, held at the Shubert on the set of *Over Here!* This time, I was not filling a prime orchestra location, next to a nominee; I was up in the last row of the second balcony with my college friend Nancy, just in front of the candy stand where I used to peddle orange drink at *Promises*.

Things started poorly, *Raisin*-wise. After the usual Tony Award ceremony opening number, the design awards went elsewhere as expected (we weren't nominated). A half-hour in came the choreography award, with Bennett—the ex-show dancer who had won two Tonys as choreographer and codirector of *Follies* in 1972—besting Donny.

A close call, I suppose; Donny had given Broadway modern-dance-infused choreography of a new and refreshing kind, but Bennett had worked magic on *Seesaw*. While the latter was closed, and a failure, it was a way for the voters to acknowledge what he had accomplished with his salvage job. It should be added, though, that a significant portion of the *Seesaw* choreography was not by Bennett. He had been understandably busy directing the show; rewriting it (personally performing surgery on Mike Stewart's existing libretto and receiving sole official credit); supervising new scenery and new orchestrations; and soothing a demoralized cast. Some of the choreography was left over from fired choreographer Grover Dale.

Surely not a factor in the choice of Bennett was that no Black director, choreographer, composer, lyricist, librettist, playwright, or producer had thus far won a Tony Award, and wouldn't until 1975. Only ten had even been nominated, including Hansberry and director Lloyd Richards for *A Raisin in the Sun*. Donny himself was the first Black choreographer to receive a nomination, in 1964, for *Golden Boy* (losing, understandably, to Gower, for *Dolly*).

Next came Ralph Carter, now a sitcom star, doing his endearing "Sidewalk Tree" number from *Raisin*. Immediately after, Ernestine lost the supporting actress award to Janie Sell (from *Over Here!*) and Ralph lost the supporting actor award to Tommy Tune, who had energized Broadway with his performance in *Seesaw*. What's more, everyone knew Tommy had choreographed his big number in that show, "It's Not Where You Start, It's Where You Finish," which Walter Kerr in the *Times* called "the nuttiest—and maybe just plain funniest—number I have ever seen in a musical."

There then followed more than an hour of unrelated awards—including a special honor to *Candide*, which had been deemed ineligible for Best Musical—capped by Virginia Capers doing her big number, "A Whole Lotta Sunlight." *Raisin* was able to get an unprecedented two separate numbers on the awards show, encompassing more than eight minutes. Bob insisted on Virginia doing her song, figuring—correctly—that Tony Awards ceremony producer Alex Cohen would so want to spotlight that newly minted TV star, Ralph, that he'd spring for two songs.

And then came blow after blow. Hal Prince, as expected, won the director award for *Candide*. This gave Donny—Broadway's first Black director/choreographer and the first to be nominated in the dual roles—two losses for the evening. Then came the Best Actor award, which Joe Morton lost to Christopher Plummer for the long-closed, lethargic musical version of *Cyrano*.

The worst moment of the evening—for *Raisin*, that is—arrived when they announced the winner of the Best Score. We were up against *Seesaw* and *Gigi*. *Gigi*?? With "Thank Heaven for Little Girls," "The Night They Invented Champagne," "I Remember It Well," and the title song, all popular hits since 1958? How could that possibly be eligible? But none of the songs had ever been performed on Broadway, so the Tony people deemed it so. The fourth nominee—signifying how poor the season was—was a nonmusical play with songs, Neil Simon's *The Good Doctor*. Like *Seesaw* and the already shuttered *Gigi*, it was a flop, with negligible incidental songs by Peter Link.

The envelope opened and the award went to: Lerner and Loewe. Jaws dropped. Poor Elliott Gould, who was presenting the award in his then-guise as a cool, counterculture movie star (as in *M*A*S*H*), looked around perplexed as nobody showed up to take the award. He finally just walked off. Lerner, no doubt, figured the nomination was a farce and stayed far away; Loewe, who had effectively retired, was disinterested in Broadway (and *Gigi*) altogether. I didn't have all that much affection for the score of *Raisin*, which I felt was hit or miss. But *Gigi?* This was, indeed, a surprise.

We then lost the book award, once again to *Candide*. Which, at least, was an altogether new piece of writing. Librettist Hugh Wheeler had changed the nature of the entire show, so his work could reasonably be considered "new," and it was arguably superior to the book for *Raisin*, which was strongest when quoting Hansberry's play verbatim.

Big Talk

Finally, two and a half hours into the ceremony, Marlo Thomas came out to present the Best Musical award. Nobody thought *Seesaw* or *Over Here!* could or should win, but after seven Tony losses in a row the *Raisin* folk were mighty nervous. But win we did.

I watched apprehensively as Bob took the stage. No pipe in view; it was the Tony Awards, after all. He was in a tux, with a fussily ruffled bright pink shirt and an oversized bowtie. Bob began to speak, as follows, and if you don't believe me you can find the 1974 Tony ceremony on the internet and cringe for yourself.

He started by explaining how songwriters Judd Woldin and Bob Brittan came to him with the idea nine years earlier. Then he thanked Lorraine; Judd and Bob; Donny McKayle; Charlotte Zaltzberg, the co-librettist who had died two months earlier. Then he thanked the "magnificent" cast and technical crew. Two minutes and six seconds in, instead of making an exit, he paused. Knowing Bob as well as I did, I turned to Nancy, way up in the second balcony, and whispered, "*Now we're in trouble.*"

Bob continued. He thanked "my mother and father, May and Moochie." There was a nervous laugh from the audience; wasn't he finished yet? As he talked about his parents, the small laugh turned into a bigger laugh of ridicule. At two-and-a-half minutes, people started to clap, louder and louder as if to say: get this man off the stage! Bob was hardly audible in the theatre, although the television audience could hear him. When he got to "there are so many people to thank," the audience broke out into cheers, or jeers, as he started mentioning investors. He finally turned and left, after three minutes and ten seconds. The Tony people immediately thereafter instituted an acceptance speech time limit, after which the orchestra starts to drown you out. Call it "the Nemiroff cue."

Next came the Best Actress award. Virginia was up against Broadway favorite Carol Channing, for *Lorelei*, and Michele Lee, who had bravely replaced Lainie Kazan during the tryout of *Seesaw* and helped turn it into an at least partially viable show. Under the circumstances, it seemed likely that the universally loved Carol would take her second Tony. But no! Virginia won, giving *Raisin* the final two awards of the evening after seven misses.

Virginia, the next day, was furious. She had gone triumphant to the press room following her win, only to find that the reporters were more interested in talking to Carol than her. "I won the Award, Channing lost!" she complained vigorously. "Why did they want to interview her? They just ignored me because I'm Black," she cried, importuning Bob and Max to do something about it.

Long Torturous Road

Two New Musicals, Someday

MEANWHILE, THINGS WERE FINALLY MOVING ALONG IN PHIL ROSE'S office, two flights up.

The years since *Purlie* had been difficult. Beginning with *A Raisin in the Sun* in 1959, Phil had produced twelve shows over twelve seasons. Only two were financially successful—the Hansberry play and William Manhoff's 1964 comedy *The Owl and the Pussycat*. The twelfth show, *Purlie*, opened in the spring of 1970. It appeared headed for success through the first summer of the run. Given Phil's lack of clout with the people then running the Shubert Theatres, though, he was forced out of the Broadway after nine months to allow the long-running *Fiddler on the Roof* to move up from the Majestic. (This to make way for *Lovely Ladies, Kind Gentlemen*, which lasted three weeks.) With no long-term booking available to Phil, he accepted the Shubert offer of the Winter Garden; only he'd have to get out in three months, to make way for the already-booked *Follies*. *Purlie* wound up at the infrequently booked ANTA for its final eight months.

Thus, the show had to endure an in-town tour from Fifty-Second Street to Fiftieth, then back to Fifty-Second. Each move meant an extra $60,000 or so to take-out the show, load it in trucks even though the moves were within two blocks, and then reassemble it in the new theatre. These excess charges were the difference between *Purlie* paying off its investment and closing at a loss.

Phil, who in the worst of times remained resolutely hopeful—hadn't they told him he'd never get *A Raisin in the Sun* on Broadway?—packed the show up and took it out on the road, for an unprofitable twelve-month tour. Faced with the end of the line, he then convinced himself that Broadway audiences were now, finally, *really* ready for *Purlie*. So he booked it into the Billy Rose Theatre—a hard-to-book "jinx-house" at the time, now the Nederlander—starting immediately *after* Christmas 1972. Thus, they missed the holiday and went headlong into the worst-attended weeks in the theatrical calendar. With no business whatsoever, *Purlie* ultimately and finally collapsed after two weeks with astounding losses.

When I first entered Helen's office in September 1973, Phil had two musicals ready to go—except for the money.

First up was—or, at least, was intended to be—*Shenandoah*, based on the provocative 1965 film of that title. James Stewart starred as Charlie Anderson, a Virginia farmer who—being a pacifist—refuses to allow his six sons to fight in the Civil War. Until they get caught up in it, at which point he inevitably picks up a rifle and fights; what else can he do? The property offered the makings of a serious musical about principle, pacifism, and death, a combination of elements that had great resonance in the final years of the Vietnam War.

As with *Purlie*, Gary Geld and Peter Udell wrote the score, while *Shenandoah* screenwriter James Lee Barrett collaborated with Phil and Peter on the book.

By early 1972, they were ready to approach their star of choice: James Stewart. Why not? He started his career in the theatre and had returned in 1970, in *Harvey*. Stewart was intrigued, but the combination of his age (sixty-four) and lack of singing skill was enough to keep him from taking up the challenge. Second choice was Robert Ryan, star of such films as *Crossfire* (which is a little-known but wonderful film worth seeking out), *The Set-Up*, *Bad Day at Black Rock*, and *Odds Against Tomorrow*. Despite Ryan's career of playing tough guys, he was actually a liberal and a pacifist—which made him perfect for *Shenandoah*. Phil set a production date for the fall of 1973, which would have put it in direct competition with *Raisin*, and had a relatively easy time lining up backers. But Ryan died just after July 4. Without a star, the money commitments vanished and there was no show.

With *Shenandoah* suddenly off the table, Phil rushed to make arrangements for his other Geld-Udell musical. *All the Comforts of Home* was a musical version of Ketti Frings's 1957 Pulitzer-winning play *Look Homeward, Angel,* based on the autobiographical novel by Thomas Wolfe. Realizing that he'd have even more difficulty raising money for this broodingly downbeat musical than he'd had with *Shenandoah,* Phil decided to make a deal with the Circle in the Square whereby the nonprofit—in their second season at their new, Broadway-area house beneath the Uris Theatre—would produce the musical at their considerably-lower-than-Broadway rates. After it opened to great reviews and played its limited engagement, Phil would swoop it up and move it over to a bigger theatre for a traditional, commercial run.

"Sure he will," I thought, as Phil announced the show in the *Times* in September, the very week we opened the *Raisin* tryout in Philadelphia.

By December, *All the Comforts of Home* had been wiped from the Circle schedule, with its March 5, 1974, opening canceled. The show remained in limbo for season after season, finally reaching Broadway in 1978 under the title *Angel.* All this for a five-performance run, which seemed hardly worth it.

Big Top

Speaking of prospective new Broadway musicals, a far more successful one was birthed one Sunday night in March 1974. Ted Goldsmith, an old-time press agent who had worked with Jeffrey on *The Pajama Game,* stopped by the office. He had an annual spring job handling the New York engagement of the Ringling Bros. and Barnum & Bailey Circus at Madison Square Garden. They were papering, did anyone want to go?

I called Bramble, who told me Ted had also offered tickets there; the circus account was headed by Lee Solters and Harvey Sabinson, Merrick's publicists.

"Do you remember Janet Gillespie? She was in our puppetry class." In the spring of 1972, I had taken an NYU course—mostly because it sounded easy—taught by one of the Muppet designers on Jim Henson's staff. I was surprised, the first day, to find Mark sitting there. It turned out that he had never quite finished his degree at Emerson College, and still needed some final credits. Mark was so good with puppets that when one was needed for a gag in *Tricks*, Biff hired Mark to make it. (Hidden in the back of the *Playbill*, you can find the unlikely credit "Gorilla Puppet by Mark Bramble.")

One of the girls in the class had left school after the second year, running off to "join the circus." Actually, to go to the Ringling clown school in Sarasota, Florida. Having graduated, she was now making her professional debut. "We should go see Janet," I said. So we did. I went with Nancy on Saturday afternoon, Mark and Kim on Sunday night.

Mark and I usually started the day on the phone, while he was opening Jack Schlissel's mail and I was sitting at my desk on Fifty-Seventh. He was all but bursting when he called the next morning.

"What do you think of this," he said. "A musical about P. T. Barnum! All about how he became a showman, and then started the circus. I could do it like a musical, only with the book interrupted by circus acts."

Mark happened to have a copy of Barnum's autobiography on his bookshelf, so he stayed up all night reading and thinking and planning and dreaming.

"Well, I don't know—" I hesitated. From the beginning, I wondered just how such a musical would work out. But Mark had more than enough enthusiasm on his own. He started putting ideas on paper right then—although it would be six long and discouraging years before Mark's *Barnum* reached Broadway.

LEADING MEN

Meanwhile, Phil Rose—nothing if not determined—plugged away at *Shenandoah*. After a wide search, he wound up with Hollywood's Jack Palance. Palance was more of a featured actor, best known for his role as the villain in *Shane*; he typically played evil, menacing characters. Far from a perfect fit for a Jimmy Stewartesque leading man, but the likeliest prospect. Phil rescheduled the show for a March 1974 Broadway opening, which would have put him directing both *Shenandoah* and *All the Comforts of Home* at once. If either of them happened as scheduled, that is, but neither did. Winter arrived, with *Shenandoah* still not capitalized and unable to go into rehearsal. In January of 1974—as *The Pajama Game* was staggering through its final weeks—Phil got a call from Michael Price, producing manager of the Goodspeed Opera House in East Haddam, Connecticut.

A local merchant named William Goodspeed opened the place in 1876. It soon fell out of use and into disrepair. After serving as a storage facility for the Connecticut Department of Transportation, the building was condemned in 1959. A group of locals—including sometime-producer Albert Selden and actress Norma Terris, who had originated the starring role of Magnolia in Jerome Kern and Oscar Hammerstein's *Show Boat*—bought it from the state and after a long renovation opened the rebuilt theatre in 1963 as a venue dedicated to discovering rarely seen old musicals. In 1965 they decided to produce an altogether new musical. *Man of La Mancha* was an instant sellout, quickly transferring to Broadway and becoming an established classic, thereby establishing the Opera House as an important tryout venue. Would Phil consider starting *Shenandoah* there?

With no investors coming in—or likely to—and Palance's agreed-upon dates running out, this was a welcome solution. If the show was as good as Phil thought it was, the Goodspeed run would serve as a full-scale, professional backer's audition. And if the show was a bust—like Phil's pre-*Purlie* musicals, *Bravo Giovanni* and *Cafe Crown*—at least Phil wouldn't be saddled with the losses. He quickly made a deal similar to the *Raisin* deal with Arena Stage, which we happily provided. Goodspeed would pay to produce the show in Connecticut, so long as Phil kept the costs in line with what they normally budgeted for the slot. The upside for Goodspeed, along with the publicity coming from a second bona fide Broadway musical trying out on their stage, would be a taste of future earnings from *Shenandoah*, should there be future earnings from *Shenandoah*. If I recall accurately, this meant one-half of 1 percent of the weekly box office gross from all first-class productions (i.e., Broadway and the National Tour), plus 5 percent of the profits.

Phil would direct the show, as planned, and bring in his chosen-for-Broadway choreographer (Bob Tucker). He also had carte blanche in casting, as long as the actors agreed to work at the applicable Goodspeed scale, which was higher than off-Broadway but lower than Broadway. This was fine with everyone involved—except Jack Palance. His agents had arranged a hefty salary of $5,000 a week, and they were not interested in him going to middle-of-nowhere Connecticut for $750 per.

Phil explained that this was the top salary at Goodspeed and nobody earned more on any of their shows; he explained that the limited capacity and low ticket prices couldn't support $5,000 a week. But no; Palance and his agents weren't interested, and that was that. I suppose their thinking was that if he went to Broadway and failed, at least he would be—by definition—a Broadway star. If he went to summer stock and failed, it would likely be seen as proof that he couldn't carry a Broadway musical. Michael Price didn't mind. Goodspeed had a large subscriber base guaranteeing practically sold-out business, and their audiences didn't expect stars; the menacing Palance, in fact, might have scared off some of the genteel, elderly subscribers.

The prior season, Goodspeed had a major hit with a production of *El Capitan*, a revised version of the 1896 comic operetta with music by "march king" John Philip Sousa. The show had done so well that it transferred—not to Broadway, but to Ford's Theatre in Washington, DC. And without a star; the leading role, Michael told Phil, was played to great acclaim by a reasonably well-known actor/singer named John Cullum.

After all that Rose-Udell-Geld had gone through, it was disheartening to once again start searching for someone to play Charlie Anderson. When Phil told Morty Halpern, his stage manager, that Palance was out, Morty said he had someone.

Morty was an old-timer—his first credit was on *Sing Out, Sweet Land!*, a 1944 Theatre Guild revue written by Walter Kerr and starring Alfred Drake just out of *Oklahoma!* His long career encompassed an impressive list of flop musicals; he almost prided himself on being hired for unworkable shows (*Shinbone Alley*, *Cafe Crown*, *The Yearling*, and *I'm Solomon* among them). Typical of his luck: after waiting more than two years for *Shenandoah*, Phil urged him to take another job he'd been offered. Ten days later, Phil unexpectedly found funding. Morty wound up with a sixteen-performance flop, *So Long, 174th Street*, instead of what would be thirty months of *Shenandoah*. The job instead went to the assistant stage manager Morty had lined up, Steven Zweigbaum.

Simultaneously with Morty's many Broadway shows and industrials, he was for twenty years production stage manager at Guy Lombardo's summer musical operation at the Jones Beach Marine Theatre. The 1973 offering had been *Carousel*, and Morty enthusiastically suggested that their Billy Bigelow would make a *perfect* Charlie Anderson: John Cullum—the same actor who had just been recommended by Michael Price.

So Phil, with a decided lack of enthusiasm, called Cullum.

The Man from Tennessee

John hailed from Knoxville, Tennessee. After graduating from the University of Tennessee and serving a couple of years in Korea, he came to New York in 1956 at the age of twenty-six determined to be an actor. He almost immediately got a job as an extra in the Phoenix Theatre production of *Saint Joan*, starring Siobhán McKenna, after which he spent several years at various regional theatres, during which he managed to thoroughly tame his strong Appalachian accent.

In the fall of 1960, he appeared in *Camelot*, playing the small role of Sir Dinadan. His distinctive voice can be heard on the cast album in the song "Then You May Take Me to the Fair," in which he promises Guenevere (Julie Andrews) that he will "vivisect" Lancelot (Robert Goulet). At the same time, he managed to befriend Richard Burton, who was only five years older but already an international star; while Burton hailed from Wales, an ocean away, both grew up in coal mining country. Cullum was assigned to understudy both Burton and featured player Roddy McDowall; he subbed for the star as King Arthur on four occasions, and ultimately replaced McDowall as the villainous Mordred.

Cullum left *Camelot* for the 1962 musical, *We Take the Town*. He had a major role—with third billing—but the show, which starred Robert Preston as the Mexican general and bandit Pancho Villa, quickly folded in Philadelphia. Yes, Robert Preston as Pancho Villa.

When Burton was cast in what turned out to be the legendary 1964 Broadway production of *Hamlet*, he told director John Gielgud that he had a perfect Laertes. Cullum joined the altogether starry cast, which also included Alfred Drake (Claudius), Hume Cronyn (Polonius), Eileen Herlie (Gertrude), Barnard Hughes (Marcellus), and George Rose (First Grave Digger).

And then came *On a Clear Day You Can See Forever*, which had traveled an especially tortured route. With Alan Jay Lerner's longtime composer Frederick Loewe having retired in 1960 (after *Camelot*) and Richard Rodgers's longtime lyricist Oscar Hammerstein having died in 1960 (after *The Sound of Music*), a Rodgers & Lerner partnership sounded invincible. *I Picked a Daisy*, a musical about extra sensory perception (ESP) and reincarnation, was announced for a March 1963 opening. Signed for the leading roles were television star Robert Horton, from the long-running *Wagon Train*; and the lesser-known Barbara Harris, who had earned personal raves in the 1961 Broadway engagement of the Chicago revue *From the Second City* and in Jerome Robbins's production of Arthur Kopit's *Oh, Dad, Poor Dad, Mama's Hung You in the Closet and I'm Feeling So Sad*. Also on board was director/choreographer Gower Champion, of *Bye Bye Birdie* and *Carnival!* but prior to *Hello, Dolly!*

It soon became apparent that the hardworking Rodgers and the unreliable Lerner were ill matched. Lerner, unbeknownst to the community and perhaps to himself, was struggling with addiction. A dedicated patient of the "miracle injections" given by a celebrity quack-doctor known as "Dr. Feelgood," Lerner grew overly dependent on the shots, which were laced with methedrine. (Dr. Max Jacobsen's clients are said to have ranged from John F. Kennedy to Mickey Mantle to Tennessee Williams, likely the only time you'll ever find those three linked in a sentence.) This explains, in part, Lerner's post-*Camelot* career: six unworkable musicals, one after another. When Lerner missed one work session too many—Rodgers learned that instead of turning up that morning, his lyricist had jetted to Capri—the composer backed out.

Lerner eventually found another collaborator: Burton Lane, of *Finian's Rainbow*, with whom he'd written songs for the 1951 Fred Astaire vehicle, *Royal Wedding* (including the exceptional balled, "Too Late

Now"). With a new title taken from what became the title song, *On a Clear Day You Can See Forever* finally made it to Boston. (Lerner imported Dr. Feelgood, keeping him in attendance during the tryout.) Top-billed, in place of Horton, was the French star Louis Jourdan, who had played the romantic lead in Lerner's 1958 film *Gigi*; Harris remained as leading lady.

Despite the impressively strong score, the show was underwritten and very much of a muddle. What's more, it became quickly apparent that Jourdan couldn't sing the robust songs or act the role in English. It was under these inauspicious circumstances that the producers of *Clear Day*—Lerner, in association with Rogo Productions ("Rogo" being *Camelot* costar Robert Goulet)—decided to cut loose Jourdan and settled on Cullum: a relative unknown for what was a starring role in a big-budget musical, but someone whom they knew full well could launch the songs to the rafters. The show moved to Broadway, opening in October 1965 to a poor critical reception and a stumbling eight-month run. Cullum managed to hold his own, although Harris—with the far flashier role—emerged as a new star.

John Cullum, circa 1974.
PHOTOFEST

After *Clear Day*, Cullum moved on to replace Richard Kiley in *Man of La Mancha*. His next big break came in 1969, with the starring role in a major new musical by the author of *The Music Man*. Meredith Willson's *1491*—about you-can-guess-who—set sail at the Dorothy Chandler Pavilion in Los Angeles. It foundered, though, in San Francisco after a mere fifteen weeks. So much for Broadway stardom; Chita Rivera, too, capsized in that one.

Cullum then joined the already opened *1776* as Edward Rutledge, the pro-slavery firebrand from South Carolina. My hunch is that this role (in a show produced by the producer of *We Take the Town*) was intended for Cullum, who had no choice but to take the starring role in the Willson musical instead. The fiery Rutledge is tailor-made for Cullum—"Molasses to Rum" sounds like it was written for his voice—and he went on to play the role in the 1972 motion picture version.

I first met Cullum when he replaced Lee Richardson as Lord Bothwell for the final five weeks of the run of *Vivat! Vivat Regina!* I also happened to see him do *Carousel* at Jones Beach, in which he appeared to be a first-class Billy Bigelow. Watching that show (or any show) in the Jones Beach amphitheater—which included a large lagoon, and in which the actors had to come way down to the apron to deliver lines into microphones—made it somewhat difficult to tell. But John could sure sing the role.

UP AT THE GOODSPEED

Phil, as director of *Shenandoah*, was lukewarm about the notion of Cullum until he heard him discuss the part. John is an intelligent actor—he might well have seen more in the script than was actually there—and he was sure to discuss the show about this Virginia farmer with his natural Appalachian accent. Once Phil, Peter, and Gary heard Cullum audition, they realized how happy they were—after going through Jimmy Stewart, Robert Ryan, and Jack Palance—to have a Charlie Anderson who was significantly younger, virile, and could actually sing the songs.

Shenandoah was slotted as the third show of the 1974 Goodspeed season. The musical before us was a 1939 Cole Porter musical called *DuBarry Was a Lady*. I had always been interested in discovering how it might hold up; it was a wild comedy written for Ethel Merman and Bert Lahr. This was the one about a nightclub janitor who is slipped a Mickey Finn and dreams that he is Louis XIV in Versailles, with the saloon singer he adores stepping into DuBarry's slippers. "Friendship" was the big song hit.

Since *Shenandoah* was already rehearsing at Goodspeed, I called Michael Price and said I wanted to stop in and could I also see the matinee of *DuBarry?* Michael welcomed me warmly and continued to welcome me up there until he retired in 2015. I fact, I introduced my kids to theatre up at Goodspeed. Michael made them feel so much at home that when I began to take them to actual Broadway theatres, they wanted to know why they couldn't go sit in Michael's office during intermission and have the bartender bring them Shirley Temples.

I didn't get much of a sense of *Shenandoah* from the rehearsal I watched; it just seemed like a bunch of young actors a-whoopin' and a-hollerin' with Phil sitting in the corner. What I was watching, it turned out, was a number called "Next to Lovin', I Like Fightin,'" which in its final form was little more than a bunch of generic southern boys a-whoopin' and a-hollerin' their frustrations.

Three weeks later, on August 12, Helen and I drove up for the opening night performance of *Shenandoah, The Only Home I Know.* That was the title at the time, the idea being that if we called it just plain *Shenandoah* the audiences would be expecting to hear the folk song of that name. "Shenandoah, The Only Home I Know" was a folk-like ballad sung by a tenor soldier in the second act, sort of a dreary substitute for a similarly slotted but superior song ("Momma Look Sharp") in the musical *1776*.

I had read the script for *Shenandoah* early on, and thought it had potential. Here was a musical with enough emotional pull that it could— if the score were strong enough—potentially measure up to Rodgers & Hammerstein. The plot tells of how Charlie Anderson staunchly refuses to let his six sons join up with the Confederate Army. His young teenager, Robert—playing soldier, wearing an army cap—is captured and taken away. Charlie and four of his boys go off to find him, leaving an older son (James) with his wife (Anne) and infant to look after the farm. James and Anne are soon killed by marauders. Meanwhile, Charlie and the other boys encounter a Union patrol; when another son is killed by a sniper, the pacifist Charlie grabs a rifle and shoots the gunman, betraying all those principles he has been singing about. "What else could I do?" he asks. The remaining Andersons return to the farm to find James and Anne murdered, but baby Martha alive. Charlie tells Martha, a prop doll in swaddling clothes, that he will make everything all right. The show closes with the family singing a hymn in church, at which point young Robert comes limping in on a tree-branch cane, back from the war.

Yes, this could make a moving musical—a moving, anti-Vietnam musical—that, for a change, was *about* something. *If* the score were strong enough. Opening night at Goodspeed, as I heard it for the first time (other than on the publisher's demo record), I felt a sinking feeling.

Out with the Old . . .

RAISIN DRIES OUT

BACK AT *RAISIN*, GROSSES IMPROVED FOLLOWING THE TONY AWARD WIN as Best Musical. Business was healthy, though not blockbuster level; given all the discounting we had already done, it was difficult to drive our way up to a full-price hit. The fall outlook, though, was less optimistic. In those days, business was traditionally weak after Labor Day, when schools started up and tourist business ground down. Then the new shows would arrive, which included the David Merrick/Jerry Herman/ Gower Champion musical *Mack & Mabel*; Angela Lansbury in the highly praised London production of *Gypsy*; and two exciting British imports, Peter Shaffer's *Equus* and the Royal Shakespeare Company production of *Sherlock Holmes*. Given the level of our advance, it became apparent that we needed to do some significant discounting. But we had been offering steep discounts all along, hadn't we?

Not helping Bob's mood was Clive Barnes's end-of-season roundup. He had been a firm champion of Donny's work on the show since the Arena Stage production, but he saw fit to call *Raisin* "presumably the last strange fruit that Robert Nemiroff is going to be able to pluck from the estate of his former wife." The harsh connotations of the reference, in 1974, would not have been oblique to most readers. Lewis Allan (a pseudonym for Abel Meeropol) coined the brutal image in his 1939 protest song, "Strange Fruit," which was popularized by Billie Holiday: "Black bodies swingin' in the Southern breeze/Strange fruit hangin' from the poplar trees." Bob plucking strange fruit from Lorraine's remains was harsh, indeed.

Booking contracts for open-ended attractions in Broadway theatres always include what is called the "stop clause." This is a figure negotiated in advance, based on the gross potential of the theatre and the estimated running costs of the show. In effect, when business remains below the stop clause figure for a certain number of weeks—in the case of *Raisin* it was the standard two consecutive weeks—the landlord had the right to give the producer two weeks' notice and eject the show.

Theatres, back then, received a percentage of the gross, out of which they paid a share of the local costs such as stagehands, musicians, and more. Nowadays, the show usually pays all expenses along with a flat weekly rental, plus an additional, smaller percentage of the gross. In either case, a show playing to full houses at full price earns the theatre owner significantly more than a show that's heavily discounted.

Over our first year, we had occasionally been below the stop clause, but never for two consecutive weeks. This is not precisely true; I recall two or three times when—after a below-stop clause week—Bob surreptitiously had people walk up to the box office and buy enough tickets, with untraceable cash, to get us over the mark. (This was technically prohibited by the theatre lease.) Treasurers, working in collusion with the theatre owner, could counter this type of activity. If they wanted to get rid of a weak show to make room for something more promising, they were known to have discouraged ticket buyers by saying a particular performance was sold out; or, if there was a good chance the show will slip below the stop clause that week, by offering to sell you "great" seats the following week. (This too was technically prohibited by the theatre lease.)

Theatre owners don't necessarily throw you out when you fall beneath the stop clause; they do, after all, want to keep the place lit. Mortgages, taxes, electricity, routine maintenance, and insurance all must be paid, even when the theatre is dark. However, the owners usually make sure to put you on provisional notice: we will let you stay open for now, but reserve the right henceforth to invoke two-week notice at any time. If a likely hit comes along, they will almost always exercise that right; maybe not if the producer is a good friend or longtime associate, but there was no loyalty to unconnected producers like Bob Nemiroff or Phil Rose.

The Bob Fosse/John Kander/Fred Ebb musical *Chicago*—starring Gwen Verdon—was a likely smash. Gwen and Bob had played the 46th Street with *Damn Yankees*, *New Girl in Town*, and *Redhead*, picking up six Tony Awards between them, and they wanted their favorite house.

The theatre owners waited patiently for us to fall below the stop clause, then immediately served notice. *Chicago* wasn't due until late January, so we were told we could stay through the final week in December. As it turned out, Fosse had a near-fatal heart attack on the first day of rehearsal, causing *Chicago* to be postponed to a May arrival. The 46th Street, though, was more than happy to fill in the time with the Maggie Smith *Private Lives*, which was selling out on tour, directed by John Gielgud and stage managed by Mitch.

Helen and I calculated *Raisin*'s prospects. The show had already recovered about $275,000 of the $350,000 investment. (This included the $75,000 bounty on Ralph Carter.) Looking at our advance sales, we estimated that we could lose $75,000 or so through mid-October, which we would likely recover and slightly exceed over the Thanksgiving and Christmas holidays. Business was sure to be weak over the winter months, until picking up in mid-March. If we had been able to remain at the 46th Street, we'd likely weather the winter in decent shape and pick up when we started getting groups in the spring; if business disintegrated altogether, we could at any time simply close.

Factoring in the costs of moving to another theatre, though, the situation became treacherous. The move—taking down the set at the 46th Street, transporting it to the new theatre, rebuilding it (with additional scenery as necessary), rehearsing it with a full complement of stagehands, and the lost box office revenue until we were ready to resume performances—would cost at least $75,000. With heavy losses likely in January and February, we might easily whittle $125,000 off the $275,000 we'd already recovered. No matter how well we might do the following spring and summer, it was unlikely we'd ever claw back those interim losses.

Regretfully, we carefully explained to Bob that our only reasonable course was to go out strong after the holidays at the end of December 1974. We were preparing a national tour for 1975; the good news was that we could cut the startup costs in half by using the Broadway physical production, instead of building a new one as planned.

"No," said Bob.

"You don't know anything," shouted Max.

Ten days later, while we were in rehearsal for the Boston tryout of *Shenandoah*, we got a call from Bob's office. So-and-so was coming over, could we please go through the files with him and also give him the checkbook?

"What?" Bob's assistant said in embarrassment, "You mean, Bob didn't tell you?"

No, Bob (of course) hadn't told us. He was insistent on keeping the show open. If his managers wouldn't come up with figures that supported his insistence on moving to another Broadway house, he would go out and find managers who would. Come up, that is, with figures that showed the wisdom of his set-in-stone decision.

Bob got his new managers; he moved the show across the street to the Lunt, which was for several reasons unsuited to the show. If you cannot sell out 1,350 seats, even on Friday and Saturday nights, what is the advantage of moving to a 1,500-seat theatre? Things, indeed, worked out as we had forecast. *Raisin* played almost a year at the Lunt, leaking money all along and never recovering the cost of the move, let alone the investment. The post-Broadway tour did poorly, as well.

BEST LAID PLANS

Helen was understandably disappointed at losing the show and the two weekly salaries it brought, but we had *Shenandoah* under way with two more musicals on the horizon. Since the closing of *The Pajama Game*, Richard had been keeping us apprised of progress on *Music Is*, an adaptation of Shakespeare's *Twelfth Night* that he was writing with Mr. Abbott. Abbott had written *The Boys from Syracuse*, a deliciously good musical adaptation of *The Comedy of Errors*; but that was in 1938, with songs from Richard Rodgers and Lorenz Hart. This time, he was working with music by Adler and lyrics by Will Holt, a minor lyricist of the time whose major credits were *The Me Nobody Knows* and Ray Bolger's *Come Summer.*

There was an even bigger inherent problem with this venture; there had recently been a hit *Twelfth Night* musical. *Your Own Thing,* which opened off-Broadway at the Orpheum in 1968, was a fast and funny protest musical featuring electric guitars, bell-bottom trousers, multimedia slides with celebrities contributing one-liners, and a rock trio called "The Apocalypse." Not only was the show modernized, the plot—with Orson, the manager of the act, falling in love with a girl dressed as a boy—fit right in with the times, just around the corner from the Electric Circus on St. Mark's Place.

Your Own Thing was a thorough delight and a significant hit, winning the New York Drama Critics' Circle Award and enjoying a national tour plus sit-down productions in Los Angeles, San Francisco, and Toronto. By the time I saw it at the Orpheum, in the summer of 1968, the girl playing the heroine Viola had been replaced by one of the most dazzling performers I had thus far come across, a young Texan named Sandy Duncan.

With the pop and rock *Your Own Thing* of recent memory, what were the chances that octogenarian Abbott and Richard Adler (of "Hey There") could turn up something better? I had already learned how to identify shows that sounded DOA from the start, and *Music Is* was one of them. Still, it was a new Broadway musical and an Abbott musical, so I was happy to sit there doing budgets. It was quite a way off, however.

Richard soon turned up something far more intriguing. He called one spring morning, a month after the closing of *The Pajama Game,* bursting with excitement. He had been talking to lawyer Eddie Colton, who represented Abbott. Colton was one of the preeminent theatrical attorneys in the business, and legendary as far as a show biz lawyer can be legendary. Having known Adler for years, Colton floated the information that another of his clients was looking to write a new musical: the great Richard Rodgers. Rodgers, in partnership with his songwriting partner Oscar Hammerstein, had been one of Broadway's most successful producers of musicals since 1946 (with *Annie Get Your Gun, South Pacific, The King and I, The Sound of Music,* and others) and continued to produce his own work until 1971. Now, he was quietly looking for someone else to do the producing. Did Adler have any Rodgers-suitable ideas?

It just so happened that he did.

Rodgers was old and ill, and no longer able to effectively write—which the world, and I suppose Rodgers himself, didn't quite yet know. His prior musicals had been the ill-starred *Do I Hear a Waltz?* (with Sondheim) in 1965, and *Two by Two* (with Martin Charnin) in 1970. *Waltz* was a troubled show that didn't gel, although the score is better than generally acknowledged. *Two by Two* was altogether drab and charmless. It got by, thanks to the presence of Danny Kaye, who sold tickets like the superstar he was but more or less ignored the material. When he tore a ligament during the run, Kaye played the role—Noah, of the Ark—in a wheelchair. The second time I saw the show, he had the wheelchair roll "out of control" down a ramp and "crash" into the stage left proscenium. "One more inch," Noah Kaye said, "and I'd be in *No, No, Nanette!*" (Stage left of the Imperial backed up against the stage wall of the 46th Street, where the Ruby Keeler revival was just then the biggest hit in town.)

Even so, a new score by Richard Rodgers still signified "blockbuster"; or at least, so everyone thought. Adler had been toying with the idea of a musical about jolly old Henry VIII, chopping off the heads of his six wives. (Adler himself was only on his third wife at the time.) Despite his super-sized ego—Richard's, that is, not Henry's—he instantly realized that Henry VIII with music by Rodgers would be a considerably easier sell than Henry VIII with music by Adler. He blurted out the idea to Colton, who quickly called back saying Rodgers would be delighted.

Rex, like *Music Is*, was two years off; but it was clearly going to be a major musical. My radar, though, instantly forecast that it was likely to be far, far closer to *Two by Two* than *The King and I*.

MAN ON THE STREET CORNER

Adler quickly brought in Sheldon Harnick, of *Fiddler on the Roof*, to write the lyrics. Sheldon had recently parted ways with Jerry Bock over disputes during the tryout of their final collaboration, *The Rothschilds*. Rodgers and Harnick had contemplated a musical adaptation of *Arsenic and Old Lace*, with book by Michael Stewart, and starring roles intended for Ethel Merman and Mary Martin, but collectively decided that the property was unworkable.

Sheldon was one of Broadway's finest lyricists, and one of my favorites; his songs were literate, clever, droll, and humane. But his best work had always been flavorful, ranging from the sardonic turn-of-the-century Jews of Anatevka, to the gemütlich charm of 1930s Budapest in *She Loves Me*, to the poker-playing politicos of *Fiorello!* His lyrics seemed somewhat restricted in the 1780 world of *The Rothschilds*, and I imagined that he would be way out of place in Hampton Court circa 1530.

When Richard added librettist Sherman Yellen—who had provided what I considered an ill-formed book for *The Rothschilds*, and whose most popular work was a sketch in *Oh! Calcutta!*—I rolled my eyes. *Rex* would certainly make it to Broadway and amass a large advance sale, and might turn out to be a good show; and sure, I was eager to work on what was likely to be the final Richard Rodgers musical. But Adler was certainly doing it the hard way.

In November, just after Nemiroff fired Helen from *Raisin*, Richard went up to New Haven for the tryout opening of the new Neil Simon comedy, *God's Favorite*. The next morning he called triumphantly: Michael Bennett—who was directing the Simon play—had agreed to do *Rex*. This impressed me. Having seen what Bennett did to salvage the disastrous Detroit tryout of *Seesaw*, and having been a fan of the choreographer since *Promises*, it seemed to me that Bennett might be able to work whatever material he got from Rodgers, Harnick, and Yellen into a hit. What's more, he was a strong enough personality to keep a meddling producer—that is, Adler—in place.

Three weeks later, Richard called in a foul and furious mood.

"Who does he think he is?" he brayed. "Jerry Robbins??"

It turns out that while Bennett—after an apparently embattled relationship with producer/codirector Hal Prince on *Follies*—was more than happy to do the new Richard Rodgers musical, his agent insisted that the director/choreographer receive 10 percent of the profits.

"*Michael Bennett?* I don't need Michael Bennett! I'll pull someone off a street corner to direct the show before I give Michael Bennett 10 percent of the profits."

The show would not reach the stage for another year and a half, but this conversation—right then and there—was the death of *Rex*. Having refused Michael Bennett's terms, Richard eventually found his way to: Ed Sherin. A former actor, Sherin was resident director at the Arena Stage in Washington during the mid-1960s. As such, he staged their most prominent play: Howard Sackler's *The Great White Hope*, which transferred to the Alvin in 1968 and had such an impact on me at fifteen. Sherin had done four plays since, but none anywhere near as effective as *The Great White Hope*. His musical experience? He was the guy they fired from *Seesaw* in Detroit when they brought in Michael Bennett.

As for Bennett, instead of *Rex* he returned to an idea of his own about a bunch of gypsies auditioning for a job in the chorus. The producer of that venture—unlike Adler—was more than glad to give Bennett an ownership position in *A Chorus Line*, and history was made. But not with *Rex*.

GOLDEN TICKET

All the while, *Shenandoah* was trying to make it to Broadway. The production at Goodspeed got generally mixed reviews, albeit with encouraging things to say along with universal raves for Cullum. The show attracted a strong local following; being the final show of the Goodspeed season, Michael Price quickly decided to extend through the end of September.

As the run progressed, we were given an unexpected lifeline. Two, actually.

Goodspeed attracted local press to their openings; further-flung critics would drift in from time to time, based on their interest in the particular show and their vacation schedule. On September 8, readers of the Arts and Leisure section of the Sunday *New York Times* found a rave—a highly emotional rave—from Walter Kerr. He confessed that he walked in prepared for maudlin sentimentality and thought he'd found just that—until, an hour in, Cullum started singing "The Pickers Are Coming," which dealt with the emotions of a father watching his young daughter going off to be married.

"Without having felt myself the least bit prepared for it," Kerr (the father of six) confessed, "I found myself embarrassedly fighting back tears." He went on to praise the show for using what appeared to be a commonplace, conventionally old-fashioned story to tackle a then-politically relevant question: At what point does it become morally proper to betray your principles and fight?

He concluded by noting the show's extended run at Goodspeed and hoping that *Shenandoah* went on from there, offering specific constructive suggestions to the authors and director. He concluded his review—and this was what we call in the theatre, for obvious reasons, a "money notice"—by advising readers that "Although *Shenandoah* looks like a stereotype, it feels like life. Trust the feeling."

While the *Times* published their Arts and Leisure section each Sunday, it was printed early in the week to allow the more time-sensitive sections—news, business, sports—to use the presses on Friday and Saturday. Thus, copies were distributed on Wednesday to the advertising agencies, whose Broadway clients greatly supported the *Times* by purchasing significant ad space. As a result, we had lined up a Broadway house even before Kerr's review was officially published on Sunday. The theatre? My old haunt, the Alvin.

This would not have been instantly possible had it not been for something that occurred a week earlier.

Back in those days, there was a rare breed of theatre creature known as the "souvenir book man." Most shows—virtually all musicals, plus many plays—had a souvenir book they sold in the lobby before, during, and after the show. This was before producers became aware that they could set the lobby awash with divers types of show merchandise. At the time, all you had to sell in the lobby was a souvenir book, and eventually—for most musicals—a cast album and perhaps sheet music.

Broadway theatre capacities, in "musical houses," ranged from 1,000 to 1,600. Should you have a show that filled those seats, and happy audiences either expecting to see a hit (before the show) or having enjoyed it immensely (at intermission and afterward), that was a significant number of potential customers streaming directly past the book man's table. Production costs of the books—12" × 9" booklets of sixteen or so black and white pages, with a colored paper cover—were minimal; and on a flop, yes, they were likely unsalable. But there was money to be made with even a moderate run; and for a hit, the book was a bonanza that multi-plied itself many times over when the show sent out a national tour, with road houses having considerably larger seating capacities.

Which is to say that the not-very-many Broadway book men com-petitively vied for the rights, often accompanied by an investment and a guaranteed advance royalty payment. Once they established a rela-tionship with a producer—even one so checkered as Phil Rose—they jealously guarded their contact.

Phil's book man was a fellow named Kal Efron. (Like many people in the business, he had a family connection: his brother Morry was a com-pany manager, specializing in national tours of megahits like *Barefoot in the Park* and *The Odd Couple*.) Kal eagerly watched the progress of *Shenan-doah*, especially since the economic downturn of Broadway meant that there would only be a handful of musicals during the 1974–1975 season.

Efron went up to see the show in the third week of the Goodspeed run, shepherding a casual acquaintance who had expressed an interest in perhaps becoming involved in Broadway. The next day, said acquaintance called Phil and invited him to Sunday brunch. Louis Sher was a mild, gentle, and likeable man. (His wife and partner, Gloria, was neither so mild nor gentle.) Phil immediately sized him up as a potential $10,000 investor, which was certainly welcome. At the end of the bagels-and-lox-and-champagne lunch, Sher handed over a check—for $250,000! Phil suddenly had a coproducer; and, more crucially, half of the $500,000 at which we had budgeted the show. When we saw the Kerr piece on the Wednesday after Labor Day, Phil—with Sher's quarter million in hand—was sure enough of funding to commit to bring *Shenandoah* to Broadway.

Show business makes strange bedfellows, yes. It turned out the mild-mannered Mr. Sher had a slight ulterior motive in undertaking and underwriting *Shenandoah*. He was a film distributor and exhibitor who specialized in foreign and independent films; known, among other things, for the 1969 3D soft-core porn film, *The Stewardesses*—"From 3D to 3XXX," to quote the ads.

Sher had been indicted on obscenity charges in 1973 for another film, *Hot Circuit*. His first trial was a mistrial; in the second he had been found guilty. He was now preparing for an appeal, scheduled for December 1974. While presenting himself as coproducer of a wholesome Broadway musical geared toward a family audience might not help his case, he figured, it surely wouldn't hurt. Thus, his $250,000 investment. As it turned out, his appeal—which was decided four months after *Shenandoah* opened on Broadway—was successful and his conviction reversed.

MAGNIFICENT MOLASSES
We opened strong at the Colonial in Boston, although once again the reviews were decidedly mixed; critics (and audiences), we found, were likely to either love it or not. Kevin Kelly of the *Boston Globe* headed his review with "*Shenandoah* is absolutely magnificent." So enthusiastic was he that he actually repeated "absolutely magnificent," for emphasis, three times in the opening paragraph.

"This farm don't belong to Virginia." John Cullum in *Shenandoah* (1975).
PHOTOFEST

The other main critic, the legendary Elliot Norton of the *Boston Post*, was equally severe. But Kelly's notice was sufficient to nearly fill the house for our five-week engagement. Enthusiasm among the cast and even the crew was so high that Phil freed up some of the investment commitments so that anyone who wished to invest could do so; cast, stagehands, many were eager to join in. When Phil reduced the minimum amount from $2,500 to a lowly $500, I figured I might as well invest, too. Despite my lack of enthusiasm, how could I refuse?

Such was the general excitement that Phil even sprung for a green piano. Given the woodsy set representing the fertile Anderson family land in the Shenandoah Valley, Phil deemed it necessary for the pit to contain a *green* Steinway baby grand. While Broadway musicals usually rented pianos, this was not easy to come by; but with money, anything can be found.

We imported the Goodspeed conductor, Lynn Crigler, to make his Broadway debut. Our pit piano player was decidedly higher grade. Don Pippin, conductor of such musicals as *Oliver!* and *Mame*, had undergone such a nerve-wracking time on two successive musicals—*Seesaw* and *Mack & Mabel*—that upon the early closing of the latter, he was happy to take a break and simply play the piano. We, of course, were glad to have him. He joined us in Boston and played the first six weeks or so at the Alvin, after which he left to more fully concentrate on the workshop of a new musical he was doing, which turned out to be *A Chorus Line*.

We moved into our house on Fifty-Second Street on December 23 for a week of previews, building toward opening night on January 7, 1975. Reactions were just as I expected; some quite good, others quite poor. The problem, in my view, was not that the show was written in the old-fashioned Rodgers & Hammerstein vein; then and now, I'd much prefer to see a great old-fashioned musical than a poor contemporary one. But to me, the sentiment in *Shenandoah* was not only cloying but synthetic. Walter Kerr found enormous truth in the show; I, alas, felt the opposite, in great part due to what I considered a highly inferior score. As I walked up to the mezzanine every night during the first act, en route to the house manager's office to do the count-up, the two child actors were singing a wretched song as they dangled their fishing poles over the orchestra pit, braying off key. On my way out of the theatre after signing the box office statement, I walked through what sounded to me like a patch of recycled *Brigadoon*.

On opening night, screenwriter/co-librettist James Lee Barrett presented us all with pre-tied, crushed velour, western-style string bowties. I hid mine in the back of a drawer and never found it again. Jeffrey Richards, who didn't work on *Shenandoah*, got one of the ties from his mother. Over more than thirty years, he has religiously worn his "lucky tie" to the Tony ceremony every time he has been nominated as Best Producer, and has thus far taken a half dozen or so awards.

Our opening night party was next door to the theatre at Gallagher's Steakhouse, a speakeasy-era eatery famous for its impressive "New York Strip" steak. (Broadway attendance business was so depressed in 1975 that Gallagher's offered us—the entire *Shenandoah* company—a 50 percent discount on food and drinks, for us and our guests, for the run of the show. So while at the Alvin, we ate well.)

An hour into the party, Phil, lyricist Peter Udell, press agent Merle Debuskey, Helen, and I piled into two cabs and headed down to the Blaine-Thompson advertising agency in the Sardi's Building. We spread out into separate offices, picking up phone extensions so we could all listen to "the call" when it came in. Eventually it did; this was a friendly pressman at the *Times* with whom Blaine-Thompson had a longstanding arrangement. He started to read the Clive Barnes review.

The first paragraph complained about "distressing sentimentality." When the reader got to Clive finding "the sweetness of that southern molasses somewhat cloying," we all heard Phil's disembodied voice over the extension: "Oh, shit!"

Which does, at least, explain why it is always better not to have the *Times* review read at the opening night party until you're certain you want your actors and investors to hear it.

Before we grimly trod back to Gallagher's displaying false bravado, the *Daily News* review came in. Headline: "*Shenandoah* Dull Civil War Musical."

The Best Decision

HOPE IT'S ENOUGH

FOR PHIL, THE CRITICAL PUMMELING WAS STANDARD PROCEDURE. Every show he ever did was a continual struggle; for every piece of good luck, there were two setbacks.

Or three. The mixed reviews—some quite good, but countered by pans from the all-important *Times*, *Daily News*, and *Post*—might have been enough to deter another producer. But Phil was a gambler and had nothing else to switch his attentions to; this was a battle he was eager to wage.

A bigger and altogether unexpected complication occurred on January 5, two days before we opened. The big shows of the season, and what were expected to be our chief competition, were two October musicals: *Mack & Mabel*, reuniting the *Hello, Dolly!* team of Jerry Herman, Michael Stewart, Gower Champion, and David Merrick, and starring Robert Preston; and *Miss Moffat*, the new Josh Logan show starring Bette Davis.

How could that new Merrick musical go wrong? Easily. The project began as a happy, nostalgic musical about early Hollywood, centering on producer Mack Sennett and his fun factory (Keystone Kops, bathing beauties, et al.). That initial version, *Hundreds of Girls*, never got onstage. When it collapsed and librettist Leonard Spigelgass departed, Herman turned to Mike Stewart, who pointed out that Sennett, in real life, had been a tyrant; Mabel Normand, his leading lady, was a cocaine addict; and the latter was directly tied to one of Hollywood's biggest murder scandals ever. Perhaps, Mike suggested that at a time when the psychologically neurotic *Follies* was changing the tone of the Broadway musical, the Mack Sennett show should center on something more than simple nostalgia.

Thus, what was to become *Mack & Mabel* had serious undertones and incorporated Mabel's deterioration into addiction, the murder of director William Desmond Taylor, and more. The fatal flaw, though, was that the composer insisted on retaining much of the *Hundreds of Girls* score. Happy, upbeat songs in the celebrated and highly popular style of Jerry Herman, yes; but unsuited to the now-troubled characters in the new *Mack & Mabel* libretto.

The long tryout underwent problem after problem, with Merrick and Gower struggling to right this wrong-footed musical. "Loaded with all the zip of a dead flounder," said the respected critic Richard Coe in the *Washington Post*. I was kept up to the minute on the travails by Mark Bramble, Jack Schlissel's apprentice company manager on the show.

The night of the final preview, Helen and I went to Sardi's after signing the *Raisin* box office statement. At 8:30, Merrick walked in.

"Hello," he said. "Have you seen"—gesturing toward the Majestic, across the street from Sardi's—"the show?"

I told him Mark gave me tickets to the opening.

"This was a tough one. Did a lot of work, but I could only get it about 80 percent where I wanted it." And he shrugged his shoulders, laconically. "Hope it's enough!"

It wasn't.

CHRISTMAS CHILD

I never could quite figure out the secret of Merrick until it was revealed to me years later by Bramble, who came to know the producer well.

"You don't understand," Mark explained. "Underneath that image he liked to present to the world, *David loved the theatre*. Finding a project, seizing it, fighting to get it on. When he was making shows he came alive, he was like a child on Christmas morning."

Underneath the forebodingly frosty and downright Machiavellian image Merrick so assiduously cultivated, it turns out that this forlorn Dickensian orphan from the slums of St. Louis had a childlike fascination in the make-believe of the theatre. How sad, in a way, that he never let anyone see it.

But then, it was this self-imposed curmudgeonly mien that enabled him to so thoroughly dominate his chosen profession. Nice little boys with a glint in their eye, David Margulois learned early on, are doomed to get tumbled and tossed by the roadside, like the young David Copperfield on his forlorn trek from London to Dover. Or like the not-so-young novice producer Merrick when he faced that Goliath-like ruffian Richard Rodgers, who blithely assumed he could wrest control of *Fanny* and toss Merrick obsequiously sniveling into the gutter.

Merrick stood firm, fully realizing the wisdom of building himself into what his competitors and victims called "the abominable showman"—a moniker Merrick himself encouraged and delighted in.

But whether he be engrossed in record-breaking blockbusters like *Hello, Dolly!* or *42nd Street*, esoteric culture clashes like *Look Back in Anger* or *Rosencrantz and Guildenstern Are Dead*, or the numerous important but unlikely-to-succeed efforts he produced under the banner of the nonprofit David Merrick Arts Foundation, the producer felt impelled to self-consciously hide his greatest secret: David Merrick was hopelessly stagestruck.

RIVIERA

Mack & Mabel opened October 6 and ignominiously folded Thanksgiving week, leaving the celebrated team of Jerry, Mike, and Gower with a collective black eye. The musical did have at least one significant result within my immediate circle.

The authors were, needless to say, upset by the show's quick demise. Come Tony Awards night the following April, the show—while a surprise and a Pyrrhic tie with *The Wiz* for eight nominations—was altogether shut out. *Shenandoah*, with six nominations, was behind not only those two musicals but the Joel Grey vehicle *Goodtime Charley* as well. As it happened, we took two of the awards to seven for *The Wiz*, with *Mack* and *Charley* altogether shut out.

Mike Stewart received a nomination for his clearly problematic book, while songwriter Jerry Herman was pointedly neglected. Not only neglected, mind you; nominations were given to two short-lived and—in my opinion, having sat through them—meritless scores, for an anti-war rock opera called *The Lieutenant* and an unfathomable Robert Wilson whatnot called *A Letter for Queen Victoria*. This was seen as a blatant slam by the *Mack & Mabel* camp; Mike was so indignant at Jerry's treatment that he placed a paid ad in *Variety* castigating the Tony committee. Instead of sitting around waiting for Tony night, Mike decamped to his place on the French Riviera. (Thank you, Dolly Gallagher Levi, for all those lovely royalties.)

Mark—having finished his preliminary draft of *Barnum* while working on *Mack & Mabel*—not unnaturally asked Mike for advice. Mike invited him to his place in Golfe-Juan, outside Cannes, offering a conducive spot to get some concentrated work done on the book. One thing led to another, as they say, and in late July came a long letter—handwritten on what they used to call aerograms, lightweight light-blue sheets of paper that when folded became a mailable envelope—explaining what had happened with Mike and that he didn't know what would happen.

As matters turned out, Mark eventually decided to come home to the apartment he shared with Kim. Work proceeded slowly on his unconventional circus musical. He approached the major Broadway composers of the time, with one after another politely apologizing that they didn't see how they could sustain a full score of what—according to Mark's early draft—seemed to require "circus songs." We even went as far as to discuss the over-aged Meredith Willson, the superannuated Irving Berlin, and the pop songwriter Jimmy Webb of "Up, Up and Away" and "By the Time I Get to Phoenix" fame. For a while, Mark worked with Harry Nilsson ("Without You," "Everybody's Talkin'") with unsatisfactory results. Among those who turned the show down early on was Cy Coleman, who in 1977 found himself a new lyric-writing partner: Mike Stewart. After many years and many misadventures, Mark would eventually prevail on Cy and Mike to write the songs for his circus musical. But only eventually.

The Corn Is Droopy

Miss Moffat, which many saw as strong competition to *Shenandoah*, was promising in a different manner. Bette Davis had been one of Hollywood's biggest stars since 1934—forty years, now—and would assuredly sell limitless tickets. The property itself, though, was suspect. Emlyn Williams's semi-autobiographical drama *The Corn Is Green* had been a major hit on both stage (London: 1938, starring Sybil Thorndike; Broadway: 1940, starring Ethel Barrymore); and on screen in 1945, starring—well, Bette Davis.

Now, Williams and director Josh Logan had decided to Americanize the play, placing the action down South and having Miss Moffatt instruct not an underprivileged Welsh student but an underprivileged American Black.

The participation of Logan—being far removed from the days of *Annie Get Your Gun* and *South Pacific*—also raised questions. His four musicals since *Fanny* in 1954 had all been distressing failures; *Miss Moffat*, his final produced musical, would make it five in a row. In addition to directing the show, Logan coproduced and collaborated with Williams on the book. As if to further the futility, Williams—who had never written a musical—wrote the lyrics as well, to music by second-rank Broadway composer Albert Hague (of *Plain and Fancy* and *Redhead*).

Miss Moffat opened its tryout in Philadelphia on October 7, 1974, to dire reviews. "A night to forget," said the *Philadelphia Daily News*. Bramble called me the next day. "Fill up the gas tank," he said, "we're going to Philadelphia."

"Why Philadelphia?" I asked.

"We got tickets for the Saturday matinee of *Miss Moffat*."

"Mark, we don't need to go to Philadelphia to see a lousy musical. We can do that *here*."

Even so, it seemed like a reasonable idea to observe just how misguided this show was at the beginning of its tryout. We piled into the car and drove down. The show was as advertised, or rather as *warned*. Just awful. What's more, it remains in memory perhaps the ugliest scenery I've ever seen; Jo Mielziner was at the end of his long career, and the show was cloaked in hideous shades of brown. Fortunately, I remember thinking at the time, the lighting designer (Mielziner) lit the show so poorly that you couldn't quite see much of the scenery.

We were fortunate in attending the first Saturday matinee, because it turned out to be the only one. Davis, who had strained her back during rehearsals in August, apparently reinjured it after she read her Philadelphia reviews. *Miss Moffat* folded then and there.

IN THE SWIM

Another out-of-town theatre party worth mentioning came several months earlier. In May of 1974, talent agent Deborah Coleman—a friend of Helen—mentioned that she had to go up to Connecticut to see a musical her client Burt Shevelove was directing, for a week, in the swimming pool at Yale University.

Yes, a musical in a swimming pool. How could one miss the opportunity to catch an eight-performance-only, Stephen Sondheim musical in a swimming pool? We immediately asked Debbie for tickets Saturday night. This was after *Company*, *Follies*, and *A Little Night Music*, at which point the composer/lyricist was just beginning to find acceptance among stodgy Broadway traditionalists who had theretofore seen his music as somewhat too intellectual for enjoyment.

The Frogs, from a play by Aristophanes, was indeed as unusual as it sounded. And it sounded waterlogged: the typically complex Sondheim score, with its typically masterful Jonathan Tunick orchestrations, was altogether defeated by the acoustics of the varsity swimming pool. The Yale Repertory Theatre production was an underdeveloped and under-rehearsed affair, given the circumstances, despite a cast headed by Larry Blyden, Anthony Holland, Alvin Epstein, and Carmen de Lavallade. Also on hand was a large, damp chorus of Yale students including the still-anonymous Meryl Streep, Sigourney Weaver, and Christopher Durang. Even so, Sondheim—albeit under water—was unquestionably worth the trek.

The memorable but mighty strange *Frogs* was ultimately reconceived, revised, and remounted by Lincoln Center Theater in 2004 with the 1974 script ("freely adapted by Burt Shevelove") now "even more freely adapted by Nathan Lane"—to little avail, even without all those reverberations.

Yale Repertory Theatre

presents a comedy written in 405 B.C. by

Aristophanes

entitled

THE FROGS

freely adapted in 1974 A.D. by
Burt Shevelove

with music and lyrics by
Stephen Sondheim

The music has been orchestrated and supervised by
Jonathan Tunick

and the orchestra and chorus are directed by
Don Jennings

Everybody jump in the pool! Soggy Sondheim, at Yale. *The Frogs* (1974).

CLEAR SAILING

By the time we started the *Shenandoah* tryout at the Colonial on November 22, we had managed to evade competition from both the Jerry Herman musical (which would close the following week, after Thanksgiving) and the Bette Davis musical. Clear sailing, yes?

Clear sailing, no. A new musical version of *The Wizard of Oz*, of all things, had undergone severe tryout troubles of its own, culminating in the firing of the director, who was replaced not by the choreographer (which is common) but the costume designer (which is highly uncommon). Two months of scrambling, it turned out, did the trick. *The Wiz* moved into the Majestic—a last-minute booking, thanks to the demise of *Mack & Mabel*—and opened on January 5. This meant that *Shenandoah* came in, two nights later, not as the first potentially decent musical of the season but as a show in competition with one the critics had highly praised the other night.

Business at the Alvin was problematic from the beginning, with Phil and the ad agency struggling to determine how to counteract the reviews. Various ads brought in some audiences, but not quite enough to stay afloat.

"If only we can hold on till the Tony Awards," said Phil.

We held on, but won only two: for Cullum as Best Actor in a Musical, and for Best Book. It was disappointing but thoroughly understandable; *The Wiz* had quickly built itself into a sellout.

Even so, John's win picked up the box office enough to convince Phil to gamble on TV. Television commercials for Broadway musicals were a recent development, thanks to the instant ticket-selling success of a commercial for the 1971 musical *Pippin*. This featured Ben Vereen and two Fosse dancers in what they called the "Manson Trio."

Shenandoah was a far cry from *Pippin*. Director Phil Rose was a far cry from Bob Fosse, too. But the *Shenandoah* solution was inspired. To begin with, we decided to make not one spot but four, to be rotated. (We quickly discovered that the two featuring Cullum were the most effective, so we limited use of the others.) We also pulled the excerpts off the stage and put them in the fields; not of Virginia, where the action took place, but of Westchester County, an hour from Broadway in the village of Pound Ridge.

Cullum was shown roaming the fields as he sings "This farm don't belong to Virginia," pulling a clump of greenery out of the ground, and on a porch with a baby, as opposed to the doll used in the show, singing the lullaby "Papa's Gonna Make It Alright." (Illustrating the resourcefulness of ad people, account executive Nancy Coyne provided her own toddler for this one.) These two spots clearly brought in crowds; not the traditional theatergoers of the day, but people interested less in ghoulish Manson/Fosse dancers and more in what appeared to be a good, old-fashioned musical.

We settled in for a fairly successful summer, and all was well until September, when Local 802—the Musicians' Union—went out on a three-week strike, which proved almost lethal to our finances. But we recovered and moved on past our first anniversary at the Alvin.

VANITY

One afternoon in the winter of 1976, I returned to the office to find Helen sitting across from a man named Richard Wolfe, from the town of New Hope in Bucks County, Pennsylvania. He had been referred by Lex Carlin, house manager of the Forrest Theatre.

Bucks County was situated on the Delaware River, just northeast of Philadelphia. New Hope was across the river from Lambertville, New Jersey, and just up the road from Washington Crossing Historic Park, which, as you might discern from its name, is where General Washington set out to cross the Delaware on Christmas night, 1776, for his surprise attack on the British forces in Trenton.

Wolfe was an interesting character. He had spent his life in the music industry, mostly as a composer and arranger. At that time, I learned, he was supporting himself by playing piano at a popular Bucks County tavern. His claim to fame both impressed and repelled me. In 1960, he had produced a single that invaded the pop charts during the summer and fall to the point that even I couldn't escape it. They sang it on the radio; they sang it on the school bus; they sang it in the bunk at sleepaway camp. The title, and it still makes me cringe: "Itsy Bitsy Teenie Weenie Yellow Polka Dot Bikini." The fortunate uninitiated can find it on the internet, at their peril.

Even so, producing such an opus—written by Paul Vance and Lee Pockriss—was an impressive credit. Richard being the first music industry person I ever talked with at length, I learned that a substantial portion of his income came from jingles, most notably a ten-second fragment of sports-like music that was played during NFL football broadcasts as they segued from game to commercial. Not a full song or a half-song even, but it was played repeatedly over the course of every game, and every time it was played—to a wide national audience—the residuals would cascade.

A theatrical neophyte, Wolfe came with a proposal. Ann Hawkes Hutton, a local clubwoman in Bucks County who was chair and founder of the Washington Crossing Foundation, and who had written books about Washington crossing the Delaware that were sold at the Washington Crossing Historic Park bookstore, had now written a play about: well, you guess.

Ann determined that her sparkling historical drama must be staged in Philadelphia as part of that summer's bicentennial celebration. And professionally produced—this work of art was not some church basement pageant but real, important, patriotic historical art that must reach the masses. Richard being the only entertainment industry person she knew—I suppose from hearing him play at the restaurant, where he was a fixture—she turned to him for guidance.

Richard had worked his way to Carlin, a well-connected theatre man in Philadelphia. Hearing the full scope of this vanity production, Lex thought of Helen; being efficient but low-powered and available enough to actually consider taking such a job, she was a good choice. He also knew that while certain theatre folk might embrace the situation as an opportunity to line their pockets, Helen was not the type to take undue advantage.

A vanity production, mind you, is just what the name implies. It is exceedingly difficult for a playwright, especially an amateur, to get their play professionally produced. If money is no object, though, you can buy anything.

This was all too apparent as we sat there with Richard, even before we read the script. (I realized, with dread, that to formulate a budget I would at some point have to read the script.) But Richard and Helen and I figured that if this lady insisted on throwing away all that money, at least we could see that it was done as economically as possible and she got what she paid for.

The main commercial theatres in Philadelphia—at that time, the Forrest and Shubert—were out of the question. They wouldn't book claptrap like this; besides, their union contracts—because they regularly booked pre-Broadway tryouts and national tours—were far more expensive than even a vanity producer could afford.

But Philadelphia had a third house with pedigree: the Walnut Street. This was—and remains—the oldest continuously operating theatre in the United States. Built in 1809 to house a circus, it converted to legit in 1812; President Jefferson and the Marquis de Lafayette attended the opening. After numerous changes in management, the Shuberts took it over in 1941. Due to its relatively intimate thousand-seat capacity, they established it as a prime spot for play tryouts (including *A Raisin in the Sun* in 1959). The house eventually fell out of favor, and in 1969 was taken over by a regional nonprofit, available during off-season dark weeks for commercial rental. It was under these auspices that we played the tryout of *Raisin* in 1973. Now, the Walnut Street—managed by Lex Carlin's brother Joe, not incidentally—was more than happy to find a full-paying rental over the typically empty summer season, especially because the locals were likely to flee the hordes of inbound tourists expected for the bicentennial July 4 celebration.

Bicentennial Gift

Helen and I went to Philadelphia in late February to give Ann and Richard a tour of the Walnut Street. *1600 Pennsylvania Avenue*—the highly anticipated new musical by Leonard Bernstein and Alan Jay Lerner—had begun its tryout that Monday to lacerating reviews ("A Bicentennial bore," said *Variety*), so we arranged our visit so that we could catch the Wednesday matinee at the Forrest.

1600 Pennsylvania Avenue was interminable and indescribably poor. During the two-hour first act, patrons got up and wandered the aisles. As the performance was sold out, I was watching from the back rail. Standing next to me, it turned out, was the composer. Bernstein was beside himself, given the awful reviews they had just received, especially so as streams of people disinterestedly moseyed about. Lerner was leaning against one of the exit doors; the pair were not communicating just then. From time to time, the new director—they had fired the original one the day before—came by for whispered consultations with Bernstein, which I was more interested in than the performance. At the same time, they fired the choreographer, our friend Donny McKayle of *Raisin*.

The following Saturday I found myself once again in Philadelphia, standing at the back of the Forrest. I had only met Lex three days earlier, but the brotherhood of theatre managers is such that he gladly slipped me back in. The show, which ran three and three-quarter hours at the Wednesday matinee, was now forty-five minutes shorter; they spent Thursday and Friday radically cutting material. It was still incoherent.

I can't imagine why I was back in Philadelphia that soon; I suppose I assumed that *1600* would close there and thought I should take the opportunity to once more hear the Bernstein score, which was in many ways highly impressive. As it happened, the show did move on to Washington, so I traveled there, too, to get a final hearing. And then it surprised everyone by staggering into the Mark Hellinger—just around the corner from *Shenandoah* at the Alvin—in May, so I saw it a fourth and final time before it closed after seven performances. "What is one to say" about *1600 Pennsylvania Avenue*, asked Clive Barnes in the *Times*. "Bring back *Rex*?"

Bernstein and Lerner's "Bicentennial gift" musical to America—which attempted to present the first hundred years of the White House featuring the president (or rather, presidents) and their several first ladies, countered by an upstairs/downstairs plot featuring a pair of nonwhite White House servants—was plagued from the start. High among the problems was the inability to get anyone to agree to undertake the leading role.

Cullum, who was well known to Lerner from *Camelot* and *On a Clear Day*, was ideal casting; but he was tied for another year to *Shenandoah*. Having lived through Lerner's methedrine-spiked behavior on *Clear Day*, he was more than glad to have a valid excuse to be out of the running. After a long conversation with the lyricist, John warned us that Lerner would be calling to seek his release and pleaded with Phil to most definitely not find a way to spring him from his contract.

Then came the musician's strike in September 1975. After two weeks of treading water, and after the press had erroneously reported that *Shenandoah* would never reopen, Actors' Equity announced that all Broadway actors were free to terminate their contracts to take other jobs. John entreated Phil to insist, when Lerner called again, that due to our financial situation we would be forced to fight—if necessary—to prevent Cullum from leaving *Shenandoah* for *Pennsylvania Avenue*.

OPTION

Broadway, and *Shenandoah*, finally reopened on October 13, after twenty-five dark days, and I went into a fairly uneventful winter save for interesting activity on the *Barnum* front.

An issue from the very beginning was the significant complication of a well-publicized, if phantom, conflicting musical about the nineteenth-century showman. Producer Alexander H. Cohen—who pictured himself as a modern-day Barnum, possessing the requisite humbug but not the creative imagination—had announced his *Barnum* for an April 1964 opening, ballyhooing it on the large billboard over the Winter Garden. Cohen's show was postponed again and again; as late as 1979, when Mark's *Barnum* was clearly under way, Alex still insisted that his *Barnum* was on schedule.

In his search for a producer, Mark had early on approached Alex. He received a quick, curt reply that Mr. Cohen was producing his own musical about P. T. Barnum and carefully proclaiming that Alex was not interested in even reading Mark's draft. (Should Cohen's version proceed using ideas originated in Bramble's draft, Mark would need to prove, legally, that Alex had access to his script.)

In fact, Alex had ordered his staff to secretly make a copy before returning it; we only knew this because the new apprentice manager standing by the Xerox machine at the Cohen office, just then, happened to be Kim. Should anyone be interested in reading Mark's first full *Barnum* draft, they can find this precise copy catalogued within the Alexander H. Cohen Collection at the New York Public Library.

In the spring of 1976, two years after the trip to the circus, Mark finally found a serious producer. Burry Fredrik, a former production stage manager of such plays as *Inherit the Wind* and *The Dark at the Top of the Stairs*, was just then one of Merrick's coproducers on Tom Stoppard's *Travesties*. Burry optioned the script—still without songwriters—for Broadway. I invited Mark and Kim for a celebratory dinner at the old Frankie & Johnnie's steakhouse, a former speakeasy then located in a second-story walkup on Forty-Fifth Street just off Eighth Avenue, across from the Majestic stage door alley. I remember noting, at the time, that this was the first time I'd spent more than $100 for a meal.

The cause for celebration was presumptive, as it turned out. Mark was to go through three other producers and multiple songwriters before *Barnum* finally opened in 1980. ("All I want now," he wrote me from Mike's place in Golfe-Juan in the summer of 1975 as he was struggling with the second act, "is to get it over with.") Within a few months of our celebratory dinner, he decided to finally leave Kim to spend his future with Mike. Mark's embarrassment over this inevitable turn of events was to cause a fragile estrangement between us for almost a decade, after which matters returned to normal until his death in 2019.

DAR

With *Shenandoah* starting its second year at the Alvin, we set out to get *The Decision* onstage. The decision of the title, by the way, was the one facing General Washington: Should I cross the Delaware or not? Imagine just how much suspense playwright Ann Hawkes Hutton was able to generate.

Why, after all, did George Washington cross the Delaware?

The answer, it goes without saying: to get to the other side. Which is what we kept telling ourselves again and again, through gritted teeth, until the Fourth of July.

Ann was a typical DAR specimen. That's Daughters of the American Revolution—although while she was clearly old, she likely wasn't sitting on the porch in 1777 when her father marched off to the Battle of Brandywine. Ann, whom we all called Sadie Hawkins, was happy to have Richard do the producing. He was just as glad to give Helen and me carte blanche to get this thing off the page and onto the stage, as it were. I did have the distinct impression that while Ann tolerated Richard—he lived in Bucks County, after all—she was altogether repelled by the thought of personal contact with theatre folk.

Did I mention that the play included six songs, music and lyrics by Ann Hawkes Hutton?

You might think that it would be difficult to find directors, designers, and actors to participate in such a venture. You would be wrong. Top-flight people, naturally, know to avoid getting caught in such a trap. But the majority of theatre professionals work all too infrequently to consider turning down paychecks. And while this was not Broadway, a patriotic play during the bicentennial celebration in Philadelphia was at least sure to be noticed. Perhaps.

We ended up with a little-known director named Arthur Allan Seidelman; where we found him, I can't recall. His one Broadway credit at the time was inauspicious, to say the least: he directed *Billy*, a 1969 musical adaptation of Herman Melville's novel *Billy Budd* that played the Billy Rose and closed opening night. The rest of the production team remains forgotten, except for our costume designers: a team called Michael Yeargan and Lawrence King. Michael Yeargan somewhat surprisingly resurfaced, twenty years later, with altogether luscious set designs for a series of musicals and plays produced by Lincoln Center Theater, beginning with *The Light in the Piazza* and *South Pacific*.

If we had a negligible production staff, our stage crew was Broadway's best. Leo took a leave from *Shenandoah* to join us, and he brought along Merrick's other two head stagehands, carpenter Teddy Van Bemmel and electrician Mitch Miller (not the music industry titan). In 1959, both Leo and Teddy left their first marriages to marry girls from Merrick musicals. Janice Herbert was in *Take Me Along*; Teddy married Chotzi Foley, who played the electrified stripper Electra in *Gypsy*. Foley changed her given name from "Charlotte" on composer Jule Styne's advice: "As long as you're playing a stripper, you might as well use a name that sounds like a stripper."

The cast was full of minimum-pay actors, mostly beginners looking to get enough work weeks to qualify for Equity health coverage. But we couldn't go to Ann Hawkes Hutton with an unknown actor to play her idol, George Washington. Who could we possibly get?

We went searching for someone, anyone with any kind of a name, to take the role. A friendly Broadway agent sent us to a fellow in Hollywood who specialized in washed up ex-TV stars looking for work. He came back with someone willing and able to take on the role, for the money: Hugh O'Brian.

O'Brian was big, really big; from 1955 to 1961, that is, when he starred in the television western *The Life and Legend of Wyatt Earp*. After that, he did occasional films and guest shots, sometimes in the persona of the Wild West lawman Earp. If he was at all prominent in 1976, it was from an ad campaign for a then-popular men's cologne, Brut by Fabergé.

We imported Hugh—who proved to be a colorless, if rugged-looking personality—from California and assembled this leaden entertainment as best we could. Following several stultifying weeks of rehearsal in New York, we loaded everyone (except the first-class Hugh) on a bus and headed down the New Jersey Turnpike.

FORGET IT

We took possession of the Walnut Street during the second week of June. I remained in Philadelphia with the show, my first time living out of a hotel room on the road; Helen stayed in New York with *Shenandoah.* Philadelphia was already blazingly hot. And already deserted; while the city fathers—and the nation—expected the "Birthplace of Liberty" to attract vast throngs for our nation's two hundredth Fourth of July, residents cleared out and tourists never did arrive. Especially not at the Walnut Street.

Hugh O'Brian ponders whether to cross the Delaware in *The Decision* (1976).

We started previews on June 17, to thundering silence. Even when General Washington did—finally, after much burrowing of brows to stormy sound effects atop the papier-mâché boulders along our banks of the Delaware—decide to cross the Delaware. There were six deadly previews, with no audience response and virtually no audience.

We opened on June 23; as opening night gifts, Hugh presented to the men sample bottles of Brut by Fabergé. Everyone just rolled their eyes. We had booked the Walnut Street for eight weeks, with a built-in two-week extension to accommodate the crowds. We barely made it through the opening week, folding on the 26th. By the Fourth of July, *The Decision* was merely a bad memory.

The Walnut Street stage remained empty until September 23, when it hosted the presidential debate between President Gerald Ford and Governor Jimmy Carter—the first such debate since the legendary night in 1960 when Kennedy trounced Nixon. President Ford did better at the Walnut Street than Hugh O'Brian as Washington had done in *The Decision*, but not all that much better.

By that point all concerned had scrubbed the entire fiasco from memory, following the sage advice of the headline from Jonathan Takiff's review in the Philadelphia *Daily News*: "The Best Decision: Forget It."

RED VOLKSWAGEN

One afternoon in early October, Jeffrey stuck his head in the door and called to Helen: "Can you get a script to Bette Davis?"

Some friend of his—I can't recall whether it was an aspiring playwright with no Broadway credits or an aspiring producer with no Broadway credits—had walked into lunch with said script. Bette Davis, presumably healed since the *Miss Moffat* debacle a year before, would be perfect. According to the aspiring playwright or producer, whichever he was.

Helen said she'd try. That afternoon, she placed a call to Robby Lantz.

Robert Lantz was an agent unlike any agent around: a gentleman with a lilt. Born in Berlin during World War I, he escaped Germany and wound up in New York after World War II. He had a limited roster on the most stellar plane: Yul Brynner, Elizabeth Taylor, Richard Burton,

Alfred Drake, and Liv Ullman were among his actors. Nonperformers included Leonard Bernstein, Lillian Hellman, Alan Jay Lerner, Peter Shaffer, and Richard Avedon. Many of these people ranked high on the temperamental scale, at least to outsiders; perhaps they were chastened into reasonableness by Robby's courtly manner.

More likely, when they got out of line—as high-tempered superstar celebrities have been known to do—Robby simply suggested that he'd walk away. He was famous for operating on a handshake; if his clients wanted to leave him, the door was always open. While he did not operate on a mere handshake with management, it was a relatively open negotiation: if Robby gave his word, you needn't rush to get papers signed.

I dealt with him a few times over the years. With other agents you were always negotiating, either trying to get them to give you something, or trying not to give *them* something. With Robby, it was more a polite conversation than a negotiation: This is what I'd like, might it be possible? You always felt that he would do whatever he could, on as reasonable terms as possible given his celebrity clients—and he expected the same from you.

Helen got Robby on the phone, sweet-talked him, in her best Jewish-southern-belle-from-Texas manner, and then got around to asking if Bette Davis was interested in reading a stage script.

She was at her house in Westport, Connecticut, he said. Perhaps we could messenger the script up there? He did not ask Helen whether the script was any good, so she did not have to say that it was. She hadn't read it, of course.

This was late in the star's career; she was nearing seventy, and in the sort of limbo that can occur when your reputation for being temperamental outweighs the advantages of having a legendary name on the marquee.

I scrawled a quick note and slid it to Helen: "Tell him we need to drive up to Westport on Thursday or Friday; we can drop it off."

Robby said he'd get back to us. He did, the next morning, with Bette's address on Crooked Mile Road. He told us that we should be there Thursday at precisely three; she was leaving for California on Saturday and had errands to run.

We drove up to Westport, making sure we were there in plenty of time. (We did not, needless to say, have any other reason to be in Connecticut.) We parked across the street and waited. At three o'clock, promptly, we walked to the door and rang the bell. No answer. We waited. No answer. We went back to the car and waited.

At 3:20 a modest red Volkswagen station wagon pulled into the driveway and parked by the front door. Out of the car came a suburban grandmother with gray hair and sensible shoes. Two minutes after she entered the house, we got out of the car and rang the bell.

The suburban grandmother opened the door smiling.

"Miss Davis, Robbie Lantz sent this script."

She took it, said a polite thank you, and closed the door.

Nothing more was ever heard of the matter. But hey, why turn down the chance to meet Bette Davis in sensible shoes?

CHAPTER TWENTY-TWO

Moving On and Away

A Trip with Cullum

As we hit the second summer of *Shenandoah*, Cullum approached Phil with an idea. Emily Frankel, John's wife since 1959, was a distinctive modern choreographer and dancer. They had been working with Emily's troupe in their in-home studio on three dance/theatre pieces inspired by Greek mythology. What were the chances of finding a theatre to present them publicly?

"Sure," said Phil. "We're dark Monday nights, we can do them at the Alvin."

And so it was that we presented what we called *Kings*, for four Mondays beginning September 27, 1976. The evening comprised John starring in Emily's version of "Oedipus," Emily in "Medea," and the pair as "Theseus & Hippolyta." We had a cast of eighteen, including the couple's ten-year-old son, John David (even then known as JD Cullum). John and Emily produced with Phil; Helen and I served as general managers.

But this wasn't the only Cullum-related activity. Phil had attended a workshop of a new play by John Bishop called *The Trip Back Down*, about a professional stock-car racer returning to his hometown, Mansfield, Ohio, to try to salvage at least something from his failed life. "You can't go home again," as Thomas Wolfe once wrote. This thought might well have been floating in Phil's mind at the time; he was still desperately seeking backing for the Geld-Udell-Rose musical version of Wolfe's *Look Homeward, Angel*.

Phil also saw, in *The Trip Back Down*, an exceptional role for Cullum. Given John's loyal dedication to *Shenandoah*—his performance, and his Tony Award, had helped us get through those first difficult months to long-run safety—Phil offered to let him leave the musical prior to the end of his contracted term in order to undertake the Broadway production of *Trip*.

Phil at the same time decided that he should override his impulse to direct his productions and allow Terry Schreiber—a respected acting coach who had directed the workshop—to remain with the play and make his Broadway debut. Phil also retained much of the cast, adding only two new actors: John, in the lead, and Doris Belack (Phil's wife) as the hero's wry sister-in-law.

The play marked a new beginning for me. In October, I finished my three-year apprenticeship and was admitted to ATPAM as a fully accredited company manager. Helen stayed over at *Shenandoah*, and I finally had a show of my own.

BALCONY

And now I stood on the stage of the Longacre. I won't say, exactly, that every theatre in existence has its own personality. But many do.

That night in 1969 at the Alvin, after my visit with James Earl Jones, was the first of many times I enjoyed that precise view from the stage of what is now called the Neil Simon. I did two shows there, *Tricks* and *Shenandoah*. What's more, I later spent several years working out of the fourth-floor offices above the auditorium. This came with my personal key to the stage door. On weekends and late at night, over the many stretches when the theatre wasn't booked, I could and would return to my original spot, looking out at the vast, dark, deep-red canyon.

Many of the theatres where I had spent time were laid out similar to the Alvin, including the first theatres at which I worked backstage: the Plymouth (where we rehearsed *Vivat*) and the Broadhurst (where *Vivat* opened). Similar, yes, and not accidentally: all three—as well as others including the Barrymore, Royale, O'Neill, and Imperial—were designed by Herbert J. Krapp, staff architect for the Shubert Brothers during the heyday of theatre construction.

The 46th Street, where we did *Raisin,* had an entirely different flavor. The first eight rows of the orchestra are on an incline, slightly more than usual; but after a mid-house crossover, the remaining fourteen rows are elevated on steep steps. Broadway's two steeply elevated older theatres—the other being the Majestic—were both designed by Krapp, for builder/architect Irwin Chanin, whose Art Moderne flair can be seen in the Chanin Building on East Forty-Second Street and the Century and Majestic apartments on Central Park West. (The Shuberts ultimately gained control of both theatres during the Depression.) This rake gives the distinct impression, from the stage of the 46th Street—and it still sounds wrong to me to call it the Rodgers—that you are enveloped by the audience. Further enhancing the effect is the presence of eight boxes, on two levels. Standing center stage, during *Raisin,* I could understand why this was the house of choice for Gwen Verdon and Bob Fosse.

The Lunt-Fontanne, where we did *The Pajama Game,* was altogether different and altogether uninviting. The orchestra floor was laid out like a shoebox, relatively narrow and exceedingly deep (with twenty-seven rows). There was also a center aisle down the middle, instead of the three-section layout of all but a few Broadway houses. (This was eventually altered to provide a large section of prime "center seats.") What's more, the Lunt mezzanine goes on forever, up to a distance where you feel that the audience can't actually see you. The Mark Hellinger was unlike the Lunt except in being equally uninviting. The orchestra floor was so wide—with forty-eight seats across at its peak, as opposed to the thirty-six at the Alvin—that you felt that the patrons on the side might as well have been sitting in a different county. This was no problem when *Shenandoah* moved to the Hellinger; we hardly ever filled those seats.

And now I was at the Longacre, similar feeling in a way but significantly different. While this pre–World War I house was only four years older than the 1917 Broadhurst, it was built on a different architectural plan. Instead of a large mezzanine floor, there was a smaller mezz and an exceedingly steep second balcony.

One supposes this had to do with advanced technology and the strength of building materials. The Shubert and Palace, also built in 1913, included second balconies. Beginning with the postwar Broadhurst, a cursory calculation shows that all but four of the twenty-seven subsequent Broadway houses opted for an extended mezzanine in place of that extra balcony.

The second balcony at the Longacre was by 1970 a distinct disadvantage. In the depressed Broadway of the time, the smaller second balcony houses—including the Cort, Belasco, and Lyceum—were considered "jinx" houses; while formerly home to distinguished hits, they now mostly housed flops. This was not some mystical jinx, mind you. Theatre owners understandably gave their one-mezzanine houses—such as the Barrymore, Plymouth/Schoenfeld, Royale/Jacobs, Music Box, and Booth—to more profitable-sounding prospective tenants.

The issue, financially, is basic: producers had learned that they could charge increasingly high prices for seats in the mezzanine. The front row of the second balcony is a region further away, unless you have a show that people are fighting to get into.

From the stage of the Longacre, the second balcony indeed looked steep. I had never seen a play from up there—by 1977, I'd long since stopped buying seats up top, although I dutifully wandered up during tech rehearsals to see what *Trip* looked like from the eaves—but I still remember what seemed like endless climbs, as a patron, up to various second balconies.

GOOD COMPANY

The Trip Back Down was uneventful, as these things go. But for the first time, I was more part of the company—the cast and backstage company—than the "office." On some shows, be they successful or not, everyone becomes a close-knit family. That was the case with *Trip*.

It was here that I cemented my relationship with Cullum. He was an exceptional singer and an accomplished actor, yes; but he was also what you might call a thinking man's actor. Many performers can talk at length about the play, and their role, and their performance; John, though, had a variety of interests on matters outside his present role. I suppose we were drawn to each other, in part because we started *Trip* with most of the company knowing each other from the prior production. Having been together almost two years on *Shenandoah* and having worked more directly with each other on *Kings*, we were—along with Phil and Doris—our own group within the group.

Doris was Phil's wife of many years—since 1946—and perhaps one could consider her his long-suffering wife, having lived through so many professional ups (i.e., *A Raisin in the Sun*) and downs (just about everything else). Her presence in *Trip* was not nepotism; she was a superb character actress, and I'd guess that her constant acting and soap opera work, over the years, brought in considerably more than her feast-or-famine husband. While her name might be little known, she is one of those familiar faces from the small and big screen. Her most noticeable role—and one that fully captured her personality—was as Rita Marshall, the acerbic soap opera producer who played foil to Dustin Hoffman in the 1982 comedy *Tootsie*. Catch it and you'll likely become a Doris Belack fan.

An Odd Couple

As for Phil, I gained further insight into his personality. He was a strong champion of the underdog, as evidenced by his start as a debt collector who favored his underprivileged debtors to his employers; his early relationships with William Marshall, Paul Robeson, and Sidney Poitier, at a time when the mere association was enough to make Phil's left-wing tendencies even more controversial; and his championship of that teen-aged waitress, with the pair supporting and instructing each other as they worked their way toward the birth of *A Raisin in the Sun*.

Phil was also a gambler. He often gambled on his shows, grasping for lifelines wherever he could find them. But most of those gambles were lost, with Helen attesting that Phil had an endless parade of impatient creditors.

The work of a company manager, back in the days before emails and instant messages, ended with a nightly phone call to the producer with box office gross. Some producers, over the course of time, were only moderately interested. A producer like Phil, though, anxiously awaited every evening's figure. On the two shows I did for him, those figures usually ranged from moderate to worse; so very many nights brought high-level disappointment.

It became apparent that Thursday was Phil's night out: I would call room 402 at the Warwick Hotel on Sixth Avenue, where Phil and friends had their weekly poker game. Central to this long-established game, whenever he was in town, was Neil Simon. It is my contention—based on my knowledge of Phil as well as the visible evidence—that this is the very card game written into Simon's *The Odd Couple.* There's a short, thickly bespectacled character named "Vinnie," and if you knew Phil you could easily see how the role could be a fond caricature.

Further cementing the similarity is the actor hired to play the role, on Broadway and the screen. John Fiedler not only looked like Phil, with the same thick glasses and balding head; he also knew him well, having created the role of Karl Lindner—the man from the Clybourne Park Improvement Association—in the stage and screen versions of *A Raisin in the Sun.* Was Fiedler, as Vinnie, doing a Phil Rose imitation? Whenever I see *The Odd Couple,* I picture Phil eagerly anteing up as that hapless card player.

BLIZZARD ALERT

Business on *The Trip Back Down* started weak and never improved.

We began previews the night after Christmas, with Phil expecting good business from holiday visitors whom press agent Merle Debuskey, Helen, and I knew would likely never come. The fatal doornail was mercilessly hammered in on opening night, January 4, 1977, by our old friend Clive Barnes. Under the headline "A Bad Trip," he called the play a mass of clichés. Which, perhaps, it was. He found only one thing to appreciate, the "absolutely exceptional" star. "Mr. Cullum, in his beleaguered, dangerous way, seemed in his acting to be answering questions the playwright had never quite thought of posing"—which, indeed, he was.

It was a long couple of months. Each week, Phil would have a critical decision to make—critical because our position was so precarious. While stronger shows (like *Shenandoah*) went into each week with at least Friday and Saturday well sold, *Trip* had little advance, meaning that our survival depended on getting in ticket buyers over the weekend. Seeing that most of the "hits" were already reasonably full, our aim was to pull in

You can't go back down home again. *The Trip Back Down* (1977).

those people who look at the Friday paper and think, (1) let's see a show this weekend; and (2) what can we still get tickets to?

Our ad budget was understandably tight; we were grossing perhaps a third of what a successful play might. Should we spring for a big Friday ad, which was decidedly not in our budget, to try to salvage the week? Or not? The space had to be reserved and committed by Wednesday, so we had long, drawn-out discussions each week with Phil and Merle. Would *Trip* sell the Friday and Saturday performances if we ran a display ad? Phil would ask again and again.

Our answer, of course, could only be maybe, possibly, hopefully.

What transpired was the following:

On the weeks when we ran a Friday display ad, we would turn on the radio Friday morning to hear that a blizzard was expected. Don't leave your homes this weekend.

On the weeks when we decided not to spring for the ad, the weather would be positively balmy for midwinter.

Our belief was that people simply weren't interested in seeing *The Trip Back Down*, good weather or bad, display ad or no. But Phil was a gambler, clutching at possible straws. As we headed into February, it became a joke between us—including Phil. The only way to guarantee snow on Saturdays was for Phil to buy an ad in the *Times*.

As we kept plowing ahead, losing week after losing week, one chance of salvation beamed to Phil like a lighthouse in a treacherous squall. Through his personal contacts in the movie world—Phil had coproduced the highly successful film version of *A Raisin in the Sun*—he floated the film rights to actor Paul Newman. Newman was at the height of his fame; he was also a champion auto racer, which must have petrified his agents every time he got behind the wheel. (He drove as "P. L. Newman.") Here was the perfect vehicle—acting vehicle, that is—for the fifty-year-old superstar from small-town Ohio, just an hour's jaunt from the town (Mansfield) where *The Trip* took place.

The importance of a film sale was not merely academic. While major hit plays were often snapped up by the studios for large sums, it was not uncommon over the decades for lesser plays to sell their screen rights for lesser sums—so much so that quite a number of ventures that looked like Broadway failures paid off their investments with the help of Hollywood money. Not only does a sizable chunk of the film payment go the investors; a successful film magnifies the number of future productions a play can expect, potentially providing substantial royalties. (For example: Ernest Thompson's 1979 play *On Golden Pond* finished its Broadway run with a loss of its entire $240,000 investment, which was recovered—many times over—from the Henry Fonda/Katharine Hepburn film and subsidiary income.) Given the doomed reception of *Trip*—which I seem to recall was capitalized at $175,000, with the lion's share again from Louis and Gloria Sher—a film sale was the only way we could hope to avoid a complete loss.

From two weeks into the run, Phil kept telling us that Paul Newman was coming next week. This went on and on, through January and February; on two occasions, Newman actually canceled his seats due to that week's snowstorm. Finally, the actor did indeed appear on a Tuesday night. I don't know that I've ever seen usherettes' eyes light up the way they did when Paul walked down the aisle.

But to no avail. Thanks, from the Newman camp, but not interested.

Displaced by Orphan, with Dog

Meanwhile, we'd run into a problem at the Alvin. A major problem.

Business had remained relatively steady since John departed on October 31. While Broadway star John Raitt and Hollywood star Howard Keel were both naturals for the replacement job, Phil instead went with a fellow named William Chapman.

A thundering baritone who played leads at New York City Opera, Chapman had some minor featured Broadway experience: the roles of Ferone, the croupier in Leonard Bernstein's 1956 *Candide* (featured in the quartet, "What's the Use?"); and the stern Reverend Lapp in Frank Loesser's 1960 *Greenwillow*. He was sturdy in *Shenandoah*, but no more. He sang the role well, but without any of the acting-through-singing inflection that Cullum added, and Raitt or Keel (both of whom eventually played the show on the road) could have brought.

Chapman opened on November 2, the very same night that Jimmy Carter won the presidential election and wasn't that auspicious? With our new Charlie Anderson, *Shenandoah* still pleased its core audience. Cullum's performance, though, was able to win over the larger group who weren't enthused by the show itself. We did fine through the Thanksgiving and Christmas holidays and settled in for another year of moderate but above-breakeven business.

And then along came *Annie*.

Annie had filled the *Shenandoah* slot in the 1976 season at Goodspeed. We needn't outline the show's history, in which a powerful New York producer—Mike Nichols, by name—took over the show; had it significantly overhauled, most significantly enlarging the character Miss Hannigan from a featured role into a crowd-pleasing, scenery-chewing star turn; and, having displaced the original producers who had been unable to arrange financing, aligned himself with two powerful coproducers: Roger L. Stevens, who brought a sizable investment plus a tryout booking at the Kennedy Center's Eisenhower Theatre; and New York theatre owner James M. Nederlander.

Our contract with the Alvin allowed us to remain at the theatre indefinitely, as long as we did not fall below the stop-clause. Unless—unless the theatre were sold, in which case there were certain circumstances under which the new owner could terminate the deal.

The owner of the Alvin, since 1963, was Konrad Matthaei. An actor and socialite from a wealthy Detroit industrial family, his most prominent acting credit outside of a recurring role on the soap opera *As the World Turns* was as Hank in the original cast of *The Boys in the Band*. I knew him from his not altogether auspicious role in the ignominious *A Place for Polly*.

A half-year into the run of *Shenandoah*, we were surprised to learn that Matthaei—who had shown no signs of distress—had lost the Alvin by foreclosure. In November 1975, it was bought from the Bowery Savings Bank by Jimmy Nederlander, making it the fifth Broadway house controlled by his family (joining the Palace, Atkinson, Hellinger, and Uris). This change of control had little effect upon us initially. And then Mike Nichols brought Nederlander into *Annie*, and one thing led to another.

Annie began its pre-Broadway tryout in early March 1977 at the Eisenhower. Even before that, though, we got a call from the Nederlanders while *The Trip Back Down* was staggering into February. *Annie* would begin previews at the Alvin on April 8; we had to get out by March 26. It seems that while our lease committed a new owner to honor our booking, that didn't apply when the theatre was bought not from the owner but from a bank following foreclosure. (Is it possible that Konrad and Nederlander somehow manipulated the foreclosure?)

We were still running at a profit; but the costs of a move—even if we could find another house—would be crushing to our overall financial picture. This forced move is precisely what turned *Purlie* from a likely success into a financial failure. And *Raisin* too, for that matter. But this was Phil "never-say-die" Rose; of course he would move the show rather than give up.

And of course, said Nederlander general manager Arthur Rubin, "I can let you have the Hellinger."

END OF RUN

The Mark Hellinger was a white elephant of a theatre around the corner on Fifty-First Street. A former movie palace, it was a flop house until *My Fair Lady* instantly changed its status when it opened there in 1956. Following that, the Hellinger played host to mostly misses, its only other profitable shows over its first thirty years being the Katharine Hepburn vehicle *Coco* and the Andrew Lloyd Webber/Tim Rice *Jesus Christ Superstar*.

The Hellinger, until 1970, was not a Nederlander theatre; it was one of two houses—the other being the Lunt-Fontanne—owned by a fellow named Stanley Stahl and general managed by Artie. The Hellinger had a huge capacity, yes, and movie palace–like trappings including a grand lobby and lower lounge. As a legit theatre, though, it had a severe drawback. The orchestra section was among the largest on Broadway, meaning that for a superhit you could sell far more full-price tickets. (In those days, nobody imagined that ticket buyers would pay orchestra prices for the mezzanine.) At the Hellinger, though, very many of the side orchestra seats had challenging sight lines. You really wouldn't want to sit there, unless it was for a sold-out hit like *My Fair Lady*.

Along with the large capacity came large operating costs, which sunk twenty of the twenty-three musicals that had played the house thus far. Artie offered Phil the Hellinger like a wolf in sheep's clothing, which you could say he was. Or perhaps a shark dressed as a minnow. Artie remained third in control at the Nederlanders until 1992, when he resigned "in order to pursue other business interests" in the midst of a district attorney investigation into the theft of $350,000 from the box office of the Lunt.

With no recourse, Phil characteristically leapt. On Saturday, March 5, we closed *The Trip Back Down* after ten previews and seventy performances. On May 6, *Annie* ran its announcement in the *Times* Arts & Leisure section with a slug at the bottom advising that "*Shenandoah* moves March 29 to Mark Hellinger Theatre."

After finishing up the paperwork on *The Trip Back Down*, Helen expected me to go back to *Shenandoah* as assistant manager. I was decidedly not interested. Having finally worked my way up to a full union manager after six years on and around Broadway, I wasn't about to take a step backward. I agreed to oversee the move and then leave once the show was safely at the Hellinger.

Shenandoah continued for four additional crowd-dwindling months at the Hellinger, finally closing on August 17, 1977, after 1,050 performances with a still significant deficit. By that point I was already in previews at the Biltmore with another musical.

Income from subsidiary rights—specifically a few tours and many stock and amateur productions—continued to dribble in over the eighteen years during which the Shenandoah Company shared in the authors' royalties, allowing the show to eventually recoup costs. When the rights fully terminated in 1994, the investors had received a profit of $81,465 on the initial $500,000 investment, a profit of 16 percent.

As it turned out, it was the right decision to move on from Helen: she would have only two more general managing jobs, both for Phil, including the long-delayed *Angel* (as they renamed *All the Comforts of Home*). Phil eventually managed to mount this third Gary Geld/Peter Udell musical at a dinner theatre on Long Island, which enabled him to raise enough money to bring the show to Broadway in May 1978.

When the call finally came for me to do *Angel*, I was most fortunately otherwise disposed, in previews for *The Best Little Whorehouse in Texas* for Jack Schlissel. So I didn't have to actually turn down Phil and Helen.

I do take responsibility—good or bad—for the casting of the leading man. Back during *Shenandoah* days, I had suggested to Phil that he try Arthur Hill for the role of the father, W. O. Gant; prior to originating George in *Who's Afraid of Virginia Woolf?*, Hill had costarred as the son Ben Gant in the 1957 Pulitzer-winner *Look Homeward, Angel*. I assured producer/director/coauthor Phil that Hill could sing, loaning him my copy of a live-theatre tape of the 1964 musical *Something More*, which starred Hill opposite Barbara Cook.

When Hill eventually turned it down (and no wonder), I told Phil that he could likely get Fred Gwynne, with whom I'd worked at Kennedy

Center on *The Enchanted* (and whom I'd singled out all the way back in *Irma La Douce*). Thus it was that Fred starred in *Angel*—opposite Frannie Sternhagen—albeit only for five performances at the Minskoff. Helen closed her office and moved over to Jeffrey's burgeoning theatrical press operation, where she remained until her death in 1983, at the age of sixty-six.

Walking with Music

During my final days with *Shenandoah*, as we were transferring the show to the Hellinger, Earl Shendell came by to drop off the bill for moving that forest-green Steinway around the corner from the Alvin.

Earl was our musical contractor, the title given to the person who supervises the musical end of the production: selecting (i.e., casting) the musicians; controlling rehearsals; managing musical instrument rentals; and troubleshooting any problems that come up along the way. If the trumpet player disappears one night, the musical contractor is the person who somehow or another finds a quick solution. With all that the stage manager, company manager, and general manager have to handle, this is an area they are glad (and relieved) to leave to someone else.

Part of Earl's fiefdom was control of Local 802 "walkers." The union contract provided that a minimum number of musicians be hired at each so-called musical house, roughly based on capacity. This was not an issue on the musicals I did; we were certain to use all the musicians we had to pay for. When plays included recorded music, the contract provided that four walkers—union members who did nothing more than walk in, once a week, and pick up a paycheck—be hired.

On *The Trip Back Down*, thus, Earl placed four people of his choosing on the payroll. The deal he made with the managers was simple: pay the walkers one check every four weeks ("cigarette money," he called it) plus the full weekly pension and welfare payments to the union. It was a bargain, especially for a cash-starved play like *The Trip Back Down*.

Earl—who seemed to have mysteriously significant pull over at 802—garnered a checkered reputation over the years. He redeemed himself in my book, for all time, in 1983 or so when he instructed us—the various managers with walkers on our payrolls—that the cigarette money game was up. Henceforth, all walkers on Shendell-controlled shows were to be bona fide musicians who had become too ill to work due to AIDS, thus allowing them to retain their health insurance. This was the first such step in the industry I was aware of, although due to the controversies and prejudices of the time it needed to be kept secret.

Stepping back to 1977, Earl asked whether I was going back on *Shenandoah*, as if he already knew that Helen intended to keep the salary for herself.

"No, Helen's on the contract."

"Anything lined up?"

"Not yet."

"Gene Wolsk has a couple of shows. I mentioned you, he's waiting for your call."

So I went to see Gene Wolsk.

The View from Times Square

BIG LEAGUE

As I started my apprenticeship in the early 1970s, the firm of Wolsk & Azenberg were Broadway's busiest general managers. This was mostly by virtue of their associations with Joseph Papp and Bernard Gersten—for whom they handled the first four Broadway transfers of productions from the New York Shakespeare Festival—and Neil Simon, whose work they started to manage and produce in 1972.

Both began their careers working for Jack Schlissel. Eugene V. Wolsk was five years older than Emanuel Azenberg, and thus—like Biff, Leo, and Mitch—came to theatre following military service. Being slightly younger than the others, it was a different war: Gene left his graduate studies at Yale Drama School in 1951 to go to Korea. Returning to New York, he managed several off-Broadway productions, then joined Merrick in 1961 as a replacement on *Carnival!* Other shows included *Tchin-Tchin* (with Anthony Quinn and Margaret Leighton) and the long-running *Stop the World—I Want to Get Off.* While Wolsk managed the Broadway production of the latter, which featured Anthony Newley and his hit song "What Kind of Fool Am I?," Azenberg took out the national tour starring Joel Grey.

Gene left Merrick after John Osborne's *Luther* in 1964, becoming general manager for producer David Black on two fall shows. The first, a revue from the Cambridge University Footlights club called *Cambridge Circus,* was imported to the Plymouth in expectations that it might match the success of *Beyond the Fringe.* It didn't, lasting only three weeks despite a cast including future *Python*ites John Cleese and Graham Chapman. Faring slightly (but only slightly) better was *Ready When You Are, C. B.!*, a Josh Logan-directed comedy starring Julie Harris. Black's next play, though, was a hit: *The Impossible Years*, with nightclub comic Alan King, opened in October 1965 at the Playhouse and ran twenty months.

Manny, too, began his career off-Broadway. For Merrick, he specialized in road companies, beginning with the brief 1962 national tour of *I Can Get It for You Wholesale* followed by *Stop the World* (in 1963) and *Oliver!* (in 1964). When Gene started work on *The Impossible Years*, the first play on which he could afford to hire a separate company manager as opposed to serving in that capacity himself, he called on Manny to come in from the road. As phone answerer and office assistant, he found a twenty-two-year-old named R. Tyler Gatchell Jr.

During the long run of the comedy, Gene came across a play he wanted to produce and arranged for the *Impossible Years* star (King) and coproducer (Walter Hyman) to finance it. James Goldman's *The Lion in Winter*—produced by Wolsk, King, and Hyman "with" Azenberg—opened at the Ambassador on March 3, 1966, starring Robert Preston and Rosemary Harris. The drama about Henry II and Eleanor of Aquitaine closed after an unsuccessful three months, although it eventually turned a profit thanks to subsidiary income from the 1968 film version starring Peter O'Toole and Katharine Hepburn.

Gene and Manny produced a second show that March, a limited engagement of Hal Holbrook's *Mark Twain Tonight* at the Longacre. Not knowing any better, they did not build in an option to share in future productions—of which there were very many.

(A *Mark Twain Tonight* tangent. Back in the days when actors toured the country in pocket-sized productions aimed for community theatres, Holbrook went to audition his act—including, among scenes from various plays, a Mark Twain sequence—at a booking convention in Ohio in 1949. When he panicked because he didn't bring a necessary prop for the audition, two strangers who were also auditioning—Mitch Erickson and Dick Corson—volunteered to run out and find what was needed. When Hal first came to New York to try to find an agent, he slept on the couch at Mitch and Dick's walk-up on Prince Street; and Dick, being a stage makeup expert, lent a hand in creating that aspect when Holbrook first brought his one-man Twain off-Broadway in 1959.)

Next for Wolsk & Azenberg came two more plays, coproduced with King and Hyman: the controversial *The Investigation* by Peter Weiss (of *Marat/Sade*) in 1966; and Carl Reiner's unsuccessful *Something Different* in 1967.

These two were general managed not by Wolsk or Azenberg but by Max Allentuck. Max was an old-timer—born in 1911, twenty-three years older than Manny. ("Stand up straight," Manny once said to me in the late 1980s. "Don't you want to look like Max when you're his age?")

Allentuck had served as general manager to Kermit Bloomgarden since 1946 on a wide array of shows, including *Death of a Salesman* and *The Music Man*. Upon Bloomgarden's temporary withdrawal from Broadway after the debacle of *Illya, Darling* in 1966, Allentuck took on the two Wolsk & Azenberg–produced shows.

Gene and Manny, considering themselves basically general managers, stopped producing (for the moment) and created a combine they called Allentuck, Azenberg, and Wolsk. They did five shows over the next two years, only one of which—the David Black–produced *George M!*—had a decent run. By this time, Gatchell had finished his union apprenticeship and served as company manager on that musical. Also working for Allentuck, Azenberg, and Wolsk was a young company manager brought over by Allentuck, Peter Neufeld.

GREEN ROOM

I got to know Max somewhat later, when he served as company manager for Manny's 1980 production of *Whose Life Is It Anyway?* Before Max ends his fleeting appearance on our pages, we digress for one of my favorite backstage anecdotes.

In 1949, Allentuck met and married an intense young Actors Studio member whose main experience at the time was small roles in four Broadway plays. She got her big break in early 1951, plucked from oblivion to take the hard-to-fill leading role in the new Tennessee Williams play. *The Rose Tattoo* was a hit, with Maureen Stapleton becoming a star overnight.

Skip to 1981. Maureen—long divorced from Max but having cordially raised their two children—has had a long career, with two Tony Awards, an Emmy, and an Oscar in the mix. But she has become something of a caricature of herself, an eccentric with a known dependence on alcohol. She remains an excellent actor but is no longer bankable due to the unreliability that comes with such excesses. Hollywood's Elizabeth Taylor decides to make her stage debut as Regina in Lillian Hellman's *The Little Foxes*. Maureen takes the second lead of Regina's sister-in-law Birdie, a lesser but critical role. Taylor is not inhibited by the thought of appearing with such a veteran scene stealer; she realizes, quite cannily, that Maureen's presence will make the show seem like something more than just another revival with a famous movie star who has never appeared onstage.

Prior to Broadway, *The Little Foxes* plays a tryout at Kennedy Center in Washington, DC. One night, President Reagan and the First Lady attend the show. Before marrying Reagan, the then–Nancy Davis had been a contract player with Taylor at MGM. Prior to that, it turns out, the still-unknown Maureen and the still-unknown Nancy had done a season of summer stock together. Like Nancy, Liz was—at the time of *The Little Foxes*—married to a GOP bigwig: John Warner, senator from Virginia and formerly Nixon's secretary of the navy.

Presidential visits to the Kennedy Center's Eisenhower Theatre are gala affairs. Following the show, the president is brought to the large backstage green room, which has an overpowering chandelier and high walls lined by layers of show posters. The cast, staff, and crew form a long line snaking back toward the stage, waiting—as economical champagne is passed around—to shake the president's hand.

The night of the *Little Foxes* visit, Liz stands with Reagan and Nancy, grandly and warmly introducing everyone by name. I can attest to the veracity of this story because the house manager of the Eisenhower—a close friend—was standing behind Liz, whispering into her ear the names of the next people in line. He called me with a firsthand report immediately after the room cleared out.

Maureen approaches the First Couple.

Liz says, "Oh, Maureen! Do you know Nancy Reagan?"

Maureen, having already started in on the champagne, responds in a voice robust enough to reach from Foggy Bottom all the way over to Capitol Hill.

"*Know* her?" she says. "Max *fucked* her!"

CHARLIE

Gene and Manny had both worked, on various Merrick shows, with stage manager Charles Blackwell. Charlie, from my days on *Promises, Promises,* was one of my favorites; as it turned out, he was one of everybody's favorites. He had started on Broadway as a dancer in Merrick's first musical, *Fanny.* Learning that Charlie had experience working in advertising, the then-novice producer sought him out for an opinion. Finding him impressively knowledgeable, Merrick soon had Charlie promoted to second ASM on the show.

He was hired as first ASM on Merrick's next musical, *Jamaica.* (As far as I can tell, Blackwell was the first Black stage manager on a major Broadway production.) He remained a Merrick regular on *Take Me Along, Carnival!,* and *110 in the Shade,* moving up to the production stage manager slot with *Breakfast at Tiffany's* and *How Now, Dow Jones.*

Breakfast at Tiffany's was a notorious failure, with Merrick closing the show during previews at the Majestic "rather than subject the drama critics and the public to an excruciatingly boring evening," he confessed. He was not without a sense of humor about the debacle: his *Playbill* bio for his next musical reads in full: "Mr. Merrick is best known as the distinguished producer of the musical, *Breakfast at Tiffany's.*"

Among a field of exceptional people, Charlie was known—along with his friendly and supportive personality—as one of the giants of Broadway; I never saw him standing next to Mr. Abbott, but I'd guess Blackwell was even taller. He was also known for his habit of embracing you—no matter who you were, dancer or stagehand, woman or man; no matter where you were, backstage or on Forty-Fifth Street—and lifting you up high off the ground. Although one doubts he did so with Mr. Merrick.

The last time I saw Charlie was in 1993, when he came backstage at a show I was directing in Pasadena. Clearly weakened by the cancer that was to end his life six months later, he *still* insisted on hoisting me off my feet.

While *Promises* was in the last year of its run, Charlie found an unconventional-for-Broadway property: Melvin Van Peebles's *Ain't Supposed to Die a Natural Death*, previously discussed in connection with Clive Barnes. Charlie brought the project to Gene and Manny, and the three of them produced it at the Barrymore in 1971.

CONNECTIONS

Ain't Supposed to Die marked the beginning of Wolsk & Azenberg's busiest spell, with four shows that season including the Tony-winning Best Play (*Sticks and Bones*) and Best Musical (*Two Gentlemen of Verona*.) They had learned—through the failure of their several self-produced shows—that they were better off working as general managers, and decided to stick to that field.

Circumstances changed almost immediately, when Neil Simon—who got to know Manny playing softball in Central Park as part of the Broadway Show League—decided to part ways with his longtime producer, Saint-Subber.

Saint—whose given name, in truth, was Arnold—had in 1963 produced Simon's second play, the long-running *Barefoot in the Park*. Producer and writer continued their association with six subsequent comedies, including *The Odd Couple* and *Plaza Suite*.

My understanding from Helen Richards, who served as company manager on several of the Simon–Subber tours and remained friendly with the staff, was that the catalyst for the split was financial. Neil's brother Danny helped supervise additional productions of the plays. At one point, Neil asked him to check a financial statement for one of the road tours. It looked fine to Danny Simon, as best he could tell, except he noticed that it included a charge for scenery. Danny knew that in this case, they had simply reused the scenery from an already-closed tour. Looking at other statements from other productions of Subber–Simon plays, it became clear that Neil—whose portion of the profits was determined by production expenses—was in effect being double billed by Saint. Whether this is accurate or not, I can't say; but it sounds like a reasonable and believable explanation.

In any event, Neil—whose wife Joan had long chafed over Saint's cavalier treatment of her husband, and who was by this time in the final stages of cancer—decided against giving his longtime producer the next play. Would Manny (and Gene) care to manage *The Sunshine Boys* and serve as nominal producers? Given that Simon comedies were prestigious cash machines, this was an offer that the general manager duo was quick to embrace.

They continued to actively manage plays and musicals over the next several seasons, including *That Championship Season, Much Ado About Nothing, The Wiz*, and the annual Simon play. A fissure began to occur in 1974. While I never thought to ask Gene or Manny about this, it was apparently over the question of producing as opposed to managing. Gene determined to produce a big musical, Josh Logan's aforementioned Bette Davis vehicle, *Miss Moffat*. Manny didn't wish to be involved—most wisely, as it transpired—so he sat it out. By mid-1975 the team had split. Manny kept Neil Simon, along with *The Wiz* and the Joe Papp account that soon included the touring companies—but not the Broadway production—of *A Chorus Line*.

While severed, Wolsk and Azenberg remained close and collegial, with a weekly tennis game into the 1990s. (One of their foursome was Frank Weissberg, a longtime theatrical attorney who became a justice of the New York Supreme Court in 1988.) Gene and Manny reunited professionally once, in 1988, at the behest of Bernie Gersten, and with me serving as their company manager. When I first became a producer in 1989—in partnership with Gene and Bernie—we did so working out of Manny's conference room.

ON THE AGENDA

When I sat with Gene at the end of April 1977, the hit Larry Gelbart comedy *Sly Fox* was in its fifth month at the Broadhurst. There were two shows for the fall; two additional shows for the winter of 1978; and three proposed musicals for the 1978–1979 season. The fall entries were revivals of major musical hits of the 1960s, not "old" musicals like *The Pajama*

Game or—for that matter—*No, No, Nanette*, but close re-creations of more recent near-classics with the participation of the original creative and design teams.

Hair, the self-proclaimed "American Tribal Love-Rock Musical," ushered in what was then a new world of music to musical theatre, attracting a younger generation of patrons who otherwise "wouldn't be caught dead" at a Broadway show. Featuring a hit-filled score by composer Galt MacDermot and lyrics by Gerome Ragni and James Rado, *Hair* was the *Rent* of its day—which, in turn, was the *Hamilton* of *its* day.

Hair, like *Hamilton*, originated at the Public Theater. In fact, it was the opening attraction (with a $2.50 top) at the house on Lafayette Street. Unlike with *Hamilton* and the 1975 *Chorus Line*, though, the Public was cut out of the Broadway transfer. A new-to-theatre producer from Chicago named Michael Butler wandered downtown to see the show; an American Indian rights supporter, he was drawn by the original poster art, which featured a vintage photo of three Native Americans with leading players Walker Daniels and Ragni, in beads, mixed in. Excited by the show's anti-war and "peace-flowers-freedom-happiness" mantra, the scion of the Butler Aviation family transferred *Hair* to Cheetah, a discotheque on Broadway at Fifty-Third Street.

When the disco *Hair* failed to attract an audience, Butler regrouped and—without the artistic or financial participation of Papp or the original director (Gerald Freedman) or designers—prepared a considerably revamped version that opened at the Biltmore on April 29, 1968. Buoyed in great part by the enthusiasm of Clive Barnes, the then-new drama critic of the *New York Times*, the show quickly attracted twin audiences: Broadway-goers adventurous enough to try something new along with non-Broadway-goers seeking the latest in pop culture.

If the reviews and word-of-mouth drew the people in, what proved irresistible were the melodious and friendly songs (including "Aquarius," "Let the Sunshine In," "Frank Mills," "Easy to Be Hard," and "Good Morning Starshine"). A rock score, yes; but not really; Canadian composer MacDermot specialized in what you might call new-wave jazz.

While lyricist-librettists Ragni and Rado could be considered hippies—Ragni, at least, was noted for his Medusa-like tresses—Galt was a jacket-and-tie family man living on Staten Island.

The show was boosted, and then some, by the addition of a new director. Tom O'Horgan, artistic director of La Mama E.T.C. (aka LaMama Experimental Theatre Club) in the East Village, had built up a reputation as one of off-off-Broadway's premiere avant-gardists. Most noticed, for obvious reasons, was his insertion into *Hair* of what was quickly dubbed "the nude scene": at the end of the first act, while the hero sings a ballad of self-discovery ("Where Do I Go?"), the actors—who have been "sleeping" under a drop that had descended from the flies and served as something like an enormous blanket draping the stage—rise from their slumber chanting "beads-flowers-freedom-happiness." If cast nudity was not officially mandated, it was more or less expected from and embraced by the so-called tribe.

Hair was an immediate hit, sprouting eight additional productions while remaining on Broadway. The original company closed on July 1, 1972, after four years and 1,750 performances—at the time, the seventh-longest running musical in Broadway history. The plan for 1977 was to present a close replica of the 1968 show under the direct control of O'Horgan, with designers Robin Wagner (sets) and Jules Fisher (lights) re-creating their work. Precisely the same as the original, yes; except that Ragni and Rado had kept the script fluid since the 1968 opening, with changes from subsequent productions haphazardly making their way back to the Broadway company at the Biltmore.

It was uncommon in those days—though not unprecedented—to revive a show merely five years after it closed. Butler's reasoning, in part, was influenced by the upcoming motion picture adaptation of the musical. It was the generally accepted belief that a show's commercial viability would be harmed once a film version was released. With Milos Forman's movie just then in production—it was filmed simultaneously with our revival and released in 1979—Butler wanted to get what he saw as his last chance to bring the *Hair* goldmine back to Broadway.

BACK TO LA MANCHA

The other revival was also a relatively recent blockbuster from the mid-1960s: *Man of La Mancha*. This was to be an even closer replica of the original, restaged by original director Albert Marre. The raison d'être was the presence of Richard Kiley, re-creating his Tony-winning performance as Cervantes.

This was being produced not for Broadway but as a national tour, albeit with an extended New York visit. The original opened at the ANTA Washington Square Theatre on November 22, 1965, and finally closed (after no less than three real estate–forced moves) on June 26, 1971, as Broadway's fourth longest-running musical ever with 2,328 performances. The gap between Broadway runs of *La Mancha* was slightly greater than the five years of *Hair*, yes; except that *La Mancha* had been revived—or, rather, quickly brought back—for a sold-out four-month run at the Vivian Beaumont beginning June 22, 1972.

This latter engagement was notable in that the thrust-stage Beaumont—with the audience enveloping the sides of the stage, and the orchestra split in something of a stereophonic wrap—replicated the show as it had appeared at the ANTA Washington Square. (Both theatres were built from the same Jo Mielziner designs, with the ANTA serving as temporary home of the newly established Repertory Theatre of Lincoln Center while the massive Lincoln Center complex was under construction.) Having seen *La Mancha* numerous times in numerous productions, I aver that it never appeared so powerful as it did at the ANTA and the Beaumont, with an extended drawbridge leading from the distant upstage wall to the isolated prison set thrust past the proscenium.

Kiley was indeed magnificent and unforgettable in the grueling role. He left the show in February 1967, replaced, as it happens, by John Cullum. Kiley then spent six months leading the national tour, after which he went on to less successful items including *Her First Roman*, an ill-conceived musicalization of Shaw's *Caesar and Cleopatra*; and the pallid 1974 Lerner & Loewe film musical, *The Little Prince*. The Beaumont engagement—reuniting Kiley with leading lady Joan Diener and two of his three other original costars—demonstrated that Broadway audiences, only a year after *La Mancha* closed, were eager to see Kiley in the role. Or to see Kiley, again, in the role.

La Mancha had continued on Broadway, post-Kiley, into 1971. There had also been a major motion picture version in 1972, released just after the closing of the show's four-month return engagement at Lincoln Center. Starring Peter O'Toole and Sophia Loren, this was lambasted by critics and audiences alike. Rather than damage the show's reputation, the film was quickly consigned to the celluloid trash pile and forgotten.

The Beaumont success suggested that audiences would gladly throng the wickets to see Kiley as Cervantes. Newspaper ads, during the original Broadway run, had carried the catchphrase: "What! You haven't even seen *Man of La Mancha* once?" For the 1977 production, the slogan became: "What! You haven't even seen Richard Kiley (The Original) in *Man of La Mancha* once?"

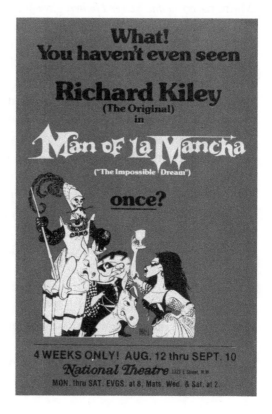

Richard Kiley, as Don Quixote, rides again. *Man of La Mancha* (1977).
MAX A. WOODWARD COLLECTION, MUSIC DIVISION, LIBRARY OF CONGRESS

Kiley had only one nonnegotiable demand in agreeing to do the tour: Joan Diener, the fiery and temperamental actress who had created the role of Aldonza—and appeared with Kiley in the 1953 musical *Kismet*, for that matter—must *not* be cast in the show. This was happily acceded to, although somewhat tricky in that Diener was married to director Marre. My observation was that Albie (as he was called, rather than Albert) thoroughly understood Kiley's request, and was not at all personally disturbed that Joan was forced to stay home.

(In 1985, Albie was enlisted to doctor the Twyla Tharp production of *Singin' in the Rain*. Featured among the cast was a young actress named Mary D'Arcy playing Kathy Selden, the Debbie Reynolds role. When Marre first attended the show, he brought the fifty-five-year-old Diener—in fiery red leather pants—along with him. A gentle propman named Barney, who had worked on the one-performance 1976 Diener/Marre fiasco *Home Sweet Homer*, gave Joan a gimlet-eyed glare and said: "If she tries to take little Mary's role, I'll scratch her eyes out.")

Gene and his not-so-silent but unbilled partner—*La Mancha* composer Mitch Leigh—guessed that while Kiley had never thus far demonstrated an ability to sell tickets, the combination of actor and role would sell well. This turned out to be a wild underestimate. The show was booked for a three-month run at the Palace beginning in mid-September 1977, preceded by a four-week August tryout at the National in Washington and followed by a six-month cross-country tour.

Given what turned out to be phenomenal demand and a string of shattered box office records from coast to coast, we prevailed on Kiley to add a second year. He and his courtly agent, Robbie Lantz, had agreed to a salary of $7,500 a week for the initial run. For the extension, we gladly gave him the 10 percent he deserved, which regularly took him up into the $15,000 range. But that came later.

STAR IN THE SPOTLIGHT

The third item on the agenda was a new musical from David Black: *Spotlight*. This was booked to follow *La Mancha* into the Palace for a February 4, 1978, opening, after a January 11 tryout at the National in Washington. Black, seeing fit to hire himself for his directing debut, opted not to take producer credit—although credit for being involved with *Spotlight*, as producer, director, or *anything*, proved negligible.

Starring in the show—about a washed-up Hollywood song-and-dance man forced out of stardom and into bankruptcy, tussling with estranged wives and children—was a bona fide washed-up Hollywood song-and-dance man, Dan Dailey. At least, he had been announced to star. Soon after I first sat with Gene, Dailey broke his hip while performing in a stock production of *The Odd Couple* and was forced to withdraw. (He died a year later, from complications following belated hip replacement surgery.) Replacing him was another washed-up former Hollywood star, Gene Barry from television's *Bat Masterson* and *Burke's Law*.

Written by a team of non-theatre folk, *Spotlight* had all the hallmarks of a classic flop. Lyricist Lyn Duddy and composer Jerry Bresler hailed from Jackie Gleason's various television variety shows; the book was by former agent Richard Seff, who was called in to try to salvage the unworkable script they were working with by a theatrical novice named Leonard Starr. Seff had entered the writing ranks with the Sam Levene/Molly Picon comedy *Paris Is Out!*, which Black produced in 1970 in association with a novice named Donald J. Trump. ("He is in the investment and real estate business," said his brief and modestly understated *Playbill* bio.)

Once I read the script, I couldn't imagine that *Spotlight* would even make it out of Washington. As it turned out, it folded in a mere four days despite some talented participants, including choreographer Tony Stevens, music director Jack Lee, and dance arranger Wally Harper. There were several bright spots in the cast, namely newcomer David-James Carroll and the already discovered D'Jamin Bartlett (from *A Little Night Music*) as Gene's wayward children, along with fiery dancer Lenora Nemetz (of *Chicago*) as the star's estranged ex-wife. Also on hand was a chorus girl with a clarion voice named Debbie Shapiro.

In the overweening ego department, let us point out that lyricist Duddy insisted—nay, *vehemently* insisted—that we bring a television set into the opening night party at the National Press Club so that all assembled could watch the TV reviews. Not a good idea, Wolsk and I advised; but who listens to us? On went the first TV review, which cited the lyrics by "the appropriately named Lyn Duddy."

Spotlight remains memorable mostly for a quote from the opening night review by *Washington Star* critic David Richards, who noted that Gene Barry dances "like an arthritic pugilist." Which he did.

Gene Barry dances "like an arthritic pugilist." And he did. *Spotlight* (1978).

Speaking of Jackie Gleason (i.e., "The Great One"), he was the star of Gene's other spring show: the national tour of *Sly Fox*. Jackie was slated to open in March in San Diego; move on after a couple of weeks to San Francisco; and work his way across the country, including a two-month stint in the Broadway production at the Broadhurst. Except Jackie turned out to be highly dissatisfied with the notion of eight performances a week and developed "heart trouble," forcing the show to fold in May in Chicago.

With a full slate of productions, Gene offered me my choice. On the one hand, I quite liked *Hair* and figured that I wouldn't mind spending time hearing the show every night. On the other hand, I liked *La Mancha* considerably more, and the presence of Kiley made it a something of a classy theatrical event—which *Hair* decidedly was not. After what seemed like a decade working as an assistant manager, though, I had finally made my way up to a Broadway show of my own. It seemed like a step backward to immediately go out on the road with *La Mancha*. As for Jackie Gleason, my week with Milton Berle and his shoe polish warned me to stay far, far away.

At the same time, *Spotlight*—despite its obvious flaws—was a new Broadway musical, which made it sound more intriguing than doing just another revival. Gene understood this, but pointed out that *Hair* would begin preproduction in May while *Spotlight* wouldn't go into rehearsal until November. If I started with *Hair*, I could always move over to *Spotlight* when the time came. In addition to *Hair*, I would help run the *La Mancha* tour from the New York office. (Our press agent, as it turned out, was the same John Prescott who had hired me at the Tappan Zee Playhouse.)

So I chose to stay on Broadway—our office on the eleventh floor of the Actors' Equity Building on Forty-Sixth Street, looked out directly over Times Square—and sign on with *Hair*. I began the following week and was immediately set to revising budgets and making arrangements for the three imminent musicals.

Chapter Twenty-Four

The Aging of Aquarius

Flopsy and Mopsy

Broadway musical juggernauts bring riches, fame, and sometimes notoriety to their creators, to the extent that on the day after they die, the headlines of their obituaries inevitably incorporate the name of said juggernaut. One *Hair* over the course of a career is an almost unparalleled achievement, satisfying enough and more than lucrative enough to last a lifetime and keep your heirs rebounding in royalties. Still, theatre folk are ambitious creatures, especially after they have once been so lavishly lauded.

At the same time, it is not uncommon for overwhelming success to lead to smoldering disputes among said creators. As the production is remounted across the nation and the world, frictions encountered the first time through often recur again and again. This happened with *Hair*. It happened with *Man of La Mancha* as well, for that matter.

Hair was a unique case, in that the assembled creators were Broadway novices. Gerry Ragni and Jim Rado met when they appeared in *Hang Your Head and Die*, a one-performance off-Broadway flop in 1964. They reunited when cast in the 1965 Chicago company of Mike Nichols's four-character off-Broadway hit, *The Knack*. Each had one Broadway acting credit, playing small parts: Ragni as a spear-carrier and understudy in the Richard Burton *Hamlet* (1964), Rado in the Wolsk-produced *The Lion in Winter* (1965).

Rado also flirted with major roles in two full-scale Broadway musicals. First came the misguided 1966 John Raitt vehicle, *A Joyful Noise*.

Rado and Donna McKechnie played the young romantic couple in the summer tryout, with both ultimately replaced for Broadway (by Clifford David and Susan Watson). According to Rado, Gerry—his lover at the time—joined him during the *Joyful Noise* tryout, the pair writing material for their hippie-themed musical in their hotel room. Rado was later announced as the third member of the romantic triangle—opposite Leslie Uggams and Robert Hooks—at the center of the 1967 Jule Styne/Arthur Laurents/Betty Comden/Adolph Green musical, *Hallelujah, Baby!* Rado chose to withdraw to concentrate on his *Hair*, which was first produced that December at the Public.

The further adventures of Ragni and Rado—lyricist, librettists, and stars of that monumental American Tribal Love-Rock Musical—proved bumpy, not only for the next nine years, at which point they rejoined for the 1977 revival of *Hair*, but for the duration of their careers. (Gerry died in 1991, at the age of fifty-five.)

James Rado and Gerome Ragni, the dawning of the age of Aquarius.
PHOTOFEST

After six months at the Biltmore, the actor/stars took *Hair* out to Los Angeles to the suitably renamed Aquarius Theatre. (This was the former Earl Carroll Theatre, built by said showman in 1938.) *Hair*, and Ragni and Rado, were the toast of the town even more than in New York.

The pair returned to the Broadway production the following spring, but the relationship ruptured abruptly: on April 11, 1969, Butler ordered them barred from performing because "their behavior onstage had become increasingly offensive." The following evening, they walked onto the stage but were ushered out of the Biltmore. A wary truce was eventually worked out, although the "peace-love-happiness" vibe was thenceforth never quite the same.

Ragni, seemingly in a fit of aggression, wrote book and lyrics for the previously mentioned *Dude*. Like the societal dropout Berger in *Hair*, Dude-the-character seemed in some ways to be Ragni-as-Everyman, traveling the Highway of Life with an enormous chip on his shoulder. (The musical was subtitled "The Highway Life.") Ragni, though, did not appear in *Dude*; as related, the semi-autobiographical role was played by eleven-year-old Ralph Carter. If that doesn't quite make sense, neither did *Dude*.

Writing the music was Galt MacDermot of *Hair*, with Tom O'Horgan directing. But only accidentally. Ragni had insisted that his friend Rocco Bufano, who had subminimal directing credits, be hired as director. When the show previewed to perplexed and furious houses, the producers asked O'Horgan to try to salvage their investment. Tom did so—while the show temporarily closed down and plunged back into rehearsals—with serious misgivings but an attitude of trying to save the day and at least keep everyone working. *Dude* remained memorably, and head-scratchingly, incomprehensible.

Neither Rado nor Butler was involved with *Dude*, perhaps exiled from the proceedings; among Dude-the-hero's antagonists were characters seen by some of the production staff as stand-ins for Rado and Butler. *Dude* opened on October 9, 1972, blazed spectacularly, and ignominiously shuttered after sixteen performances.

Rado, at the same time, was writing music, lyrics, and (in collaboration with his brother Ted Rado) book for his own musical, *Rainbow*.

More formally known as *The Rainbow Rainbeam Radio Roadshow*, the story told of an Everyman (character name: Man) who has been killed in Vietnam, just like Rado's character in *Hair*. The show opened on December 18, 1972, at the off-Broadway Orpheum Theatre on Second Avenue, closing after forty-eight performances—four times as long as *Dude*, but who's counting? A quick failure, though nowhere as visible as Ragni's folly.

When we went into preproduction for the 1977 revival of *Hair*, Ragni and Rado were back in tandem. (As I sat across from them at our first meeting, I couldn't help but think of them—for reasons unknown, or perhaps due to Gerry's Medusa cut—as "Flopsy and Mopsy," an image that has endured ever since.) I would say that they were speaking as one, except it was Gerry who did most of the talking and all of the complaining. They had a new opus in the works at the time, a musical known under various names but most frequently as *YMCA*, although it was never professionally produced. They continued working away at various projects over the years, with none of their post-*Hair* shows (other than *Dude* and *Rainbow*) making it to full production.

GALT AT THE KEYS

Galt, alone among the trio, followed *Hair* with a second Broadway hit—not as monumental, but a bona fide artistic and financial crowd pleaser. While the Public Theater was cut out of *Hair* before it reached Broadway, they nevertheless invited MacDermot back for more. The 1967 production of *Hair* had been the opening attraction at Papp's house on Lafayette Street, but his New York Shakespeare Festival had been producing Shakespeare in the Park since 1954 (with a permanent base, the Delacorte, established in 1962). The summer season consisted of two or sometimes three classics—mostly but not exclusively Shakespeare—presented outdoors, in Central Park, free to the public. In 1971 they decided to try something different: instead of presenting Shakespeare intact, they commissioned a musical version of the Bard's comedy *Two Gentlemen of Verona*.

One of the supreme playgoing highlights of the winter of 1971 had been John Guare's fancifully caustic *The House of Blue Leaves*, an off-Broadway hit at the then-new Truck & Warehouse Theatre. (This was a converted garage on East Fourth Street, which is presently the home of New York Theatre Workshop.) The excellence of the writing presumably impelled Papp and Gersten to commission Guare and Mel Shapiro (director of *Blue Leaves*) to collaborate on the book for the musicalized *Two Gentlemen of Verona*. Guare also served as lyricist, Shapiro as director. Given that this would be a contemporized Shakespearean musicalization for swingin' Central Park in those "summer of love" days, who better than Galt to write the music?

As we have seen, *Two Gents* was triumphant, moving to a successful Broadway run along with two national tours, leaving the competition (i.e., *Follies*) in the shade. While *Two Gents* took that season's Tony Award for Best Musical, and Guare and Shapiro won for the Best Book, the Best Score award went not to Guare and MacDermot but—understandably so—to Stephen Sondheim for *Follies*.

For Galt, that was the end of the successful road. The fall of 1972 saw not one but two all-time disasters, both of which have already been discussed: Gerry Ragni's *Dude* and the space-mess *Via Galactica* (with lyrics by Christopher Gore). These two mammoth miscues, despite some interesting music buried beneath the big-budget trappings, dropped a combined $1,800,000 within seven weeks—back in the days when $1,800,000 was a lot of money.

Galt in fact had an earlier disaster, an ocean away, that is generally overlooked. *Isabel's a Jezebel*—Isabel being a Grimm Brothers heroine whom in this telling spent two acts copulating over and over and over—opened on December 15, 1970, at the Duchess on the West End, with book and lyrics by William Dumaresq. Being from the composer of *Hair*, just then flying high down the lane at the Shaftesbury, the musical was highly anticipated but quickly consigned to the annals of instant flopdom.

I don't suppose these failures much bothered MacDermot: his only interest, it seemed to me, was making music. The *Hair* goldmine—with ASCAP royalties for life and beyond from "Aquarius" et al.—left him more than financially set, as well it should. While Gerry and perhaps Jim needed to show the world that they could "do it again," Galt seemingly remained content sitting at the keyboard with his merry band. He did, in fact, form and fund his own merry band (which he called the New Pulse Jazz Band).

The composer's only return to Broadway after that dire fall of 1972 came in 1984, when Papp produced *The Human Comedy*, based on William Saroyan's 1943 novel. With book and lyrics again by Dumaresq (of *Isabel's a Jezebel*) and direction by Wilfrid Leach (who had enjoyed great success with Papp's 1981 production of *The Pirates of Penzance*), the show was well received at the Public. Papp insisted on transferring it uptown to the Royale (now Jabobs), where the contemplative sung-through and simplistically staged musical was wildly out of place and quickly withdrawn.

I missed *The Human Comedy*, being on the road during the thirteen-performance run. Galt nevertheless recorded the production—with full cast, full orchestra, and the full eighty-six musical tracks (yes, eighty-six!)—and in 1997 saw fit to belatedly release the album on his own record label. It is foolhardy to judge the power of a musical by a recording alone; and the score is surely imperfect, saddled as it is with more than a few inept stretches from the lyricist. Even so, I find *The Human Comedy*—which I'd term an eclectic folk-oratorio—to be a remarkably tuneful musical cornucopia. My guess is that Galt didn't bat an eye over the demise of *Dude*, *Via Galactica*, or *Isabel's a Jezebel*. The outright dismissal of the heartfelt *The Human Comedy*, though, might have been a wound that remained until his death in 2018.

BUTLER AND TOM

Despite or perhaps because of the success of *Hair*, none of the authors chose or were chosen to work with producer Butler again. He continued to retain the first-class rights to the musical, so the authors were obligated to participate in the 1977 revival. Butler—and the original *Hair* investors—also retained a significant share of the authors' income from the then-upcoming film version, which turned out to be sizable.

Butler produced one show between the two productions of *Hair*. *Lenny*, by a former Broadway stage manager named Julian Barry, with direction and incidental music by O'Horgan, opened in May 1971 directly across from the Biltmore at the Brooks Atkinson. Due in great part to Cliff Gorman's bravura performance and to Tom's outrageously absurdist staging—the accoutrements including strippers, storm troopers, and supersized puppets—*Lenny* shook up the Broadway establishment quite as much as *Hair* had. (To my eighteen-year-old eyes, *Lenny* was novel and entertaining but somewhat less offensive—despite the inclusion of arguably censorable material—than it aspired to be.) *Lenny* is all but forgotten despite a successful 453-performance run, overshadowed by the 1974 Barry-scripted film version directed by Bob Fosse and starring Dustin Hoffman.

Following the late-May opening of *Lenny*, O'Horgan was called in to replace Tito Capobianco, an Argentinian director then with the New York City Opera, on the similarly controversial *Jesus Christ Superstar*. While some can and did question its artistic merit and O'Horgan's high-flying wildness, this was the only new musical to sell out in a crop that included *Follies* and *Two Gentlemen of Verona*.

Contrary to what might be assumed, the first Andrew Lloyd Webber/Tim Rice hit was not a British musical, per se; based on the internationally successful concept album, the show was initially staged on Broadway. The authors and producer Robert Stigwood chose not to replicate O'Horgan's flashy production elsewhere. Produced in London ten months later in a less outrageous production directed by Jim Sharman, *Superstar* ran eight years—becoming, for a time, the West End's longest-running musical ever—as opposed to the Broadway version's twenty months at the Hellinger.

Two months into the run of *Superstar*, O'Horgan returned with a musical that he conceived and coproduced. *Inner City* was a "street cantata" compiled from poet Eve Merriam's book of sardonic nursery rhymes, *The Inner City Mother Goose*. Unfortunately, the show had none of the power or musicality of the just-closed *The Me Nobody Knows* or the then-current *Ain't Supposed to Die a Natural Death*.

"Masochism is New York's way of life," Clive Barnes headed his pan in the *New York Times*. The Shuberts, in their wisdom, saw fit to force *Ain't Supposed to Die* out of the Barrymore to make way for *Inner City*. *Inner City* closed in March 1972 after a forced three months, while *Ain't Supposed to Die* continued at the Ambassador through the end of July.

Tom would go on to direct six additional Broadway shows, each dire and amassing an astoundingly low total of thirty-four official performances combined. This left him all but unemployable from 1989—when *Senator Joe*, a fantastical modernist rendition of events drawn from the life of Senator Joseph McCarthy, collapsed after three previews at the Alvin—until his death in 2009.

Split Ends

Hair was in something of a tangle when I started in May. Given the successful and recent history of the show, many elements were predetermined. The theatre was prebooked: we would be returning to the home of the long-running original production, the Biltmore on West Forty-Seventh Street (now the Samuel J. Friedman).

The Biltmore was high atop the list of Broadway's least desirable houses, a status magnified by it being one of the few then-remaining independent theatres not controlled by the Shubert, Nederlander, or Jujamcyn chains. (Producers keen to get into a Shubert house—any Shubert house—would take the Cort or Belasco if that's all that was on offer, in the hopes they'd be upgraded if the present tenant unexpectedly closed, as occasionally happened.) Over the five years since *Hair* ended its initial run in July 1972, bookings had been sparse. During the first nineteen months, there was only one play, a vanity production that lasted one performance (plus one week of previews). The Biltmore had seven lackluster bookings prior to the return of *Hair*, with the house sitting entirely vacant for a fourteen-month stretch encompassing the entirety of 1975.

Given the lucrative success of the original production, Butler had the funding readily at hand—although, as it turned out, from an unconventional source. He also had a full array of advertising and promotional materials; the show's ad campaign was well established. The press agents who had closed out the original run—the fourth set Butler had gone through—could pick up where they left off, as opposed to needing to try to educate audiences on just what this musical called *Hair* was about.

The production design, too, was set and time tested; the designers, veritable Broadway newcomers in 1968, were now among the theatre's best. Robin Wagner had gone on to shows ranging from *Promises, Prom-*

ises to *Jesus Christ Superstar* to *A Chorus Line*. Jules Fisher's lighting credits in the interim included *Nanette*, *Superstar*, *Pippin*, and *Chicago*. Both had teamed with O'Horgan and Butler on *Lenny*.

While Robin and Jules were very much in evidence, their designs—which had been used in numerous *Hair* productions worldwide—were simply pulled out of the files. The two were consummate professionals, as was Tom. Galt, meanwhile, was unobtrusively present, content to assemble his band (including some *Hair* veterans) and oversee the sound of the music.

Ragni and Rado? Not as easy to please. Impossible to please, rather, especially Gerry. The crux of the problem was the question of casting. They—and again, it was Gerry who did the speaking and the objecting—were continually obstructive, seeming not to know what they wanted. It wasn't until several weeks into previews that it became apparent that Gerry *did* know what he wanted. He had created the more-or-less-autobiographical role of Berger back when *Hair* premiered at the Public in 1967, remaining in the role through the run at Cheetah and opening the show on Broadway and in Los Angeles. (Rado had not officially joined the cast, as the fated-to-be-drafted Claude Hooper Bukowski, until the O'Horgan production at the Biltmore.) Now, as Gerry stormed and fumed about the casting in general, it became clear: the forty-one-year-old coauthor apparently wanted to play this teenaged high school dropout himself, resulting in an unrelenting campaign against our leading men.

"Maybe Jim and I should just go up there and play it," he'd joke. But none of us were laughing—not even the balding forty-five-year-old Rado, who clearly realized that he would look ludicrous if he once again donned the hippie beads and hairpiece. As it was, Gerry and Jim would occasionally make a cameo appearance in our production—hauling up the aisle in police uniforms at the end of the first act, after the culmination of the nude scene—threatening to arrest the audience on obscenity charges.

MEMORIAL DAY

Three weeks into the preproduction period came the Memorial Day weekend. Leo Herbert threw a grand picnic at the grand—or at least, historically and culturally distinctive—house he was renting in Glen Ridge, New Jersey. An actual Frank Lloyd Wright–designed house, a "Usonian style" three-bedroom known as the Stuart Richardson House. Hexagonal shaped in everything, even the shower. (Janice Herbert complained that it was especially hard to vacuum the floors, given the rounded walls.) The low-flung one-story house, indeed, blended so well into the surrounding trees that you could barely pick it out.

Leo had long lived on West Forty-Sixth Street, in a nineteenth-century carriage house removed from the street by an alley leading to what is still called Clinton Court—an infamous haunted house, according to legend. Leo was a mountain of a man impervious to danger, but Janice (by that point in *Hello, Dolly!*) and their young daughter were not impervious to the drug addicts on the streets of Hell's Kitchen in the late 1960s. So they moved off to a succession of rental houses in and around Montclair, New Jersey, a quick jump during noncommuter hours through the Lincoln Tunnel to Broadway.

Backstage anecdotal digression: *Dolly* begins with a highly effective star entrance. There's no overture; director Gower Champion wanted the eyes of the audience glued to his staging—rather than a conductor waving a baton—from the start. The curtain rises on a snappy turn-of-the-century vamp, written by dance arranger Peter Howard, with the chorus entering and singing a brief verse. ("Call on Dolly . . ." it starts.) During a second, briefer vamp, a full-sized trolley—pulled by a dancing horse consisting of two female dancers—trundles on with three seated women, faces covered by newspapers they are reading as the car bounces along. The middle woman drops the paper on cue, revealing the star a mere forty-five seconds in.

During Ethel Merman's run in the show, Janice was one of the so-called swing dancers, whose job is to fill in for any chorus members who might be ill, injured, or on vacation. One matinee, Leo's daughter—who more or less grew up backstage—happened to be sitting in the wing as Merman climbed up onto the trolley to await her entrance.

"Hello, Heather," said Merman in her friendliest, talking-to-a-sweet-little-girl manner. "Where's your mom?"

"Oh," said the six-year-old Herbert, "she's the horse's ass."

On went the trolley, Ethel's prop newspaper shaking violently as she tried to suppress uncontrollable laughter.

PICNIC
Back to Memorial Day, 1977, and Leo's picnic at the Frank Lloyd Wright house. Mostly stagehands were in attendance, with assorted others. The rounded, corner-less house was packed, as was the large landscaped garden with sunken pool. A crowd was gathered around one of the attendees; as I neared, I discovered that this was not a stagehand but actor Clive Revill, best known for playing Fagin in Merrick's Broadway production of *Oliver!*

I was momentarily drawn to Revill, not for *Oliver!* but because he had starred in the *Irma La Douce* that had so impressed me when I was eight. Finding his discourse somewhat boring—or more likely, the talk of a shy Kiwi (i.e., New Zealander) cornered by stagehands in the back yard—I quickly walked away.

Outnumbered by carpenters, electricians, and prop men, some of whom I knew but most of whom I didn't, I gravitated to a quiet tree. There I found a relatively young woman—a few years older than I, it seemed—with a sunny-faced child by her side. She was clearly out of her element within this group of strangers, as was I; we got to talking.

She introduced herself as Kim Herbert's girlfriend. Four of Leo's children ultimately went into the family business (i.e., props), but his younger son for a while tried to break away and become an actor. His one Broadway credit was as a member of the American replacement cast for the Royal Shakespeare Company production of *Sherlock Holmes*, which had recently closed a year's run at the Broadhurst. Revill, though not American, had joined the replacement cast as Professor Moriarty, which presumably explains why he was at the party that day.

As we chatted, the woman mentioned that she answered phones at Manny Azenberg's office. This sounded familiar to me; she then went on to say that she was also a casting director.

"Wait a second," I said. "Wasn't that you at the meeting on Friday?"

We had just fired our casting director, who had been assistant to Biff's assistant at the Merrick office and whom we had all called Eve

Harrington. (She was highly ambitious, although without the people skills you'd want in a casting director.) Gene had brought in a replacement who did occasional casting for Manny, so Mary Jo Slater and I had just sat across from each other in the rehearsal studio while Gerry Ragni railed on. Dressed for Memorial Day rather than in office clothes, we didn't immediately place each other.

We instantly got on well, spending the rest of the afternoon chatting with each other and with Mary Jo's well-behaved but keenly observant seven-year-old. When the holiday season rolled around several months later, Mary Jo insisted that I go see the boy play Tiny Tim in a church basement on the Upper East Side. Imagine my surprise—and my relief—to find that Christian was *good*. Even at that age he was a canny and intelligent actor, clearly the most professional person on the stage of that *Christmas Carol*.

Mary Jo Slater and seven-year-old Christian (1977).
COURTESY MARY JO SLATER

THE NEW TRIBE

MJ quickly assembled a full cast, supplementing the actors Tom and the authors had already seen and liked—most of whom fit well into the "tribe"—with a dynamic group of newcomers to play the major roles.

Sheila, the female lead, was played by Ellen Foley. She had the requisite strong voice, more than capable of taking center stage with "Easy to Be Hard" and "Good Morning Starshine." Ellen quickly demonstrated that she was also a fine comic actor. Sharing the honors was the unique Annie Golden as Jeanie, the very-much-pregnant "welcome, sulfur dioxide" wastrel. Annie was also filming the role, under an agreement brokered by Rado and Ragni that would allow her to do both projects simultaneously. When we ultimately delayed our opening, she was forced to withdraw from her stage role; since she was such an asset to us, we agreed to have her remain in the ensemble and play as many performances as she could make from the film set in New Jersey.

Hud, the so-called "Colored Spade," was played by an altogether dynamic newcomer named Cleavant Derricks. Among the "White Boys" trio of girls was another newcomer named Loretta Devine; not long thereafter she created one of the title roles (Lorrell) in *Dreamgirls*, while Cleavant took a Tony as James Thunder Early in that musical. (Ben Harney, the other male lead in the Michael Bennett musical, had been in *The Pajama Game* revival.) Also among the members of our tribe were Charlayne Woodard, even then a fireball of talent; and fourteen-year-old Kristen Vygard as Crissy, singing "Frank Mills."

Our cast also included an arrestingly interesting young actor just out of Tufts University named Peter Gallagher, whom we added to our tribe and assigned to understudy Claude (the Rado role). Midway through our extended preview period, MJ—who had just taken over the casting of the still-running original production of *Grease*—asked if we'd mind if she stole Peter away from us. Leave the chorus of a not-likely-to-run revival to take over the leading role in a Broadway hit? Gene and I were glad to release him, albeit with a complaint from Gerry. It was poetic justice in a way, as Gallagher was needed to replace Treat Williams, who had just then been pulled from *Grease* to play the Ragni role in the film version of *Hair*.

343

And then there was the question of the leading men, Berger and Claude.

Berger was our bigger problem, in that the aging Ragni seemed predisposed to reject anyone playing "his" role. It was finally cast with a musician (as opposed to an actor) named Doug Katsaros; his only Broadway credit at the time was as dance arranger of the ill-fated 1976 Gower Champion musical *Rockabye Hamlet* (and was *that* a mess). While admittedly not an actor, he sang the role with elan and had something of the free-spirit style and "ratty-matty-oily-greasy" hair of Ragni, circa 1968.

David Patrick Kelly, at twenty-six, was as far as I can tell the only *Hair* veteran in our group: he had played Claude in the final Butler-produced company of the show, which opened in David's hometown of Detroit in 1970. O'Horgan had then featured Kelly as Sgt. Pepper in a not-quite-Broadway Beatles spinoff called *Sgt. Pepper's Lonely Hearts Club Band on the Road*, an extravaganza "conceived and adapted by Robin Wagner and Tom O'Horgan." Produced by *Superstar*'s Robert Stigwood—who had specifically not invited Tom to stage the London production of that musical, presumably at the insistence of authors Lloyd Webber and Rice—*Sgt. Pepper* played two months at the Beacon (on upper Broadway) in 1974 without causing a stir and without successfully transferring to Broadway, the road, or anywhere.

Sometime later, other producers took the idea of mock-Beatles replicating the famous foursome—which had disbanded in 1969—onstage and turned it into a multi-company hit under the title *Beatlemania*. This opened the night after Leo's Memorial Day picnic, a few weeks before our revival of *Hair* went into rehearsal. It turned out to be an enormous if thoroughly unexpected Broadway hit, topping out at more than a thousand performances. If there was indeed a potential audience for *Hair* during the summer of 1977, they were thronging to the Winter Garden before we even got onstage at the Biltmore.

Long Hot Summer

INTO THE DARK

WEDNESDAY, JULY 13, DAWNED HOT AND HAZY. OR PERHAPS NOT; I WAS not awake to face the dawn. But it was mighty hot; as Irving Berlin once wrote, "we're having a heat wave," and literally so. While it's foolhardy to put full faith in what you pull up on the internet decades later, one weather site suggests that this was the first day of the hottest heat wave in pre–climate change New York history: nine consecutive days with an average high over ninety-seven degrees.

Manny Kladitis, company manager of *Sly Fox*, was going home to Cleveland for a visit and asked me to cover for him. Whereas *Hair* was still three weeks from the first preview, I was happy to do so. I went with him to the Broadhurst on Tuesday night so he could introduce me to the star. Robert Preston, American's favorite *Music Man* (having won Tony and Oscar for playing Professor Harold Hill), had taken over the role of Foxwell J. Sly from George C. Scott.

I first met Pres two years earlier in the bathtub, at *Mack & Mabel*, a prop bathtub, with "soapsuds" painted on. I had gone backstage looking for Leo, who introduced us in the wings.

My observation was that Pres enhanced the play. Scott had a larger-than-life bluster that illuminated Gelbart's comedy with explosive bursts. Pres brought to the stage his personal warmth and humor. His presence permeated the entire play in a manner that Scott, despite his onstage dynamism, did not. Every time Scott went off to sit in his dressing room, the play somewhat deflated despite the sustained comedy writing.

I went to the Broadhurst the next sweltering evening. While I was familiar with the house from the run of *Vivat*, I was now there as management and thus able to stand inside the box office and watch the patrons file past the ticket windows. The Broadhurst box office had a feature I've never seen elsewhere. Between the two windows was a built-in map of the house's 1,166 seats, orchestra, and mezz. When I say map, it was an actual wooden map, seat-by-seat, with three-inch-deep slots cut into the wood representing each location. After the curtain went up each night, the treasurers would carefully place the unsold tickets for the next performance in their assigned slots.

Thus, you had a visual and actual map of precisely what seats were available. Contrary to what might be assumed, practiced treasurers don't simply sell tickets row by row. There is an art to making a not-exactly-sold-out house *look* full. You want ticket buyers to feel, as the play begins, lucky to be able to get a seat, and you want the performers—insecure stars, particularly—to think that the show is sold out. One hundred empty seats, clumped together, look like one hundred empty seats. Spaced out among almost-filled rows, you can give the visual impression that the place is full when it is not.

When the performance was sold out, this wall map would be all but empty, with only the so-called emergency seats in the rack. When the show was poorly sold, though, the rack was a thicket of tickets. If there were hundreds of unsold seats—as was the case when I returned to the Broadhurst some years later as replacement manager of *Amadeus* and we ran into rough weather—they wouldn't bother to "rack" the far sides and upper stretches. We all knew they were empty.

FLASHLIGHT FROM THE MEZZ

After signing the box office statement at *Sly Fox*, I went over to Joe Allen's restaurant to meet Gene to discuss revised *Spotlight* budgets. Little did we know—although we certainly guessed—that the poster for *Spotlight* would soon be hanging on Joe's wall of shame along with other fabled flops.

We were having drinks while awaiting dinner when the kitchen lights dimmed off, around 9:30, and the background music ground out.

"Power's off, hold on everybody," offered a friendly waiter.

There was sufficient lighting from the candle lamps on the tables, so we continued examining the budget pages. Five minutes later, someone started tapping on a glass as if to introduce a speech at a wedding.

Joe Allen himself, standing by the flop-poster-laden brick wall leading from the bar, chirped up. "The whole block is out, the kitchen is totally down. Finish your meals if you already have them, otherwise I'm afraid we're going to have to close up."

Stepping out onto Forty-Sixth Street, Gene and I looked toward Eighth Avenue. The streetlights and lamp lights were out, the marquees of the Imperial and 46th Street Theatres dark. "Better head over to the Broadhurst," we immediately thought.

The two-block walk was eerie. There were headlights from traffic, of course. But it was difficult crossing the avenue with no red lights to stop the cars and buses staggering uptown.

We passed the Majestic and St. James—dark and quiet—and headed through the stage door of the Broadhurst. The inner entrance was lit by the emergency lights on the stairs. We heard a roar of laughter—a *big* roar of laughter.

We went through the inner pass door to the backstage area. Stagehands were holding flashlights to the ground, to keep people from tripping on cables and scenic pieces. We walked over to Henry Velez at the stage manager's desk, lit by a battery-operated flashlight. Henry, who had been Charlie Blackwell's assistant on *Promises*, saw us and shrugged.

Another big laugh. We stuck our heads through the wings.

There was Pres on our side of the stage and costar Jack Gilford over stage left, firing off jokes at each other. About the delay, about each other, about whatever they came up with. Peering out into the house—I could stick my head inside the show portal, because it was dark—I made out two usherettes sitting on the bottom steps at the front of the mezzanine, shining flashlights on the stars like weak follow spots. With the pair ad-libbing away, *Sly Fox* turned into a vaudeville slugfest between canny comedians.

Where were you when the lights went out? Robert Preston
in *Sly Fox* (1976).
PHOTOFEST

They hammed it up for another ten minutes, with us and the rest
of the cast—lining the wings—enjoying the show biz tales as much as
the patrons. Eventually the house manager came to the stage manager's
desk to say that the Shuberts had sent word to all their houses to clear
the audience and shut down. Henry walked over to Preston—who did
a classic take at the appearance of this non-costumed stage manager, in
desert boots, appearing in the nineteenth-century hotel room set—to
whisper the news.

"Time to go home, everybody," Pres said warmly. "They say that the
entire city is blacked out. Please be careful."

Another roar of applause and everyone went home in the darkness of the Great Blackout of 1977. Everyone except Pres. He kept his car in the outdoor garage adjacent to the Imperial. When he finally got over there, they explained that his car was parked in the elevated section of the garage, impossible to access without the elevator.

In any case, the lucky audience got its never-to-be-forgotten money's worth with that impromptu duo act. Or more than its money's worth, since the tickets for the incomplete performance were fully refundable.

TANGLES

Previews of *Hair* began on August 3. It was plain within days of going on sale that our preliminary advertising was not impelling audiences to buy tickets. If Butler hoped that last-minute buyers would clamor for seats once we started previews, that proved not to be the case. When we couldn't fill the house that first Saturday night, even with discounted tickets available, our fate was all too clear.

Business was moderate, mostly generated by the half-price TKTS booth in Times Square, which opened in 1973. We pulled in enough to avoid large weekly losses, but the revival of *Hair*—from start to finish—engendered little enthusiasm.

There was a more fundamental issue. *Hair*, in 1968, had been coarse and dangerous but joyfully exuberant. In 1977, the danger was gone and the coarseness barely noticeable.

As for the production itself, Katsaros and Kelly were both more than satisfactory as the male leads. Doug brought the same sort of unpredictability to Berger that Ragni had, although with less danger; David gave a steady and sure performance as the hero who gets drafted. But that wasn't quite good enough under the circumstances. My guess is that the fact that Tom urged that David—whom he had twice worked with—be cast in the show was enough to set Gerry against him from the start. This was magnified in his reaction to Doug—who, most obviously, was far younger than Gerry.

If there was a flaw in the calculation of reviving *Hair* for Broadway audiences in 1977, Ragni and Rado weren't ready to recognize it, so they took it out on the actors playing Ragni and Rado. Gerry, who had a talent for needling the opposition, wore down O'Horgan and Butler to the extent that by the end of three weeks it was agreed that Katsaros and Kelly must be replaced. But in no case, Tom and Michael insisted, would Gerry be allowed to take over as Berger.

Tom, who disagreed with the firings, refused to take part; Butler left town to go off to be with his polo ponies. Gerry and Jim ran from the confrontation, so it fell to me to fire both David and Doug, separately but at the same time. I did so as gently as possible, making it clear that I did not agree with the choice. David said thanks and agreed to stay until his replacement was ready. (He has continued to turn out fine performances into the third decade of the new century, with films by Spike Lee and David Lynch plus the Broadway musical *Once*—in which he played "Da"—notable among his credits.) Doug, apparently unaccustomed to earning a Broadway-level salary at that point in his career, chose to remain in the cast as a tribe member and understudy his replacement. He too has gone on to an active show business career, as an orchestrator/arranger.

The new Berger was an actor unknown to me named Michael Hoit. The new Claude, also unknown, was B. G. Gibson, who had been in O'Horgan's *Sgt. Pepper* with Kelly. But the star performances weren't the problem: the show itself was faded, with the East Village buoyancy bleached out after less than a decade. There was nothing to do but wait till the opening and see if the reviews provided a lift.

FLAMBOYANTLY OUTRAGEOUS

Most interesting to me, among the team of *Hair* creators, was O'Horgan. Given the steadily uneasy presence of the lyricist/librettists, he was not actually called upon to direct the revival; rather, his position was to restage and restore the show to what it had been. The complication was that the memory and definition of "what it had been," to the several people who had been there, was somewhat variable.

Butler wanted to see the show with which he had conquered the entertainment world. Ragni and Rado more narrowly defined *Hair* as what they saw from their center-stage position. Galt, meanwhile, was the easiest to please; he just wanted the music to sound as good as it did when he himself had been up there, on the Biltmore stage in 1968, playing the electric piano.

Tom, I think, had the best notion of what to do; more or less replicate what had been while adjusting for what had come in the intervening decade. Some of what looked refreshing back during the dawning of the Age of Aquarius was now passé; thanks in great part, mind you, to the enormous influence *Hair* had when it first opened. But Tom did not have the freedom to adjust the focus of the show as he might have seen fit; while a man of great creative theatricality, he had little interest in and no appetite for a round of skirmishes with the others. Instead, he simply put the show back on the boards, conforming to the specifications and sometimes conflicting demands of Ragni, Rado, and Butler.

I was able, in the time I spent with Tom, to recognize a strong knowledge of—and love of—the theatre. This was from an avant-garde standpoint, yes, but highly intelligent. He at one point noted, ruefully, that he couldn't get hired to do what he creatively wished to do; producers only turned to him when they wanted something flamboyantly outrageous like *Hair*, *Superstar*, and *Lenny*. He would have been more than happy to try his hand at the classics, and might well have been able to find new truths in old works. But given his well-noted excesses, he was seen as too risky to hire unless it was excesses you were specifically looking for.

And so Tom was fated to basically sit aside, year after year, away from Broadway in his loft on Broadway—which, mind you, was quite a place, at 840 Broadway, on the southeast corner of Broadway and Thirteenth Street. (The ground floor, at the time, served as the headquarters of the *Village Voice*.) Tom's loft had a bird's-eye view of midtown from the wall of large windows. Being an advanced collector of exotic musical instruments from around the world with unlimited funds (for a time, anyway, thanks to *Hair* and *Superstar*), the other walls were hung with his massive collection. It was here that I beheld and held a serpent, the seventeenth-century wooden horn that was an ancestor of the modern tuba.

Cautionary Tale, Big City

Among the O'Horgan/*Hair* team, the person I worked with most directly was stage manager Galen McKinley. He was a slight, sprightly thirty-year-old with a wicked smile and a perennial glint in his sparking grey eyes, which matched the sparkle of the diamond in his ear. Not your typical Broadway stage manager, by a long shot. Even so, when things got difficult and I watched him battle, conquer, and tame the typically chauvinistic house stagehands at the Biltmore, I decided Galen was altogether up to the job.

I only later learned just how he came to be Tom's preferred stage manager. The story as I heard it, hopefully bordering on the accurate, in broad sketches: Galen arrived in New York in 1964 as a sixteen-year-old runaway from rural Maryland. The forty-year-old Tom found him on the street, literally, and took him home. The on-again/off-again relationship was stormy. While Tom mentored the teenager, he was also "mentoring" a Wall Street type whom he was encouraging to break from the bonds of conformity, to say the least. Galen soon moved in with the latter, whose name was Harvey. When Galen went to California to help set up the 1969 San Francisco production of *Hair*, he took Harvey with him. Later that year, the Chicago production opened with Galen as stage manager.

Tom called Galen back to New York in 1971 to serve as production stage manager of *Lenny*, with Harvey listed in the program as "assistant to Mr. O'Horgan" on both *Lenny* and *Jesus Christ Superstar*. For *Inner City*, Harvey was promoted to title page billing as associate producer, after which the former financial analyst finally broke with Galen and moved back to San Francisco. He was to become the first openly gay man elected to the city's Board of Supervisors, and on November 27, 1978—after sponsoring a bill banning discrimination—Harvey Milk was assassinated by a political opponent.

I was oblivious to all of this at the time, mind you; I simply found Galen to be highly unusual but thoroughly capable. There was no reason for me to have even heard of Harvey Milk; he didn't become famous (posthumously) until his murder a year after our revival of *Hair*. The closest I came to the counterculture at that point, I suppose, was a dinner that a group of us—including Tom, Jim, Gerry, Butler, and Galen—had after the show one night at a French bistro in the West Village. The special guest was Timothy Leary, the psychedelic psychologist from Harvard who is mentioned in one of the *Hair* lyrics. Then there were two visits to Studio 54 in the first months of its existence, the first to set up our opening night party and the second for the actual event. I made my appearance and got out quick.

Galen's life after *Hair* and the death of Harvey continued as rockily as it had begun. I heard the coda from Frank Marino, the stage manager on my musical after *Spotlight*; Frank had been assistant stage manager to Galen on *Superstar*. While I have been unable to verify precisely what happened, the result is factual.

On February 14, 1980, Galen—who typically house-sat while Tom was out of town—threw a Valentine's Day party at O'Horgan's loft. Said party was populated, it is said, by a group of Brazilian (?) sailors whom Galen saw fit to entertain with drugs, etc. At one point, the sailors decided it would be fun to stand out on the window ledge—in the cold and wind—to view the Empire State Building twenty blocks north. When Galen's turn came, the navy decided it would be a fine joke to lock the window. When they remembered Galen was out there freezing and opened the window, he was gone. If you ever wondered how you might find a naked thirty-two-year-old smashed on a downtown sidewalk on a freezing Valentine's eve, there's your explanation.

It is reported that mutual friends of the trio scattered Galen's ashes—and, in 2009, Tom's ashes—over the same spot in San Francisco Bay where they had scattered Harvey's. Apocryphal, perhaps; but not quite so farfetched given the tangled history.

TOWNHOUSE

Corporately speaking, most commercial theatrical productions at that time were set up as limited partnerships. The capitalization—or at least, the minimum permissible capitalization specified in the partnership papers—was placed in savings accounts, treasury bills, or other such interest-bearing devices. The managers would draw on funds as needed, initially for fees, bonds, down payments on sets and costumes, advertising costs, and such. As the show went into rehearsals, we'd switch to a weekly transfer to cover outlays.

In the case of *Hair*, I didn't know precisely what sort of arrangement Butler had made. What I did know was that when we needed money, we would look to his associate producer, a fellow of indeterminate origin named Eric Nezhad. The necessary funds would appear in time.

At one point as we entered our second month of previews, the money did not arrive. Butler nonchalantly shrugged, so we had to explain to him that if we didn't meet the cast payroll, Actors' Equity would pull the funds from our security bond and force the immediate closing of the show.

This produced action, and I was instructed to meet Eric at 29 Beekman Place. Beekman Place is a highly exclusive enclave on the East River, a two-block stretch that runs from Forty-Ninth to Fifty-First Streets. (All good show biz fans know the street from the opening lyric of the musical *Mame*, which goes "St. Bridget deliver us to Beekman Place.")

I was delivered to Beekman Place not by St. Bridget but by taxicab. What I found was not simply a typically grand townhouse but a seven-story *mansion*.

The door was opened by a formally dressed housemaid accompanied by a dark-suited guard. The name Nezhad proved sufficient to gain entrance.

I was escorted through the lavish wood-parqueted entry hall, then up a grand curving staircase into another lavish entrance hall. They led me through a living-room-sized sitting room to the rear of the house into what I suppose you'd call a solarium, featuring a round glass table with four chairs, trees growing out of large planters, and—on three sides— large picture windows. You did not feel as though you were looking at the East River; you felt as though you were *on* the East River.

I have since learned that Manhattan townhouses are purposely deceptive; you never know what's behind those oaken doors. Of course, there are townhouses and then there are *townhouses*.

When 29 Beekman Place was sold following the owner's death many years later, the house—initially owned by William S. Paley of CBS—was marketed as having 12,260 square feet including ten bedrooms, nine bathrooms, eight fireplaces, three terraces encompassing an additional 1,500 square feet, and need I go on?

A slight, well-dressed, dark-haired fifty-something woman of culture was sitting at the table reading from a suede folder of letters, her back to the river and a most obviously authentic French antique tray with teapot, teacup, toast caddy, and preserves by her side. Nezhad stooped to her ear, quietly explaining the check that he was presenting for her to sign. She nodded in agreement, sent the very slightest sidelong glance my way, signed her name, and dismissively turned back to teacup and toast without giving me further notice.

Eric took the check and ushered me out of the solarium. He led me through the house down to the entranceway, where a manila envelope had magically appeared on a side table. The check was in triplicate, with two carbons. He detached a copy for himself, put the check in the envelope, licked it shut, and handed it to me.

"Don't we need it certified?" I asked.

"The car will take you; our banker is waiting." And with that, I was off in a limo to a stately Madison Avenue bank with a foreign name.

FAMILY TIES

Back at the office, I told Gene about my visit to the East River.

"Did you see the signature?" he said.

I showed him the carbon. There was no name printed on it, but it was signed "Ashraf Pahlavi."

"Do you know who that is?" he asked, expecting I would.

I didn't, being at the time altogether ignorant of international affairs.

"*That*," he said, "is the sister of the Shah of Iran."

Not merely the sister of the Shah of Iran. The twin sister of the autocratic king, who in February 1979—after a thirty-eight-year reign—would be overthrown in the Iranian Revolution and forced into exile. It turns out that the backer of *Hair* was, yes, the sister of the Shah of Iran, who was herself apparently up to her oil-soaked ears in political intrigue, CIA plots, and allegedly pilfered millions. Eric, who was a nice enough fellow, was not professionally an associate producer; rather, he seems to have been a registered attaché to the Iran Embassy.

On September 14, the day before what had been our planned opening night, the news from Cannes was that Princess Pahlavi's Rolls-Royce was attacked by two hooded terrorists with machine guns. She managed to escape injury, although her personal assistant was killed.

The Saturday after the attack, I returned to the Biltmore between shows at about 6:00 p.m. As I signaled the treasurer to buzz me through the lobby, house manager Frank Hopkins—who was inside the box office, at the ticket window—frantically gestured for me to meet him inside.

"There's a bomb scare, we got a call. The police are on their way."

I started down the center aisle, then thought it was probably not the best idea. From the back of the orchestra, I looked at the stage, lit by work lights. All seemed serene.

"Is anyone back there?" I asked.

"The doorman said everyone's out for the break."

I went back through the lobby and onto Forty-Seventh Street, awaiting the police. *Hair* was a ragtag, prop-heavy show, with the skeletal unit set open to the back wall and items stashed in every possible corner of the backstage area. How could they even begin to comb the stage?

And so I waited—five, ten minutes. The half-hour call wasn't until 7:30, so we had time. A couple of wardrobe people approached the stage door with takeout dinner; we told them to stay on the street.

The traffic in front of the theatre, heading toward Eighth Avenue, crawled in typical Saturday summer twilight fashion. A police cruiser finally approached but drove right past me, stopping in the line of cars at the red light on the corner. I walked over and called through the open window to the officer in the passenger seat.

"Hey, aren't you here for us?" I asked.

"No," he said casually, "the bomb squad is down the block, they'll be right here."

And the officer driving the car leaned over and said sardonically, and I quote: "Yeah, we heard there was a *bomb* in this theatre."

That's Broadway: even the street cops are critics.

When the bomb squad arrived, they took a blasé look backstage—all the junk piled upstage and in the wings—gave us the all clear, and drove away into the twilight, and the show went on.

Ending of the Age (of Aquarius)

Previews continued, with neither business nor the show improving. The new Berger, Michael Hoit, was not quite as good as Doug Katsaros had been; the new Claude, B. G. Gibson, was markedly inferior to David Patrick Kelly—so much so that over the Labor Day weekend it was determined that Gibson must be fired as well. We pushed off our September 15 opening for three weeks to allow time to comb through the casting also-rans and settle on a third Claude.

We didn't waste the opening date, though. Opening nights are registered in advance with the Broadway League—at that time, the League of New York Theatres—to avoid conflicting openings. Thursday nights are the preferred slots, specifically because the *New York Times* has a heavy pre-weekend readership on Friday. (While that no longer quite applies in today's media world, Thursday remains the night of choice.) When calling in the cancellation, we simultaneously switched *Man of La Mancha* from earlier that week into Thursday.

La Mancha opened on the fifteenth at the Palace to excellent business, although we were still not prepared for the record-breaking grosses we would generate in "barns" across the country. The production was very good, with Emily Yancy—who had played the final five months of the original *La Mancha* run—as Aldonza. Kiley, at fifty-five, had aged into the role; while superb back in 1966, he now brought elements of weariness and despair to his creation of the addled knight-errant.

In the hunt for the next Claude, Tom, Gerry, and Jim uneasily settled on another new-to-Broadway actor named Randall Easterbrook. He was rushed into rehearsal and onstage, with two full playing weeks before facing the critics. Hoit, with a three-week head start, was more proficient; but neither even began to approach Katsaros or Kelly, to say nothing of Ellen Foley, Cleavant Derricks, Annie Golden, and Kristen Vygard, all of whom were giving standout performances within days of the first preview back in July.

We opened, finally, on October 5, to be greeted by Richard Eder—the new drama critic of the *Times*, Clive Barnes having been stolen away by a munificent offer from the *Post*. Eder was direct enough: "Nothing ages worse than graffiti," he began, continuing to note that *Hair* "is too far gone to be timely; too recently gone to be history or even nostalgia."

While I rarely agreed with Eder during his short reign—which he started, mind you, with a lukewarm review of our *La Mancha*—he wasn't in this case wrong. Not that *Hair* didn't retain its strengths; considering the production before the departures of Katsaros and Kelly, it was a more than satisfactory staging of the show, retaining much of its raffish charm. But necessary? Hardly, not in the fall of 1977.

I had an adverse reaction when the show was subsequently revived on Broadway in 2009, with an altogether new production team, to significant acclaim. In 1968, the acting company seemed to be, in part, authentic hippies off the streets of St. Mark's Place. The 1977 actors, while too young to be actual hippies, had at least grown up in the era—the Vietnam War didn't end until 1975—and they were able to give the impression of the communal street tribe so necessary to the show. In 2009, I felt as though I were watching singer/dancers *pretending* to be hippies, their research likely restricted to watching the *Hair* movie and other Hollywood renditions of Those Turbulent Times. No dirty toenails, if you know what I mean.

Producers of shows that audiences do not wish to see, by nature, tend to hope that word of mouth will build business; that great reviews will bring crowds; that "good weather" will change fate; and on and on. Butler, having lived through and profited by the smashing success of the original *Hair*, wasn't fooled. He went through the motions, spending a respectable amount of the Shah's sister's money on post-opening ads so nobody could say he didn't give the show a chance. But it was clear from the first preview that the 1977 *Hair* was unnecessary and unlikely to flourish. The audience response, from the start, was mild; the people who chose to buy tickets seemed to enjoy the show, but with none of the wild enthusiasm that was required. This was the age of *A Chorus Line* and *Annie*, mind you—plus *Beatlemania* for those so disposed.

We ran five more weeks, closing on November 6. The best that can be said, I suppose, is that by combining our forty-three-performance run with seventy-nine previews and the rehearsal period, the cast members wound up with twenty workweeks. That was enough to qualify for a full year of Equity healthcare coverage, which was something, anyway.

But it turned out that the Age of Aquarius, in 1977 at the Biltmore, was no more.

Chapter Twenty-Six

Cameo

The Injured List

BUT THE MOST MEMORABLE PART OF THE *HAIR* EXPERIENCE, FOR ME, occurred midway through previews. Arriving for the Wednesday matinee on the steamy final day of August, I headed backstage to check in with Galen.

"Good," he said, seeing me. "You're on."

"I'm on *what?*"

"No. You are *on*. At this performance."

We had been going through a barrage of injuries. Our production was performed by a cast of twenty-eight. The show has what could be considered three leads (Berger, Claude, Sheila); five major featured characters (Jeanie, Hud, Crissy, Dionne, Woof); plus an all-purpose singing-and-dancing ensemble of—in our case—twenty, which is referred to not as the chorus but the tribe. Not twenty, actually; eighteen plus two "swings" who were general understudies for the entire tribe. *Hair* being something of a loosely plotted story told in the manner of a free-form musical revue, there was always a lot going on, with the tribe members picking up numerous brief identities within the course of the evening. In a typical musical, these are deemed "bits" and "specialties," with additional Equity payments for each. In *Hair*, this was less formal.

The job of the swing is to know the assignments of all the ensemble members (but not the principals), so that they can jump in for any missing dancer or singer. When there are multiple absences, existing chorus

359

members might move over to perform the missing actors' specialties, in which case the swings cover the resulting gaps. With multiple absences, then, the goal becomes not to cover everything but to make it look like nothing is noticeably missing: a six-person dance section can likely make do with five or even four, in an emergency, but a vocal duet (like the Shakespeare-derived "What a Piece of Work Is Man" in *Hair*) will not work with only one singer.

Hair, with its cast jumping, crowding, climbing through the audience across the seatbacks, and more, was a roughly physical show. Not in comparison to an intensive dance musical, like Fosse's *Pippin* or Bennett's *A Chorus Line*; but those are necessarily cast with trained dancers, who undergo rigorous pre-show warm-up routines and are at least prepared for minor mishaps. The kids in a show like *Hair* just got up there and worked themselves into a frenzy, as staged; missteps, collisions, slipped disks, and the like happened with frequency.

We had started the week with four absent tribe members, while another two were injured but performing the sections of the show they could handle (i.e., singing the songs but not doing the steps). Tuesday night we lost another actor, leaving us with thirteen fully functioning tribal bodies (including the two swings) in place of the full group. Galen—part of whose job was to figure out how to reassign the actors in case of absence—had more or less managed to fill out the stage the prior weekend. But with the additional Tuesday night casualty, he simply didn't have enough bodies available to work with.

What was missing, ultimately, was someone to play a briefly onstage character called Hubert. Midway through the first act, a way-out-of-place tourist couple wanders up the aisle and is pulled onstage by the tribe, the wife in a big old-lady wig and a dress with corsage, the husband with an old-fashioned flash camera strapped around his neck. The tribe, needless to say, pokes fun at them. Did Gerry and Jim purposely write this to approximate the supposed reception of anthropologist Margaret Mead on St. Mark's Place? Seems so; the Tourist Lady is referred to—in the script, though not onstage—as Margaret Mead.

It is in this context that Berger and Claude lead everybody in the title song, explaining to the tourist couple just why they have "shining, gleaming, steaming, flaxen, waxen" hair. After which the Tourist Lady announces, like a good Margaret Mead stand-in, that she is accepting of this newly discovered hippie culture reveling in "male plumage" in a solo called "My Conviction." At the end of this she opens her dress—rigged to tear apart down the middle—to reveal that she is in fact a man. "Don't tell Hubert," she whispers to Claude and Berger. And off goes the tourist couple, to great laughter and applause.

As with all the smaller parts in the show, the Tourist Lady and Hubert were cast with tribe/ensemble members who were for that section pulled out of the general action. The "Hair" number was performed by the entire cast less the two actors playing the tourist couple, who stand witnessing the song. With seven injured or missing bodies, Galen simply didn't have enough bodies for the title song. The tribe member playing the Tourist Lady—a likable fellow called Perry Arthur, who a decade later went on to write the book and lyrics (under his full name, Perry Arthur Kroeger) for O'Horgan's cataclysmic swansong *Senator Joe*—was healthy and present. Given his big solo "My Conviction," he couldn't be switched out. Hubert, whose part consisted principally of reacting to the tribe, was altogether necessary to the action; but of all the bits and specialties in the show, it was the one that could most practically be filled by someone pulled off the street. Or in this case, by a company manager who strayed too close to the stage manager's desk.

HUBERT

"Well, I suppose I could get away with it," I was more or less forced to say, "but I don't know what to do. Anyway, I'm certainly not going to fit into the costume." The injured actor who regularly played the role was slight.

"Not a problem," said Galen. "You're already wearing your costume."

Now, in those days, audiences had already started dressing informally—especially at a counterculture musical like *Hair* (and in part due to the increased audience that first began to attend Broadway during the original runs of *Hair*, *Superstar*, and *Grease*). It was an unwritten policy, though, that front-of-house management—anyone who was there officially interacting with the audience—need wear a jacket and tie. Or a dress or pantsuit, in the case of the then relatively few female company managers. This was soon to change. When I soon thereafter worked for producer Liz McCann, who was anything but a snappy dresser, she took one look at me in jacket and tie at our first preview and said: "What, are you going to a funeral?"

But at *Hair*, it was jacket and tie. On that steamy summer afternoon, I was wearing my one lightweight summer suit; I had gotten it because it seemed like a good idea for hot days, but I found it too traditional for my taste. By East Village standards—or even by any standards—it was what you might call "square." For Hubert, the New Jersey tourist accompanying Margaret Mead? "That's perfect," said Galen.

A wardrobe tangent: I purchased that suit on my first visit to Brooks Brothers, which I also found too traditional for my taste. Waiting in the fitting room along with me was a sixty-something man whom I realized was Cy Feuer, the all-powerful producer of *Guys and Dolls*, *How to Succeed in Business Without Really Trying*, and other musicals. But *How to Succeed*, in 1961, had been his last hit, followed by flop after flop after flop. One of the Brooks salesmen, obviously having been told who was in the fitting room, ran in and eagerly approached Cy.

"Mr. Feuer! I just love your shows!" (Feuer smiled, silently.) "I saw *Mame* four times, and *Sweet Charity*." (The smile turned icy.) "And *Chicago*, with Gwen and then Liza, the best of all! Your musicals are great, the best!"

Feuer kept smiling, darting daggers until he was rescued by the tailor. I'm the only one there besides Feuer himself who knew that he was being praised not for *his* shows, but those produced by his direct competitor, Bobby Fryer.

Anyway, I'm standing there with Galen by the stage manager's desk in my Brooks Brothers' Haspel suit.

"What do I do?"

"You've seen the show. Just follow Perry, he'll lead you. And scrunch over as much as you can, so you look short."

After signing the box office statement, I went down to wardrobe. They creased my jacket, rolled up one pant leg, gave me a 1950s fedora and bow tie, and drew on a scraggly mustache. I went up to Galen, running the show from the stage manager's desk. He gave me a sideways glance and said, "Now I've seen it all."

As Doug Katsaros (playing Berger) was working his way through "Going Down"—a lesser known but effective song from the show—I headed out to the lobby. Perry dashed in, after his quick change to the housewife dress, to join me. On the applause, we walked down the aisle, with the cast "noticing" us and physically pulling us up onstage.

The actors, directed to be amused by these strange invaders, reacted uproariously—not having been alerted to just whom would be filling Hubert's bowtie.

At the Office

Following my twelve minutes onstage, I washed off the mustache, smoothed my suit, and returned to the office. I explained to Gene what had happened. "Nobody can say we're not a full-service operation," he said.

After catching up on the afternoon's work, it was back for the evening performance. At evening's end, Galen said: "I'll try to figure something out for tomorrow. But you might want to wear that suit."

The next day, as I was signing that week's payroll, I had two calls.

First, Galen.

"So, who's going on tonight?" I asked.

"Same as last night."

Another call came in from the business agent for Actors' Equity, sternly accusing us of breaking the collective bargaining agreement, which forbids having an actor onstage without a contract filed with the union.

I began to explain the situation, of which they were obviously already aware, hence the call.

"It doesn't matter, you can't do it," she said, demanding that we sign a formal contract for a full week (as opposed to the performances played), plus pension and welfare contributions. "And," she added punitively, "you'll have to join Equity. That's five hundred dollars. Sorry"—in a manner that suggested she wasn't.

"Well," I said slowly, "Four of the injured actors have already run out of sick days. We were going to pay them anyway; but if Michael Butler has to pay me, we'll just have to make up the money by docking the injured actors. *You* can explain that to them."

"Anyway," she grumbled, "you still have to be an Equity Member."

"Five hundred dollars induction? Gee. Good thing I already have an Equity card," said I, hanging up. I drew up a contract with myself and that was that, except to say that I chose not to dock the actors.

ACCOLADES

Gerry Ragni seemed to like my performance, claiming that I was "the best Hubert we ever had." Over the years, on the half-dozen occasions he ran into me thereafter, he greeted me not by name (which he had no need to remember) but as "the best Hubert." This is not as extraordinary as it might sound. Hubert, an uncomfortable and exceedingly square character from out-of-the-East-Village orbit, was always—by necessity—played by one of the tribal singer/dancers disguised by a costume change. I was clearly not, by any stretch of the imagination, a singer/dancer pulled from the tribe; so it stands to reason that I might have been far more convincing in that particular role. I was surely the only Hubert who wore his own suit.

Mary Jo Slater came to catch up on the show Thursday; she was in the midst of finding replacements for Katsaros and Kelly. She was pleasantly surprised—in the way that you might be surprised by your dog playing a chord, any chord, on the piano—by my performance. Seven-year-old Christian said, simply, "Well, I think you should still keep your regular job."

He turned out to be a cannily perceptive lad. A few summers later, we went to see *Damn Yankees* starring Joe Namath—yes, Joe Namath—at the outdoor Jones Beach Marine Theatre. The performance culminated in the big, pseudo-Fosse second act dance number "Two Lost Souls," in which they saw fit to place Namath in an office chair with the chorus rolling him back and forth across the wide stage while they danced. Afterward, stage manager Morty Halpern introduced us to the former Super Bowl–winning quarterback. Christian told him that he was just back from playing *Oliver!*, which followed *Damn Yankees* into the Starlight Theatre in Kansas City. "They were all still talking about your performance," Christian told Namath with a perfectly innocent face. "Said they'd never seen anything like it."

Ad-Lib

Friday night of my week onstage, one of our injured-but-performing actors needed to stay home in bed. In the further reshuffling, Galen assigned me an additional role. The centerpiece of the second act is an extended hallucinatory drug trip, which starts with "Walking in Space"; continues with "Abie, Baby," a retelling of the Gettysburg Address; climaxes with the nightmarish "Three-Five-Zero-Zero" ("ripped open by metal explosion"), inspired by a poem by Allen Ginsberg; and culminates with the gently folk-like "What a Piece of Work Is Man."

While one of the girls—playing the *Hair* version of Lincoln, stovepipe hat festooned with sewn-on dreadlocks—delivers the Gettysburg Address, General Grant (in a Union Army coat) shambles on. At one point, he stops to speak; in our production Grant was encouraged to ad-lib.

I prepared my joke and donned General Grant's uniform, which was so small that I couldn't move my shoulders. I stood in the wings at the beginning of the "trip," entering as directed during the Civil War segment. When it came time for my ad-lib, I confidently plunged into it. I instantly learned, though, that when the audience starts to laugh, you must keep your concentration or else you might freeze up midsentence; forget what you are about to say; and stand there frozen like a proverbial deer in the headlights, only worse in the unforgiving follow spot as the seconds tick away like hours.

Given that this freeze came within the hallucinatory nightmare dream sequence, I eventually (after seemingly endless turmoil) realized that my best option was to forget the joke—not *forget* the joke, which I'd already done—and get out of the spotlight. So after an expectant wait on the part of the audience (and the cast and the conductor), I simply gave an oversize shrug of the shoulders—almost splitting the seam of the too-tight coat—to suggest that I was finished, which I certainly was, and disappeared into the wing as the onstage nightmare resumed.

After the performance, Tom gave me a pleasant look with an elevated bushy eyebrow and said, gently, "Next time, you might want to *not* tell that joke." Which you can be assured I didn't over the rest of what turned out to be my seven-performance run.

As an opening night gift, Tom gave me a photo he had somehow managed to have taken from the front mezzanine. There is Hubert in his beige Haspel suit, being accosted by an incredulous Cleavant Derricks and surrounded by a dozen or so tribe members including a spaced-out Annie Golden at my elbow; Perry Arthur in white gloves and pearls, clutching his/her *Playbill*; and a most-bemused David Patrick Kelly who can't quite believe what he is seeing. A picture is worth a thousand words, and my kids—born twenty-odd years later—find it most entertaining.

The author (as Hubert, in fedora) being accosted by Cleavant Derricks in the 1977 revival of *Hair*. Those looking on include Annie Golden (half-hidden on far left), Perry Arthur (in dress with pearls), and David Patrick Kelly (in front of the "earth" sign with headband and glasses).

Epilogue
Onstage

BILTMORE

So, WHERE WAS I AT TWENTY-FOUR?

Standing where I wanted, doing what I wanted.

The Biltmore was just five blocks from the Alvin, where I took the stage on that Monday night eight years earlier. But everything, at that Wednesday matinee in 1977, was different.

The two houses were not dissimilar, despite the seating capacities. (The Biltmore had 948 seats at the time, against 1,334 at the Alvin.) Here there was an unusual-for-Broadway single aisle running up the center of the orchestra, and there were no box seats climbing the side walls. But the two had been built by the same architect, almost simultaneously.

The difference I felt, when I made my unexpected stage debut, was not a matter of capacity. From the various stages I'd stood upon—the Broadhurst, Plymouth, 46th Street, Lunt, Hellinger, Washington's Eisenhower, Philadelphia's Walnut Street, Boston's Colonial, and more—the empty auditoriums seemed like friendly canyons: cool, deep, reassuringly contemplative—as was the Biltmore, when I previously had reason to step onstage.

Now, though, there was an elemental added element: the audience. Hundreds of faces. Given that I was standing there during two cheerfully upbeat musical numbers, hundreds of beaming faces. The plush—or

The view from the stage of the Biltmore.

faux-plush—red rows at the Alvin were inviting, in the darkness. The seats at the Biltmore were invisible, replaced by people.

We've heard many laughs, all of us who attend plays and musicals—often explosive ones. But I abruptly realized there's a great difference—in terms of sonics and impact—when you are standing on the other side of the footlights. Explosions erupt in front of you; sometimes from the full house, sometimes starting in one area and spreading row by row.

With luck, you might personally set the match with your line delivery or sight gags. (The author or director, perhaps, can claim a bit of credit for this.) Waves of laughter, cascades of laughter. All you can do is stand there, wait, and—being a professional—make sure you keep from reacting. We know about the sound of music; but the roar of laughter, heard from the stage, is not to be forgotten.

From my earliest visit, I had seen the theatre as a place of refuge: cool, dark, shaded. As soon as I gained professional access to Broadway theatres, my favorite spot—before the show, between shows on matinee days, during rehearsals—was on the aisle surrounded by rows of empty seats. I spent hours and hours, at the Shubert during *Promises*, at the Alvin during *Shenandoah*.

Onstage at *Hair*, I discovered the other side of the equation. In place of that placid darkness: light, with as many watts as Jules Fisher could throw at me—Jules Fisher not only in a generic sense, being the most innovative lighting designer of the time, but as the designer of *Hair*.

What's more, I could actually feel *heat* from all that wattage. For someone who reveled in the cool, sheltered atmosphere of the huddled audience, I was startled by the opposite: the ultra-brightness of stage lighting, the warmth generated, the explosive reaction of hundreds of people in the throes of enjoyment. So this, it seems, is what happens—what had always been happening—on the other side of the footlights

The Biltmore was flooded by the roar of the crowd and a full complement of colored stage lights. The Alvin was silent, bathed in moody shadows cast by that lone ghost light.

LIFE IN THE THEATRE

So, where was I?

I had planned on a life in the theatre since before it occurred to me to plan on anything. My appetite was whetted by the discovery of cast recordings; ignited by *The Music Man* at the Majestic, in the fall of 1960; and cemented by the one-two punch of *Carnival!* and *Irma La Douce* in 1961.

The die was cast when I was old enough, at fifteen, to pick and choose and attend whatever shows I wished. My future was molded, permanently, on the night after my sixteenth birthday when I stepped into the ghost light on the stage of the Alvin.

I quickly thereafter set my course, determining to skip years of school so that I could get out quicker, start sooner.

I began working in the theatre before even moving into my dorm room in the fall of 1971; on my first day of college, I started working eight shows a week. Didn't matter to me that I was ushering, or selling candy, or even proverbially sharpening pencils. I was there, every night, sitting in the dark and breathing the air of show business.

My goal was to have access to a real, professional theatre job waiting for me by the time I graduated, which is how matters worked out.

This was done, in great part, by concentrating solely on life in the theatre. No teenage years, none of those dear old school days or wild wasted college antics fondly cherished by many. Not even a solitary vacation ever, other than theatre-work related treks to my alternate universe of Boston, New Haven, Philadelphia, and Washington.

I had meanwhile found a family—literally so, literally in the theatre. Within three weeks at the Merrick office, I met Leo Herbert, Mitch Erickson, and Mark Bramble, who remained among my closest friends for the rest of their lives. At the same time and in the same place, I found a handful of other enduring friends, a group that would be added to as I progressed from show to show. For someone who walked in at eighteen virtually friendless, I suddenly and unexpectedly found I did, after all, have a home.

This was to remain the case for years: my world, and my family, began at the stage door. It wasn't until 1994 that I met my wife, Helen Lang, a non-show-business "civilian." I realize now that until then, all of my friends—including the three women I had lived with along the way—had come from onstage or backstage. Where friendship was concerned, for me, there was no business *but* show business.

But I was, through it all, doing precisely what I wanted.

I was well on my way to my goal of becoming a theatrical producer—although my enthusiasm with time would be tempered, in part by the roundabout discovery that I was actually a writer. But that came later.

For now, it was Broadway, night after night at some theatre or other. My offstage observations end much as they began:

Onstage, wondering what happens next.

Acknowledgments

Between performances on matinee day (1985).
PHOTO BY ARTURO E. PORAZZI

IT IS SOMETHING OF A CLICHÉ TO THANK EVERYONE FOR EVERYTHING they ever did. Let me acknowledge, though, that without the innumerable people who crossed my path over the course of these pages, there wouldn't have been quite so many observations to observe. To quote the Bard—or was it Stanislavski?—there are no small actors, merely players.

A clutch of folk has provided information, advice, permissions, and assorted assistance. I offer appreciation, in random order, to the following: Max A. Woodward, John Handy, Heather Herbert Mays, Cheri Herbert, Kim Sellon, Mary Jo Slater, Jeffrey Richards, Ken Bloom, Michael Yoscary, Arturo E. Porazzi, Ann Churchill-Brown, Esther Margolis, Richard W. Kidwell, Bill Rosenfield, and Stephen Sondheim. I also salute the efforts of and illustration permissions from Mark Eden Horowitz, Vincent Novara, and Thomas Barrick of the Music Division of the Library of Congress; Philip Birsh and Andrew Ku of *Playbill*; Howard Mandelbaum of Photofest; and Sylvia Wang of the Shubert Archive. And without the supportive folk at Applause Books, you wouldn't likely be perusing these pages or e-pages.

Finally, I thank my wife, Helen, who has remained by my side through many days and nights of theatre-going—some more enjoyable than others—since 1994; and my now-adult children, Johanna and Charlie, who grew up adjacent to my Broadway world. The three of them have met some of the people and heard some of the stories, but these pages should help them finally make some sense of it all. Perhaps.

Index